Strategy and Human Resource Management

3rd editi

MANAGEMENT, WORK AND ORGANISATIONS

Series editors: **Gibson Burrell**, The Management Centre, University of Leicester
Mick Marchington, Manchester Business School
Paul Thompson, Department of Human Resource Management,
University of Strathclyde

This series of new textbooks covers the areas of human resource management, employee relations, organisational behaviour and related business and management fields. Each text has been specially commissioned to be written by leading experts in a clear and accessible way. The books contain serious and challenging material, take an analytical rather than prescriptive approach and are particularly suitable for use by students with no prior specialist knowledge.

The series is relevant for many business and management courses, including MBA and post-experience courses, specialist masters and postgraduate diplomas, professional courses and final-year undergraduate courses. These texts have become essential reading at business and management schools worldwide.

Published

Emma Bell
READING MANAGEMENT AND ORGANIZATION IN FILM

Paul Blyton and Peter Turnbull
THE DYNAMICS OF EMPLOYEE RELATIONS (3rd edn)

Paul Blyton and Peter Turnbull (eds)
REASSESSING THE EMPLOYMENT RELATIONSHIP

Sharon C. Bolton
EMOTION MANAGEMENT IN THE WORKPLACE

Sharon C. Bolton and Maeve Houlihan (eds)
SEARCHING FOR THE HUMAN IN HUMAN RESOURCE MANAGEMENT

Peter Boxall and John Purcell
STRATEGY AND HUMAN RESOURCE MANAGEMENT (3rd edn)

J. Martin Corbett
CRITICAL CASES IN ORGANISATIONAL BEHAVIOUR

Susan Corby, Steve Palmer and Esmond Lindop
RETHINKING REWARD

Ian Greener
PUBLIC MANAGEMENT

Keith Grint
LEADERSHIP

Irena Grugulis
SKILLS, TRAINING AND HUMAN RESOURCE DEVELOPMENT

Geraldine Healy, Gill Kirton and Mike Noon (eds)
EQUALITY, INEQUALITIES AND DIVERSITY

Damian Hodgson and Svetlana Cicmil (eds)
MAKING PROJECTS CRITICAL

Marek Korczynski
HUMAN RESOURCE MANAGEMENT IN SERVICE WORK

Karen Legge
HUMAN RESOURCE MANAGEMENT: anniversary edition

Patricia Lewis and Ruth Simpson (eds)
GENDERING EMOTIONS IN ORGANIZATIONS

Patricia Lewis and Ruth Simpson (eds)
VOICE, VISIBILITY AND THE GENDERING OF ORGANIZATIONS

Alison Pullen, Nic Beech and David Sims (eds)
EXPLORING IDENTITY

Jill Rubery and Damian Grimshaw
THE ORGANISATION OF EMPLOYMENT

Hugh Scullion and Margaret Linehan (eds)
INTERNATIONAL HUMAN RESOURCE MANAGEMENT

Colin C. Williams
RETHINKING THE FUTURE OF WORK

Diana Winstanley and Jean Woodall (eds)
ETHICAL ISSUES IN CONTEMPORARY HUMAN RESOURCE MANAGEMENT

For more information on titles in the Series please go to www.palgrave.com/business/mwo

Series Standing Order

If you would like to receive future titles in this series as they are published, you can make use of our standing order facility. To place a standing order please contact your bookseller or, in case of difficulty, write to us at the address below with your name and address and the name of the series. Please state with which title you wish to begin your standing order.

Customer Services Department, Macmillan Distribution Ltd,
Houndmills, Basingstoke, Hampshire RG21 6XS, England, UK

Strategy and Human Resource Management

3rd edition

Peter Boxall
Professor of Human Resource Management, University of Auckland, New Zealand

and

John Purcell
Associate Fellow of the Industrial Relations Research Unit at Warwick University Business School, UK and a Deputy Chairman of the Central Arbitration Commitee, ACAS, UK

First edition 2003
Second edition 2008
Third edition 2011

Published by
PALGRAVE MACMILLAN

Palgrave Macmillan in the UK is an imprint of Macmillan Publishers Limited, registered in England, company number 785998, of Houndmills, Basingstoke, Hampshire RG21 6XS.

Palgrave Macmillan in the US is a division of St Martin's Press LLC, 175 Fifth Avenue, New York, NY 10010.

Palgrave Macmillan is the global academic imprint of the above companies and has companies and representatives throughout the world.

Palgrave® and Macmillan® are registered trademarks in the United States, the United Kingdom, Europe and other countries.

ISBN 978–0–230–57935–4

This book is printed on paper suitable for recycling and made from fully managed and sustained forest sources. Logging, pulping and manufacturing processes are expected to conform to the environmental regulations of the country of origin.

A catalogue record for this book is available from the British Library.

A catalog record for this book is available from the Library of Congress.

10 9   8   7   6   5   4   3   2   1
20 19 18 17 16 15 14 13 12 11

Printed in China

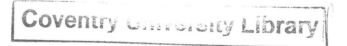

Contents

v

List of boxes, figures and tables

Tables

Introduction

The last thirty years witnessed a major growth of interest in strategy and human resource management. Reacting to the dramatic growth of new technology, of competitive change, and of regulatory reform, business leaders, and their counterparts in the public sector, looked for ways to design and implement more successful strategies. Consultancy practices responded to this explosion of interest. So too did the academic field of strategic management. It moved on from its base in prescriptive texts on 'business policy'. Academically, strategic management is now characterised by a range of theoretical schools, by extensive research, and by large academic conferences. Business schools have invested enormous resources in the teaching of strategy, both in MBA programmes and in the 'capstone courses' of major undergraduate degrees.

The situation is much the same in HRM. The term first gained prominence in the United States, where the most influential textbooks were initially published and where leading journals such as *Human Resource Management* and *Human Resource Management Review* are based. Outside the United States, the significance of HRM has been recognised in the launch and growth of the *Human Resource Management Journal*, the *International Journal of Human Resource Management* and the *Asia Pacific Journal of Human Resources*, among others. Within business schools, and across more traditional academic departments, there has been an explosion of courses and publications concerned with the management of work and people. It may have been fashionable to treat personnel management as a 'Cinderella' subject in the 1970s but few universities today treat HRM with quite the same disdain.

The growth of interest in strategic management and HRM has not, however, been accompanied by sufficient concern for integrating these two important fields of theory and practice. This was our argument for writing the first edition of this book and remains our overriding goal in this third edition. Too much of the literature in strategic management continues to downplay or disregard the human issues which affect the viability and relative performance of firms. Similarly, too much of the literature in HRM carries on the preoccupation of the personnel management literature with individual techniques – such as particular types of selection tests or performance appraisal formats – and fails to pay sufficient regard to the way that the value of particular techniques varies across contexts. Both bodies of literature have their characteristic weaknesses. On the strategy side, it is the failure genuinely to appreciate the ways in which the management of work and people is strategic to organisational success. On the HRM side, it is the failure to look up from the nooks and crannies of currently fashionable techniques to study the bigger picture, to perceive the ways in which patterns of HRM relate to broader business problems and need to vary with the organisation's particular environment.

Strategy and Human Resource Management is not organised around the classical sub-functions of HR practice – selection, appraisal, pay, training, and so on – with the word 'strategic' slipped in front. The sub-functional domains of micro-HRM do not dominate the design of chapters as if they were self-contained 'solutions'. Instead, the book is designed around the need for a critical analysis of how HRM affects organisational performance. We are concerned with understanding the role that HRM plays in strategic management, with examining how HR strategy impacts on an organisation's chances of survival and its relative success, and with how HR strategy varies across important organisational, industry and societal contexts. In tackling these questions, we are committed to what we call an 'analytical approach' to HRM. This means we try to understand what managers do and why they do it before we offer any sort of prescription for what they should do or how they could do things better. In other words, empirical description and theoretical explanation should come before policy prescription. This is an approach which is uncompromisingly about research but, wherever possible, we try to bring the story to life with the more interesting illustrations – cases and vignettes – with which we are familiar and, wherever possible, we insert references to valuable internet sites. In the book's companion website, we provide case studies and lecture notes for every chapter.

In this edition, all chapters in the book have been rigorously reviewed and updated. As before, we argue that HRM is an essential organisational process which serves multiple goals, and that these goals are subject to strategic tensions. The framework presented in Chapter 1 contends that not only are firms typically concerned with securing cost-effective labour and with some degree of organisational flexibility but that social legitimacy and managerial power also play important roles in their HR activities. This framework acts as a touchstone throughout the book. It is reinforced in Chapter 2, where we argue for the centrality of human resource strategy within any credible understanding of business strategy – and not as some kind of dubious appendage to it. Our view is that an effective HR strategy is a necessary, though not a sufficient, condition of business viability. In addition, for those firms that survive, HR strategy may help to support some form of sustained competitive advantage. Differences in the quality of HRM help to explain differences in relative performance.

In Chapter 3, we continue to analyse the debate within strategic HRM over the role of context ('best fit') and universalism ('best practice'). Our review of the evidence now includes greater material on national cultures and social institutions. We have reorganised our discussion of fit so that the evidence is presented on three levels: societal, industry and organisational. We think this is a better structure for analysis of specific situations. We retain the conclusion that firms either adapt to their specific context or they fail. There is a basis, however, for a concept of best practice when it is founded on underpinning principles that help managers to achieve better outcomes. As might be expected, we continue to work studiously with the resource-based view of the firm (Chapter 4), with the notion that intangible assets can build distinctive and enviable positions of competitive strength. This remains a very important body of work which quite obviously links the strategy and HRM fields. We try in this area to make some of the obtuse ideas more accessible and to ensure we have an argument that goes beyond the self-evident truths.

The central section of the book (Chapters 5 to 8) aims to identify and expound major principles that underpin key choices in HR strategy. This means we are less interested in talking about specific HR practices than we are in pinpointing critical theoretical principles that run across HRM. In this edition, Chapter 6 has been reorganised and Chapter 7 has been renamed and enhanced to underline the importance of mutuality or reciprocity in employment relationships. As in the second edition, in order to make sense of the enormous clutter in HRM, we emphasise the value of understanding organisational HR strategies as clusters of HR systems (Chapter 8). While organisational politics often ensure that there are some overlapping features, each HR system in a firm is aimed at a different workforce group. Understanding HR strategy in this way helps to us to see patterns in it, within and across organisations, and over time.

Areas much less often visited by writers on strategic HRM include the evolution of HR strategy across cycles of industry change and the shape of HR strategy within multidivisional and multinational firms. These have been concerns of ours – we see them as important in the dynamic picture and in the larger world of capitalist competition – and they continue to play a key role in the final section of the book (Chapters 9 and 10). The book's final chapter includes a summary of the main themes in the book and relates HRM to important developments in strategic planning and management accounting. Overall, we think that *Strategy and Human Resource Management* is a novel synthesis of the HRM–strategy nexus: you be the judge.

PETER BOXALL
JOHN PURCELL

Acknowledgements

I am very grateful for the support of Professor Greg Whittred, Dean, Professor Jilnaught Wong, Senior Associate Dean, and Professor Hugh Whittaker, Head of the Department of Management and International Business, at the University of Auckland Business School. Collectively, they have made it possible for me to remain research-active while serving as the School's Associate Dean of Research. I am also indebted to a range of colleagues who have taught me a lot in our strategic HRM research over recent few years, including Keith Macky, Peter Haynes, Giles Burch, Tim Bartram and Siah Ang. Similarly, I am very grateful to my students in the postgraduate diploma of HRM, all of whom are practitioners, bringing the touchstone of the 'real world' into the classroom. I am, as ever, deeply indebted to my friend and partner in this work, John Purcell. John's support of my sabbaticals at the University of Bath enabled this book to become a reality and to reach its third edition in eight years. Working with John is always an enriching experience. I have benefited greatly from his challenging critique and his insight into the critical processes of HRM, honed through a distinguished research career and extensive engagement with practitioners. We both thank Palgrave Macmillan for commissioning this third edition. At Palgrave Macmillan, we especially thank Ursula Gavin, Ceri Griffiths and Keith Povey. As ever, my heartfelt thanks go to Marijanne for her unfailing interest in my work and to our sons, Chris, Andy and David, whose careers help me to see the world of work from a fresh perspective.

2010   PETER BOXALL

My thanks go to Professor Paul Marginson at the Industrial Relations Research Unit at Warwick Business School for appointing me as a Research Professor in the period 2007–10 and providing all kinds of support. In particular, I wish to thank Mark Hall for his friendship and sharing with me his deep understanding of consultation, or what we call in this book 'employee voice'. While I was at the IRRU I was also working at the Advisory, Conciliation and Arbitration Service (ACAS). It is a rare privilege for an academic to have the opportunity to try to turn theory into practice. My colleagues in the Strategy Unit – Kimberley Bingham, George Boyce, Rachel Suff, Sarah Podro, Lydia Bradley and Nicole Ranieri – helped me hugely in debating the practical implications of 'good practice' and the limits of regulation. One outcome was the design of the ACAS Model Workplace, an interactive tool for managers, and employee representatives, to use to evaluate their employment relations. I hope that some of this practical application is reflected in this third edition. Both Peter Boxall and I share a bond in always wanting theory to inform practice and for practitioners to be able to appreciate the origins and outcomes of their decisions. This is why we embarked on the book a decade ago. I am most grateful to Peter for his friendship and support, and critical debates over many years over analysis, expression and big ideas, and for the depth of his scholarship. Kate Purcell has, for over forty years, kept me focused on what is important in work, life and play. My debt to her is beyond compare.

2010   JOHN PURCELL

The authors and publishers would like to thank the following for permission to reproduce copyright material: **Professor M. Beer and Professor B. Spector** for Figure 3.2 from Beer, M., Spector, B., Lawrence, P., Quinn Millis, D., and Walton, R. (1984) *Managing Human Assets*, copyright previously held by New York: Free Press; **California Management Review** for Figure 9.3 from Williams, J. (1992) 'How sustainable is your competitive advantage?', *California Management Review*, 34(3): 29–51; **Cornell University Press** for Table 5.2 from Herzenberg, S., Alic, J. and Wial, H. (1998) *New Rules for a New Economy: Employment and Opportunity in Postindustrial America*, Ithaca, NY: ILR Press; **Emerald Group Publishing Ltd** for Figure 5.2 from Haynes, P. and Fryer, G. (2000) 'Human resources, service quality and performance: a case study', *International Journal of Contemporary Hospitality Management*, 12(4): 240–8, and Figure 9.4 from Dyer, L. and Shafer, R. (1999) 'Creating organizational agility: implications for strategic human resource management', in Wright, P., Dyer, L., Bourdreau, J., and Milkovich, G. (eds) *Research in Personnel and Human Resource Management (Supplement 4: Strategic Human Resource Management in the Twenty First Century)*, Stanford, CT, and London: JAI Press; **Harvard Business School Publishing** for Box 4.3 and Figure 4.2 from Leonard, D. (1998) *Wellsprings of Knowledge: Building and Sustaining the Sources of Innovation*, Boston, MA: Harvard Business School Press, Figure 11.1 from Kaplan, R. and Norton, D. (1996) *The Balanced Scorecard:*

Translating Strategy into Action, Boston, MA: Harvard Business School Press, and Figures 11.2–11.3 from Kaplan, R. and Norton, D. (2001) *The Strategy-Focused Organization*, Boston, MA: Harvard Business School Press; **John Wiley & Sons Ltd** for Figure 7.2 from Campbell, J. P., McCloy, R., Oppler, S. and Sager, C. (1993) 'A theory of performance', in Schmitt, N. and Borman, W. (eds) *Personnel Selection in Organizations*, San Francisco: Jossey-Bass; **Oxford University Press** for Table 7.2 from Rose, M. (1994) 'Job satisfaction, job skills, and personal skills', in Penn, R., Rose, M. and Rubery, J. (eds) *Skill and Occupational Change*, Oxford: Oxford University Press; Figure 4.3 from Lepak, D. and Snell, S., (2007) 'Employment sub-systems and the "HR architecture"', in Boxall, P., Purcell, J. and Wright, P. (eds) *The Oxford Handbook of Human Resource Management*, Oxford: Oxford University Press, and Figure 7.7 from Guest, D., (2007) 'Human resource management and the worker: towards a new psychological contract?', in Boxall, P., Purcell, J. and Wright, P. (eds) *The Oxford Handbook of Human Resource Management*, Oxford: Oxford University Press; **The Free Press** for Figure 3.3 from Porter, M. (1985) *Competitive Advantage: Creating and Sustaining Superior Performance*, New York: Free Press; **Sage Publications** for Box 5.1 from Parker, S. and Wall, T. (1998) *Job and Work Design: Organizing Work to Promote Well-being and Effectiveness*, Thousand Oaks, CA: Sage; Figure 5.1 from Vandenberg, R. J., Richardson, H. A. and Eastman, L. J. (1999) 'The impact of high involvement work processes on organizational effectiveness: a second-order latent variable approach', *Group and Organization Management,* 24(3): 300–39; Figure 7.3 from Windolf, P. (1986) 'Recruitment, selection, and internal labour markets in Britain and Germany', *Organization Studies*, 7(3), and Figures 7.5–7.10 from Rousseau, D. (1995) *Psychological Contracts in Organizations*, Thousand Oaks, CA: Sage. Every effort has been made to contact all copyright-holders, but if any have been inadvertently omitted the publishers will be please to make the necessary arrangement at the earliest opportunity.

1

The goals of human resource management

Our mission in this book is to examine the ways in which human resource management (HRM) is critical to organisational success. We are interested in how HRM affects the fundamental viability and relative performance of organisations. The logical place to begin is with the analysis of management's goals in HRM. What is management trying to achieve in organising work and employing people? What sort of motives underpin human resource management? This is the question we pose and seek to answer in this first chapter. The chapter begins by defining the key characteristics of HRM. We then identify and examine the principal goals or motives that can be discerned in management's HRM activities. This leads into a discussion of the strategic tensions and problems that management faces in pursuing these goals. We conclude with a summary and an outline of what lies ahead in the book.

Defining human resource management

HRM refers to all those activities associated with the management of work and people in organisations. In this book, related terms such as 'employee relations', 'labour management' and 'people management' are used as synonyms for HRM. While there have been debates over the meaning of HRM since the term came into vogue in the 1980s, it has become the most widely recognised term in the English-speaking world referring to the activities of management in organising work and employing people. The term is not restricted to organizations in the Anglo-American sphere: it is also popular in the Francophone and Hispanic worlds, among others.

We do not wish to use the term loosely, however. Definitions are important. They should not be rushed or glossed over because they indicate the intellectual terrain that is being addressed. They suggest the relevant 'problematics' of the field – that is, they suggest what needs to be discussed and explained. Before proceeding, our definition will be clarified and elaborated.

HRM: an inevitable process in organisations

Let's suppose you are a self-employed individual running your own small business. The business, however, is starting to take off. You have more orders from clients than you can cope with. You have some capital and your bank manager, who likes your financial performance so far and thinks you are a good risk, is prepared to lend you some more. The minute you decide you want to hire your first employee, you are engaged in the initial stages of human resource management. You are moving from a situation in which self-employment and self-management has been everything to one in which the employment and management of others will also be critical. Your ideas may not be well shaped at this stage but as you start to think more seriously about what kind of help you need and take some steps to make it happen (for example, by networking among talented friends or advertising the job on the internet), you are entering the world of HRM. Once someone has actually joined you as an employee, you have really begun the process of HRM in earnest. You have started to expand your business in the anticipation of improving its potential and, if you wish to survive, with the intention of making money through employing the talents of other people. You have embarked on a process that brings opportunity at the same time as it creates a whole new world of problems for you. (For example: How are you going to involve this person in decision making? What will you do if they are not much good at the job and coping with them turns out to be very time-consuming? If they are good at it, how will you keep up with their income and career aspirations?)

This simple illustration underlines the fact that it is virtually impossible to grow businesses (and, for that matter, any kind of formal organization) without employing people. HRM is a process that accompanies the expansion of organisations: it is a correlate of entrepreneurial success and organisational growth. One of the key metrics commonly used to measure the size of organisations is the number of people employed. The world's largest company by revenue in 2009 – Royal Dutch Shell – employs 102,000 people.[1]

---

[1] http://money.cnn.com/magazines/fortune/global500/2009/snapshots/6388.html, accessed 20/5/10.

The third largest company by revenue in 2009, Wal-Mart Stores, employs around 2.1 million people.[2] These differences in employee numbers say something about the difference between oil production and retail organisations in terms of technological intensity (the oil industry requires huge capital investments while supermarkets remain relatively labour intensive) but both of these organisations need large numbers of people to do what they do. In the public sector, workforces can also be very large. The British national health service, for example, employs 1.4 million people.[3]

The idea that we might need to justify the process of HRM in organisations is, thus, rather absurd. We may well wish to analyse the effectiveness of a firm's approach to HRM and make some changes but we inevitably come back to some kind of 'human resourcing' process (Watson 2005). You simply cannot grow and maintain organisations without at least some employment of other people. Longstanding firms may go through periods in which they need to lay off people – possibly very large numbers of people – to improve their cost structure but hardly any business will survive unless it is employing at least some people on a regular basis. If everyone is laid off and their final entitlements paid to them, the process of HRM will cease – but so will the firm.[4]

HRM: managing work and people

Our conception of HRM covers the policies and practices used to organise work and to employ people. In other words, HRM encompasses the management of work and the management of people to do the work. Work policies and practices are to do with the way the work itself is organised. This includes its fundamental structure, which can range from low-discretion jobs where supervisors exercise a high level of control through to highly autonomous jobs where individuals largely supervise themselves. It also includes any associated opportunities to engage in problem-solving and change management regarding work processes (for example, through quality circles or team meetings). Employment policies and practices, on the other hand, are concerned with how firms try to hire and manage people. They include management activities in recruiting, selecting, deploying, motivating,

---

[2] http://money.cnn.com/magazines/fortune/global500/2009/snapshots/2255.html, accessed 20/5/10.
[3] http://www.ic.nhs.uk/statistics-and-data-collections/workforce/nhs-staff-numbers/nhs-staff-1999--2009-overview, accessed 20/5/10.
[4] Except in the case of 'shell companies' which are defunct but may be revived when someone acquires the rights to the name and decides to use them.

appraising, training, developing and retaining individual employees. In addition, they include processes for informing, consulting and negotiating with individuals and groups and activities associated with disciplining employees, terminating their contracts and downsizing entire workforces. As this makes apparent, the management of work and people includes both individual and collective dimensions. People are managed through employing and relating to them as individuals and also through relating to them in larger groups.

HRM: involving line and specialist managers

Given this wide remit, it should be obvious that HRM can never be the exclusive property of HR specialists. As an essential organisational process, HRM is as an aspect of all management jobs. All firms have 'workforce strategies' (Huselid, Becker and Beatty 2005), whether or not they have specialist HR people on their staff. Line managers – those who directly supervise employees engaged in the operations of the firm – are intimately involved, usually hiring people in their team and almost always held directly accountable for the performance of that team. In larger organisations, there may be permanent in-house HR specialists contributing specialist skills in such technical aspects of HRM as the design of selection processes, the formation of Equal Employment Opportunity (EEO) policies, the conduct of collective employment negotiations, and training needs' analysis. There may also be specialist HR consultants contracted to provide such important services as executive search, and assistance with major reformulations of salary structure and performance incentives. In the UK, the Personnel Manager's Yearbook lists 90,000 HR specialists working in 13,000 organisations.[5] In the USA, there are more than 250,000 members of the Society for Human Resource Management, making this organisation the world's largest voluntary association of HR specialists.[6] These figures underline the importance of this kind of work in advanced economies. All specialists, however, are engaged in 'selling' their services to other managers (senior, middle and first-line), in working together with other members of the management team to achieve the desired results. In this book, the acronym 'HRM' is therefore used to refer to the totality of the firm's management of work and people and not simply to those aspects where HR specialists are involved.

---

[5] http://www.wlrstore.com/apinfo/personnel-managers-yearbook.aspx, accessed 20/5/10.
[6] http://www.shrm.org/about/pages/default.aspx, accessed 20/5/10.

HRM: building individual and workforce performance

HRM can usefully be understood as a set of activities aimed at building individual and workforce performance. On the level of individual performance, HRM consists of managerial attempts to influence individual ability (A), motivation (M), and the opportunity to perform (O). If managers want to enhance individual performance, they need to influence these three variables positively (Blumberg and Pringle 1982, Campbell, McCloy, Oppler and Sager 1993). This is true in any model of HRM, whether we are talking of one in which employees have relatively basic skills (such as fast-food services) or very advanced qualifications (such as brain surgery). Using mathematical notation:

$$P = f(A, M, O)$$

In other words, individuals perform when they have:

- the ability (A) to perform (they *can do* the job because they possess the necessary knowledge, skills and aptitudes);
- the motivation (M) to perform (they *will do* the job because they feel adequately interested and incentivised); and
- the opportunity (O) to perform (their work structure and its environment provides the necessary support and avenues for expression).

The AMO framework is depicted in Figure 1.1. We should note here that it is not only HRM that affects the AMO variables. Employees are motivated and enabled not only through incentives (such as pay and promotion) and work processes (such as supervisory help and co-worker support) but also through the wider organisational environment, including such things as the quality of information systems and the level of funding available. It is easier to perform

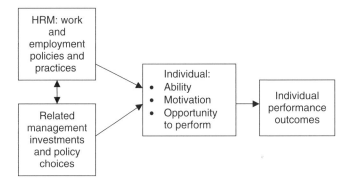

Figure 1.1 The AMO model of individual performance

when a firm is financially successful and management decides to plough its wealth back into new technologies and better staffing budgets.

The mathematical shorthand we use here, $P = f(A,M,O)$, is not meant to be mystifying or off-putting. It is simply a useful way of indicating that no one knows the precise relationships among ability, motivation and opportunity. There is no exact formula here but we do know that all three factors are involved in creating employee performance. Good ability alone will not bring performance: the worker must want to apply it. Similarly, motivated workers with good abilities cannot achieve much if critical resources or organisational support are lacking. The AMO framework is something that we will refer to regularly, and develop in a more sophisticated way, in this book.

The managerial effort in human resource management, however, is not solely concerned with managing individuals as if they were independent of others. It does include this but, as we have indicated, it also includes efforts to organise groups of employees and manage whole workforces. Figure 1.2 sketches the role of HRM on this collective level. Again, we do not know the precise relationships here but we do know that HRM plays an important role in building workforce organisation and collective capabilities and the general climate of employee attitudes. It typically includes attempts to build work systems that coordinate individuals in some kind of way, such as permanent teams, finite project groups and 'virtual teams' which coordinate through intranets and the internet. It may include attempts to build collaboration across departmental or hierarchical boundaries and networks operating across work sites, countries and time zones. These sorts of work organisation activities, along with various kinds of recruitment and development activities (including, at times, company takeovers), are attempts to build workforce capabilities. Managers try to build 'critical mass': the stock of knowledge and

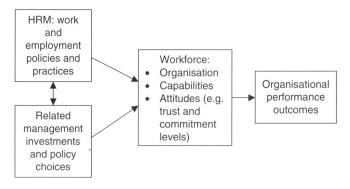

Figure 1.2 HRM and workforce performance

skills they need to fulfil the firm's mission. Finally on the collective level, HRM includes management actions that affect the attitudinal climate of the workplace. Management's stance towards employee voice is a key influence here and a variety of collective variables – such as trust levels, commitment levels and the quality of cooperation – are in play.

HRM, then, needs to be understood as a management process that operates on more than one level. It includes attempts to manage individuals and attempts to build a functioning workforce. HRM is about building both human capital (what individuals can and will do that is valuable to the organisation) and social capital (relationships and networks among individuals and groups that create value for the organisation) (Ghoshal and Nahapiet 1998, Leana and van Buren 1999, Snell 1999). These levels are obviously connected. While there is often much that individuals can achieve through their own skills and drive, they are always acting within a larger social context. They are inevitably affected by the quality of workforce organisation and capabilities and the attitudinal climate in which they are embedded. The need to understand HRM as concerned with both individual and collective performance will be an important theme in this book.

HRM: incorporating a variety of management styles and ideologies

As our discussion so far should indicate, management often adopts a variety of approaches to managing employees: variety of management practice is a fact of life in HRM. In the larger organisations, it is quite common for one approach to be taken to managing managers, another approach to permanent non-managerial employees, and yet another to temporary and 'contract' staff (Pinfield and Berner 1994, Harley 2001, Kalleberg et al. 2006). In unionised organisations, such as public sector hospitals, there can be different employment regimes for each occupational group with each of these negotiated in separate contractual negotiations and then enforced or 'policed' with a high degree of seriousness. In this light, Osterman (1987) refers to a range of 'employment subsystems' in firms. Lepak and Snell (1999, 2002, 2007) talk of a 'human resource architecture' in which management chooses different HR systems for different groups based on their strategic value and the uniqueness of the skills that each group possesses.

Not only are there key differences in style within firms but differences in styles across firms are also widely observed. In terms of the way firms approach employee voice, we see a broad range of styles from paternalistic ones through to workplace 'partnerships' in which there is much greater recognition of employee rights and interests (Purcell, 1987, Purcell and Ahlstrand 1994, Budd 2004). At one extreme, managers seek to 'command and control' and allow very limited avenues, if any, for employees to express disagreement with management policies. This is not necessarily going to stop employee discontent because employees can still resign, or can sabotage operations in ways that are not easy to detect, but attempts to exercise managerial power in a unilateral way are a common style. At the other end, there are companies that are committed participants in collective bargaining with employee unions, which produces a structured and legally enforceable way of recognising employee voice. In European societies, many companies complement union negotiations with such vehicles as consultative committees or works councils or develop such structures when unions are absent (for example, Marchington 2007, Purcell and Georgiades 2007). In between, there is a range of ways in which managers can open up channels for employee voice, including open-door policies, regular team meetings, and employee forums or 'town hall' meetings (Freeman, Boxall and Haynes 2007).

Our definition of HRM, then, allows for a wide variety of management ideologies and styles. The notion of HRM is largely used in this sense in the United States where the term covers all management approaches to managing people in the workplace. Some approaches involve unions while others do not (see, for example, Noe, Hollenbeck, Gerhart and Wright 2005). It must be admitted, however, that most styles of labour management in the US *private* sector do not involve dealing with unions.[7] This fact can mean that students of HRM there have much less exposure to theory on union–management relations than is typical in Europe and in the old Commonwealth countries of Canada, South Africa, Australia and New Zealand.

In Britain, the rise of practitioner and academic interest in HRM sparked a debate about the term's meaning, its ideological presuppositions, and its consequences for the teaching and practice of Industrial Relations. Storey (1995: 5) defined HRM as a 'distinctive approach to employment management', one which 'seeks to achieve competitive advantage through the strategic deployment of a highly committed and capable workforce, using an integrated array of cultural, structural and personnel techniques.' Similarly, Guest (1987) developed a model of HRM as a strongly integrated management approach in which high levels of commitment and flexibility are sought from a high quality staff. Some commentators went further and saw HRM as a workplace

---

[7] In 2009, US private sector union density (based on membership) stood at 7.2% of employed wage and salary earners: http://www.bls.gov/news.release/union2.t03.htm, accessed 20/5/10.

manifestation of Thatcherite 'enterprise culture', as an ideology that would make management prerogative the natural order of things (see, for example, Keenoy and Anthony 1992).

For research purposes, defining HRM as a particular style is obviously a legitimate way to proceed. It opens up useful questions such as: What practices constitute a high-commitment model of labour management? In what contexts is such a model likely to occur? Are the outcomes of such a model actually superior?

We are interested in all styles of labour management, and the ideologies associated with them, and pursue the sorts of questions about particular models just noted. However, for the purposes of exploring the links between strategic management and HRM, we find that a broad, inclusive definition of HRM is more appropriate. The terrain of HRM includes a variety of styles. We are interested in which ones managers take in a particular context and why, and we are interested in how different styles work. The strategy literature requires this kind of openness because it recognises variety in business strategy across varying contexts (see, for example, Miles and Snow 1984, Porter 1980, 1985). It implies that there is no 'one best way' to compete in markets and organise the internal operations of the firm. If we are to truly explore the HRM–strategy nexus, we need relatively open definitions on both sides of the equation.

HRM: embedded in industries and societies

HRM, then, is a process carried out in formal organisations – some small, some large, some very large, including multinational firms and the huge government departments of large countries. While recognition of this fact is essential, the academic study of HRM has been criticised by scholars in the companion discipline of Industrial or Employment Relations for focusing too much on the firm and ignoring the wider context of the markets, networks and societies in which the firm operates (see, for example, Rubery and Grimshaw 2003, Blyton and Turnbull 2004, Rubery, Earnshaw and Marchington 2005). We think this is a fair criticism. The different HR strategies of firms are better understood if they are examined in the wider context that helps to shape them, something we shall certainly be arguing throughout this book. Work and employment practices are not entirely developed within a firm or controlled by that firm's management. In Granovetter's (1985: 481) famous phrase, firms are 'embedded in structures of social relations'.

We will shortly be arguing that HRM is profoundly affected by the characteristics of the industries in which the firm chooses to compete. This is a fundamental premise in strategic management theory in which industries are seen to vary in structure and profitability (Porter 1980) but was also demonstrated long ago in Blauner's (1964) sociological analysis of the nature of work across different manufacturing environments. He categorised industries according to four types of technology: craft (in which products are made in small, distinctive, customised batches), machine-tending (in which production is highly mechanised, as in textile production), assembly-line (in which workers are located along a conveyer belt which propels the partially completed product towards them, as in car assembly), and continuous-process technology (highly automated, '24/7', production, as in oil refining). The nature of work varies enormously across these four types. According to Blauner (1964), workers deploy a greater range of skills, have greater control and generally experience a greater sense of meaning in craft and continuous-process industries, as compared with machine-tending and assembly-line industries. The problems of how best to motivate workers naturally vary across these working conditions.

One can also observe enormous variations across service industries (Herzenberg, Alic and Wial, 1998). Simply contrast the experience of working in a major commercial law firm, with its extensive basis in professional education, its elite clients with complex problems, its comfortable, well-appointed offices and its high level of pay, with that of working in most of the retail sector, where jobs require much less education, where the public can be rude and demanding, where employees may be monitored by mystery shoppers, and have much lower pay levels! In addition to the variation that exists across manufacturing and service industries, it is also useful to consider the public sector as a set of 'industries', embracing government departments, the armed services, public health providers, state schools, and many others. Organisations in these areas, just like firms in private sector industries, face distinctive challenges and demonstrate characteristic ways of handling HRM that mark them out from other industries (see, for example, Sherer and Leblebici 2001, Kalleberg *et al.* 2006, Bach and Kessler 2007).

We will also be arguing that along with industry differences, HRM is deeply affected by differences between societies. Although globalisation is a powerful set of forces, the different characteristics of nation states still exercise a major impact on the HR strategies of firms. Nations provide a range of resources that affect workplaces and workforces: they provide some level of physical infrastructure (roading, ports, power, and so on), provide some form of political and justice system (ranging from autocracy to democracy), some kind of economic system (usually a variation of capitalism or a blend of capitalism and communism), some degree of general education, and some level of social order. These resources are of various kinds and of variable quality across nations but they are always significant in the way they affect what firms can achieve (Porter 1990). Some differences are more immediately visible than others. A less visible, but deep-seated, element of the way societies vary concerns cultural differences, the 'beliefs, values, and attitudes shared by people ... that guide their thoughts, reasoning, actions, and interactions' (De Cieri 2007: 510). As we shall explore in Chapter 3 of this book, cultural differences in attitudes to work affect *how* management can operate in different countries and are not easily set aside by companies wanting to impose a particular management style from elsewhere.

The role of industry and societal factors in influencing the HR strategies of firms is an important theme in this book. The implicit model of HR practice as something entirely within the control of management in the individual firm is something we work hard to avoid.

What are the goals of HRM?

Human resource management, we have argued, covers a broad range of activities associated with managing work and people and shows a huge range of variations across hierarchical levels, occupations, firms, industries and societies. This confusing detail and profound diversity naturally begs a fundamental question: what are employers seeking through engaging in HRM and how do their goals for HRM relate to their broader organisational goals? What are the underpinning objectives of employers? In terms of the 'level of analysis' involved, our question concerns the goals that characterise whole employing units: that is, firms or, where these are diversified and devolved in labour management, business units or establishments within them.

The task is a difficult one. It has never been easy to define the goals of labour management in the firm. In a classic analysis, Karen Legge (1978: 3) noted that most textbooks on (what was then) personnel management sidestepped the issue by briefly referring to some statement such as, 'the optimum utilization of human resources in order to achieve the goals and objectives of the organization'. She pointed out that this kind of vague, ill-defined statement begged a number of important questions, including the question of *whose* interests were being served and what was meant by optimisation. Ignoring such troublesome questions, the textbooks moved quickly into the traditional exposition of personnel practices, depicted as ends in themselves (rather than as means or methods which might be relevant in some contexts and counter-productive in others).

One can, to some extent, sympathise. In asking about a firm's goals for HRM, we face the problem that these goals are often implicit (Purcell and Ahlstrand 1994, Gratton *et al.* 1999b). Only the larger firms have formal or explicit goal statements for their HR strategies (Kersley *et al.* 2006). Even when they do, we need to be careful in taking them at face value. In HRM, aspirational rhetoric or ideology may mask a more opportunistic and pragmatic reality (Marchington and Grugulis 2000, Legge 2005). Broad policies are always open to the interpretations of managers, both general and specialist, and sometimes their active subversion. Furthermore, particular patterns of HRM are laid down or 'sedimented' at certain critical moments in an organisation's history (Poole 1986) and managers find themselves working within these traditions without necessarily being able to explain how all the pieces got there. Goals may not be seriously analysed unless some kind of crisis emerges in the firm's growth or performance that forces reconsideration and restructuring (Snape, Redman and Wilkinson 1993, Colling 1995). Our task, then, is better understood as trying to infer the general intentions or motives underpinning labour management, recognising that we are studying a complex, collective process, built up historically in firms and inevitably subject to a degree of interpretation, politicking and inconsistent practice. It helps if we analyse the goals of HRM in terms of two broad categories: economic and socio-political goals (Boxall 2007).

The economic goals of HRM

Cost-effective labour

We argue in this book that the primary problem facing firms is to secure their economic viability in the industries in which they have chosen to compete. Economic viability means that a firm generates a return on investment that its shareholders consider 'acceptable' or which meets the obligations it has to its bankers and other lenders (Cyert and March 1956, Kaysen 1960, Williamson 1964). It is not essential for a firm to 'maximise' profits but it is essential to provide investors and lenders with the kind of financial returns that sustain their commitment to the organisation. Shareholders and other finance-providers form part of the political coalition of stakeholders that sustains a firm (March 1962, Cyert and March 1963: 42–3). Management needs to ensure it meets their demands for a worthwhile return from the risk they are taking. The consequences of failing to generate an acceptable profit are that managers may be sacked, firms may be sold off, or they may be broken up and reabsorbed into other parts of a larger organisation.

It helps to tease out more fully what this implies for the organisation, including its HRM. In order to build a viable business model, management must, in fact, meet four fundamental conditions. First, managers must develop products or services that an economically worthwhile group of customers wants to buy. Marketing theory has long emphasised the fundamental principle that management needs to identify a group of customers whose needs the firm can potentially serve at a profit (Kotler and Keller 2006). However, a second condition applies. The firm will not be profitable simply through an astute targeting of customer needs. It will fail unless it actually implements its marketing promises. This means that it must stabilise a production system that delivers its promised products or services to customers in a reliable way (Rubery 1994, Rubery and Grimshaw 2003). This depends on having the necessary technology or know-how and operational processes for producing the product or service, and leads to a third, closely related condition. The firm must hire and manage the kind of labour it needs in a way that is affordable. In other words, management needs to establish a *cost-effective* system for managing the work and people the business requires (Geare 1977, Osterman 1987, Godard 2001). All of this implies one final condition: the firm needs the financial backing that will make its marketing, production and human resource management possible (Reynolds 1987, Besley and Brigham 2009). Sometimes this funding comes solely from the owner–manager or from family members but, in larger organisations, it typically comes from securing investment from shareholders and loans from bondholders or bankers.

Cost-effectiveness is a dual concept. It incorporates the idea that firms need people who are effective, who are skilled at what the firm needs them to do, while also motivating them to perform at a cost (wages, benefits, training, and so on) that the firm can afford to pay. A viable model of HRM is one that delivers on the grounds of *both* effectiveness *and* cost. Because the characteristics of industries vary (Blauner 1964, Porter 1980), we can therefore expect that viable models of HRM will vary across industries. For example, in the discount retail sector, where standard, low-priced goods are sold in bulk, consumers often shop around for the lowest prices, competition among firms is often intense, and even minor cost differences can threaten a firm's viability (Jany-Catrice, Gadrey and Pernod 2005). In such circumstances, stores have some long-term managers and experienced employees to provide a reliable 'backbone' to operations but otherwise do enough in HRM to attract less experienced workers, such as part-time student workers and new migrants, who are paid the kind of wage that is adequate in the retail sector (Siebert and Zubanov 2009). This is typically at, or not much above, the legal minimum wage (Osterman 2001). Managers do not expect most of these workers to stay for the long term but provide a basic setting in which they can gain some working experience and move on. Their business model typically turns on providing sufficient, rather than superior, service standards because customers are more price than quality sensitive. As a result, expensive models of HRM, which incorporate more rigorous employee selection, higher pay, and extensive internal employee development, are unusual in this industry (Boxall 2003). The simple fact is that they would not be cost effective.

On the other hand, as Godard and Delaney (2000: 488) explain, high-skill, high-commitment HR strategies are more often found in industries where the production system is capital intensive or where high technology is involved. They cite the example of nuclear power plants:

> in a nuclear power plant employing many workers, the costs of poor morale, [labour] turnover, and strikes can be high, so the benefits of HRM innovations will tend to be high. Firm size may also introduce important economies of scale, reducing the costs of HRM innovations per worker. Thus, in this plant, the benefits of new practices can be expected to exceed the costs. In a small, low-technology garment factory employing unskilled labour, the opposite may be true.

In capital-intensive conditions, the actual level of labour cost will be quite low (10 per cent or less of total cost) but workers will have a major effect on how well the technology is utilised (Blauner 1964). It thus pays to remunerate and train them very well, making better use of their skills and ensuring their motivation is kept high. As they find ways of making the equipment meet or even exceed its specifications, the unit costs of labour fall and productivity rises. Thus, in this kind of industry context, the firm can easily sustain high wage levels. It is more important *not* to alienate this kind of labour, because of the productivity impacts of disruptions to production, than it is to worry about wage levels (Blauner 1964: 136, 180).

These examples help to illustrate the point that it is wrong to confuse wage levels with *unit* labour costs or to confuse cost minimisation with cost-effectiveness (Osterman 1987). In certain cases, where product markets are very competitive and where technology is limited and the work is labour intensive, labour costs are decisive in the assessment of cost-effectiveness (Boxall 2003). In these situations, cost-effectiveness does broadly equate with labour cost minimisation because labour cost levels have such a huge impact on the survival of firms. This is why so much clothing, footwear and toy manufacture has moved to low-wage countries such as China and Cambodia. On the other hand, more complex and capital-intensive research and design functions can often be kept in high-wage countries where a small team of well-paid designers uses advanced computing equipment and keeps in close contact with their marketing colleagues and with retail buyers external to the firm.

Clearly, then, the problem of securing cost-effective labour, of making labour productive at reasonable cost, invites some careful thinking about costs and benefits in the industry concerned. There are indeed situations where labour costs can make or break the firm. When this occurs in manufacturing, firms worry about where to site production facilities to take advantage of lower labour costs. When it occurs in services, firms typically use employment practices that keep their service costs competitive: wages paid are relative to 'the going rate' in the local labour market (but rarely superior to it), the training investment is only sufficient to ensure basic quality, and employee turnover levels can be high. Or, if the service can be offered over the internet, managers may think about outsourcing or offshoring it to lower-cost countries. Quality may be no better than average but this may be quite acceptable with customers if the price is right. On the other hand, there are situations where labour costs are not in competition but the interaction between labour and technology needs to be carefully managed to achieve high productivity. Here, high levels of HR investment pay high dividends and help to protect against disruption or downtime. Similarly, there are areas in the service sector, such as professional services, which are knowledge-intensive. Here, managers see the value of investing in higher salaries, extensive career development, and time-consuming performance appraisal because these practices foster the kind of expert interactions with customers that make it possible for the firm to secure and retain high value-added business.

In summary, the fundamental economic motive that can be observed in HRM is concerned with making labour productive at an affordable cost in the industry concerned. In effect, managers ask: what HR systems are cost-effective or 'profit-rational' in our specific market context? In capitalist societies, the pursuit of cost-effectiveness runs across the management of labour in all business organisations and also makes its impact in public sector organisations through their budget constraints and contracting requirements.

Organisational flexibility

Cost-effectiveness is not, however, the only economic goal we can discern in HRM. Cost-effective labour is essential to economic viability in a given context. In other words, given a particular market or budget and a certain type of technology (among other things), it is about management's drive to make labour productive at competitive cost. However, change is inevitable and so an element of flexibility is also essential if the firm's model of HRM is to remain viable over time. In recent years, many firms have, of necessity, adopted some HR practices designed to enhance capacity to change or build 'organisational flexibility' (Osterman 1987). The word 'organisational' is used here because employers typically seek forms of flexibility which extend beyond, but encompass, their labour management (Streeck 1987). Concern to achieve an appropriate degree of flexibility has grown since the 1980s.

In thinking about the HRM goals that firms pursue in the area of organisational flexibility, it is useful to distinguish between *short-run* responsiveness and *long-run* agility. Short-run responsiveness includes attempts to bring about greater numerical (or 'headcount') flexibility (measures which make it easier to hire and shed labour) and greater financial flexibility (attempts to bring greater flexibility into the price of labour) (Atkinson 1984). Thus, firms engaged in very cyclical activities often seek to relate their permanent staff numbers to their calculation of the troughs in business demand rather than the relatively unpredictable peaks, seeking to offer overtime and bring in temporary or 'seasonal' staff if, and when, the workload surges. This is common in the retail sector, for example (Siebert and Zubanov 2009). In other cases, managers seek to pay workers a mix of wages and profit-related bonuses, with the latter fluctuating in line with company financial fortunes. In both these cases, the emphasis is on adjusting labour costs to fit with changes in business revenues. Short-run responsiveness also includes attempts to hire workers who are cross-trained or 'multi-skilled', combining roles that have historically been kept in separate job descriptions. Such 'functional flexibility' (Atkinson 1984) helps the firm to maintain a lower headcount but cope better with marginal improvements in product design or production processes.

Long-run agility, on the other hand, is a much more powerful, but rather ambiguous, concept (Dyer and Shafer 1999). It is concerned with the question of whether a firm can build the ability to survive in an environment that can change radically. Does the firm have the capacity to create, or at least cope with, long-run changes in products, costs and technologies? Can it adapt to change as fast or faster than its major rivals? What elements of its HR strategy might need to be flexible to achieve this? While some firms aspire to long-run agility, organisational ecologists such as Carroll and Hannan (1995), who study patterns of organisational birth, growth and decline in industries, observe that it is very hard to achieve because core features of organizations are hard to change once laid down in the early stages of establishment and growth.

A key challenge to the agility of manufacturing firms in recent times has come from the major cost differences between companies with operations in the developed world and those with operations in newly industrialising nations. When manufacturers in lower-cost countries find ways of making the same products at the same quality and delivery benchmarks but do so at much lower prices, established firms operating in high-wage countries either adjust their HR strategies or go out of business. A case in point is one of Britain's most innovative manufacturing firms, Dyson. The firm, an international leader in vacuum cleaner technology, shifted its production facilities to Malaysia in the year 2000. Relocation to Malaysia delivered lower unit costs than was possible in the UK and also ensured proximity to key parts' suppliers, thus improving the firm's location in its supply chain. Some 550 British workers were laid off in the process and HR strategy now revolves around managing a dual workforce: one in the UK where research and development (R&D) staff are employed and one in Malaysia where the products are assembled.[8] This shift in production facilities and labour forces has made Dyson a more agile firm, enabling it to invest more heavily in R&D and to expand production. The company sees its long-run ability to survive as relying on innovation in its core products or technologies. Making a difficult change to its production and HR strategy has enabled it to focus more effectively on this goal. Agility, then, may mean that the firm needs the capacity to make quite radical changes in HRM.

Human resource advantage

The achievement of economic viability is clearly the fundamental priority for management. It is the most pressing problem that management faces: without securing their financial viability, firms fail (Reynolds 1987). However, firms that survive are engaged in an ongoing process of trying to build and defend competitive advantages (Porter 1980, 1985). Advantages may be temporary or more sustained. The sort of production switching we have just talked about in the Dyson case is more likely to enhance viability than it is to bring about a sustained advantage. The firms that do it first enjoy some temporary advantages in performance but their offshoring moves are highly visible and are based on well-known information about cost differences in different countries. As other manufacturers follow suit, profits typically return to normal (Hayes and Pisano 1996). High-tech manufacturing firms, like Dyson, generally seek a more enduring form of advantage through some distinctive feature that is not so easily copied. Dyson has clearly built up a leadership position that depends on the innovativeness of its products, which stems from the quality of the highly skilled executives and designers who drive this. This is a form of

---

[8] For a summary of the company's history, see http://en.wikipedia.org/wiki/James_Dyson, accessed 25/5/10.

differentiation in the quality of human resources, a form of 'human resource advantage'.

A firm has some kind of human resource advantage when it builds a superior, hard-to-imitate capability through the special quality of its human resources. Human resource advantage can be broken down into two dimensions (Boxall 1996, 1998). The first of these is 'human capital advantage', which a firm enjoys when it employs more talented individuals than its rivals. A human capital advantage rests on the outstanding intellectual, emotional and physical performances of individuals employed in the firm. Depending on the firm's business philosophies and financial strategies, this advantage may simply relate to an elite group of highly talented individuals, typically executives and other employees whose skills generate special value, or it may be more deeply embedded throughout the entire workforce. The second dimension of HRA is 'organizational process' or 'social capital advantage', which occurs in those firms that have developed superior ways of combining the talents of individuals in collaborative activities. It is possible to hire brilliant individuals, and this can bring important breakthroughs for a company, but fail to make best use of their potential as a result of poor organisational processes in such areas as teamwork, cross-functional communication and problem solving. Thus, more powerful forms of human resource advantage occur when both the human capital and organisational processes of an organisation are superior to those of its rivals.

In the long run, just about all firms need to think, in some way, about human resource advantage but the extent of their investment in HRM varies from 'elite' to more 'egalitarian' models. Studies in the service sector imply that firms rarely build an elite model of HRM for the majority of their workers when they are locked into the cost-based competition that occurs in low-skill services (Boxall 2003). In low-skill services, technology is often used to substitute for workers and customers will typically take part in self-service if the price is right. The firm may have some elite elements in its staffing (for example, in its management of marketing and supply-chain experts) but it is unlikely to invest more than its executives consider necessary in its general workforce. The goal of building human resource advantage in a more extensive or egalitarian way throughout a workforce is more of a possibility in differentiated service markets where a group of affluent customers is prepared to pay a premium for a higher quality of service (Boxall 2003). This is observed, for example, in professional services and in such expensive services as luxury hotels and top-tier retirement villages. As a result, firms will often invest in more selective recruitment, greater development and better reward of their front-line staff in order to meet these more discerning customer needs.

Thus, the extent to which human resource advantage is based on elite or egalitarian models is variable. We will analyse and explore the possibility of human resource advantage further in this book, particularly in Chapters 4, 5 and 9. What we wish to emphasise at this stage is that the need to support the firm's viability is the fundamental economic driver in HRM. This rests on achieving a cost-effective approach to managing people and some degree of flexibility over time. As the competitive struggle unfolds, however, firms need to consider how HRM can support or develop competitive advantage, either through management of an elite core of employees or, in certain conditions, more generally across the workforce.

The socio-political objectives of HRM

Social legitimacy

While the pursuit of economic objectives is fundamental to HRM, it does not fully account for the strategic behaviour of employers. Firms are economic actors but they operate in societies, in which there are laws that attempt to control how managers employ people and in which there are customs, or widely shared expectations, for how people should be treated in the workplace. This means that some degree of *social legitimacy* must also be seen as a motive in HRM.

The reasons for this are not hard to discern. Employment laws vary significantly across nations, accounting for significant differences in HRM across different national boundaries (Gooderham, Nordhaug and Ringdal 1999). There are fundamental differences, for example, between Anglo-American employment systems, in which management typically contracts with individual employees rather than unions, and those that prevail in the 'Rhineland countries' of Germany, France and the Netherlands where 'social partnership' models accord a strong role to trade unions and to works councils in which elected employees have a say over HR policy (Paauwe and Boselie 2003, 2007).

The idea that firms need to adapt to the rules and customs of different societies is widely acknowledged in the social sciences. Economists talk of 'varieties of capitalism' (Hall and Soskice 2001), recognising the ways that economic institutions vary across nations. In the Anglophone world, the 'liberal market' model is dominant. In this variety of capitalism, shares are widely traded in stockmarkets, corporate takeovers are commonplace, and both labour-market regulation and customary attitudes to employment are more individualist and less collectivist (Gospel and Pendleton 2003). Unionisation is relatively low, and declining in the private sector, and there are few sanctions against lay-offs when times are tough (Freeman, Boxall and Haynes 2007). Firms that step out of this environment and hire a workforce in major continental European countries such as France or Germany enter a much more highly coordinated and regulated variety of capitalism. They typically find that it is important to work with trade unions and works councils and find it much more difficult to make unilateral decisions about the workforce. This was graphically illustrated in the global financial crisis of 2008–9 when some American and British managers were kidnapped – or 'bossnapped' – in French companies and forced to renegotiate deals involving major redundancies.[9] French workers sought to send the message that Anglo-American cultural assumptions about hiring and firing labour would not be treated so charitably in France. These events were viewed with incomprehension in the USA where labour contracts are more easily terminated, often requiring no advanced notice or compensation. In many European countries, collective dismissals or redundancies must be justified to the works council or the union. In some countries, like Sweden and Germany, the state has an 'active labour market strategy' to provide job and training subsidies to keep workers in employment. National context is important, especially at times of economic difficulty.

The need for firms to adapt to their social environment is, of course, strongly underlined by sociologists, such as DiMaggio and Powell (1983, 1991), who bring an 'institutional perspective' to the analysis of firms, examining the ways in which organisations are influenced by a range of expectations in wider society. In a major review of this perspective, Scott (2008: 50–9) defines 'three pillars of institutions': the 'regulative', the 'normative' and the 'cultural-cognitive'. Regulative pressures are the most obvious. They include the different codes of employment law that we have just highlighted in our discussion of varieties of capitalism. Organisations can be coerced to comply with legal rules, if the state deems this necessary and has the power to do so. Normative or moral pressures are also fairly apparent, evidenced in the way that firms come under pressure to conform to prevailing social values and norms around how to treat people in the workplace. For example, in the Anglophone world, the last 50 years have seen a growing movement to foster equal employment opportunity, to eliminate discrimination on such grounds as gender, race, sexual orientation, and physical disability, and the largest companies increasingly invest in practices that foster diversity and social inclusion (Kossek and Pichler 2007). Few companies that are large enough to be 'household names' are untouched by this important social trend. To be sure, a lot of this expectation is now embedded in regulation but much of it is conveyed

---

[9] See, for example: http://business.timesonline.co.uk/tol/business/industry_sectors/industrials/article5974895.ece, accessed 20/5/10.

through norms of behaviour that were much less prevalent in earlier times. Finally, there are cultural–cognitive pressures, which include the ways in which people customarily think and behave in a society. Hofstede's (1980, 1983) pioneering work on national culture has emphasised the ways in which people in some societies are more individualistic than they are in others, more comfortable with status and power differences, more prone to avoid uncertainty, and so on. These are more subtle, deep-seated pressures and managers may not discern their true significance if they are simply passing through a country on a short business trip. Those who stay to live and build a business typically find that they affect how HRM can be conducted, as we will discuss in Chapter 3.

The key implication we wish to emphasise at this stage is that prevailing notions of legitimate or appropriate behaviour in how people are employed affect the standing of organisations (Suchman 1995, Scott 2008). This is certainly true in societies where labour laws are not simply enacted but also effectively enforced through government agencies and/or trade union action. As Lees (1997) argues, it is therefore important that social legitimacy is recognised as an employer goal in HRM alongside the more market-oriented ones. Not only are there legitimacy issues for firms operating in one society but there are extremely complex legitimacy issues when firms operate in multiple societies (Kostova and Zaheer 1999). In general, therefore , employers are concerned with ensuring their social legitimacy *while simultaneously* pursuing cost-effective HRM (Boxall 2007). More broadly, of course, the quality of the firm's reputation as an employer is only one aspect of its social legitimacy, which also includes such things as its impacts on the natural environment. There is a range of contemporary movements designed to encourage greater social responsibility in business and broader corporate reporting, including the notion of the 'triple bottom line' (financial, environmental and social) (Elkington 1997).

In practice, we see significant variation in the extent to which employers take legitimacy goals into account in their labour management. At one extreme, there is a group of employers in any society who try to avoid their legal responsibilities. In the UK, for example, there is an ongoing problem with the employment of new migrants in unsafe conditions. This was tragically illustrated in the drowning of 23 Chinese workers while harvesting shell-fish at Morecombe Bay in 2004.[10] There are sectors of the British economy, such as catering, where research has revealed that a significant number of employers do not pay the minimum wage (Edwards and Ram 2006). Most employers

---

[10] See, for example, 'Another Morecombe Bay is waiting to happen', *The Guardian*, Tuesday 28 March 2006, p. 28.

in Britain, however, comply with their responsibilities under employment law and under government regulations for occupational safety and health. Their legitimacy goal is legal compliance. Compliance is the baseline legitimacy goal for employers who wish to avoid prosecution and bad publicity, a risk in any society in which labour laws are efficiently enforced. It is apparent, however, that some firms, at least, operate beyond this baseline. For example, some firms are now actively competing for Equal Employment Opportunity (EEO) awards or for favourable rankings in lists of the best companies to work for or the most family-friendly workplaces.[11] These tend to be larger, better-known firms, but some are also innovative small firms, with a strong interest in building their standing as an 'employer of choice'. Some see the achievement of the Investors in People (IiP) standard,[12] based on a commitment to training and development linked to business needs, as a dimension of legitimacy while for others being recognised for corporate social responsibility, including in employment, is a desirable goal.

Managerial power

As with economic motives, where we see both attempts to stabilise cost-effectiveness in the short run and the need to build flexibility and competitive advantage if firms are to survive into the longer term, it is useful to think about management's socio-political motives in a dynamic way. All firms can be seen as political systems in which management holds legitimate authority but one in which management decisions are nonetheless subject to legal and moral challenge (Donaldson and Preston 1995). What is management trying to achieve in the politics or governance of the workplace as time goes by? The evidence suggests that management exhibits a fundamental desire to enhance its power as a stakeholder, a tendency that can have both positive and perverse consequences for the organisation.

In a classic study of management ideology and power, Reinhard Bendix (1956: xxiii) argued that 'ideologies of management are attempts by leaders of enterprises to justify the privilege of voluntary action and association for themselves, while imposing upon all subordinates the duty of obedience and of service to the best of their ability'. Similarly, Gospel (1973) refers to management as having a less openly acknowledged 'security objective' alongside the profit (cost-effectiveness) motive, a goal to maximise managerial control

---

[11] http://money.cnn.com/magazines/fortune/bestcompanies/2009/, accessed 20/5/10; http://www.greatplacetowork.co.uk/, accessed 20/5/10; http://www.workingmother.com/BestCompanies/, accessed 20/5/10.
[12] http://www.investorsinpeople.co.uk/Pages/Home.aspx, accessed 20/5/10.

over an uncertain environment including threats to its power base from work groups and trade unions. We can see this in the way the managers of multinational firms tend to favour investment in countries with less demanding labour market regulations (Cooke 2001, 2007b). We can also see it at industry and societal levels, in the tendency of employer federations to lobby, over time, for greater freedom to manage and to resist new employment regulations seen to be diminishing managerial prerogative. And we see it in the actions of those firms in which managers wish to minimise the pressures exerted by external shareholders and watchdogs. De-listing from stockmarkets is growing among firms in which a dominant (often, family-based) interest has sufficient capital to buy out other shareholders.[13]

Power, of course, has negative connotations but we should be careful not to rush to such a judgement. An appropriate level of management power is positive. It is needed so that management can coordinate the interests of the diverse stakeholders on whom the organisation depends, an assumption of good governance which has long been recognised (Blau 1964, chapter eight). Most people would recognise that there is a natural tendency in positions of authority, or in conditions of risk, to try to ensure one can act effectively: it is unhelpful to firms if managers are hopelessly checked at every point when they need to make important decisions for the sake of the organisation. Like other organisational actors, managers need the power to act, they need some degrees of freedom or the job is impossible (Clegg and Haugaard 2009, Gohler 2009).

However, there is always the potential for power-seeking behaviour to become perverse, bringing about consequences that are counterproductive for an organisation's well-being. Economists studying managerial behaviour inside the firm have long emphasised the fact that the interests of shareholders and managers do not perfectly coincide. Williamson (1964), for example, argues that while managers need to generate an acceptable level of profit, their motives also include enlarging their salaries, enhancing their security, and increasing their status, power and prestige. In the branch of organisational economics known as 'agency theory', managers are seen as agents whose interests overlap with, but also diverge from, those of the firm's principals or owners (Jensen and Meckling 1976, Lazear 1999, Tomer 2001). Managers, like other stakeholders in organisations, can use their power to pursue their own interests, including their personal rewards. Evidence for this perspective is not hard to find. The global financial crisis of 2008–9, for example, has given rise

---

[13] See, for example, *The Economist*, 25 November–1 December, 2006, p. 96.

to widespread criticism of the way in which banking executives have profited enormously from annual bonus payouts based on short-term performance targets while the long-term health of their organisations has been undermined, or fatally compromised, by ill-informed and excessive risk-taking (Stiglitz 2010).[14] Although the worst excesses are in banking, the executive bonus culture has actually been more widespread. It has been encouraged by the growth of private equity firms and hedge funds, which have promoted highly leveraged company acquisitions and speculative investments based on predictions of share price movements rather than on more conservative valuations of a company's assets and liabilities. This trend to 'financialization' (Sisson and Purcell 2010: 91–4) has brought an increasing emphasis on managing managers through pay-for-performance schemes.

Thus, while management is generally concerned about social legitimacy, at least to the extent of legal compliance in societies where there is a risk of legal enforcement, and sometimes well beyond this, we also observe management, as a stakeholder, playing a longer-run political game. The tendency of management is to act, over time, to enhance its power base, something which can have both positive and negative consequences for the organization.

Strategic tensions and problems in HRM

We have identified some fundamental or underpinning motives in HRM (Figure 1.3). We have split these into economic and socio-political goals because the firm is not simply an unconstrained economic actor: it is an economic entity located in a social context. Firms need a cost-effective approach

Figure 1.3 The goals of HRM

---

[14] For the OECD's review of the problem, see http://www.oecdobserver.org/news/fullstory. php/aid/2931/Corporate_governance:_Lessons_from_the_financial_crisis.html, accessed 19/5/10.

to HRM in the industries in which they compete while also needing legitimacy in the societies in which they are located. If they fail on these two criteria, they will generally not survive. Over time, firms need to develop some degree of flexibility in their HRM and their managers need to secure enough power to be effective. Firms that survive are concerned with how to build and defend competitive advantages. This implies some thinking about 'human resource advantage', not necessarily for the entire workforce but at least for elite elements in it. Such a discussion naturally arouses suspicion that the pursuit of these goals is far from straightforward. This is indeed the case. The strategic management of work and people in the firm inevitably involves management wrestling with 'strategic tensions' and problems, including trade-offs between employer and employee interests. We turn now to a discussion of the key tensions and problems that management faces.

The problem of labour scarcity

One of the main problems facing management stems from the fact that firms need to compete not only in product markets but also in labour markets (Windolf 1986, Rubery 1994, Coff 1997). In all countries where forced labour has been eliminated, workers are free to resign and seek alternative employment. Firms must compete with others to secure appropriately skilled staff. The general severity of labour supply problems waxes and wanes with the level of economic growth. Organisations are often inundated with job applicants and have less difficulty recruiting in major recessions when unemployment levels are high. However, the challenge of recruiting the *quality* of labour they need tends to remain an issue. Well-resourced and well-recognised organisations, those that have the ability to pay high salaries and offer career development opportunities, tend to dominate the labour market. As a result, many small firms remain fragile, tenuous organisations with ongoing recruitment problems (Storey 1985, Hendry, Arthur and Jones 1995, Hornsby and Kuratko 2003). The goals of building a stable production system, including a cost-effective supply of motivated employees, and building some capacity for development of the business, are seriously compromised if the firm cannot make competitive job offers and keep the labour it has. It then struggles to build the capabilities it needs to meet its business objectives or respond to its clients' demands. In the extreme, the tension associated with labour scarcity can become a full-blown 'capability crisis', threatening the firm's reputation and viability.

Labour scarcity is a problem that can afflict entire industries and not simply undercapitalised firms or new firms struggling for recognition. In the oil industry, shortages of the specialised workers needed on offshore drilling platforms remains a problem despite the global recession of 2008–9.[15] In the British trucking industry, there have been major shortages of drivers because of difficult working conditions: drivers have responsibility for valuable vehicles and dangerous loads, work long hours in stressful driving conditions, and are often away from home (Marchington, Carroll and Boxall 2003). Many people who hold driving qualifications prefer to work in a local factory or service industry where their lifestyle can be more normal.

In the health sector, labour scarcity is a worldwide phenomenon: competition for workers with internationally transferable skills continues to strain the resources of public and private health systems all over the world. The UK government's list of skill shortages, used to indicate immigration opportunities, currently includes around 30 categories of medical specialists.[16] As recruiters in rich countries comb the globe for scarce labour, there can be kick-on effects and ethical problems: health services in third-world countries, for example, can be denuded of expensively trained health professionals by first-world 'poaching'. Similarly, small countries, such as New Zealand, can find that capable managers are constantly being recruited to more challenging and better paid jobs in much larger countries where the big companies offer extensive career opportunities (Gilbert and Boxall 2009). Labour scarcity is therefore a multi-layered problem: it can cause severe problems at organisational, industry and societal levels.

The problem of labour motivation or control

As suggested by the AMO framework, a second major problem is associated with the motivation of employee behaviour if and when workers are actually hired. Motivation is a fragile variable. The employment contract is an exchange relationship but, unlike the sale and purchase of commodities, it involves an ongoing, unpredictable interaction between the parties. Future behaviour matters but neither party can accurately predict it when they sign up. Both are taking risks. As the pioneering industrial relations writers, Sidney and Beatrice Webb (1902: 658) put it, the labour contract is 'indeterminate'. Does the worker really have the skills they say they have and will they offer a conscientious level of effort over time, helping the employer reach their productivity objectives? On the other side of the coin, will the employer impose

---

[15] http://www.offshoreoilandgasjobs.com/1673.html?*session*id*key*=*session*id*val*, accessed 20/5/10.

[16] http://www.skillclear.co.uk/Skills-Shortage-Occupation-List.pdf, accessed 20/5/10.

work pressures that are intense or make the worker suffer working conditions that are unsafe? Will the level of work pressure be subtly (or, perhaps, crudely) increased over time without any renegotiation of rewards? Such a process of work intensification without compensation can undermine the initial trust extended to the employer by the worker and invite some form of retaliation which then damages the firm's performance (for example, reduction of work quality, absenteeism, disinclination to 'go the extra mile', and resignation). Overall, will the 'wage-effort bargain' become more or less satisfying for the parties? Will the parties achieve some kind of satisfactory balance in their relationship?

With employment relationships, as with marriages, it is impossible to anticipate all this in advance and silly to think that any written contract of employment could ever cover all the possibilities (Williamson, Wachter and Harris 1975, Roehling 2005). As Cartier (1994: 182) puts it, 'the contract of employment is inherently incomplete'. As a result, the law of employment gives employers the right to issue what are commonly known as 'lawful and reasonable orders', but herein lies the rub. The simple fact is that employer control of the behaviour of other human beings is always limited. As Keenoy (1992: 95) argues, 'no matter how extensive the controls, in the final analysis, management is reliant on employee cooperation'. When individuals are instructed to carry out work tasks, their discretion is never fully taken away from them (Bendix 1956, Organ 1988, Hardy and Clegg 1996). This means that the employer, like the employee, must exercise some trust, relying on workers to use their judgement in productive ways. For example, no matter how much 'scripting' there is of how to deal with customers in shops, the individual employee still decides whether to be helpful to customers or to be plainly rude in a way that alienates them, something we have all experienced.

While it is true that employers typically have greater economic power and may use it to impose terms on workers (Webb and Webb 1902), we should not imagine that employees are passive or lack power resources, even in low-wage, low-skill conditions. All employees have some power over their own actions and those with know-how that is critical to production, and who are not easily replaced, have greater power. For example, in Edwards and Ram's (2006: 909) study of a selection of Indian restaurants in Britain, chefs were 'in relatively short supply and the quality of their cooking was critical to the success of the restaurant'. This meant that they were granted greater autonomy in how they ran the kitchen and could sometimes get extended leave to visit family in India, a concession rarely available to waiters. Workers also gain greater power when they are prepared to act in concert (Coff 1999), as is frequently demonstrated in those strikes which shut down operations and impose major costs on employers. It pays, therefore, to think of employment relationships in terms of a 'bargaining model': the parties are 'mutually dependent' and each has some room to bargain with the other party over time (Edwards and Ram 2006: 897).

There is a huge body of literature examining the relationships between employer and employee interests in the workplace and their implications for motivation and workplace performance. Researchers in industrial relations and the sociology of work emphasise the fact that there are important conflicts of interest in the workplace (see, for example, Clegg 1975, Kelly 1998, Blyton and Turnbull 2004, Budd 2004). An important perspective is 'labour process' theory (LPT), which analyses the tensions between employer attempts at control and worker resistance (Braverman 1974, Burawoy 1979, Thompson and Harley 2007). Conflicts over income (for example, what share of revenue goes to profit and what to wages?; what relativities should there be across occupational groups?; to what extent is it fair to pay for performance differences within occupational groups?) and over the control of work (for example, who makes decisions about work processes?; what staffing levels should be maintained?; how fair is the workload?) are seen to affect the basis for workplace cooperation. Many scholars emphasise the role of voice institutions in improving the balance of interests. The general argument is that management should work with worker representatives in processes of collective bargaining, information sharing and consultation, to enhance fairness and build a work climate characterised by trust and mutual respect. A willingness on management's part to share control is seen as important to developing a stable 'social order' in which both the firm and its workers can work productively and reap the rewards they value (Watson 2005, 2007).

Organisational psychologists also emphasise fairness or equity concerns in the workplace, including employee concerns with the justice of their rewards and workplace decision-making processes (see, for example, Folger and Cropanzano 1998, Folger 2005). The process of building trust and positive motivation to perform is seen to depend on the employer creating a track record of fairness in HR decisions. In terms of conceptual frameworks, the notion that individuals have a 'psychological contract' with their employer has become increasingly important (Rousseau 1995, Guest 2007). A major gap between what management promises and what management delivers in the psychological contract inevitably affects both an individual's capacity to trust and their level of commitment. Psychological researchers have also conducted extensive work on the motivational properties of work itself, on the ways in which it can be made more interesting and challenging (Cordery and Parker 2007).

In this book, we bring together these perspectives on motivation. The key point we wish to emphasise is that a tension around employee motivation or control is inevitable in the employment relationship. Motivation is an ongoing concern for individual managers and for management collectively. At their worst, motivational challenges can be expressed in forms of collective action (such as lowered work norms and strikes) or in high levels of individual resistance (such as dysfunctional levels of absenteeism and employee turnover). Such challenges can affect management's legitimacy, depress productivity and threaten the firm's viability.

Change tensions in labour management

The reality of change also creates tensions. The need to establish a stable production system, while also pursuing some degree of flexibility, poses major dilemmas within management strategy (Osterman 1987, Brown and Reich 1997, Adler, Goldoftas and Levine 1999). How much weight should management place on strengthening its production routines to make the firm more efficient and how much weight should be placed on building flexibility for the future (Wright and Snell 1998)?

To illustrate the difficult choices involved, suppose a firm developing a new line of business decides it wants a high degree of flexibility. It faces a context in which unemployment levels are presently high. In this context, management decides to employ all operating staff in the new business on short-term or temporary employment contracts. This means the firm can shed labour or downsize more easily if it has to. A problem emerges, however, when the labour market improves: many of the more highly productive workers take the opportunity to move to more secure jobs elsewhere (why should they work on a short-term contract when they can obtain a permanent job, one that will help them gain home loans and make their families more secure?). In this labour market context, the firm finds that it fails to recruit and retain as well as its competitors or to reach their level of production quality. Too much emphasis on flexible employment starts to threaten its chances of survival. It will have to think again about how to employ people.

Imagine another firm, which employs all its labour on well-paid, permanent contracts to build a loyal workforce (traditionally called 'labour hoarding'). This works well for quite a time but the firm's sales are sensitive to consumer discretionary spending and they decline sharply when an economic recession comes along. The firm has products with excellent long-term prospects but greater flexibility is needed in its staffing structure to ensure it can weather these sorts of short-term variations in demand. It feels forced to make some lay-offs, a process that tarnishes its 'psychological contract' with its employees, and spurs management to think about whether all staff should actually be on permanent contracts.

As these illustrations make apparent, both of these scenarios represent undesirable extremes. Both firms need to consider how to strike a better balance between short-run and long-run. For example, in the recession of 2008–9, many firms in the UK and in Europe sought to avoid lay-offs by reducing the working week or encouraging employees to take leave on reduced pay in order to retain skills and employee goodwill.[17] Further, as the scenarios make clear, the problem of how to cope with change not only creates dilemmas within management strategy but brings trade-offs with the security interests of workers. In Hyman's (1987: 43) memorable phrase, capitalism is a system in which 'employers require workers to be *both* dependable *and* disposable'. The most resilient firms are those which can evolve a clever balance between stability and flexibility while maintaining employee trust and confidence. This is much easier said than done.

Tension between management power and social legitimacy

As emphasised above, some level of social legitimacy typically matters to firms. Social legitimacy can be thought of as having an inward and an outward face: there needs to be an appropriate 'social order' within the firm, which inevitably connects to the firm's reputation in wider society. An important strategic tension lies in the fact that establishing an appropriate social order depends on management accepting some constraints on its power. Historically, this has not always come willingly from management and action by trade unions and the state have often been necessary to enforce it, as we shall explain in Chapter 5. In countries such as the UK, France and the USA, the growth of trade unions in the early to mid-twentieth century saw the legitimacy challenge spill over from the shopfloor onto the streets. These countries, and many others, experienced waves of strikes and social disruption until unions won recognition from employers and gained the right to collective bargaining to improve workplace safety, reduce workloads, and lift wages. Collective bargaining enabled workers to 'jointly regulate' their employment conditions with management (Flanders 1970). Unions also turned to national political activity, lobbying political parties and, in many countries, forming their own. As a result, progressive social legislation – which brings organising rights and

---

[17] See http://business.timesonline.co.uk/tol/business/economics/article6685682.ece, accessed 20/5/10.

minimum conditions to all workers – has largely eliminated this sort of challenge in advanced industrialised countries. There are exceptions, of course. Stubborn management resistance to employee influence is still apparent in a minority of firms (Freeman 2007), something which can require the intervention of labour courts or government mediation services. There is also the fact that there are large low-wage sectors in advanced countries, which are targeted by unions and community coalitions in 'living wage' campaigns (see, for example, Juravich and Hilgert 1999, Nissen 2000). The existence of low-wage environments still generates political concern throughout the rich countries (Kazis and Miller 2001).

In addition, public attention is increasingly focused on how management uses its power in developing countries. An important contemporary development concerns the ethics of human resource management in global supply chains in which managers seek out production sites which offer both lower costs and greater freedom to manage (Cooke 2001, 2007b). But the exercise of this power can bring legitimacy challenges. Multinational clothing and footwear companies are increasingly concerned that they do not acquire a reputation for sourcing their products from contractors employing Third-World labour on exploitative terms.[18] Gap Inc, for example, employs more than 80 people in its corporate social responsibility department to develop standards and monitor employment practices across an extensive supply chain of around 1,500 production sites in some 50 countries.[19]

Key questions concern what level of rights should be universally available to workers and respected by companies. The International Labour Organisation (ILO), established in 1919 and incorporated into the United Nations in 1946, is the 'tripartite UN agency that brings together governments, employers and workers of its member states in common action to promote decent work throughout the world'.[20] Its decent-work agenda includes attempts to ensure workers everywhere can freely join unions and engage in collective bargaining while also aiming to eliminate forced labour, child labour and discrimination in employment (Hughes 2005).

Following from the fundamental issue of the baseline level of labour rights that management should respect, a key question concerns whether companies can successfully audit their own performance in this area. To bring third-party

---

[18] See, for example, 'Labour Behind the Label', http://en.wikipedia.org/wiki/Labour_Behind_the_Label, accessed 20/5/10.

[19] Gap's response to reports of child labour being used at one of its sub-contractors can be found at: http://www.gapinc.com/GapIncSubSites/csr/Goals/SupplyChain/Program/SC_Addressing_Child_Labor_Program.shtml, accessed 20/5/10.

[20] http://www.ilo.org/global/lang--en/index.htm, accessed 20/5/10.

scrutiny into the assessment of ethical employment practice, a New York-based organisation called Social Accountability International has developed an international standard called SA (Social Accountability) 8000.[21] SA 8000 is based on key conventions drawn from the ILO, the Universal Declaration of Human Rights and the UN Convention on the Rights of the Child. It thus incorporates standards on child and forced labour, union rights, employee discipline, and health and safety, among others. Companies seeking this standard must be audited and certified by an accredited audit agency. While modelled on the well-known ISO quality system, SA 8000 requires auditors to consult with workers and their unions, and includes a mechanism for workers to bring complaints about non-compliance. Another way in which global companies can attest to the legitimacy of their HRM is through membership of the 'Ethical Trading Initiative', an alliance of companies, non-governmental organisations and trade unions, which requires independent verification that codes of employment practice are being implemented.[22]

In summary, therefore, when management reaches employment agreements with workers and their organisations, and thus willingly constrains its own power in certain ways, the legitimacy of the employment regime in the firm is usually enhanced. Furthermore, when management in international companies openly embraces the ILO's decent-work agenda, including fundamental labour rights, its legitimacy in both its home country and around the world is very likely to be improved. It is readily apparent, however, that there are many firms which try to 'fly under the radar', in which the tension between management power and social legitimacy is being resolved at a much lower level, including firms in which managers breach the minimum wage and working conditions and seek to avoid providing channels for employee voice.

Complexity and politics in management

What we have said so far should indicate the kind of complexity that is involved in managing work and people. The fact that we can highlight the sorts of problems firms face in pursuing their HRM goals does not mean that it is easy to solve any of them. Complexity grows as organisations grow and as they become more diverse. Management faces 'cognitive limitations' in developing good strategy, a problem that has bedevilled management attempts to develop astute frameworks for problem analysis and goal setting in HRM. Despite the growing attention to HRM since the 1980s, boardroom and top management

---

[21] http://www.sa-intl.org/, accessed 20/5/10.
[22] http://www.ethicaltrade.org/, accessed 20/5/10.

debates have often been hamstrung by lack of agreement on how reports on strategic HR matters should be structured. The problem was summed up by a group managing director in Purcell and Ahlstrand's (1994: 61) study of HRM in multidivisional firms who commented that the board in his company 'had decided on thirty priorities in the last few years, with the people ones being the most woolly, the hardest to measure, and the easiest to forget.' In this light, much of this book is dedicated to examining confusing HR issues that affect management policy and exploring frameworks that can help structure the management of work and people in a way useful to managers.

But management's problems in HRM are not simply cognitive. Strategic management is not just mentally hard, it is politically fraught. Never mind the politics between management and labour, some of the worst politics are on one's own side. Besides the personal power struggles that take place between ambitious managers in organisations, management can be split between disciplines and across levels of the hierarchy. Marketing and operations executives, for example, may clash over how best to provide customer service when there are pressures on company margins (Batt 2007). The desire of marketers to personalise customer service may be resisted by operations managers who are accountable for increasing efficiency, which often implies reducing costs through staff reductions and using technology to standardise how customers are treated. This will then affect HR executives, who become the proverbial meat in the sandwich: they will have to carry out the lay-offs that deliver the cost reductions and cope with the impact on employee attitudes. Batt (2004) also provides a vivid illustration of conflict within management across hierarchical levels. She describes how senior management in one company wished to introduce self-managing teams on the grounds that they would enhance productivity but supervisors and middle managers successfully resisted the initiative, which would radically change their roles. Implementation became impossible without their willing cooperation. Such an illustration reinforces the point that change in labour management can be as much about politics and power within management, as it is about economic rationality.

Variations in institutional supports and societal resources

Finally, supposing management understands the problems of HRM well enough and is well resourced and well disposed in political terms to handle them, we return to the fact that firms are embedded in industries and societies, as scholars of comparative employment institutions, such as Rubery and Grimshaw (2003), emphasise. Small firms are clearly very dependent on state support which includes, very critically, systems for vocational education and training in their sector (Winterton 2007). Firms in societies in which they and their competitors rely on 'poaching' rather than training to develop the staff they need are very vulnerable in a hot labour market: the undercapitalised ones may simply fail to attract the workers they need, finding that customers desert them and they lose their reputation.

It is wrong to assume that these issues simply afflict small firms. So-called 'global' firms are also affected by the dominant ways in which a society organises its human resource development. As is well known, large British manufacturers have been at a disadvantage for some time. German firms, for example, have enjoyed major advantages in manufacturing arising from superior technical training systems to those typically found in English-speaking countries (Steedman and Wagner 1989, Wever 1995). As Winterton (2007: 327) explains, 'the higher skill level of the German workforce is generally seen as a source of competitive advantage, permitting German firms to focus on higher value-added market niches'. On the other hand, he also explains that German firms do not have it all their own way: US and UK firms often find it easier to make the changes necessary to bring in 'lean production' and more flexible ways of working. The slow pace of the German institutional structure, with its layers of industrial negotiation and consultation, can act as a costly drag. Firms in the Anglophone world often take advantage of their more fluid decision-making structures. This helps to make the point that the industry and societal context both constrains and enables firms to perform.

Overall, therefore, firms are not masters of their own destiny in HRM even if managers perceive the issues well and want to act effectively. We will be arguing that management does enjoy a realm of strategic choice to make distinctive decisions in HRM but the extent of that realm varies: the choices are never entirely in management's hands.

Summary and structure of the book

This book adopts a broad, inclusive definition of HRM because we aim to explore the various ways in which HRM is critical to the survival and relative performance of firms and other organisations. Human resource management includes the firm's work systems and its employment practices. It embraces both individual and collective aspects of people management. It is not restricted to any one style or ideology. It engages the energies of both line and specialist managers (where the latter exist) and typically entails a range of messages for a variety of workforce groups.

This chapter has discussed the goals or motives that we see underpinning the management of work and people. Human resource management is a process which serves more than one critical goal. The fundamental economic goal in HRM is concerned with developing a cost-effective system of labour management that supports the firm's financial viability in the industries in which it competes. This goal implies a second one: achieving a degree of flexibility in HRM if the firm is to remain viable as the economic context changes. A third economic motive involves seeking ways of supporting or developing competitive advantage through the quality of HRM in the firm ('human resource advantage'), although this is often pursued for an elite group of employees rather than the entire workforce. These economic goals are accompanied by two socio-political ones: social legitimacy and management power. At the same time as they are seeking economic viability, management needs to think about how to secure legitimacy in the societies in which the firm operates. At a minimum, this should mean employing labour according to legal requirements and taking important social customs seriously but, in reality, we know that there are some firms that do not operate legitimately. In the dynamic picture, we also observe management seeking to enhance its power. Much of this is appropriate because management needs a secure power base to coordinate the stakeholders who contribute to the firm. However, it can become perverse, as recently illustrated in the controversy over the ways in which management has used its power to inflate its personal rewards in the banking sector, at the expense of shareholders and the wider community.

As this suggests, pursuing these goals inevitably involves grappling with strategic tensions and problems. These include the problem of labour scarcity, which hamstrings firms that are weak in the labour market and which can afflict entire industries and societies. Labour motivation is an inevitable challenge in all firms because employment relationships rely on human discretion and the control of human behaviour is always limited. The need to grapple with change brings trade-offs between company survival and employee security while management's pursuit of power can bring major challenges to the firm's legitimacy. The cognitive and political issues associated with these problems are a major problem in themselves. And, even where the firm is well resourced and astutely led, there are serious challenges posed by the industry and societal contexts in which firms are embedded.

We have a job to do, so what lies ahead? In Part 1, three chapters look at the key bridges that link strategy with HRM. Chapter 2 explores the meaning of strategy, contrasting the strategic problems of firms with the strategies they adopt to tackle them. It examines the ways in which the quality of HRM inevitably affects the process of strategic management and can be used to improve it. In Chapter 3, we set up definitions of strategic HRM and HR strategy and consider the ways in which managers actually adapt their HR practices to their environments. This chapter underlines the 'law of context' in HRM. While finding serious fault with 'best-practicism' in HRM, it does, however, find value in the identification of general principles of HRM. Chapter 4 explores the ways in which HRM might contribute to competitive advantage. This means engaging with the resource-based view of the firm, a key body of thought in strategic management that is laced with perplexing human issues. Along with an emphasis on the fact that firms are embedded in an economic and social context, it is a perspective which informs much of the rest of the book.

In Part 2, the book contains four chapters which aim to lay the basis of a strategic theory of labour management after the previous section has undermined simplistic concepts of 'best practice'. It explores general principles that can be used to guide the strategic choices firms make in managing work and people. The first two chapters explore issues that are inherently collective. In Chapter 5, we examine work systems in the light of the changing economics of production and, in Chapter 6, we explore the variety of ways in which employees can express their voice or exert some influence over workplace decisions. This is followed by Chapter 7 which focuses on the management of individual employment relationships within this larger context. In Chapter 8, we draw the various pieces from this part of the book together through a typology outlining major HR systems and a model of the key links between HR systems and performance inside the 'black box' of the firm.

In Part 3 of the book, we apply strategy concepts and general principles of labour management to the analysis of HR strategy in complex and dynamic contexts. In Chapter 9, we set out a model of how HR strategy evolves across cycles of industry growth, maturity and decline/renewal. Then, in Chapter 10, we discuss research on the nature of HRM in the most complex contexts currently known: multidivisional and multinational firms. The final chapter (Chapter 11) summarises the book's most important themes and asks the 'where to from here?' question, examining ways in which the understandings of strategy and HRM developed in this book might be practically applied to improve the strategic management processes in contemporary firms.

part 1

Connecting strategy and human resource management

2

Strategy and the process of strategic management

What do we mean by 'strategy' and 'strategic management' and what role does HRM play in them? How might HRM play a more powerful, more effective role in strategic management? This part of the book is dedicated to these important questions. Because of diverse conceptions of strategy, the role of the first chapter in Part 1 is to establish a definition of this troublesome word. In so doing, we consider the ways in which strategy is formed and re-formed in organisations: the process of strategic management. As the chapter will make clear, strategic management is a human process beset with both intellectual difficulties and political challenges. Senior executives, in particular, are critical to the quality of the process. How well organisations handle the strategic management process therefore depends on how effectively they manage their managers, one of the central concerns in HRM.

Strategic problems and the strategies of firms

As many writers have pointed out, the notion of strategy is subject to a confusing variety of interpretations. Much of the early literature in the field of strategic HRM leapt into the fray with little recognition that the notion of strategy needs careful handling. In order to describe what we mean by the word, it helps if we start with the negative. What definitions or conceptions of strategy are not helpful?

Defining strategy: misunderstandings

First, as Henry Mintzberg (1978, 1990, 1994) has long argued, it is unhelpful to equate strategy with 'strategic plan'. A strategic plan is a formal document setting out an organisation's goals and initiatives over a defined time period. *defining* Strategic plans are characterised by a variety of formats. For example, the time horizons vary. Some firms use three-year plans, others use five-year plans, and still others, in industries such as mining characterised by long-term invest-ments and controversial environmental issues, there are plans that run for 25 years or beyond. Other variations include the range of goals targeted, the activities that are planned for, and the ways in which the functional areas of the business are integrated with one another. Strategic plans are more likely to be found in large, complex companies which have major problems with coordinating efforts towards common goals (Grant 2005). It is hard to see how any multidivisional firm – facing the task of allocating its capital across business units – could cope without them. It is easy to see why such 'vast, diverse' firms as General Electric developed corporate planning in the 1960s (Whittington 1993: 71). Such complex firms need to engage in strategic plan-ning in order to enhance communication across organisational levels and to negotiate goals in an array of business units located across diverse political environments (Jarzabkowski and Balogun 2009). Strategic plans are also more likely to be found in public sector organisations which have requirements to disclose their goals and principal activities to politicians and the public. There are also certain industries where formal planning is *de rigueur*. It is impossible, for example, to undertake major construction projects, such as a new hotel or office tower in a city, without formal planning for the financial, architectural, material, labour and environmental implications. Official permission is rarely forthcoming without it.

However, the formality of strategic planning is unusual in small businesses, which often account for as much as half the private sector economy, even in the world's richest countries. Does this mean these firms have no strategy? Certainly not. It is possible to find strategy in every business because it is embedded in the important choices that managers and other employees of the firm make about what to do and how to do it. In other words, when careful observers make the effort, it is possible to discern the firm's strategy in its behaviour: in the characteristic ways in which the organisation tries to cope with its environment (Freeman 1995). As will be explained further below, we intend to base our understanding of strategy on the 'strategic choice' per-spective. A firm's strategy is the set of strategic choices that is revealed in the characteristic ways it behaves.

This conception of strategy means we should 'treat with a grain of salt' the strategic plans we do find in the kind of organisations that use them. Formal planning documents rarely describe all of the organisation's strategic behaviour or keep track of all of its 'strategic learning' over time (Mintzberg 1990). We are not wanting to imply, however, that planning is therefore unhelpful. Far from it. As we will explain further in Part 3 of the book and in the final chapter, the research suggests that *good* planning is very valuable in HRM. We are not anti-planners. The point we are making here is that strategy is best discerned in behaviour, not in formal planning documents.

Second, we need to be careful with the popular distinction between 'strategy' and 'tactics' or between 'strategy' and 'operations'. This is a problem that has crept into management jargon from the military origins of strategy. In classical Greek, 'strategos' is associated with the role of the general, the high-level, orchestrating commander (Bracker 1980). In popular usage, we still tend to associate strategy with the top leader who articulates a vision, or who makes great decisions at a distance from the action, and who lets lower-level staff work out the details later. A major problem with this imagery is the way it tends to imply that the goals or ends we decide on are much more important that the tactics, or means, that we use to reach them.

In reality, this is a dangerous way of thinking because reliable delivery on the ground, in credible, day-to-day operations, is essential to the success of any business, as management theory is increasingly recognising (Kaplan and Norton 2001). Operational mistakes can often be fateful for an organisation. Take a major retail organisation or chain store, for example. It may have great goals for business success but if management cannot efficiently organise the daily handling of its sales – stocking of shelves, staffing of shifts, greeting of customers, and processing of transactions – its chances of staying in business are slim. In other words, both our goals or desired ends (what we intend to achieve) and our means (how we intend to go about it) are critical to our success. In every business, there are certain operational routines that are strategic to success. Going back to the military sphere, much of the German performance in the First World War is not attributed to the leadership at the top, which was plagued with division and debate over the appropriate objectives for the war, but to German 'tactical excellence' on the ground: to the adaptable behaviour of well-trained soldiers in the field who coped better than most with the chaos that the fighting inevitably created (Ferguson 1998: 308–10).

In business, astute leaders realise the importance of taking care with *both* ends and means. They do not diminish the importance of the latter. This is a reason why, in some enduring organisations, only those who have worked their way up from the fundamental roles at the base of the organisation can ever hold the top management posts (Pascale 1985). Historically, many of the largest firms have structured their internal management development programmes so that new recruits with management potential are required to spend time learning what matters to the firm's customers, suppliers and employees (Boxall and Gilbert 2007). With a suitable apprenticeship in the 'engine room' of the firm, they get a chance to learn what is critical in the fundamental disciplines – marketing, production, finance and human resource management – that sustain the business model.

In adopting this perspective, some may think we are debasing the currency of strategy. Where do we draw the line between the strategic and the non-strategic? It must be admitted that this is often a difficult thing to discern, not least because the environment changes in ways that surface new issues that become strategic. Take the internet, for example. Ten to fifteen years ago, it seemed that retailers, particularly the small ones, could ignore its implications for sales and distribution processes. Now hardly anyone in retail can afford to be complacent about it, large or small: a retailer's web pages help potential customers to locate its products, search for items in the stock, and make purchases over the internet. Failure to use the internet can now be devastating for a retail business.

It seems we need some way of discerning where the strategic issues lie. One thing we must definitely avoid is the profligate application of strategy language simply to impress. This is something of a disease in the HRM literature. Very often writers in HRM have slapped the word 'strategic' in front of the old sub-functional categories of selection, appraisal, pay, and training to produce, as if by magic, a book on 'strategic HRM'. David Guest makes exactly the same point about much of the transition from personnel management to HRM – the covers of some textbooks changed but very little in between them (Guest 1987: 506). As he points out, and as many managers know, the titles of personnel departments often changed with little attempt to review the nature of the work they do. This kind of self-serving use of language leaves students and practitioners with no basis for distinguishing between the critical or strategic issues involved in running firms successfully and those which are of lesser significance. In the definitions that follow, we will attempt to provide a more meaningful set of markers.

The problem of viability

We are now in a position to move from the negative to the positive. In our view, strategy is best defined by making a distinction between the 'strategic problems' firms face in their environment and the strategies they adopt to address them (Boxall 1998: 266). This means we believe that there is a real business environment, a reality 'out there' that firms must deal with. The environment – political, economic, social and technological – is not a fiction. The stark fact is that sooner, rather than later, firms face 'intelligent opposition' from rivals (Quinn 1980). They can also face threatening regulation from the state and major fluctuations in markets. Even the most powerful firms, seemingly in control of their environment, will eventually face some kind of turbulence that threatens their position, as was revealed in the global financial crisis of 2008–9. Not only did the crisis destroy seemingly invulnerable banks, or take them out of private ownership into government hands, but it had major repercussions for firms well beyond the banking sector (Stiglitz 2010).

The most critical challenge that the firm faces, then, is that of survival: the problem of becoming and remaining viable in its chosen market (Suarez and Utterback 2005). In order to be viable, firms require 'table stakes': a set of goals, resources and capable people that are appropriate to the industry concerned (Hamel and Prahalad 1994: 226, Boxall and Steeneveld 1999). Decisions about these 'table stakes' are strategic: they are make-or-break factors. Get the system of these choices right – or right enough – and the firm will be viable. Miss a key piece out and the firm will fail, usually quickly (Reynolds 1987). In other words, when we use the word 'strategic' to describe something, we mean that it is something that is critical to survival. It will be fatal if we get it wrong.

Carrying forward our discussion in Chapter 1, Figure 2.1 summarises the four essential elements we see in any viable business model. One element is

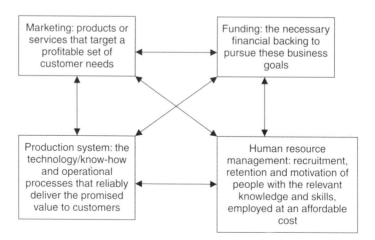

Figure 2.1 Four critical elements in a viable business model

concerned with marketing. The firm needs to develop products or services that can potentially meet a profitable set of customer needs. It will fail if it simply produces something that no one wants to buy or that they might desire but cannot afford to buy. It also needs a stable production system, a credible way of making that product or providing that service. Thus, suitable production technology or know-how and reliable operational processes are critical to survival. Production technology is integral to manufacturing while productive know-how is vital in the service sector. In many industries in both sectors, information technology, in the form of computing and communication technologies, has become an essential aspect of the production system. But there will be no production without people. The two are heavily interdependent. Even where robotics is involved, the business will need the managers and other employees who have the knowledge and skills that are necessary to its functioning. In a viable business, they are motivated to perform in a way that is affordable. Finally, it needs the financial backing to pursue its goals. A firm's leaders may have great ideas for performance but unless they have the finance to back the venture, they lack the complete set of 'table stakes' to enter, and stay alive, in the game.

As an illustration, take the case of a company launching a new High Street or Main Street bank. As Freeman (1995: 221) emphasises, much of a firm's strategy is formed in a 'package' when the original choice of industry is made. A bank has to act like a bank: it comes with the territory. To be credible at all, it must have a similar profile of products or services to competing banks. It must also have the premises and the technologies that will help it to process deposits and facilitate lending, plus the skilled staff who can make it happen 'with the gear' on the day. Finally, it needs the funding that will underpin these investments, something that fell over catastrophically in those banks that failed in the global financial crisis of 2008–9. In the USA, the Federal Deposit Insurance Corporation maintains a list of bank failures.[1] By November 2009, 115 banks had failed so far in the year due to 'capital erosion'.[2] This illustration should underline the point that all four of the critical elements of viability that we have identified are essential: a failure in one part will compromise all the others.

While Figure 2.1 naturally over-simplifies the ambiguities and complexities that are involved in the problem of viability, we use it to emphasise two critical principles about the role of HRM in a firm's strategy. First, Figure 2.1

---

[1] http://www.fdic.gov/BANK/HISTORICAL/BANK/index.html, accessed 19/11/09.
[2] http://www.dailymarkets.com/stocks/2009/11/02/us-bank-failures-zoom-to-115, accessed 19/11/09.

highlights the fact that there is no solution to the problem of viability *without* capable people. Appropriate human capabilities are strategic to the success of every firm. It is only people that pose the questions, 'What goals are appropriate for our business?' and 'What resources are relevant to our goals?', and take an interest in making the answers a reality. This is desperately obvious but it has to be said because there are dozens of books on strategic management which assume that good strategy appears out of nowhere: human beings, and human resource management, do not seem to be involved. Nothing could be further from the truth. An appropriate approach to HRM – a suitable way of managing work and people – is one of the necessary elements in business success. A competent level of HRM is not sufficient on its own but it is necessary for business viability.

Furthermore, the two-way arrows in Figure 2.1 underline a second principle. They depict the fact that the four elements of marketing, production, people, and funding *interact* with each other over time. This means, for example, that the choices we make in human resource management not only flow from our marketing and production choices but they have a way of 'boomeranging' back on these functions. Take the case of an apparel or clothing manufacturing firm that aims to be a low-cost producer. It hires workers to perform highly defined but not very flexible jobs to implement this marketing strategy and it focuses hard on efficiency, reinforcing standard ways of making garments and investing no funds in employee training beyond the immediate job. Such a firm may well make plenty of lower cost garments at adequate quality standards, but never be able to make the kind of complex, branded clothing that commands a price premium. This is because its workforce has not been developed or rewarded for a more flexible, higher-quality mode of production. The competitive goals of such a firm will not be easily turned around. They are limited by its historical approach to managing its employees, a problem that will not be overcome quickly, if at all, as noted in comparative studies of the British and German clothing industries (Steedman and Wagner 1989, Lane 1990). The point is this: the history of any firm is both a help and a hindrance. It stabilises or reinforces an approach to running the company that enables management to contemplate some futures but makes other aspirations extremely difficult because the firm's established 'routines' have simply not been focused on these other approaches (Nelson and Winter 1982).

The problem of viability, then, is the most fundamental strategic problem facing the firm. It is an interactive and dynamic set of concerns involving marketing, production, HRM and finance. There are critical choices about goals and means in each of these functions, and in how they fit together, which make or break a business. A viable business model is one which puts these pieces together in a profitable and sustainable way.

The problem of sustained advantage

While the problem of viability is the fundamental strategic problem, there is a 'second-order' or higher-level problem that lies beyond it. Firms that survive are engaged in a struggle to build and defend competitive advantages. A firm which builds a relatively consistent pattern of superior returns for its shareholders has developed some form of 'sustained competitive advantage' (Porter 1980, 1985) – or achieved what the economic theory of the firm has traditionally called 'rents': profits above those that can normally be earned in conditions of 'perfect competition'. Chief executives are often incentivised for this higher level game: they may, for example, be promised certain bonus sums if the firm's profitability significantly exceeds the industry average or if its share price beats the average of its rivals over a certain time-frame. Their goal, if you will, is not to support perfect competition (which might be a goal of politicians) but to engineer *im*perfect competition favouring their firm.

How long such superior performance can be sustained is, however, variable. As explained in Chapter 1, many advantages are simply temporary. It doesn't take what economists call 'perfect competition' for imitative forces to set in. There simply have to be serious rivals – as there are in most markets – who observe that someone has achieved an unusual level of profitability and seek to compete it away (Porter 1980). It is better to think of 'barriers to imitation' as having different heights and different rates of decay or erosion (Reed and DeFillippi 1990). And, as Barney (1991) reminds us, there is also the possibility of 'Schumpeterian shocks'. This refers to the great Austrian economist, Joseph Schumpeter's view that capitalism involves 'gales of creative destruction' (Schumpeter 1950: 84). These are major innovations in products or processes, which can destroy whole firms and the industries they inhabit. As he pointed out, this is a lot tougher than price-based competition.

The question of how to achieve competitive advantage is the dominant concern in the strategic management literature. Following theorists like Porter (1980, 1985, 1991), strategy textbooks in the last thirty years have typically assumed that competitive advantage is the dependent variable of interest in the whole subject. In our view, this emphasis is important but somewhat unbalanced. It focuses too much on how firms might make themselves different. Firms are inevitably different – in good, bad and ugly ways – but we think it is more balanced to use the notion of two strategic problems or dependent variables – viability and sustained advantage. In other words, firms must meet certain base-line conditions that make them similar to other firms (in the industries and societies in which they are based) while also having the opportunity to make gains from being positively different.

Our emphasis on the problem of viability is broadly consistent with the arguments of sociologists including 'organisational ecologists' (such as Carroll and Hannan 1995) and 'institutionalists' (such as DiMaggio and Powell 1983 and Scott 2008) who examine the processes that account for similarity among organisations. Recognition that firms face pressures to conform in order to gain wider approval – or 'social legitimacy' (one of the key goals discussed in Chapter 1) – and have economic reasons to adopt successful strategies in their industry has grown in the strategic management literature (see, for example, Oliver 1997, Peteraf and Shanley 1997, Deephouse 1999). In saying, then, that competitive advantage is a desirable end, we are not wanting to convey the impression that firms that pursue it will become completely different from their rivals. They will not. They will retain many similarities but one can also expect some distinctive traits.

Take the low-cost airline industry, for example. In terms of competitive strategy, companies follow a very similar formula: they focus on the short-haul market (including the lucrative tourist destinations), tend to use one or two styles of airplane to reduce maintenance costs, carry higher loads of passengers, reduce turn-around times and keep their aircraft airborne for longer ('machine uptime', if you like), offer fewer of the staffing entitlements common in 'legacy' airlines, charge for optional services, and foster inter-net booking enormously.[3] All of this helps to reduce operating costs and raise productivity, supporting the low-pricing strategy, and makes these low-cost airlines similar to each other and discernibly different from 'full-service' carriers. However, there can still be differences in their strategies: for exam-ple, in the extent to which they use primary or secondary airports and in their HR strategies. Research by Gittel and Bamber (2010) and Harvey and Turnbull (2010) in this industry points to markedly different approaches to managing people between 'high-road' and 'low-road' HR models. Although such contrasts can be over-simplified, in the former, company executives see their business model of cost reduction as consistent with fostering individ-ual commitment and working in a cooperative, 'mutual-gains' approach with unions. This means working with employees to find ways of reducing non-labour costs while enhancing service performance, something exemplified in the case of Southwest Airlines (Gittel and Bamber 2010). In the low-road

---

[3] See, for example, http://www.guardian.co.uk/business/2006/oct/06/theairlineindustry. travelnews2, accessed 25/5/10.

model, executives are not convinced that such 'touchy-feely' practices (Gittel and Bamber 2010: 176) will support cost reduction. They practise a more contingent approach to employee interests and aim to remain union-free, something that can help to enhance flexibility when downturns come, which they regularly do (Blyton and Turnbull 2004, Harvey and Turnbull 2010: 231). As this example suggests, one can expect to find a blend of similarity and difference in a detailed analysis of business strategies in any industry.

The strategies of firms

In this context, the *strategies* of firms are their particular attempts to deal with the strategic problems they face. They are the characteristic ways in which the managers of firms understand their goals and develop resources – both human and non-human – to reach them. Some strategies are better than others in the context concerned: some address the problem of viability extremely well and others are simply disastrous – with every shade of effectiveness in between. The very best strategies are those which reach beyond the problem of viability to master the 'second order' problem of sustained advantage. When key requirements for viability are not addressed by a firm's strategy, its leaders either learn quickly where they are failing or the firm will fold up. In this sense, all firms have strategies but some have strategies that are much smarter than those of other firms. This is exactly what we observe in practice. The fact that someone has a strategy does not mean they are successful. It simply means they have a characteristic way of behaving in their environment.

As noted earlier, we should not make the mistake of equating the strategies of firms with formal strategic plans. Following the 'strategic choice' perspective (Child 1972), it is better if we understand the strategies of firms as *sets of strategic choices*, some of which might stem from planning exercises and set-piece debates in senior management, and some of which emerge in a stream of action. The latter, called 'emergent strategy' by Mintzberg (1978) in a classic paper, is an inevitable feature of strategy. Once a firm commits to a particular strategy, such as a decision to enter internet banking, it is inevitable that the process of carrying out that commitment will involve learning, which will shape the strategy over time. Resource commitments of this kind provide a structure or frame within which strategy evolves.

And, as mentioned earlier, in defining a firm's strategy as a set of strategic choices, we are saying that it includes critical choices about ends *and* means. A firm's strategy contains 'outward' and 'inward' elements. Firms face the problem of choosing suitable goals and the problem of choosing and organising appropriate resources to meet them. In effect, our 'strategic choice' definition draws on a 'configurational' or *gestalt* perspective (Miller 1981, Meyer, Tsui and Hinings 1993, Veliyath and Srinavasan 1995). To be successful, firms need an effective system of choices involving all the key dimensions of the business: marketing, production, human resource management, and finance.

This definition means we do not use the terms 'business strategy' and 'competitive strategy' interchangeably (Boxall 1996). As the word implies, *business* strategy is the strategy for the whole of the business, for all the critical functions it needs and how they should relate to each other. A business is a system, not a single component. Competitive strategy is concerned with the marketing goals and policies embedded in the business strategy: with what customers are targeted, with which products or services, and with how the firm positions itself in relation to competitors for these customers. It is an aspect that interacts with, and evolves with, other aspects of the business strategy over time. This is not an attempt to downplay competitive strategy. There is no doubt that decisions about market positioning are extremely important, as we have already indicated. However, they constitute only one element of a business strategy, which must be effectively related to the other essential parts if the business is to be successful.

Our discussion so far implies that business strategy is composed of a cluster of strategies covering the critical functions of the business: marketing, operations, human resources and finance. Another way of putting this, using stakeholder theory, is to say that business strategy includes key choices involving all the stakeholder groups: it covers critical aspects of the firm's relations with customers, suppliers, employees, investors and regulators (Hill and Jones 1992, Donaldson and Preston 1995). Business strategy is the system of the firm's important relationships, a system that could be well integrated around common concerns or which might have various weak links and 'foul-ups'. As noted before, there is nothing in this definition to say that a firm's strategy is particularly clever.

A key issue associated with the strategic choice perspective is the question of what we are implying about the *extent of choice* available to firms. It is widely accepted in the strategy literature that firms in some sectors have greater 'degrees of freedom' than others enjoy (Porter 1980, 1985, Nelson 1991). Some environments are more benign – more 'munificent' – than are others (Pfeffer and Salancik 1978). Some firms are heavily constrained by competitive forces pushing them towards intense margin-based competition (something suppliers of supermarkets regularly complain about) while others enjoy a much more dominant position (companies like Microsoft come readily to mind). Consistent with John Child's (1997) re-formulation of the strategic choice perspective, we believe it is important to steer a path between 'hyper-determinism', on the one hand, and 'hyper-voluntarism', on the other. That is, firms are neither fully constrained by their environment nor fully able to create it. Adopting a strategic choice perspective means that we see firms as experiencing a varying blend of constraint and choice somewhere in between these two extremes. The 'choice' in 'strategic choice' is real but its extent is variable.

Before moving on, we should note that this definition of strategy is based at the business-unit level. This level is, in fact, the most logical one at which to define strategy because different business units are organised around markets or segments of markets which require different goals and clusters of resources (Porter 1980, Ghemawat and Costa 1993). Theory and analysis in strategy stems, almost entirely, from the business-unit level (Porter 1985, Kaplan and Norton 1996). However, we should note that more complex frameworks are needed to encompass corporate strategy in multidivisional firms. Questions about 'parenting' – about which businesses to buy and sell, which to grow organically and so on – are vital in multidivisional firms. We examine the different ways multidivisional firms take these choices and the role of *corporate* human resource strategy in Chapter 10.

The process of strategic management

If we take this view of strategy, strategic management is best defined as a process. It is a process of strategy making: of forming and, if the firm survives, of re-forming its strategy over time. As we have already indicated, this may involve elements of formal planning, including the application of analytical techniques such as industry analysis and portfolio analysis (Porter 1980, 1985, Whittington 1993, Grant 2005). It may involve set-piece debates among directors and executives, framed around policy papers and financial proposals. It may also involve *force majeure* if key power brokers – John Child's (1972, 1997) 'dominant coalition' – impose their will where they have the ability to do so. It will also, as Mintzberg emphasises (1978, 1990, 1994), inevitably involve a learning process as the managers of firms find out what works well in practice for them – or, we might add, what works better for their rivals. The transition in the strategy textbooks from titles such as 'Business Policy' and 'Strategic Planning' to 'Strategic Management' indicates a realisation that strategy making is a mixed, impure, interactive kind of process.

This description of the strategic management process implies that it is hard to do it well. Following Eisenhardt and Zbaracki (1992) and Child (1997), we see strategic decision making as difficult in two key ways which need exploring in more depth: it is mentally or 'cognitively' tough and it is often politically fraught.

Strategic management and human cognition

Human cognition is a psychological term for thinking processes, for our ability to process information and make decisions. Research on cognition recognises the validity of Herbert Simon's observation, in his classic *Administrative Behavior*, that human beings are subject to 'bounded rationality' (Simon 1947). We cannot know everything about our environment, nor can we easily manipulate more than a handful of key ideas in a problem-solving situation: we are limited in the number of variables we can actively 'work on' as we wrestle with an environment that is much more complex than that. Our search for information is 'incomplete, often inadequate, based on uncertain information and partial ignorance, and usually terminated with the discovery of satisfactory, not optimal courses of action' (Simon 1985: 295).

While criticising the concept of optimisation or maximisation in conventional economics, we must be careful, however, to note that Simon (1985: 297) was not saying that human behaviour is irrational:

> On the contrary ... there is plenty of evidence that people are quite rational: that is to say, they usually have reasons for what they do. Even in madness, there is almost always method, as Freud was at great pains to point out. And putting madness aside for a moment, almost all human behavior consists of sequences of goal-oriented actions.

As Simon indicates, we can generally find goals or the element of *intent* in human action. When studying strategy in firms, we can find intent in both formal planning and in Mintzberg's (1978) 'emergent strategy' of action, a point that Mintzberg, unfortunately, fails to make clear. The nature of the intent may shift, and it may not be very clever in the eyes of rivals or through our own hindsight, but it is there.

Following Simon (1947), management theory does not typically employ the assumptions of 'homo economicus': that tradition within economics, which keeps alive a view of economic agents acting with all the information they need and with no debilitating debates or frustrating compromises over the firm's desirable direction or internal organisation. As many academics have quipped, this view of business behaviour is largely unjustified but it makes the maths easier! Certainly, whoever thought of it first had no experience of university administration or any familiarity with the management of major organisations.

On a practical level, management can ill afford to assume it holds perfect knowledge or has outstanding problem-solving abilities. The work of strategic management, of finding a desirable path for the firm and managing its resources accordingly, is complex work that takes place in an environment of risk and uncertainty. As we have emphasised, it involves *systemic* factors – the problem of thinking not only within 'silos' but of identifying and linking a range of critical issues across the business. Box 2.1, drawn from various sources (Belbin 1981, Isenberg 1984, Simon 1985, Barr, Stimpert and Huff 1992, Eisenhardt and Zbaracki 1992, Hambrick 1995), summarises some of the main findings of research on the cognitive problems of decision making in firms. The overall effect of this research should be to induce some humility in the face of complex decisions. In respect of strategic decisions, it is much better to be 'often in doubt but seldom wrong' than 'seldom in doubt and often wrong'.

Box 2.1   Human cognitive issues affecting strategic management

1. We have reasons or goals for our actions but some of them are not very smart by other people's standards. Our powers of reasoning and our understanding of the world vary considerably.

2. We often have to act without knowing everything we'd like to: complexity and uncertainty are facts of life, especially in strategic management. Managers rely on 'mental models' which simplify and may distort the changing nature of their environment.

3. We often commit emotionally to a failing course of action and 'throw good money after bad'. People do not like to lose face.

4. We tend to search for confirming rather than disconfirming evidence to support our views (which is a common trap in employee selection, for example).

5. In problem solving, we often leap to a favourite or preferred solution without disciplining ourselves to diagnose the problem more deeply, mapping causes and consequences, generating real alternatives, and remaining truly open to the criticisms and refinements offered by others. Existing 'mental models' (about major cause–effect relationships in our world) tend to limit the range of our thinking about solutions to new problems.

6. No single executive in a large business is likely to have all the answers to complex, ambiguous problems: strategic management in large organisations needs teams of people with complementary strengths and styles.
7. Even if the need for management teamwork is recognised, knowledge of how things are done, and of how the firm might best respond to competitor threats or new technology, may be dispersed throughout the firm, not held exclusively by far-sighted or 'heroic' executives.
8. The management process tends to repeat yesterday's success formula. It can take a long time to change the focus on 'what worked before' in a business. This opens up profitable opportunities for firms whose people can think differently. One firm's mindset or 'strong culture' is another firm's competitive opportunity.

Barr, Stimpert and Huff (1992) provide an interesting illustration of the cognitive problems of strategic management. They examine the quality of strategic decision making in two US railway companies in the 1950s, a time when rail faced growing competition from other transport modes, particularly the growing trucking industry. Between 1949 and 1973, the number of major railway companies roughly halved (down from 135 to 69). Barr *et al.* examined the efforts of two companies, the Chicago and North Western (C&NW) and the Chicago, Rock Island and Pacific (Rock Island), to handle this threatening environment. C&NW survived but Rock Island went bankrupt in the mid-1970s. Barr *et al.*'s analysis of 50 letters to shareholders written by the directors of these companies is revealing. As the environment began to turn against the rail companies in the 1950s, both companies blamed *external* factors for their poor performance – such as the weather, government programmes, and regulation. By about 1956, however, management at C&NW began to change its mental model, focusing efforts on *internal* factors (associated with costs and productivity) that management could control more effectively. This set in train (so to speak) a progressive learning process in which management strategies were improved by trial-and-error. This kind of shift in mental model did not occur at Rock Island until 1964, when an abrupt change of thinking occurred, by which time it was too late.

Barr *et al.* suggest that Rock Island's directors may have been caught in a 'success trap': having been prosperous for many years, they tended to dismiss the need for change even though the post-war environment was steadily moving against rail transport. This study is interesting because it demonstrates the way in which a dysfunctional mental model – one in which notions of cause-and-effect are well wide of the mark – can persist among the members of a senior management team. Not only was the environment clearly difficult but there were other firms – such as CN&W – that were handling it better.

Strategic management and organisational politics

Cases such as the demise of the Rock Island railway point to the role of cognitive strengths and weaknesses in strategic decision making. There is no doubt that cognition – cleverness – counts for a lot in company success. Most of the research on human cognition, however, overlooks the fact that strategic decision making is not simply about dealing with complex mental challenges in threatening environments. More than this is involved: politics matter, particularly in larger organisations. Strategic management is also about steering a course in a politically constituted organisation (Child 1972, 1997, Eisenhardt and Zbaracki 1992).

The point is well made in Child and Smith's (1987) study of Cadbury's attempts to transform itself in the 1960s and 70s. Facing the concentration and growth of retailer power and rising oligopolistic competition in a saturated home market, Cadbury needed strategic renewal. It needed to move away from some key elements of 'Cadburyism' – including a huge range of products and some key HR policies such as life-time commitment – towards a more efficient model of manufacturing with better technology and fewer but more flexible (and well-paid) workers. The leaders who made this change happen were people who handled the cognitive problems well. They cleverly perceived which parts of 'Cadburyism' needed to change and which ought to be enduring. However, as Child and Smith (1987: 588) explain, they also had the power to influence events, the political position and credibility needed within the firm to effect change: 'The Cadbury transformation relied on the exercise of power as well as on the persuasive force of vision and its attendant symbols.'

Because firms are coalitions of stakeholder groups (Cyert and March 1963), we must expect that any major initiative involves *political* management, particularly where investors must be persuaded to support the initiative or where employee groups are being asked to make changes that threaten their interests, as was the case in the Cadbury transformation. This is one of the straightforward implications of the stakeholder theory of the firm (Hill and Jones 1992, Donaldson and Preston 1995) and of 'resource-dependence' theory (Pfeffer and Salancik 1978). In a nutshell, firms are beholden to stockholders (who supply financial capital) but they are also dependent on any stakeholder group (such as suppliers and key customers) that contributes resources that are valuable to the firm. Labour is powerful in this sense, as we noted in Chapter 1. Workers – employees and contractors – do not need 'equal power' to have influence with management, they simply need the power to affect performance in some significant way. This is almost invariably the case. It follows that dealing with the power of labour is something that should concern executives in all firms, irrespective of whether the workforce is unionised. Dealing with the power of non-management labour is one of the most visible of the power dynamics in firms. It often hits the media. Less eye catching but equally powerful is the loss of key employees who cannot be replaced, people with particularly scarce skills and good performance records who exercise their personal labour market power.

Much of the political difficulty of strategic management occurs within the management structure itself. Organisations offer managers opportunities for personal aggrandisement (Williamson 1964). The large enterprises of our time – the *Fortune 500* companies for example – provide management 'careerists' (Rousseau 1995) with a huge domain for self-serving behaviour. Intra-management political problems are of two main types. On the more 'macro' level, departments acquire power when they are central to the fundamental strategy on which a business is founded (Boeker 1989). Managers who head the historically strong departments often fight change even when the larger picture indicates that strategic change is now needed. For example, a firm in which production has historically led the way may well suffer from serious managerial in-fighting if the marketing department grows in significance and starts to challenge production's power base.

On the more 'micro' level, individual managers have personal reasons to advance their own interests irrespective of whether they are located in a powerful department. Perhaps the most significant problem presented by this feast of opportunity is the way consideration for one's personal future often encourages managers to keep quiet about problems, to filter the bad news. Alternatively, individuals may try to fix blame onto their supervisors, subordinates or peers as a way of displacing attention from their own performance (Longenecker, Sims and Gioia 1987).

When most managers in a team are afraid of introducing conflicting opinion, the organisation can suffer from 'groupthink' (Janis 1972), a syndrome where executives close down debate prematurely and take decisions with negative consequences. The decision by the US cabinet to invade Cuba at the Bay of Pigs in April 1961 is one of Janis's famous examples. In her classic study of flawed decision making in a selection of great historical events ('from Troy to

Vietnam'), *The March of Folly*, Barbara Tuchman (1996: 302–3), finds many cases of the tendency:

> Adjustment is painful. For the ruler it is easier, once he [*sic*] has entered a policy box, to stay inside. For the lesser official it is better, for the sake of his [*sic*] position, not to make waves, not to press evidence that the chief will find painful to accept. Psychologists call the process of screening out discordant information 'cognitive dissonance', an academic disguise for 'Do not confuse me with the facts.' Cognitive dissonance is the tendency 'to suppress, gloss over, water down or "waffle" issues that would produce conflict or "psychological pain" within an organization.' It causes alternatives to be 'deselected since even thinking about them entails conflicts.' In the relations of subordinate to superior . . . its object is the development of policies that upset no one.

The tendency to look after oneself is recognised by those branches of organisational economics, such as agency theory, which acknowledge that managerial interests can diverge from those of stockholders (McMillan 1992, Rowlinson 1997), as noted in Chapter 1. In the current chapter, it is simply important to observe that the politics of executive ambition adds complexity to the broader stakeholder-based politics we find in organisations.

The role of HRM in improving strategic management processes

Given intellectual limitations and political complications, what can be done to improve the quality of strategic decision making in firms? And what role might human resource management play in this task?

The importance of executive recruitment and development

In the light of what we know about cognitive problems, including the fact that human performance becomes increasingly variable in jobs of high complexity (Hunter, Schmidt and Judiesch 1990), it seems obvious that HRM should play a major role in improving the quality of strategic management. The greater the uncertainty and discretion involved in work, the more important it is to hire or develop people of high ability, with a well-rounded intellectual and emotional profile, who have a capacity to think critically, creatively and flexibly. This is particularly true at the apex of organisations because the performance of companies tends to reflect the quality of their 'upper echelons' (Hambrick 1987, 1995, Norburn and Birley 1988). Failure to recruit and retain suitable managers will hamstring company performance, a problem that is prevalent in small countries that lose managerial talent to the greater opportunities available in the global labour market for executives (Gilbert and Boxall 2009).

There is plenty of evidence that company directors and chief executives act on this common-sense principle. The enormous resources they invest in executive recruitment and search ('headhunting') testifies to the significance they place on hiring the best senior managers they can. In 2008, executive search firms who are members of the Executive Search Association employed around 6,000 consultants in 70 countries, undertook some 50,000 'senior-level search assignments' for clients, and grossed US$11 billion in revenue.[4] On top of this, there are all the firms that are not members of this association and all the resources invested inside companies that handle their own executive recruitment. Added to the investment in executive recruitment is another enormous investment in executive development, incorporating executive education, such as MBA programmes, in-house training, and one-to-one coaching. One of the smaller elements in this is the executive coaching industry but this alone may already have passed the US$1 billion mark in revenues.[5]

There is also evidence that senior HR specialists orient their jobs to focus on critical activities associated with managing managers. In a study of human resource directors in the largest New Zealand corporates, Hunt and Boxall (1998) found a strong emphasis in their work priorities on developing executive capability and performance. In line with findings in the UK (Marginson *et al.* 1988), the primary concern of most of the senior HR specialists in the study was the management of managers, including recruitment, remuneration, development, succession planning and termination. One stated that they 'worked constantly' with the CEO of the company: 'looking at managers, identifying strengths and weaknesses, seeing who will go further and who needs to go' (Hunt and Boxall 1998: 772–3). Arguably, constituting and renewing the top team, including the chief executive, should be regarded as the most strategic concern of all in human resource management (Boxall 1994). In large organisations, the resources allocated to managing senior executives sit within the larger approach to managing managers that starts with promotion or recruitment to first-line management (Boxall and Gilbert 2007).

---

[4] https://members.aesc.org/eweb/DynamicPage.aspx?Site=aesc.org&WebKey=06f4aca5-286a-4ed7-879d-3706c1ab8598, accessed 25/5/10.
[5] http://www.executivecoachcollege.com/state_of_coaching_industry.htm. accessed 25/5/10.

The role of team building

But we should not think that the strategic management process will improve solely as a result of selecting or developing higher-performing individuals. Team processes are also vital to performance. This means that selection practices that assess not only 'person-job fit' but also 'person-team fit' have something to offer (Burch and Anderson 2004), as do team-building activities for existing management teams. This is emphasised in the work of Stuart Hart (1992) who defines five styles of strategy-making (Table 2.1). Hart's (1992) typology is useful because it specifies roles not only for executives but also for other members of the organisation under different modes of strategy making. We can see a major shift in the way senior managers and other members of the organisation are expected to behave from the command model at one end to the generative model at the other. Different modes might be appropriate to different contexts (a command style is often needed in crises) while firms might benefit from gaining the ability to combine different modes.

Table 2.1 Styles of strategy making

Descriptors	Command	Symbolic	Rational	Participative	Generative
Style	(Imperial) Strategy driven by leader or small top team	(Cultural) Strategy driven by mission and a vision of the future	(Analytical) Strategy driven by formal structure and planning systems	(Procedural) Strategy driven by internal process and mutual adjustment	(Organic) Strategy driven by organisational actors' initiative
Role of top management	Commander: provide direction	Coach: motivate and inspire	Boss: evaluate and control	Facilitator: empower and enable	Sponsor: endorse and support
Role of organizational members	Soldier: obey orders	Player: respond to challenge	Subordinate: follow the system	Participant: learn and improve through self-evaluation against agreed criteria	Entrepreneur: experiment and take risks

Source: adapted from Hart (1992).

In a survey of the opinions of US chief executives, Hart and Banbury (1994: 266) find some evidence that 'firms which combine high levels of competence in multiple modes of strategy-making appear to be the highest performers.' Consistent with resource-based view of the firm (which we explore in Chapter 4), they suggest (p. 255) that:

> a firm dominated by the command mode of strategy-making relies on the idiosyncratic capabilities of a single (or a few) individual(s). Should this person(s) leave the organization or be attracted away by competitors, the firm's strategy-making capability would be severely impaired. In contrast, a firm using symbolic, transactive[6], and generative processes of strategy-making demonstrates a more complex, deeply embedded capability requiring the concerted effort of hundreds (or even thousands) of people. Such an organization possesses a difficult-to-copy asset that could yield competitive advantage. Thus, firms able to accumulate several process skills into a complex strategy-making capability should outperform less process-capable organizations.

The value of a mix of strategy-making abilities is an excellent point but Hart and Banbury's (1994) research does not tell us *how* firms can develop such a repertoire. A small group of researchers and consultants has, however, tried to identify ways in which teamwork in organisations can be made more effective. One of the most celebrated frameworks is associated with the work of Belbin (1981, 1993). Belbin's model of team roles has been used to analyse the strengths and weaknesses of many senior management teams.

According to this theory, it is a mistake to construct management teams simply based on the functional expertise of individuals (that is, their abilities in marketing, finance, operations, or other such disciplines). Belbin argues that the most effective management teams enjoy a healthy mix of complementary *teamwork* styles (such as, how people characteristically behave during team activities). Such teams have at least one clever and highly creative individual (a 'plant'), are chaired by someone who knows how to use the talents of others, and contain a spread of other useful styles (for example, a 'monitor–evaluator' to provide some dispassionate intellectual appraisal of the plant's ideas, and a 'completer–finisher' who will ensure sound organisation and follow-through) (Belbin 1981: 93–9).

Belbin's ideas have been psychometrically evaluated and developed further by the British management consultancy, Robertson Cooper Ltd (2003).[7]

---

[6] We have changed the 'transactive' label to 'participative' in Table 2.1.
[7] http://www.robertsoncooper.com/Pages/Products/Teamable/Teamable.aspx, accessed 25/5/10.

Table 2.2 A typology of team roles

Team role	Offers the team	Should aim to develop
Specialist	Their technical skills and professionalism	A fuller involvement in the team beyond their technical skills
Leader-Coordinator	An ability to encourage and coordinate others, to listen, to persuade and to build consensus	Their ability to move from decision making through to action
Driver	Urgency, a willingness to assume responsibility and a desire to make things happen	Their ability to consult others carefully and not simply rely on their personal drive to take others with them
Innovator	An ability to come up with creative ideas and original approaches in challenging circumstances	Their ability to listen to others and to connect with current priorities in the team
Explorer-Networker	Strong interests in new ideas and in people and an ability to network with them	Their ability to move from exploring and talking to making things happen
Analyst	Strong analytical abilities, a rigorous capacity to weigh up ideas and think through the implications	Their ability to empathise as well as challenge critically
Team coach	An ability to get on well with nearly all people, listen to their feelings and offer personal support	Their ability to handle tough decisions where validating everyone's feelings is not going to work
Completer-Achiever	An ability to manage the details and ensure the job is done on time and to high standards	Their ability to see when their approach is too critical of the efforts of others or too 'perfectionist'

Source: adapted from Robertson Cooper Ltd (2003).

A brief summary of their evolution of the Belbin team roles is shown in Table 2.2. While they explain that individuals typically have strengths in one to three of these roles, they emphasise that it is not helpful to use role analysis to stereotype oneself or other people. It is much better if individuals participate as fully as possible in team activities and learn to develop new abilities.

Clearly, the development of better teamwork in management, and more broadly, depends more than anything on the support of the chief executive. The CEO plays a critical role in setting the style of participation within the senior management team and, through them, throughout the organisation.

He or she can decide that team-building processes are important or can ignore the issue. Even when a company has built a more participative culture, every time a new chief executive is appointed there is potential for decision making to revert to an autocratic or closely held style. Business organisations are not constituted as democracies. Disproportionate power keeps reverting into the hands of senior management. This should remind us how central executive appointments are to the long-term success of the firm.

Conclusions

This chapter provides a basis for examining the role of HRM in strategic management. It is important to pause and reflect on the nature of strategy and strategic management before leaping into theory and research on strategic HRM. Doing so will help to restrain us from superficial conclusions and misleading advice.

We have defined strategy by distinguishing between 'strategic problems' the firm faces in its environment and the characteristic ways it ties to cope with them (its 'strategy'). As common sense tells us, the word 'strategic' implies something that is seriously consequential for the future of the firm. The fundamental strategic problem is the problem of viability or survival. To be viable, a firm needs an appropriate set of goals and a relevant set of human and non-human resources, a configuration or system of ends and means consistent with its survival in the context in which it operates. Along with an appropriate approach to marketing, operations management and finance, this means that firms need a cost-effective approach to HRM. Without certain kinds of capable and motivated people, firms are simply not viable.

We take issue, then, with anyone who wants to downplay the significance of HRM in the firm. We find fault with those strategy texts which imply that key human resource concerns are not strategic. There is really no need for HR specialists to hang their heads in shame around the executive table, as if the critical dimensions of HRM were not important to the firm's success. As we shall argue further in the next two chapters, effective human resource strategy is a necessary, though not sufficient, condition of firm viability. We shall also examine the debate over the ways in which 'human assets' might help the firm to build a sustained competitive advantage (which can be thought of as a 'second order' or higher-level strategic problem). As we have argued in this chapter, however, firms that achieve some form of competitive advantage will not be completely different from those that do not – due to the need of all firms in the industry to have 'table stakes', features that make them similar to each other, and due to the need for firms that wish to be perceived as legitimate in society to comply with laws and adapt to social conventions.

Strategy, then, is a set of strategic choices, some of which may be formally planned. It is inevitable that much, if not most, of a firm's strategy emerges in a stream of action over time. Strategy has both 'outward' and 'inward' elements – it includes both the firm's goals and the important means it uses to pursue them. How well these elements are conceived and coordinated is very variable. Saying that firms have strategy does not mean they are successful in their environment. Some firms fail, some secure viability with adequate returns, and some find ways of out-performing others for periods of time.

Strategic management, therefore, is the process used in the firm to develop critical goals and resources. It is a mixed, impure, interactive process, fraught with difficulty, both intellectually and politically. Improving the process of strategic management has a lot to do with HRM. It involves making some critical HR decisions about talent management, about the recruitment and development of key managers, but it also involves astute team-building activities, within the senior management team and throughout the organisation. There is some research suggesting that firms that develop multiple modes of strategy making are likely to be superior performers. Developing and sustaining highly participative styles of strategic management is not easy, however. Business organisations are not democracies. Power keeps reverting to those at the top, a phenomenon that reinforces the critical importance of people decisions at the apex of firms.

3
Strategic HRM: 'best fit' or 'best practice'?

Perhaps one message – more than any other – is communicated in job advertisements for HR directors: whatever you do, help the firm to make its HRM consistent with its strategic direction, *integrate* HR strategy with the wider business strategy. To many people this piece of advice seems obvious and straightforward. But is it? Could it be interpreted in quite different ways? Building on the concepts clarified in the previous chapter, our task in this one is to explain the main ways in which it has been argued that HRM should be integrated into strategic management and to consider the evidence for these claims.

The theory of strategic HRM does not, in fact, advocate a single way of linking HRM to strategy. Most theoretical debate around this nexus has been consumed with a contest between two approaches. One approach, the 'best fit' school, is associated with the contingency approaches that are prevalent in the theory of strategic management. It argues that firms must adapt their HR strategies to other elements of the firm's strategy and to its wider environment. In other words, what constitutes a good HR strategy will depend on the specific context. This school invites a string of questions about which are the most critical contextual variables and how they are best connected. The other approach advocates 'best practice', a form of universalism. It argues that all firms will be better off if they identify and adopt those HR practices which are shown to be 'best' for organising work and managing people. This is not straightforward either: it begs questions about how best practice models are defined and about whose interests are best served by them. This chapter subjects these two approaches to close scrutiny. We examine in each case what the research and theoretical critiques have to say and we reach an assessment of the relative merits of each approach. Readers will find that we take a very broad view of the research in reaching our conclusions and laying a basis for subsequent analysis in this book. The questions we are concerned with are critical to managing the whole of the business and a narrow view of the studies only published in the HRM journals would be woefully inadequate. To begin with, we need to flesh out our definition of strategic HRM and its companion term, human resource strategy.

Defining strategic HRM and HR strategy

As Chapter 1 made clear, we do not associate HRM with any particular philosophy or style of management. Simply in terms of work organisation and opportunities for employee voice, we see all sorts of variations in employer behaviour. Work organisation varies from highly prescribed 'command and control' models through to high-involvement or high-discretion ones and employer strategies towards employee voice vary from very paternalistic and anti-union styles through to union–management 'partnerships'. The practice of HRM incorporates all of these patterns and many more. We are interested in identifying, analysing and tracking trends in all significant patterns of managerial behaviour over time.

What difference does it make, then, when we apply the adjective *strategic* to HRM? As explained in Chapter 2, our understanding of strategy is based on a 'strategic choice' perspective – something which can be applied to the whole of strategy and to its constituent parts, including human resource strategy. In this interpretation, the application of the adjective 'strategic' implies a concern with the ways in which HRM is critical to the firm's survival and to its relative success. There are always strategic choices associated with labour management in the firm – whether highly planned or largely emergent in management behaviour – and these choices are inevitably connected to the firm's performance. These choices are made over time by the whole management structure, including line managers and HR specialists (where they exist).

As explained in Chapter 2, it is helpful to think of strategic choices on two levels: they either play a role in underpinning the firm's viability (make-or-break choices) or they contribute to some kind of sustained competitive advantage, helping to create major differences in the quality of business performance. In adopting this understanding, we follow Dyer (1984) in referring to a firm's *pattern* of strategic choices in labour management (including critical ends and means) as its 'organizational human resource strategy' – or its 'HR strategy', for short.

To illustrate what we mean by strategic choices in HRM, take the case of a management consulting firm that aims to join the elite cluster of firms that are global in their reach (Boxall and Purcell 2000). Firms such as PricewaterhouseCoopers, McKinsey and KPMG are among the leaders in this industry. What might it take to join them? There is no doubt that firms in this elite group must have highly selective recruitment and strong development of staff to ensure they can consistently offer clients high quality service on complex business problems. In this echelon of professional service firms, a synergistic blend of certain human resource practices – such as proactive recruitment channels, high entry standards, challenging, high-discretion work, high pay, the prospect of entering into partnership, and extensive professional education – is critical to business credibility. Firms of this type which are focused on competing through advanced and rare expertise need these types of HR practices to attract and retain the talented people they want (Dooreward and Meihuizen 2000). On the other hand, we can draw something of a line between these critical elements of HRM and other aspects which are not really important. It is unlikely, for example, that there is much hanging on the firm's choice of job evaluation systems. Job evaluation systems allocate jobs to pay grades based on the skill, effort and responsibility they involve. If any one of a range of such systems supports its remuneration goals in recruiting and retaining highly qualified consultants, or does not perversely undermine them, then the choice among different systems is not critical. Similarly, the contracting out of payroll or benefits administration in such a firm is not a strategic dimension of its HRM. It is not difficult to meet the requirements of employment contracts in these areas and elite firms are not differentiated from lesser firms on this basis. What is vital, however, is that the firm's leaders put together the *system* of truly critical HR practices and investments that will help the firm to join the elite group of professional firms in this sector. However, it would be unwise to think that the firm's labour market reputation will be made quickly or that viability in the sector will be achieved solely through HR strategy (as our discussion of the resource-based view of the firm in the next chapter will make clear).

As a field of study, therefore, strategic HRM is concerned with the strategic choices associated with the organization of work and the use of labour in firms and with explaining why some firms manage them more effectively than others. It is helpful to spell out this definition in a very practical manner. Suppose an HR Director is asked by a chief executive to conduct a review of the quality of HR strategy in a firm. What should such a review entail? We suggest the questions shown in Box 3.1:

Box 3.1   Three sets of questions for a review of HR strategy in a firm

Strengths and weaknesses in human resources

How well does the firm's human and social capital help it to perform? In relation to the firm's goals, what strengths and weaknesses are apparent in the firm's management of its main employee groups?

Competitive risks and potential in HRM

What threats does the firm face in its HRM (e.g. from under-performing work systems, from employee dissatisfaction or from labour market competition)? What opportunities does the firm have to improve its HR performance relative to its industry rivals? Does the firm's HRM have the potential to contribute to sustained competitive advantage? If so, how?

Assessment of strategic HR management processes

How effective are the firm's HR planning and reporting processes? What data are available on HR performance and how are they used for evidence-based strategic decisions, especially when linked to data on other critical variables like customer satisfaction and product or service quality? How can such strategic management processes be improved?

As the three sets of questions in Box 3.1 make clear, this kind of analysis is far from straightforward. In many firms, a major effort in data gathering would be needed to answer the questions. A study of these questions nearly always reveals the need for better ways of measuring HR performance in the firm, as advocates of the 'balanced scorecard' have noted (Kaplan and Norton 1996: 144–5). There is still a marked tendency in firms to treat HR practices as ends in themselves and a lot of work is needed to map their links to one another, to other management activities and to important performance variables (an issue we explore in Chapters 8 and 11). The second question involves not only data analysis but some kind of theory about how to make HRM more effective in the firm, about how to improve the strategic management of human resources in it. This is the nub of the debate between advocates of best fit and best practice, which is the focus of this chapter.

Before exploring this interesting debate, we should note some complications in our conception of human resource strategy. First, as noted in our definition of HRM in Chapter 1, we should not assume that HR strategies are uniform within firms. It is wrong to conjure up the image of HR strategy as a single set of critical practices for managing work and people in the firm. The vast bulk of the evidence suggests otherwise: firms rarely adopt a single style of management for all their employee groups (see, for example, Osterman 1987, Pinfield and Berner 1994, Harley 2001). It is better to think of HR strategy as a cluster of HR systems, as depicted in Figure 3.1. Questions of social legitimacy and internal political pressures mean there will usually be overlaps in HR practices across HR systems within an organization: for example, there may be common ways of handling leave entitlements and common ways of dealing with personal grievances. There are some companies in which opportunities for shareholding are opened to all employees, and so on. However, there are also substantial differences across HR systems. Each HR system is aimed at organizing the work and managing the employment of a major workforce group. It is quite common for there to be one HR system for management, another for core operating workers, and one or more models for support workers and specialists of various kinds. This is something we explore more fully in Chapters 4 and 8.

Second, we have been talking as if the firm is a single business unit. As explained in our definition of strategy in Chapter 2, this is the easiest way to develop theory in strategic management. Reality, however, is much more complicated. Difficulties arise with multidivisional firms, operating across a variety of markets. To what extent should lower levels of management be free to adapt HR strategies suited to their unique contexts? If they do this (and it

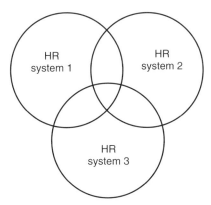

Figure 3.1 An organisation's HR strategy as a cluster of HR systems

is common), is there a role for corporate HR strategy in such firms and, if so, what should it be? Can corporate HR strategy provide some form of 'parenting advantage' which adds value to what business units can achieve without corporate influence? This question is explored in Chapter 10.

A third complication arises with international firms (as many multidivisional firms are). Where firms compete across national boundaries, in what ways should they adapt their HR strategies to local conditions? How should HRM be organized when the firm operates in more than one society? This is one of the key concerns of the field of international HRM (Evans, Pucik and Barsoux 2002, Sparrow, Brewster and Harris 2004, Dowling, Festing and Eagle 2008). We address this problem in the course of this chapter and extend our analysis in Chapter 10. Overall, our understanding of HR strategy is summarised in Box 3.2.

Box 3.2   Key characteristics of human resource strategy

- consists of critical goals and means for organising the firm's work and managing its people
- inevitably affects the firm's chances of survival and its relative performance
- is made by the whole management team and not simply by HR specialists (where they exist)
- is likely to be partly planned and partly 'emergent' in management behaviour
- is typically 'variegated' – while there are overlaps, firms typically have different HR systems for different employee groups (e.g. different models for management, for core operating workers, and for support staff)
- like strategy generally, is easiest to define at the business-unit level
- is more complex in multidivisional firms in which different business units face different markets and in which there are political interactions between the corporate, divisional and business-unit levels
- is more complex in firms that operate across national boundaries because of the impact of different societal contexts.

On the basis of these definitions and clarifications, we are now in a position to examine the debate between 'best fit' and 'best practice' in strategic HRM.

Strategic HRM: the best-fit school

As indicated in our chapter introduction, the best-fit school of strategic HRM argues that the variety we see in HRM in the real world implies that managers inevitably tailor their HRM to their specific context. Furthermore, they are wise to do so: firms under-perform and may fail if they do not adapt to their environment and if they fail to integrate the different parts of the business effectively. The best-fit literature contains both broad analytical models and more specific theories. In this section, we will outline these and consider the research evidence and conceptual critiques.

Best fit: broad analytical frameworks

In the late 1980s and early 1990s, the Harvard framework (Beer *et al.* 1984) provided one of the first major statements in the HRM canon on the issue of how managers should make strategic choices in HRM (Figure 3.2) (Poole 1990, Boxall 1992). In this analytical framework, managers in firms are encouraged to set their own priorities in HRM based on a consideration of stakeholder interests and situational factors. HR outcomes, in turn, are seen

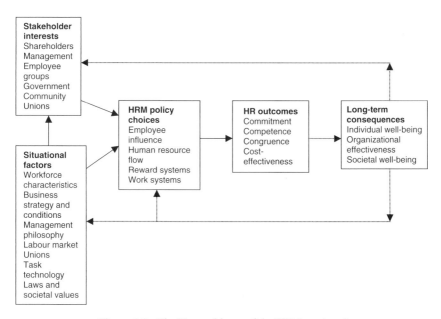

Figure 3.2 The Harvard 'map of the HRM territory'
Source: Beer *et al.* (1984).

as having longer-term impacts on organizational effectiveness and on societal and individual well-being.

In terms of our understanding of HR strategy, the most important chapter in the Harvard text was the last one in which the authors sought to integrate the huge range of HR choices that might be adopted by considering the differences between 'bureaucratic', 'market' and 'clan' models of HRM, a set of categories that draws on the work of Ouchi (1980). The bureaucratic model is seen as concerned with 'control and efficiency', using traditional authority and such staples of personnel management as job descriptions and job evaluation to provide order and equity (Beer *et al.* 1984: 179). This HRM approach is regarded as relevant to markets with stable technology and employment levels. The market HRM approach, on the other hand, aims to treat employees more like sub-contractors, fostering short-term exchanges and performance-related pay systems. This is seen as relevant to fast-changing environments such as high-fashion merchandising, advertising and professional sports (*ibid.*: 180). Finally, clan HRM systems are seen as building more diffuse kinship links, fostering shared values, teamwork and strong commitment in organisations seeking 'long-term adaptability' (*ibid.*: 181). This is seen as relevant to firms pursuing quality and innovation. Combining aspects of two or even three models is seen as useful when facing complex environments (*ibid.*: 184).

While the links between HRM goals and the firm's business strategy and environment are only very briefly sketched in the book, the main message is that HR strategies can, and should, vary based on contextual factors and that firms should aim to develop a relatively consistent style. Beer *et al.* (1984: 178, 184) argue that 'HRM policies need to fit with business strategy' and with 'situational constraints' while also envisaging a role for management values (*ibid.*: 190–1). The goal of fit with broader business strategy and with the the environment of the business, followed by internal consistency in HR choices, was argued to be the essential purpose of HRM.

The Harvard framework was followed by a range of similar models (see, for example, Dyer and Holder 1988, Baron and Kreps 1999). In Dyer and Holder's (1988) framework, management is advised to aim for 'consistency between HR goals . . . and the underlying business strategy and relevant environmental conditions' (with the latter, like the Harvard framework, including influences such as labour law, unions, labour markets, technology and management values). In Baron and Kreps's (1999) framework, managers are advised to consider the impact of 'five forces' on HR policy choices: the external environment (social, political, legal and economic), the workforce, the organisation's culture, its strategy and the technology of production and organisation of work. This advice is not offered in a simple, deterministic fashion: managers still have choices (such as where to locate plants in manufacturing) but once some choices are made, certain environmental consequences do follow: so, if you locate in the USA, rather than Honduras, US laws, culture and labour markets inevitably come into play. The goal of achieving internal consistency in whatever model of HRM is adopted – otherwise known as 'internal' or 'horizontal' fit – is then strongly emphasised by Baron and Kreps (1999).

Like the Harvard authors, if not more emphatically, Dyer and Holder (1988) and Baron and Kreps (1999) argue for a contingent understanding of HR strategy or the necessity of moulding HRM to the firm's particular context. Dyer and Holder (1988: 31) conclude that 'the inescapable conclusion is that what is best, depends'. Baron and Kreps (1999: 33) assert that 'in HRM, there is no one size that fits every situation' and argue that no model should be adopted unless the benefits outweigh the costs. None of these frameworks is inherently anti-union or takes the view that HRM is restricted to one style. The message in terms of HR strategy is one of fit or adaptation to the firm's broader business goals and its environmental context.

Best fit: research and critique

The broad frameworks just described have been important as analytical models that help managers to identify options and make choices in their own environments. In terms of theoretical development, however, progress depends on picking particular variables in these frameworks and subjecting them to formal research, typically through surveys and/or case studies. We must examine these studies if we are to be rigorous in any debate between best fit and best practice. There is an enormous body of research we could call on here and it does not sit solely within the HRM field. There is a range of studies in related fields such as comparative industrial relations, international business, strategy, and operations management. To help organise the evidence, we will look at research on three analytical levels – society, industry and organisation. Such a structure can be useful for undertaking a management review of contingencies that might affect HRM in a company.

Societal fit

Societal fit is about the question of whether organisations adapt to the characteristics of the societies in which they are located and whether they are wise to do so. We should recall here the discussion of the goals of HRM in Chapter 1. As explained, firms that wish to be socially legitimate need to comply with the labour laws of the countries in which they have operations, something which is emphasised in the institutional perspective in organisational studies (see, for example, DiMaggio and Powell 1983, Scott 2008). In reality, compliance with labour law is variable, with some firms seeking to avoid their legal responsibilities in any society. However, the evidence suggests that different labour regulations, including laws on union recognition, collective bargaining and workplace consultation, do account for major variation in HR practices across countries, vindicating the institutional perspective (Gooderham *et al.* 1999, Paauwe and Boselie 2003). An obvious contrast is between countries in the Anglo-American world and those European countries in which unions are recognised as 'social partners'. In the latter, employees have much stronger statutory rights to collective bargaining and workplace consultation (see, for example, Frege and Kelly 2004, Gooderham, Morley, Brewster and Mayrhofer 2004). The overall point is that the behaviour of firms *is* heavily shaped by labour law and all firms *ought* to comply with it if they wish to be responsible corporate citizens.

However, societal fit in HRM relates to a range of economic and social factors that extend well beyond the law. It also includes adaptation to national economic conditions, including the relative difficulty of recruiting suitable labour in local labour markets. Research shows that when economic growth in a country is strong and labour markets are tight, firms adjust their employment practices to cope: managers tend to respond with more generous pay offers and more motivating conditions (Jackson and Schuler 1995, Gamble 2010, Kaufman 2010). The converse is true when economic growth is slow or negative, as in the economic downturn experienced in many countries in 2008–9. In these conditions, firms 'hold the whip hand' in negotiations over pay and conditions. Even if they don't shed labour, managers often institute a hiring freeze and cut back on overtime work. While this recession was global, the effects were variable across countries: the negative impact on people was much greater in the USA and the UK than in Australia, for example, where unemployment rates remained lower.[1]

Alongside this critical economic factor, there is the issue of differences across countries in cultural norms, in the ways people instinctively behave. There is now a major body of literature in international business stemming from Hofstede's (1980) classic study of a databank of 116,000 employee attitude questionnaires collected in IBM's international subsidiaries over the period from 1967 to 1973. Hofstede (1983: 76) defined culture as 'collective mental programming ... the conditioning we share with other members of

---

[1] See http://en.wikipedia.org/wiki/Late-2000s_recession, accessed 25/5/10.

our nation, region or group but not with members of other nations, regions or groups'. Hofstede's study distinguishes cultures that are high on 'individualism', in which people focus on their own self-interests and perhaps those of their immediate family, from those that are high on 'collectivism', in which people are much more concerned with the collective welfare of their wider family groups and communities. He also distinguishes societies low in 'power distance', in which employees prefer egalitarian types of decision making and are relatively comfortable questioning the boss, from those high in power distance in which people are more approving of social inequalities and more readily accepting of autocratic styles of authority. On top of this, there are differences across cultures in the extent to which people cope positively with novel and unusual situations ('uncertainty avoidance') and in attitudes to gender roles. Cultures with sharp distinctions between male and female roles and in which competitiveness is highly valued are more 'masculine' while, in more 'feminine' cultures, both sexes show stronger nurturing values. Another dimension, added later, concerns 'long-term versus short-term orientation' in a culture, with Asian cultures typically taking a more patient, long-term attitude to life and business (Hofstede and Bond 1988).

The vast majority of evidence suggests that these sorts of differences in cultural attitudes do find their way into HR practices. In a major review of international HRM, Aycan (2005) describes a wide range of research showing that practices in such areas as selection, performance appraisal and pay are affected by such dimensions as the extent to which individualism is fostered over collectivism and the extent to which it is considered legitimate to challenge authority. In Anglo-Saxon and in Dutch cultural contexts, for example, it is common to consider people as individuals who can be selected, evaluated, rewarded and dispensed with on their individual merits but such assumptions risk failure in more collectivist cultures where an over-emphasis on individuals can threaten group harmony and challenge important status differences. This makes some common Anglo HR practices, such as individually based performance-related pay, dangerous cultural exports. In another highly cited study similar to Hofstede's work, *Riding the Waves of Culture*, Trompenaars and Hampden-Turner (1997: 4–5) comment that:

Pay-for-performance . . . can work out well in the USA, the Netherlands and the UK. In more communitarian cultures like France, Germany and large parts of Asia it may not be so successful, at least not the Anglo-Saxon version of pay-for-performance. Employees may not accept that individual members of the group should excel in a way that reveals the shortcomings of other members. Their definition of an 'outstanding individual' is one who benefits those closest to him or her.

Various studies in the international business literature suggest that organisations are more effective when managers work with the grain of these cultural differences rather than against them. For example, Newman and Nollen (1996), in a quantitative study of 176 work units in one US company operating in 18 European and Asian countries, find that higher financial performance is associated with those units where management practices are more congruent with the local culture. Similarly, but in an in-depth case study of two Russian companies, Michailova (2002: 183) finds that the attempts of expatriate American managers to foster employee empowerment, often regarded as an enlightened management principle in US organisations, can be dysfunctional in Russia: Russian employees, who are more accustomed to directive and paternalistic leadership styles, often perceive participation in decision making as 'avoidance of responsibility and lack of professionalism or as a burden that brings more work to the lower level'.

These sorts of studies do not imply that multinational firms *completely* adapt to local conditions. Rather, the evidence suggests that they *substantially* adapt to national institutions and cultural norms while still seeking to take advantage of their proprietary technologies (Cooke 2007a) or their service know-how (Gamble 2010). This process is well illustrated in a study by Doeringer, Lorenz and Terkla (2003) of the HR practices of Japanese multinationals with transplants in the USA, the UK and France. These plants are required to meet Japanese productivity benchmarks and usually have Japanese managers appointed to them to lead and monitor local management. Examination of the ways they have sought to organise work and employment over the last 20 to 30 years provides a kind of 'natural experiment' on the interaction between HRM and societal institutions and cultural norms. Doeringer *et al.* (2003: 271) conclude that there is 'almost no evidence' of Japanese management practices 'being transferred intact to Japanese transplants'. What they do show, however, is that *work* processes associated with Japanese quality-oriented production systems (such as problem-solving in quality circles, teamworking, and worker responsibility for quality) are much more likely to have been diffused than *employment* practices associated with pay, skill, promotion systems and the like. This makes a lot of sense: the transplants need work processes that are consistent with the economics of production in the industry but can be much more flexible in relation to employment practices. The latter are much more driven by national laws, by local labour markets, by union contracts, and by deep-set social attitudes. In the UK, for example, Japanese firms have learnt to work with a higher level of unionisation than they find in the USA and have been found to adapt to British attitudes to bonus systems (which often favour simpler and 'less subjective' systems to those found in Japan) and to the status differences in British society between technicians and production workers. In France, among other things, Japanese firms have learnt to accept that supervisors will typically be appointed directly to a position of responsibility based on their personal achievements in France's national system of educational qualifications and without any prior experience (for an excellent overview of national differences in approaches to vocational education and training, see Winterton 2007). The French elite model of education, with all its hierarchical rungs, is not easily sidestepped. This contrasts sharply with the Japanese practice of promoting from within based on extensive shopfloor experience.

In other studies, even less of the Japanese approach to work and employment is found to be diffused across countries. A compelling example is Wilkinson *et al.*'s (2001) case study of two Japanese-owned multinationals operating in Malaysia, which draws on Kenney *et al.*'s (1998) distinction between 'learning factories' and 'reproduction factories'. The Japanese firms in this study use their Japanese plants to foster their product innovation and to iron out the bugs in the production system (that is, these plants are the 'learning factories'). Once problem solving by highly trained and well paid Japanese workers has played its part, they then mass produce the standardised products in Malaysian plants (their 'reproduction factories'). In the latter, less skilled and much lower paid workers assemble what are essentially pre-designed and quality-engineered products. A subsequent study by Morris, Wilkinson and Gamble (2009) of Japanese and Korean firms operating factories in China finds the same phenomenon there, as does Shibata's (2008) study of Japanese transplants in Thailand. Such studies challenge the assumption that multinational companies *want* to export their HR practices around the globe. As Edwards and Kuruvilla (2005) argue, much of the literature in international HRM makes the faulty assumption that multinational firms somehow want to export the way they manage people from the richer countries to the less developed ones. As they argue, research on the 'international division of labour' often reveals the reverse: many firms go offshore to take advantage of lower labour costs and less demanding labour regulations (see also Cooke 2007b). They are not seeking to export their high-cost models of HRM but to escape them, as we shall explain further in Chapter 5.

Where, then, have we come to? The studies we have discussed help us to see that national boundaries are not impermeable barriers in HRM: multinational firms search out ways of making money through transferring their financial capital and, often, the core elements of their production systems across them. On the other hand, once they land in a country, they face the human elements of running a business that are essentially local (Hofstede and Bond 1988). Firms arriving in a new country come into contact with national labour laws, with local labour markets, with people carrying different cultural expectations, and with specific systems for trade union recognition and for vocational education and training. All of these labour factors help to *localise* HR practices, ensuring that in each country a large measure of adaptation to the customary employment practices takes place. Furthermore, multinationals are often heading to these countries precisely because they offer lower-cost models of HRM. They know that reducing their reliance on the high-cost labour markets in their home country will increase their survival chances.

Industry fit

While societal fit emphasises the way national features affect HRM, the notion of industry fit encapsulates the relationship between firms and the economic, technological and socio-political factors that are specific to their particular industry. Again, the question is: do firms adapt to their industry contexts and are they wise to do so? The industry is a critical level of analysis in strategic management, as long emphasised by Michael Porter (1980), and as affirmed by strategy researchers who have uncovered 'industry recipes' in the ways firms strategise (Spender 1989). The existence of industry recipes shows that firms tend to imitate what is seen to work in their industry, and this includes approaches to managing people. Research in organisational behaviour has also underlined industry differences. Chatman and Jehn (1994), for example, show that different industry characteristics, such as different types of technology and different rates of growth, affect organizational cultures.

Industry, however, is a rather complex or 'fuzzy' variable (McGee 2003: 276). When we say 'industry', we are, in fact, thinking about various levels at which differences in management behaviour can occur: differences between broad sectors, differences between industries within sectors, and differences within industries across customer segments or 'strategic groups'. The highest level is the broad sector in which HRM takes place: no one needs much convincing that there are major differences between the private sector, in which firms need to make profits to survive, and the public sector, something which is readily confirmed by major studies and reviews (see, for example, Kalleberg *et al.* 2006, Bach and Kessler 2007). Public-sector HRM is not profit driven but it is subject to the directives of governments, which vary as economic conditions and political agendas change. Public sector organisations are typically larger and more bureaucratic than those in the private sector, as well as being much more highly unionised (Freeman, Boxall and Haynes 2007). Not only are public sector managers more constrained by their political masters, but they must learn to live with more prescriptive employment contracts that restrict their discretion in HRM, and may face conflict-laden collective negotiations whenever they seek to make change.

Then, within these broad sectors, there are further important differences. HRM in the private sector varies between manufacturing and services and varies markedly within each domain. Within manufacturing, analysis of the different types of production technology helps to reveal important differences in work systems. Blauner's (1964) classic study, which we highlighted in Chapter 1, traced differences in how people are managed across craft, machine-tending, assembly-line and continuous process industries. As a general rule, the greater the investment in production technology required in the industry, the greater will be the economic incentive to invest in the people who are employed to keep it working. Subsequent research in manufacturing confirms major differences in HRM between capital-intensive and labour-intensive production conditions. For example, Snell and Dean's (1992) study of 512 US metal manufacturing plants shows that heavier investments in individual employees, including more extensive screening and training practices, are associated with plants using advanced manufacturing technologies (AMT) such as computer-integrated manufacturing systems. The value of such investments, however, is likely to be questioned by managers when the industry they are operating in is characterised by a stable, low-technology environment (Kintana, Alonso, Olaverri 2006). As we shall explain in Chapter 5, labour-intensive, low-tech manufacturing is much more likely to be associated with pressures to outsource production to low-wage countries.

We see similar patterns within services, which we will also be examining in more depth in Chapter 5. As mentioned in Chapter 1, there are enormous differences between working in, say, a law firm, which is run by highly qualified, highly paid professionals, who work whatever hours are needed to get the job done for the client, and working in a discount retailer, which employs casual, low-paid labour, often students and new migrants, on an hourly rate for the job. That the service sector encompasses a range of industries from those that are expensive and esoteric, such as professional and consulting services, through to those that are low-cost and routine, including retail, fast-food, and cleaning services, is regularly emphasised in the industrial relations research (see, for example, Katz and Darbishire 2000, Appelbaum, Bernhardt and Murnane 2003, Batt 2007). Because services are labour intensive, managers seek to maintain labour costs at a level that will offer the prospect of economic survival in the industry concerned. The general observation in service industries is that the greater the knowledge required to deliver the service or the higher the quality of the service, the higher will be the price of it and the greater will be the investment in recruiting, paying and developing the people who deliver it (Boxall 2003). High-investment models of HRM are cost-effective in those service industries where customers will pay the premium prices that make the firm's high-cost labour sustainable.

Let us now take this down to the strategic-group level. Industries are not uniform: they consist of clusters of firms, often targeting the same group of customers, whose strategies tend to fit into a similar configuration (Porter 1980, Suarez and Utterback 2005, Peteraf and Shanley 1997). Mobility barriers between these strategic groups make it costly and time-consuming for other groups of firms in the industry to challenge their 'strategic space' (McGee 2003). Take, for example, the hotel industry in which there are firms targeting wealthy travellers (4-star and 5-star hotels), those targeting mid-range travellers who do not need the full amenities of an elite hotel (3-star and 2-star hotels), and those targeting the low-cost traveller (1-star hotels and backpacker hostels). These can be seen as distinct strategic groups of firms with major investments required to move from one category to another. Barring a war, a terrorism incident or a natural disaster, it is laughable to think that backpacker hostels actually compete with the higher-quality strategic groups in hotels, although all are notionally in the 'hospitality industry'. Not only do the mobility barriers between groups include investments in facilities but studies show that those firms at the luxury end of the hotel industry invest more heavily in their staff in order to deliver superior customer service (Lashley 1998, Knox and Walsh 2005, Sun, Aryee and Law 2007). Strategic-group effects can also be seen in US studies of rest homes (Eaton 2000, Hunter 2000) where HR investments (in training, pay, career structures and staffing levels) are greater in firms that target higher-value niches (more expensive rest homes with better facilities and a higher level of nursing care). Thus, HR investments vary not only between industries but tend to vary enormously within any industry in which there are major quality differences.

Overall, research confirms that industry characteristics make a major impact on the ways firms manage work and people. At the highest level, there are broad differences between private sector and public sector HRM. There are therefore major variations across industries within each sector and, in addition, contrasts between customer segments or strategic groups within industries. Not only do we see major differences in HRM across these categories but the process of adapting to the economic realities in one's industry niche is important for competitive survival. It seems, again, that firms adapt to their context, and they are wise to do so.

Organisational fit

The process of cascading down the layers of industry fit leads us inevitably to our last type of fit: organisational fit. The issue here is whether managers can, and should, mould their HR strategies to fit in with other critical features of their particular business, including its wider strategy and its structural features. Most contingency research starts by looking at the correlation between two variables. A rather simple example is the relationship between organisational size and HRM. In a major review of studies on contextual influences in HRM, Jackson and Schuler (1995) show that larger organizations are more likely to have due-process procedures, use more sophisticated staffing and training practices and have more developed 'internal labour markets' (that is, a structure of more specialised jobs and more extensive career hierarchies which provide greater scope to promote and develop people from within), among other features (see also the major review of studies on HRM in small firms by Cardon and Stevens 2004). None of this will come as a surprise to anyone who has worked in both small and large firms or in the same organization which started small and became much bigger. Larger firms inevitably need more formalised practices to manage larger numbers of people and to cope with more diverse occupational groups. In addition, employees often bring greater expectations to larger firms. Individuals being recruited to larger organisations are likely to be screened through multiple channels and will often ask to see a job description and ask questions about how their pay fits into the job hierarchy. Those joining a small firm are much more likely to agree the details directly with one person – the owner – and are much less likely to see written documentation. There is clearly strong support for the idea that the size of an organization makes a major difference to the kind of HR practices management adopts and to the level of formalization involved in HRM.

A second kind of organisational fit overlaps with this phenomenon. This is the observation that HRM varies across organisational life-cycle stages, such as birth, growth and maturity (Baird and Meshoulam 1988). For example, in a study of 2,903 small to medium-sized US family firms, Rutherford, Buller and McMullen (2003) find that managers in firms experiencing high rates of growth consider employee development their biggest problem but perceive much less difficulty with employee retention. This is not surprising: fast growth can make a company exciting to join but stretches managers in terms of trying to develop the employee capabilities they need. In comparison, firms not experiencing growth have the greatest difficulty recruiting. These could be failing firms which are stymied in terms of their ability to grow precisely because no one wants to join them. We think life-cycle theory is an important line of analysis in HR strategy and explore it more fully in Chapter 9.

Among the most influential models of organisational fit in HRM are those that have argued that the key issue in organisational fit concerns the link between competitive strategy and HR strategy. In this line of thinking, it is seen as critical to bring HR strategy into line with the firm's desired market position (sometimes called 'external' or 'vertical' fit): in other words, management should do what it takes in HRM to enable the firm to meet the customer needs it is targeting. We should make two initial clarifying points about this idea. First, when theorists advocate fitting HR strategy to competitive strategy, they are usually talking about matching HR practices to the marketing strategy of a *particular business unit* which operates in a particular industry. This should not be confused with the much more complex question of how to develop HR strategy in a multidivisional organisation in which the parent company presides over diverse divisions and business units, something we discuss in Chapter 10. Second, theorists are generally talking about how management should manage *core operating workers*: those most intimately involved in making the product or providing the service. Theoretical models in this area are not generally about how managers themselves should be managed, which is a different question altogether (Boxall 1992, Boxall and Gilbert 2007), and something we will consider in Chapter 8.

The most heavily cited work on this kind of fit in strategic HRM is associated with a theoretical model developed by Schuler and Jackson (1987). Their model, and a subsequent stream of papers (Schuler 1989, 1996), has proven very influential for the way it spells out the connections between competitive strategies, desired employee behaviours and particular HR practices. Schuler and Jackson (1987) argue that HR practices should be designed to reinforce the behavioural implications of the various competitive strategies defined by Porter (1980, 1985). A giant in the strategy field, Porter (1980, 1985) advises firms to specialise carefully in competitive strategy (Figure 3.3). In his view, firms should choose between cost leadership (achieving lowest unit costs in the industry), differentiation (based, for example, on superior quality or service) or focus (a 'niche play' in cost or differentiation). They should avoid getting 'stuck in the middle' or caught in a strategic posture which is mixed – neither fish nor fowl, one might say.

Schuler and Jackson (1987) use Porter's framework to argue that performance will improve when the HR practices in a business mutually reinforce competitive strategy (Figure 3.4 teases this out). To arrive at a desirable set of HR practices, they argue that different competitive strategies imply different kinds or blends of employee behaviour. These inferences are drawn from

Competitive advantage

	Lower cost	Differentiation
Broad target	Cost leadership	Differentiation
Narrow target	Focus: Cost leadership	Focus: Differentiation

Competitive scope

Figure 3.3 Porter's typology of competitive strategies

Source: Reprinted with the permission of The Free Press, a Division of Simon & Schuster, Inc. © All rights reserved. For Porter (1985).

a major review of existing literature. If, for example, management chooses a competitive strategy of differentiation through continuous product innovation, this would call for high levels of creative, risk-oriented and cooperative behaviour. The company's HR practices would therefore need to emphasise 'selecting highly skilled individuals, giving employees more discretion, using minimal controls, making greater investment in human resources, providing more resources for experimentation, allowing and even rewarding occasional failure, and appraising performance for its long-run implications' (Schuler and Jackson 1987: 210).

Desired competitive strategy
(cost leadership, differentiation or focus)

↓

Required employee skills and behaviours
(for example, extent of predictability in behaviour, degree of teamwork, extent of concern for quality, propensity for risk taking)

↓

Supportive HR practices
(choices in staffing, appraisal, remuneration, training, etc.)

↓

HR outcomes
(employee skills and behaviour relevant to desired competitive position)

Figure 3.4 Linking HR practices to competitive strategy

Source: Adapted from Schuler and Jackson (1987).

On the other hand, if management wants to pursue cost leadership (that is, to attain lowest unit costs in the sector), the Schuler and Jackson model implies something a lot less attractive to the average employee. It suggests designing jobs which are fairly repetitive, reducing employee numbers and wage levels, training workers as little as is practical, and rewarding short-term results.

Although competitive posture is complex and two-dimensional, typologies, such as Porter's, can be misleading (Murray 1988, Miller 1992, Cronshaw, Davis and Kay 1994), as we will discuss below, the fundamental idea is that business performance will be better when there is alignment between competitive strategy and the management of core operating workers inside the business. In evaluating such a claim, we come back to our two questions: do managers relate their HR practices to their competitive strategies and are they wise to do so? In answering the first question, it helps if we distinguish between firms operating in service industries and those operating in manufacturing. A leading study in services is Batt's (2000) analysis of four market segments in call-centre work in the US telecommunications industry. These segments vary in terms of the complexity and value of the employee–customer interaction. At the low end, there are low-margin interactions of short duration, typically with predetermined scripts and with strong technological monitoring of call-centre workers. At the high end, there are high-margin, low-volume interactions relying far more on employee skill and discretion where technology is much more of an enabler than a monitor. One statistic alone is telling: at the low-margin end, operators deal with an average of 465 customers per day, in the two mid-range segments they deal with 100 and 64, and at the top end they deal with an average of 32 (Batt 2000: 550). Batt (2000) finds significant differences in the contours of HR strategy across these market segments with skill requirements, the degree of discretion allowed to employees and pay levels all higher among firms competing at the high-margin end of the call-centre market.

Studies of specific service industries like this one on call centres, and those on hotels and rest homes referred to earlier, generally support the notion that HR strategy is closely related to competitive positioning in services. A close relationship between competitive strategy and HRM can also be discerned in professional services. In their study of Dutch and German management consultancies, Dooreward and Meihuizen (2000) discern two broad strategic types: firms oriented to efficiency and firms oriented to expertise. The former offer 'standard solution(s) to familiar problems in an efficient way' while the latter promote 'an individual professional's ability to offer new, client-specific solutions to new, unusual problems' (Dooreward and Meihuizen 2000: 43). These are tendencies, not hard-and-fast categories, but they are associated with differentiation in HR strategies. Expertise-driven firms try to hire highly intelligent 'free spirits' and retain them through challenging, high-discretion work, while those oriented to efficiency have a much more bureaucratic model of HRM.

When it comes to firms operating in services, therefore, research suggests there are quite strong links between different kinds of competitive position and investments in HRM. It is not that hard to see why. Firms that compete through more esoteric forms of knowledge or through higher service quality need to employ more highly qualified people and pay them more, which translates through higher labour costs directly into higher prices. Customers that can afford them are used to the fact that professional and higher quality services are going to cost them more.

The picture in manufacturing is more complex because contemporary manufacturing technologies and processes can make it possible for firms to be simultaneously pursuing quality improvements and cost reductions, along with improvements in such other manufacturing performance indicators as delivery time and product flexibility (see, for example, Jayaram, Droge and Vickery 1999, Das and Narasimhan 2001). The notion of a trade-off between cost and quality, implied by Porterian models of strategy, is not necessarily helpful in understanding HRM in contemporary manufacturing. How managers try to organise HRM for a manufacturing firm's core workers tends to be related to technological choices and innovations in production processes (Purcell 1999). When a manufacturing firm has expensive investments in advanced technology, which requires highly skilled and careful handling, managers are likely to spend money building employee competencies and fostering employee commitment (Steedman and Wagner 1989, Godard 1991). This is important *even if* their competitive goal is to achieve the lowest unit costs in the industry. The issue is this: where there are high 'interaction risks' between specialised capital assets (in which the firm has major 'sunk costs') and the behaviour of workers, managers are likely to adopt employment models that foster greater expertise and buy greater loyalty and care. Such investments, however, are of questionable value in a stable, low-technology environment, as noted above.

It helps if we look outside the HRM literature and consider the in-depth research on manufacturing management. In an impressive array of studies published in the *Journal of Operations Management*, scholars such as Boyer *et al.* (1997), Kotha and Swamidass (2000), Das and Narasimhan (2001) and Shah and Ward (2003) find that the performance of firms adopting advanced manufacturing technology is better when they make commensurate improvements in the people 'infrastructure' that enables the technology to function.

The common theme is the value of ensuring HR strategy fits with more complex manufacturing goals and greater investment in manufacturing technology. Similarly, in an important longitudinal study, de Menezes, Wood, and Gelade (2010) find that British firms investing in Japanese-style lean manufacturing systems, such as integrated computer-based technology and total quality management, perform better when they integrate these costly changes in production strategy with a more empowering style of HRM and extensive employee training. These studies provide some of the best evidence we currently have of the value of a good fit between HRM and operating strategy.

The manufacturing research we have just cited shows the importance of thinking about the wider fit among competitive goals, operations management and HRM. Services marketing thinkers are calling for the same kind of integrative modelling in services (Lovelock, Patterson and Walker 2007), but the research is less well advanced. We have been hamstrung for many years by management researchers channelling their energies into their particular silo – be that marketing, IT, operations, HRM, accounting or finance – and what is needed now is a much better integration of these disciplines in different types of business context. The contingency approach leads naturally into this more 'configurational' or systemic understanding of strategy because people realise that making a business successful is likely to depend on much more than simply aligning two management variables (for a recent review of configurational theory, see Short, Payne and Ketchen 2008). In fact, one should be careful about any kind of aligning between two variables until one has a sense of all the main variables that may need some kind of integration. There are some very difficult methodological issues involved in studying the interaction among multiple management variables but the task is a vital one if management theory is to be more useful to practitioners.

In conclusion, then, we have looked at the case for best fit on three levels: the societal, the industry and the organisational. These three levels of analysis, each rather complex, demonstrate the overwhelming impact of context on HRM. In arguing a case for the wisdom of adapting HRM in an organisation to its particular context, one could simply pick out one of two killer blows: employment law, for example. Most firms in the Anglophone world respect the employment laws of the societies in which they operate and, because social legitimacy is an important goal in HRM, all firms would be wise to do so. A case for best fit in HRM could be argued on this simple point alone. The case only becomes more compelling as we look at other contextual factors, such as local labour market conditions, varying cultural norms, unique industry characteristics, differences in organisational size, different operating strategies, and so on. It would be strange indeed if managers did not adapt to, and take advantage of, these differing circumstances.

Strategic HRM: the best-practice school

Those who advocate the best-practice approach start from a different premise to contingency theorists. In best practice thinking, a universal prescription is preferred. The staunchest advocates of best practice argue that all firms will see performance improvements if they identify and implement best practices. This brings quite a different understanding of the problem of integrating HR strategy with the rest of business strategy. Integration with strategic management, in this conception, is about top management identifying the 'leading edge' of best practice, publicising commitments to best practices, measuring progress towards them and rewarding lower-level managers for implementing them consistently.

Before proceeding, we should note an initial difficulty with this school of thought: a lot of writing on best practice moves fairly quickly into prescription without making its basic assumptions explicit. In a classic critique of the best-practice genre in what was then personnel management, Legge (1978) asked the question: For *whom* is 'best practice' best? *Whose* goals or interests are being served? If 'best practice' serves both shareholder and worker interests, it is hard to object to it.[2] Similarly, if we agree that some practice is bad for both parties, it should be avoided. But what if a practice is good for corporate returns but bad for workers? This is often the case with downsizing: share-markets seem to rate companies more highly for doing it, a cold comfort for the workers laid off and for those left behind whose workload may just have become much more stressful. When this kind of trade-off emerges, do workers get a real voice in deciding the issue (Marchington and Grugulis 2000)? Best-practice models are typically silent on these sorts of tensions. Those emanating from the USA do not typically mention or argue for the sort of strong employee voice institutions seen in Europe, such as unions and works councils, which can help to protect employee interests when trade-offs occur.

Furthermore, what if a practice is good for executives but not good for either shareholders or waged workers? This is the problem, arguably, with many exit packages used for senior executives dismissed or 'let go' because

---

[2] Although consumers and environmentalists might still object to some practices (for example, when a firm is making high profits and paying high wages but prices are extortionate or the firm is a bad polluter).

of disappointing performance: *they* benefit but the company and its other employees typically lose out. In fact, the whole area of executive remuneration – staying or going – has become highly controversial, including in the USA. As Kochan (2007: 604) explains, American 'CEO pay relative to the average worker (has) exploded from a ratio of 40:1 in the 1960s and 70s to over 400:1 today'. This trend may be best for senior US executives but many others, both within the USA and looking at US practices from the outside, regard the trend as an aspect of American HR practice which is socially divisive and undesirable.

How are we going to proceed with a discussion of 'best practice' in the light of the problem of interest conflicts? Given that explicit assumptions are largely lacking, we need to consider implicit ones. In our view, the most common implicit assumption in the best-practice literature is that 'best practices' are those that enhance shareholder value. We think, however, that a useful test of any best-practice claim is the extent to which it also serves employee interests. One would not expect to see a perfect alignment of interests but it is likely that the most sustainable models of HRM over the long run are those that enjoy high levels of legitimacy among people within the firm and in wider society. On the basis of this caveat, we step gingerly forward.

Best practice: micro foundations and macro models

Despite their tendency to gloss over basic assumptions, studies of individual best practices within the major categories of micro HRM – such as selection, training and appraisal – do have a very long tradition in Western psychology and management theory. During both World Wars, for example, a lot of British and American energy went into improving practices for officer selection and also into the training and motivation of (non-combatant) production workers (Eysenck 1953, Eilbert 1959, Crichton 1968). The academic discipline of Industrial Psychology gained great momentum as industrial psychologists studied the prediction and development of human performance. In the area of employee selection, for example, they usefully compared different practices for selecting individual employees (such as ability tests, personality inventories, 'biodata' obtained through application forms or from an individual's curriculum vitae ('cv') or résumé, references, and various types of interviews), assessing their validity in terms of subsequent performance (usually as rated by supervisors).

Based on this tradition of work, some micro aspects of best practice *are* widely acknowledged by researchers and practitioners (Delery and Doty 1996: 806, Youndt, Snell, Dean and Lepak 1996: 838). In the selection area, hardly anyone would advocate unstructured interviewing over interviews carefully designed around job-relevant factors. Similarly, no one would advocate input-based performance appraisal for senior executives (such as measures of time-keeping) over processes that examine results achieved (such as profit generated and growth in market share) or the kind of behaviour demonstrated in working with colleagues and clients. The selection and performance appraisal fields are two areas where we can point to an extensive body of research that assists management to carry out these processes more effectively. While there are still major debates and a raft of new problems, as recent reviews attest (Latham, Sulsky and MacDonald 2007, Schmitt and Kim 2007), there is quite a lot of agreement on what constitutes 'bad' or 'stupid' practice, on the one hand, and 'sensible' practice, on the other, when we talk about practices in selection and performance appraisal.

At least, this is a fair generalisation *within* our specific cultural mind-set or 'blinkers'. We are talking here about selection and appraisal within a Western cultural frame of reference, dominated by US and British research. In this cultural tradition, we are generally comfortable with the idea that management should try to predict, appraise and reward *individual* performance, as noted in our discussion of research on best fit. In fact, a lot of high-performing employees will be angry and disloyal if their individual merit is not recognised (Trevor, Gerhart and Boudreau 1997). The sort of research discussed earlier helps us to remember, however, that such a high emphasis on individualism may be considered counter-cultural or subversive in societies which place a heavier emphasis on group identification and interpersonal humility. As a result of this, many psychologists nowadays, including those writing in the *Journal of Cross-Cultural Psychology*, will openly acknowledge that cultural factors are important (for example, Smith 2004). It is decidedly helpful when industrial psychologists identify themselves as working on HRM *within* a particular cultural domain (such as, Warr 2007: 283–8).

The interesting and difficult question we face in a book about strategic HRM is whether best-practice thinking can work on a more macro level, on the level of *HR systems* (Becker and Gerhart 1996), a notion that is critical to our understanding of HR strategy. As noted in the definitions at the beginning of this chapter, firms often have more than one HR system. HR systems are aggregations of HR practices that managers have built over time to organise the work and manage the employment of a major workforce group. In most theoretical models, the key group of workers is the firm's core operational workers: the largest category of workers who make the products or deliver the services. Research often tries to identify what proportion of this core group is covered by a particular set of practices (Osterman 1994, 2000). A key theme that these models share with the literature on best fit discussed above is the idea that HR systems should be synergistic (see, for example, Dyer and Reeves 1995, Delery and Shaw 2001): that practices should be 'bundled' or clustered to reinforce desired effects.

There are, in fact, writers who have set out to offer models at this higher, more systemic level. In the USA, one model that has attracted a high profile is associated with Jeffrey Pfeffer's (1998) seven practices 'for building profits by putting people first', shown in Table 3.1.

What comes through Pfeffer's list is a desire to carefully hire and develop talented people, organising them into highly cooperative teams, and employing them in a way that builds their commitment over the long term (through high pay, employment security and as much egalitarianism and openness as possible). Recruiting and retaining talented, team-oriented, highly motivated people is seen to lay a basis for superior business performance or competitive advantage. This is one well-known model which has been widely propagated through books and conferences.

It does not, however, stand up well on a reality test – that is, when we look at the actual HR practices of US firms. There are cases of individual firms aiming to behave in the way Pfeffer advocates but research by industrial relations scholars on the actual diffusion of HR practices shows that they are very much in the minority (Kaufman 2010). For example, when we observe the general trends in pay in the USA, noted above, the trend is actually towards executive elitism and away from the egalitarianism that Pfeffer (1998) advocates. Similarly, the US data suggests that job security declined in the 1990s and teamworking, present in around 40 per cent of firms with at least 50 employees, did not expand (Osterman 2000, Batt 2004). In a more recent study of diffusion, using a nationally random sample of US workplaces, Blasi and Kruse (2006: 572) find that 'self-managed work teams were used by some sites for some employees but their adoption for most employees is rather modest'. It is

Table 3.1 Pfeffer's seven practices

1	Employment security
2	Selective hiring
3	Self-managed teams or teamworking
4	High pay contingent on company performance
5	Extensive training
6	Reduction of status differences
7	Sharing information

Source: Pfeffer (1998).

not only the industrial relations scholars who are pinpointing the lack of diffusion of managerial 'best practice'. Based on a major study of 661 US firms, which finds major variation in HR models across different organisational contexts, the prominent industrial psychologists, Toh, Morgesen and Campion (2008: 877) conclude that 'any prescriptions for a set of universal HR "best practices" must be informed by the contextual factors that surround their use'. One would think that this kind of study, published in the elite *Journal of Applied Psychology*, would make an impact. Best-practice writers, however, are not necessarily deterred by this kind of empirical observation. They are typically making a normative argument, an argument about what *ought* to be, not what is, and do not enquire very far into the question of what managers actually do and why they do it.

There is now a major body of literature in which various academics have attempted to define macro models of best HR practice. This literature is very diverse and at least three terms have been employed. One stream of literature stems from the work of the Harvard academic, Walton (1985), and is commonly called 'high-commitment management' (HCM) (Wood 1996). As this implies, the emphasis in this model is on winning employee commitment to the organisation's goals through positive incentives and identification with company culture rather than trying to control their behaviour through routine, short-cycle jobs and direct supervision. Another school of thought traces back to Lawler (1986) and is concerned with 'high-involvement work systems' (HIWSs). Here, the emphasis is on redesigning work to involve employees more fully in decision making and on the skill and motivational practices that are needed to support this process (see, for example, Vandenberg, Richardson and Eastman 1999). A third term, 'high-performance work systems' (HPWSs) has sparked widespread interest over the last 10 to 15 years and is now the terminology many people use when they talk of best-practice models of HRM. Cappelli and Neumark (2001) trace the term's popularity to an influential public report, *America's Choice: High Skills or Low Wages!* (Commission on the Skills of the American Workforce 1990). This report, concerned about the fate of US jobs and highly critical of traditional work organization, argues the case for substantial investment in 'high-performance work organization' and higher skills. HPWSs are commonly understood to involve reforms to work practices to increase employee involvement in decision making and companion investments in employee skills and changes to performance incentives to ensure they can undertake these greater responsibilities and want to do so (Appelbaum *et al.* 2000). They constitute an attempt to roll back the kind of 'Taylorist' or highly specialised, de-skilled jobs which were a key part of the US system of mass production (something we will discuss further in Chapter 5).

Models of best practice: research and critique

What, therefore, does research and theoretical critique have to say about the best-practice approach to HR systems? The first and most obvious difficulty with the approach was pointed out early on by Becker and Gerhart (1996): there is too much diversity in lists of best practices. Pfeffer's (1998) list of seven practices is actually reduced from an earlier list of 16 practices (Pfeffer 1994) and there have been major variations between theorists not only in the number of practices needed for an HR system but in which ones to include. A big part of the problem, as Becker and Gerhart (1996) and Purcell (1999) point out, is that many theorists simply list practices and do not specify the pathway or intervening variables through which they are supposed to improve business performance so we are not sure *how* they are supposed to be best.

Leaving aside definitional issues, the major objection to the idea of a universally valid set of best HR practices is the socio-cultural one. As emphasised in our review of the best-fit literature, there is overwhelming research evidence that firms adapt their HR practices to their unique contexts. And this is the key point: they are *wise* to do so because social legitimacy is an important aspect of a firm's multidimensional HR performance. Some practices – such as an employee grievance procedure and forms of consultation – are legal requirements in countries like the UK. Governments have decided they should form part of employer practice for ethical and political reasons. Simply on the fact of societal regulation of labour markets, we must discount the idea that there can be universally valid lists of best practice.

Similarly, as Hofstede (1980), Trompenaars and Hampden-Turner (1997) and many others remind us, there really is a problem with trying to specify a set of cross-culturally best HR practices because there are significant differences across countries in cultural values. Even if we are talking about the same practice, such as selection interviewing, the application of it can vary very significantly. In New Zealand, for example, where government policy supports biculturalism (English and Maori are both official languages), it is not uncommon for Maori job applicants to request a *whanau* (family, kinship-supported) interview. In such an interview, family members and close friends speak to the merits of the job applicant because it is considered culturally offensive to indulge in self praise or 'blow your own trumpet'. This is still a selection interview but it is not what American or British writers think of when they use the term.

As Becker and Gerhart (1996) imply, we would be wise to dispense with the idea that there can be lists of HR practices that are universally relevant. A more appropriate line of thinking is to accept that there will always be socio-cultural variations in how HRM is organised and look to systems or configurations of HR practices that have a kind of 'functional equivalence' or 'equifinality' (Delery and Doty 1996). In other words, it is possible to envisage systems that are designed to serve certain ends but which recognise variety in the actual practices that are used in different industries and different societies to express these principles.

In effect, Appelbaum and Batt (1994), whose work on models of high-performance work systems has been highly influential, adopt this kind of approach. When looking beyond the USA for HPWS models, they identify four that provide interesting lessons: Swedish 'sociotechnical systems', Japanese 'lean production', Italian 'flexible specialisation' and German 'diversified quality production'. Each of these models (all of which have internal variations) are embedded in national laws, customs and management styles that vary from the USA. Just comparing institutional features in three of these countries shows major differences (Table 3.2). As Appelbaum and Batt argue,

Table 3.2 Some key differences in employment relations in three national contexts

	USA	Japan	Germany
Unionisation	Very low level (below 10% of private sector workers).	Well-established enterprise unions in the large corporations.	Strong, industry-based unions with key involvement in vocational training (among other areas).
Power sharing: institutions	Collective bargaining only in workplaces where there is majority worker support.	Collective bargaining at set annual time ('shunto' – the Spring Offensive) plus well established consultative processes.	Industry-based collective bargaining plus very established tradition of co-determination (works councils and worker directors).
Management attitudes to joint governance	Apart from some cases of union-management 'partnerships', strong management resistance to any form of power sharing with unions.	Japanese executives work with strong cultural norms that emphasise consultation and have often been officials in the enterprise union.	German managers have adjusted to co-determination and, while grappling with flexibility problems, see advantages in consensual decision making.

Sources: Taira (1993), Appelbaum and Batt (1994), Wever (1995), Towers (1997), Freeman (2007).

it is very difficult to transplant foreign models of high-performance work systems to the USA because of these socio-political contexts. While they support the idea of greater voice mechanisms for US workers, they realise that this will have to be worked out in an American way. Most commentators on the USA recognise that the chances of major reform there towards European-style works councils or worker directors are extremely small (Towers 1997, Freeman 2007).

The line of argument found in the work of Appelbaum and Batt (1994) was reinforced with the publication of *Manufacturing Advantage* (Appelbaum *et al.* 2000). This book looks at US-style HPWSs in three industries: steel making, clothing manufacturing and medical electronics manufacturing. The studies in this book were all conducted at the plant level, identifying the particular HR practices used in each industry and measuring performance as objectively as possible in terms of the productivity indices relevant to the production processes concerned. They involve surveys of worker responses to HR reforms and do not rely on managerial reports of either company results or worker attitudes. In the main, the studies are supportive of the idea that both companies and employees have benefited where HPWSs have been implemented in these industries. There are other influential studies in the steel industry (Ichniowski, Shaw and Prennushi 1997, Arthur 1999, Ichniowski and Shaw 1999) and in automobile manufacturing (MacDuffie 1995). The latter studies have actually looked at HR systems in similar plants across countries (most notably comparing the USA and Japan). This has enabled these studies to pick up principles of work design that have become common across the two countries while also observing culturally embedded HR practices that have not.

As Ichniowski and Shaw (1999) show in their study of US and Japanese steel plants, the US plants that have achieved similar operational performance to Japanese ones have done so through adopting the principles of employee-driven problem-solving seen in Japanese plants while customizing employment practices (such as selection tests and pay systems) in a way that is more compatible with local law and cultural norms. Their work indicates the way in which the debate about best practice needs to evolve: away from the idea that we can have exact replicas of 'best practices' in all industries towards studies of HR systems or models that are established on a core set of common principles but inevitably show intelligent adaptation of specific practices across contexts.

Do studies such as those by Ichniowski and Shaw (1999) in steel plants and MacDuffie (1995) in automobile manufacturing give us a basis for asserting that there are best HR practices that will deliver higher value across all industries or across strategic groups within an industry? No, they do not. These studies have the virtue of identifying the technologies, work processes and employment practices actually used in these industries and measuring the operational outcomes relevant to them. Understanding these distinctive features means we are less likely to assume they will work in other production environments. Appleyard and Brown (2001) underline this point in a study of the semiconductor manufacturing industry in Japan, Korea and the USA, contrasting the role of key occupational groups in this industry with that described by MacDuffie (1995) in automobiles and Ichniowski et al. (1997) in steel. In semiconductor production, problem-solving processes are dominated by highly skilled professional engineers and not by operators or technicians. The latter two occupational groups have an important role to play but the production process is more technologically intensive than either steel or automobile manufacturing. While operators and technicians bring their knowledge into problem-solving activities, it is the involvement and skills of highly qualified professional engineers, including software and equipment engineers, which is decisive in finding solutions to production quality issues and breakdowns.

What the sets of studies we have just cited offer is a thorough examination of production and HR systems in the field and a rigorous assessment of whether new HR systems will pay off in terms of the characteristics of production in that industry or competitive cluster within it. We can be pretty confident from studies of steel-finishing production systems that HR approaches which significantly enhance operator engagement in problem solving do improve machine up-time, quality and on-time delivery in this industry (Ichniowski et al. 1997, Ichniowski and Shaw 1999, Appelbaum et al. 2000). Within this particular environment, we can envisage improvements in shareholder value from these HR systems.

We can be more confident of such findings when research exercises use longitudinal methodologies that rule out or heavily discount other causes of performance variation. We have this with the steel industry studies just mentioned but it is far from easy to conduct this kind of study (Wright, Gardner, Moynihan, and Allen 2005, Gerhart 2007a). The only research we have that addresses the cost-effectiveness of HPWSs across a broad swathe of industries over time, and at a high level of rigour, is not flattering. This is the work of Cappelli and Neumark (2001), who use a national probability sample of US manufacturing establishments, assessing work practices and outcomes in firms in 1977 and then again some 20 years later. They conclude that HPWSs raise labour costs and that this implies that employees benefit through average remuneration rises, a picture reinforced by Osterman's (2006) study of the wage impacts of high-performance work organization in US manufacturers. However, the statistical case for productivity benefits is weaker and the effects on profitability are unclear. In this context, firms would be wise to be sceptical about the economics of such systems, as Godard (2004) argues. They may well offer benefits but they will not be cost-less and the relationship between benefit and cost needs careful assessment in their *particular* context.

Conclusions

In the light of all this, where do things stand in the debate between best fit and best practice? If we want to identify a winner, it is obviously a clear win to the best-fit camp on the evidence of what firms actually do. Research on what firms do – descriptive research – makes life very difficult for the more extreme advocates of best practice. It demonstrates that methods of labour management are inevitably influenced by context, including a range of economic and socio-political factors. And it also shows that there are very good reasons for adaptation to context including the need to fit in with social values and to adapt to industry characteristics. Does this fact invalidate all best-practice thinking? Should the best-practice people pack up their tents and go home?

We think there are three ways in which it is possible to take some value out of the best-practice approach rather than discarding it completely. First, as we explained above, there are aspects of best practice in the micro domains of HRM that are valuable providing we recognise their contextual limits. When companies commit to an executive selection process, for example, they are well advised to avoid invalid predictors of executive performance. Similarly, if they commit to performance appraisal, they are well advised to work hard on dealing with the 'rating errors' that research has shown will inevitably rear their ugly heads (Latham *et al.* 2007). However, all of this takes place within a cultural and legal context. The relevant best-practice prescriptions in these domains have been developed in an individualist Anglo-American frame of reference and should have regard to Anglo-American laws on discrimination and equal opportunity (Kossek and Pichler 2007).

Second, when we come to study specific industries, it is clearly possible to identify HR systems that embody a set of principles while fostering astute local adaptations in different production sites around the world. The research by Doeringer *et al.* (2003) and by Ichniowski and Shaw (1999), among others, shows the way in which management might emulate a core set of principles while cannily adapting to the specific context. Tayeb (1995: 600), for example, underlines the astute capacity of Japanese managers in Britain to implement their core philosophies on 'quality and built-in control . . . and harmonious employee-management relationships' while adjusting sensitively to

'British employees' cultural attitudes and values'. In a high-tech firm she studied, Japanese managers did not require 'the famous morning rituals performed in many Japanese companies . . . nor did they experiment with . . . plant-based unions' (*ibid.*: 600). There is a role for identifying better HR systems within particular industry contexts as these evolve, bearing in mind that such systems will more likely be based on 'equifinality' (aiming to achieve similar performance outcomes) than on exact lists of practices.

The second point leads us to a third, more general one. Following Becker and Gerhart (1996), we think there is scope to identify some general principles in HRM and, in fact, much of this book is dedicated to this task. Building on the arguments in this chapter, it is helpful to make an analytical distinction between the surface level of HR policy and practices in a firm and an underpinning level of HR principles (Figure 3.5). This is not a perfect distinction but it helps to reconcile the tension between best fit and best practice in strategic HRM. We are most unlikely to find that any theorist's selection of best practices (the surface layer) will have universal relevance because context always matters. It is, however, possible to argue that at the level of the underpinning layer there are some desirable principles which, if applied, will bring about more effective management of people. In effect, it is possible to argue that, 'ceteris paribus' (other things being equal), all firms are better off when they pursue certain principles in HRM (Youndt *et al.* 1996: 837, Edwards and Wright 2001).

What sort of principles do we have in mind? We have, in effect, already been arguing for three underpinning principles. First, both in this chapter and in Chapter 1, we have claimed that a good performance in HRM involves dealing with multiple goals. There are multiple 'bottom lines' in HRM, including economic and socio-political goals which involve managing trade-offs and dynamic tensions. This is a fundamental perspective or principle that informs

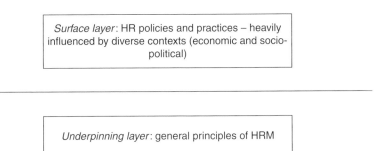

Figure 3.5 The 'best fit' versus 'best practice' debate: two levels of analysis

all of our analysis. Second, the pursuit of economic and socio-political goals means that firms inevitably adapt their HRM to their specific context *and* they are wise to do so. This is the 'law of context', if you like, which we have been at pains to demonstrate in this chapter. Third, we have argued that all models of HRM work through their impacts on employees: they all work through the 'AMO' variables, on the individual level, and through employee attitudes, on the collective level, as we described in Chapter 1. At the heart of this is a principle concerned with alignment: with the need to align management and employee interests, at least at the level of a contract that meets the base-line requirements of both parties. As a general rule, all firms benefit from policies and practices that help them to align their interests with those of employees. In any context where workers have good labour market choice or develop powerful union organization or enjoy strongly enforced labour market standards, this principle becomes more apparent – but it is always there. Research on how employees respond to different kinds of managerial policy and behaviour, and the links from these responses to the firm's performance, is going to be very important in this book and is likely to lead us to other important principles.

In Part 2 of the book, we engage in a process of 'searching for general principles' in the management of work and people and in the final part we look at how these play out in dynamic and complex contexts. In effect, the book is grounded on the assumption that *both* general principles *and* specific contexts play an important role in the theory and practice of strategic HRM. No one can seriously argue against the importance of best fit or contextual thinking in HRM (although some still try). However, there remains a valuable role for a concept of best practice if it means a concern for underpinning principles that are relevant across the diverse contexts in which managers actually try to manage work and people.

4

Strategic HRM and sustained competitive advantage

In this section of the book, we are concerned with concepts and models that build bridges between strategic management and HRM. As Chapter 3 made clear, contingency theory is important in this regard, especially when we locate HR strategy within a more holistic, systemic understanding of business strategy in which the various management disciplines, including marketing, HRM, operations and finance, need to be integrated. The strategic HRM literature is also heavily infused with a branch of strategic management known as the resource-based view of the firm (RBV). Relating the RBV to the best-fit/best-practice debate we have just been discussing, one might say that strategy theorists who work with the RBV aim to discover how a firm can build an *exclusive* form of fit. Fit is valuable and doing it better than others is clearly very valuable. How might a firm develop, interrelate and manipulate its resources – human and non-human – to become the best adapted, the most consistently profitable of all firms in its industry, despite the efforts of other firms to emulate or undermine it? This is the nub of the debate in strategic management around sustained competitive advantage. This chapter aims to explain what is meant by the RBV, defining key concepts and exploring major models. In so doing, it examines the ways in which HRM may help to lay a basis for sustained advantage.

The resource-based view of the firm: origins and assumptions

The resource-based view is usually sourced to a remarkable book by a University of London Professor of Economics, Edith Penrose (1959). At the time, texts on the economics of the firm were dominated by discussion of 'equilibrium' conditions under different forms of competition. The main focus of these texts was on the relative merits of different types of market, including 'perfect competition', oligopoly and monopoly. While valuable in debates about market regulation, the traditional analysis ignored very important issues inside the 'black box' of the firm's operations, leaving the study of entrepreneurship and business management in a very rudimentary state within the discipline of Economics.

Arguing that her interest was different from that of the standard texts on the firm, Penrose set out to build a theory of the growth of firms. She made the basic, but critical, observation that the firm is 'an administrative organization and a collection of productive resources', distinguishing between 'physical' and 'human resources' (Penrose 1959: 31, 24).[1] Her understanding of the quality of the firm's human resources placed heavy emphasis on the knowledge and experience of the management team and their subjective interpretation (or 'images') of the firm's environment (showing an early grasp of the kind of cognitive problems of strategic management discussed in Chapter 2). Her analysis proceeded from what has become a fundamental premiss in the theory of business strategy: firms are 'heterogeneous' (Penrose 1959: 74–8). As Nelson (1991: 61) puts it, competition ('perfect' or otherwise) never entirely eliminates 'differences among firms in the same line of business' and these differences account for major performance variations.

Penrose's ideas lay dormant for some time. Her work was not brought within the mainstream of strategic management theory until it was rediscovered by Wernerfelt (1984) and then by a string of other strategy writers from the late 1980s (see, for example, Dierickx and Cool 1989, Barney 1991, Conner 1991, Grant 1991, Mahoney and Pandian 1992, Amit and Shoemaker 1993, Peteraf, 1993). The result has been an explosion of interest in the resource-based perspective, focusing on the ways in which firms might build unique clusters or 'bundles' of human and technical resources that generate enviable levels of performance. Major reviews of the strategic management literature now routinely recognise the RBV as a major body of thought concerned with explaining sources of competitive advantage (see, for example, Hoskisson, Hitt, Wan and Yiu 1999, Lockett, Thompson and Morgenstern 2009).

In effect, the growth of the RBV has provided a counterweight to the marketing-oriented models of strategic management that were dominant in

---

[1] In passing, we might note that Penrose was one of the first theorists to adopt the 'human resources' terminology.

the strategy textbooks of the 1980s. The best known of these models was associated with the works of Michael Porter (1980, 1985), discussed in the context of best-fit theory in Chapter 3. These models place greatest emphasis on critical choices associated with competitive strategy – primarily, choices about which industry to enter and which competitive position to seek in it. In so doing, these models make some fairly heroic assumptions (Boxall 1992, 1996). For example, they assume that the firm already has a clever leadership team which can make these sorts of choices effectively. They assume that the human resource issues that arise when particular paths are chosen, such as hiring and motivating a capable workforce, are straightforward. They assume that culture change, when it might be needed to shift direction, is also unproblematic. In contrast, it is *exactly* these sorts of people issues that the resource-based view regards as strategic. In the RBV, the quality of the management process and of the firm's workplace culture are seen as major factors that explain enduring differences in business performance (Barney 1991, 2000).

It can, however, be argued that the RBV is itself imbalanced, placing undue emphasis on the internal side of the old SWOT acronym (strengths, weaknesses, opportunities, threats). In a response to criticism from resource-based theorists, Michael Porter argues that 'resources are not valuable in and of themselves, but because they allow firms to perform activities that create advantages in particular markets' (Porter 1991: 108). Similarly, Miller and Shamsie (1996: 520) argue that the RBV needs 'to consider the contexts within which various kinds of resources will have the best influence on performance.' In a study of the Hollywood film studios from 1936 to 1965, they demonstrate how knowledge-based resources (such as the exceptionally creative skills of key writers and cinematographers, and big budget coordinating abilities) were more valuable to the studios in the relatively uncertain and turbulent environment of the 1950s when the advent of television seriously affected movie-going habits. On the other hand, in the more stable conditions of the late 1930s and the 1940s (movie-going was very popular before and during World War II[2]), property-based resources (such as networks of theatres and long-term, exclusive contracts with particular actors) were more valuable for studio performance. In other words, the human talents that helped the studios to 'think and act outside the square' were indeed valuable when the context became less predictable.

---

[2] For example, some 90 million Americans went to the movies every week during World War II. See http://www.digitalhistory.uh.edu/modules/ww2/combatfilms.html, accessed 26/5/10.

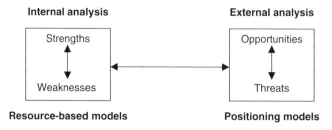

Figure 4.1 Internal and external dimensions of the strategic problem
Source: Adapted from Barney (1991).

Wernerfelt (1984: 173) did recognise the interplay of resources and markets when he said there is a 'duality between products and resources'. In other words, the strategic problem has both internal (strengths, weaknesses) and external (opportunities, threats) dimensions (Figure 4.1). These dimensions – what Baden-Fuller (1995) calls the 'inside-out' and the 'outside-in' perspectives on the strategic problem – are interactive over time. The point is well-made. One should not get carried away with either external or internal perspectives: both are necessary for a sufficient view of a firm's strategy. It seems safe, however, to suggest that what the resource-based perspective has achieved is a *re-balancing* of the literature on strategy, reminding people of the strategic significance of internal resources and their development over time.

Resources and barriers to imitation

What, then, are the basic definitions and concepts associated with the RBV? In the resource-based perspective, resources are not simply understood as assets in the formal accounting sense (which can be disclosed on a balance sheet) but include any feature of the firm with value-creating properties (Hunt 1995: 322). This means that aspects of the business that are not formally owned by it, such as the talents and interactions of the people who work in it, are not ignored but come within the realm of analytical interest. Wernerfelt (1984: 172) defined resources in the following way:

> By a resource is meant anything which could be thought of as a strength or weakness of a given firm. More formally, a firm's resources at a given time could be defined as those (tangible and intangible) assets which are tied semipermanently to the firm. Examples of resources are: brand names, in-house knowledge of technology, employment of skilled personnel, trade contacts, machinery, efficient procedures, capital, etc.

In an interesting study of chief executive opinion about the value of different kinds of resource, Hall (1993) found that CEOs rated the quality of employee know-how and their firm's reputation with customers as their most strategic assets. It is easy to see why the RBV is so attractive to human resource specialists – here at last is a body of thought within strategic management in which people issues figure prominently.

Clusters of resources, understood in this broader way, can be sources of competitive advantage. Barney (1991, 2000), one of the most influential and accessible theorists in the RBV school, distinguishes between a competitive advantage which a firm presently enjoys, but which others will be able to copy, and *sustained* competitive advantage, a characteristic which rivals find themselves unable to compete away, despite their best efforts. In his conception, resources are valuable when they enable the firm to take advantage of market opportunities or deal particularly well with market threats in a way that competitors are not currently able to. The task is to manage these valuable resources in such a way that rivals are frustrated in their efforts to imitate or out-flank them.

Using some fairly awkward terminology, RBV theorists are interested in the conditions that make desirable resources 'inimitable' and 'non-substitutable' (Barney 1991). What can be done to ensure others do not simply imitate or copy a firm's strengths or find ways of substituting for them that achieve the same ends? The key characteristics of desirable resources, then, are that they are valuable and inimitable (with inimitability covering both direct and indirect forms of copying) (Hoopes, Madsen and Walker 2003).

As Coff (1997, 1999) and others point out (for example, Grant 1991, Kamoche 1996), it is important to add 'appropriability' to this list of traits. Not only must the firm be able to generate and defend sources of high performance[3], but the RBV assumes that the firm is able to capture the benefits for its shareholders. This is easier said than done because the firm is a network of *stake*holders. Some stakeholders, such as senior executives, have access to the kind of information and power which can enlarge their share of the firm's bounty. Where they are concentrated in a small geographical area, such as the City of London or Wall Street, the result can be quite extreme competition for very high bonus payments in millions of pounds or dollars. Qualities of desirable resources are shown in Box 4.1.

---

[3] In the RBV literature, high financial performance is often described as 'rent', an old-fashioned term in Economics for profits above the normal level in competitive markets.

> **Box 4.1 Qualities of desirable resources**
>
> - Valuable: capable of delivering superior competitive results
> - Inimitable: very hard to imitate or copy, either directly or indirectly
> - Appropriable: capable of benefiting the firm's shareholders.

Having defined these sorts of desirable traits, Barney (1991) notes that such resources are not immune to 'Schumpeterian shocks'. The great Austrian economist, Joseph Schumpeter, referred to the propensity for capitalism to generate 'gales of creative destruction' – radical breakthroughs which disturb technologies or basic concepts of business (Schumpeter 1950). In the transportation sector, for example, inventions such as railroads, automobiles, and airplanes have had enormous impacts on the ways of providing transport that preceded them. We are currently living through a time when computerisation, telecommunications and the internet are making a major impact across various industries. The vast majority of firms cannot insulate themselves from such radical trends but there is scope for firms to differentiate themselves in ways which are relatively sustainable in a *given* competitive context.

The issue is one of how management might build valuable, firm-specific characteristics and 'barriers to imitation' (Reed and DeFillippi 1990, Rumelt 1987), which make it hard for others to copy or invalidate what the successful firm is doing. What, then, are the key barriers to imitation noted by resource-based theorists?

Unique timing and learning

Models proposed in the RBV typically place emphasis on the way that historical learning acts as a barrier to newcomers and slower rivals. Theorists cite the value to firms of 'unique historical conditions' (Barney 1991: 107), 'first-mover advantages' (Wernerfelt 1984: 173) and 'path dependency' (Leonard 1998: 35). They argue that valuable, specialised resources (sometimes called 'asset specificity') are developed over time through opportunities that do not repeat themselves (or not in quite the same way). Competitive success does not come simply from making choices in the present (as positioning models of strategic management seem to imply) but stems from building up distinctive capabilities at critical junctures and over considerable periods of time.

In simple terms, RBV theorists argue that a sense of time and place matters: if you are not there at the time things are happening, you cannot expect to be successful. Others will take up the unique learning opportunity. As Woody

Allen once quipped, 'eighty percent of success is just showing up'. Shakespeare expressed the same sentiment in a famous line from *Julius Caesar*: 'there is a tide in the affairs of men, which taken at the flood, leads on to fortune.' In other words, you have to be there when the tide is turning and seize your opportunity at the best moment. This could be at a time when a new technology is being developed, a new market is being opened up, or a new management methodology is being developed. If you are there at such moments, you can build business experience, important connections or complex know-how ahead of others. There is now good evidence, for example, using a data set that spans a 24-year period, that those British firms that first learnt to integrate the HR and operational practices needed to support 'lean manufacturing' have outperformed later adopters in terms of productivity (de Menezes, Wood and Gelade 2010).

The special value of timing and learning is widely understood in the business community. The difficulty of securing a firm's presence in an area where it has no experience is often a reason for take-overs. Directors of firms often feel they cannot make a mark in a new industry (or a new region) without buying an established player who has built up the necessary client base, employee skills and operating systems. The international accounting firms very often expanded this way in the 1970s and 1980s, taking over much smaller, but well regarded, firms around the world. The small firms thus absorbed provided important political connections, a pool of appropriately qualified staff and a well-established client base. Naturally, the owners of these firms also benefited enormously from the historical learning of the international firm, gaining access, for example, to special audit techniques, management consulting methodologies, and training systems developed at considerable expense elsewhere.

Social complexity

The phenomenon of historical learning or 'path dependence' is intimately linked to a second barrier to imitation – 'social complexity' (Barney 1991, Wright, McMahan and McWilliams 1994). As firms grow, they inevitably become characterised by complex patterns of teamwork and coordination, both inside and outside the firm. As we emphasised in Chapter 1, successful firms become strong clusters of 'human and social capital' (Lovas and Ghoshal 2000: 883). Productive work communities, such as outstanding schools and universities, take time to build and are inherently complex systems. The network of these internal and external connections is a kind of natural barrier to imitation by rivals, a prime reason why firms in some industries try to recruit an entire team of employees. Loss of all or most of an outstanding team of staff can decimate an organisation's reputation. Something like this happened in 1957 when eight scientists and engineers working on the development of the silicon chip resigned from the Shockley Semiconductor Laboratory, a research and development company led by the Nobel laureate physicist, Bill Shockley: 'Their mass departure cut the productive heart out of the laboratory, leaving behind a carcass of men working... on the four-layer diode project plus a bunch of aimless technicians and secretaries' (Riordan and Hoddeson 1997: 252). The group left to form Fairchild Semiconductor. The rest, as they say, is history.

Mueller's (1996) discussion of 'resource mobility barriers' is one that places strong emphasis on socially complex attributes of firms. Mueller argues that sustained advantage stems from hard-to-imitate routines deeply embedded in a firm's 'social architecture' (Mueller 1996: 774). By contrast, he sees little enduring value accruing to the firm from top management's codified policy positions (which are easily imitated because of their public visibility). Indeed, he (1996: 771, 777) implies that little value is created by those senior managers who are highly mobile:

> Corporate prosperity not seldom rests in the social architecture that has emerged incrementally over time, and might often predate the tenure of current senior management... The social architecture is created and re-created not only or even primarily at senior management levels in the organization, but at other levels too, including at workgroup level on the shopfloor.

According to Mueller, outstanding *organisational* value is more likely to come from persistent, patient management processes that, over time, encourage skill formation and powerful forms of cooperation deep within the firm. A key factor in here must be the quality of the motivational incentives inside firms that foster skill-building and cooperation. As Gottschalg and Zollo (2007) argue, many forms of competitive advantage depend on strong interest alignment between companies and critical groups of employees.

Causal ambiguity

A third type of resource barrier noted in the RBV literature – causal ambiguity – is more controversial. As with social complexity, ambiguity about the cause/effect relationships involved in the firm's performance is an inevitable outcome of firm growth (Barney 1991, Reed and DeFillippi 1990). It can take some time to figure why an established firm has become successful and to discern how successful it really is. There is no doubt that firms wanting to acquire other firms should be very careful in the 'due diligence' process that precedes (or ought to precede) the purchase of another business. There are inevitably elements of ambiguity about a firm's performance, as there are about the performance of individuals and teams.

Having said this, it is likely that causal ambiguity is over-rated as a barrier to imitation (McWilliams and Smart 1995). Human rationality is always bounded, as was noted in Chapter 2, but if one pushes the notion of causal ambiguity too far, management is virtually meaningless, as is theory (Priem and Butler 2001). The 'paradox of causal ambiguity' has been explored by a study in two US industries: textiles and hospitals (King and Zeithaml 2001). This study examined the way senior and middle managers perceive the competencies of their organisations and their links to competitive advantage. Interestingly, the study was one in which chief executives were very keen to participate (which is quite unusual given 'survey fatigue' among managers in the USA). It involved finding out how other members of their senior team and a cross-section of middle managers understood the firm's resources and their impacts. CEOs were interviewed and the other managers selected in the 17 firms were surveyed (with very high response rates). The study contains evidence that high-performing firms benefit from building consensus across management levels about the resources that enable them to out-perform rivals. An understanding of the key competencies and the most important links among them *ought* to be high. This does not mean, however, that all the micro aspects of particular competencies will be transparent because there is always some degree of ambiguity embedded in organisational culture and employee know-how. As we explore further below, 'tacit knowledge' is always present in organisations.

The findings of this study are consistent with the arguments of advocates of the 'balanced scorecard' (Kaplan and Norton 1996, 2001, 2004, 2006) who claim that, given enough effort, it must be possible within business units to evolve a broad theory of how the business works or might work better (see Chapter 11). Not only this, but the benefits of having agreement about where we are going and how we can get there must be more valuable than confusion and working at cross-purposes! It seems, therefore, that while causal ambiguity will always be present to some degree, it is likely to be a less important barrier to imitation than the processes of historical learning and social interaction that characterise established firms.

Competencies, 'table stakes' and dynamic learning

The discussion so far might convince us that the RBV contains some important insights but leave us wondering what we can do about it. How can all this talk of valuable resources and barriers to imitation be made useful?

One of the more popular frameworks is associated with the work of Hamel and Prahalad (1993, 1994). They argue that competitive advantage, over the long term, stems from building 'core competencies' in a firm which are superior to those of rivals. Their notion of core competence is very close to the concept of 'distinctive competence' discussed in the older strategy texts as something that the firm does particularly well. Their definitions of the term (shown in Box 4.2) place strong emphasis on analysing a firm's collective skills: skills found in the complex teamwork embedded in the firm.

The writings of Hamel and Prahalad are important for leaders of multidivisional firms (discussed in Chapter 10). CEOs and directors of these firms are encouraged to identify the underlying clusters of know-how in their companies that transcend the artificial divisions of 'strategic business units' – or which might do so, if they were appropriately managed. Sony's 'unrelenting pursuit of leadership in miniaturization' – manifesting itself in various products over time – is one of Hamel and Prahalad's standard examples (Hamel and Prahalad 1994: 119). Another example, offered by Goold *et al.* (1994) is that of Canon which has deliberately sought to integrate development engineers in different strands of the business to exploit fibre-optic technology.

Box 4.2   Hamel and Prahalad's notion of 'core competence'

A 'core competence':

- is a bundle of skills and technologies that enables a company to provide particular benefits to customers
- is not product specific
- represents ... the sum of learning across individual skill sets and individual organizational units
- must ... be competitively unique
- is not an 'asset' in the accounting sense of the word
- represents a 'broad opportunity arena' or 'gateway to the future'.

Source: Excerpted from Hamel and Prahalad (1994: 217–28).

Hamel and Prahalad (1994) argue that companies which make the effort to understand their core competencies (and envision the core competencies they ought to build) are much less likely to get left with outdated products or miss important new applications of a knowledge base. In effect, their work is an argument for developing a 'knowledge-based', rather than a product-based, understanding of the firm. This might be a simple distinction to make but it suggests quite a profound change in the way corporate directors review company strengths and analyse their strategic opportunities.

A similar analysis is advanced by Leonard (1998) who uses the word 'capability' instead of 'competence' (but is concerned with the same idea). Her framework helps executives to identify the distinctive or 'core capabilities' underpinning their products or services. Core capabilities are 'knowledge sets' composed of four dimensions: the 'content' dimensions which include the relevant employee skills and knowledge and technical systems, and the 'process' dimensions which include managerial systems, and values and norms (Box 4.3). Her framework is perhaps the most helpful in terms of spelling out the HR implications. This is because managerial systems include the critical HR practices needed to recruit, develop and motivate employees with the relevant skills and aptitudes (Leonard 1998: 19). Employee development and incentive systems are a key part of her notion of core capability. She also emphasises the interlocking, systemic nature of the four dimensions and the resulting tendency of core capabilities to become 'core rigidities' over time, unless firms learn to practise continuous renewal. According to Leonard (1998: 30), every strength is also simultaneously a weakness. The recognition that firms can also have weaknesses or 'distinctive inadequacies' is an aspect of the RBV that ought to be given greater attention (West and DeCastro 2001). Some weaknesses can result from having 'too much of a good thing', as Leonard implies, while others can simply be 'bad things' (such as not developing sufficient skills in environmental analysis and change management).

Box 4.3   The four dimensions of a 'core capability'

1. *Employee knowledge and skill*: This dimension is the most obvious one.
2. *Physical technical systems*: But technological competence accumulates not only in the heads of people; it also accumulates in the physical systems that they build over time – databases, machinery, and software programs.

Box 4.3   (Continued)

3. *Managerial systems*: The accumulation of employee knowledge is guided and monitored by the company's systems of education, rewards, and incentives. These managerial systems – particularly incentive structures – create the channels through which knowledge is accessed and flows; they also set up barriers to undesired knowledge-creation activities.

4. *Values and norms*: These determine what kinds of knowledge are sought and nurtured, what kinds of knowledge-building activities are tolerated and encouraged. These are systems of caste and status, rituals of behavior, and passionate beliefs associated with various kinds of technological knowledge that are as rigid and complex as those associated with religion. Therefore, values serve as knowledge-screening and -control mechanisms.

Source: Reprinted by permission of Harvard Business School Press. From Leonard, D., *Wellsprings of Knowledge: Building and Sustaining the Sources of Innovation*, p. 19. © 1998 Harvard Business School Publishing Corporation. All rights reserved.

In outlining her model of how firms might develop outstanding capabilities, Leonard (1998: 5–16) discusses the interesting case of Chaparral Steel, a very successful US 'minimill'. While only the tenth largest steel producer in the USA at the time of this study, Chaparral enjoyed a reputation as a world leader in productivity (1998: 6):

in 1990, its 1.5 person-hours per rolled ton of steel compared to a US average of 5.3, a Japanese average of 5.6, and a German average of 5.7. Chaparral was the first American steel company (and only the second company outside of Japan at the time) to be awarded the right to use the Japanese Industrial Standard certification on its general structural steel products.

With strong values and incentives supporting the creation of new knowledge, Chaparral employees have pushed the company's equipment well beyond its original specifications (1998: 11):

The rolling mill equipment its vendor believed [was] limited to 8-inch slabs is turning out 14-inch slabs, and the vendor has tried to buy back the redesign. The two electric arc furnaces, designed originally to melt annual rates of 250,000 and 500,000 tons of scrap metal, now produce over 600,000 and 1 million tons, respectively.

Leonard (1998: 15–16) explains how Chaparral has achieved these results through building an 'interdependent system' of employee skills and technical systems supported by HR policies, practices and cultural values:

> Chaparral's skills, physical systems, learning activities, values and managerial philosophies and practices are obviously highly interdependent. Competitively advantageous equipment can be designed and constantly improved *only* if the workforce is highly skilled. Continuous education is attractive *only* if employees are carefully selected for their willingness to learn. Sending workers throughout the world to garner ideas is cost-effective *only* if they are empowered to apply what they have learned to production problems.

Leonard's model, therefore, places emphasis on the fact that cleverly developed systems of this kind – where the parts do reinforce each other in powerful ways – are very hard to imitate. This is certainly the view within Chaparral. Leonard (1998: 7) notes that the CEO is happy to give visitors a full plant tour, showing them almost 'everything and . . . giving away nothing because they cannot take it home with them'. This kind of story lends some support to the argument made earlier that even if we have a good understanding of why a firm is successful (low 'causal ambiguity'), the unique path that company has travelled and the social complexity this brings remain significant barriers to imitation.

'Table stakes' and distinctive capabilities

While sources of valuable differentiation are very important in the RBV, it is worth injecting a note of caution here. A problem with some writing in the RBV is the tendency of authors to focus only on sources of idiosyncrasy, thus exaggerating differences between firms in the same industry. As we argued in Chapters 2 and 3, all viable firms in an industry need some similar resources in order to establish their identity in the minds of customers and to help secure legitimacy in broader society (Carroll and Hannan 1995, Deephouse 1999, Peteraf and Shanley 1997). For example, retail banks must act like retail banks (having the requisite information technology and the typical range of services, such as the capacity for speedy cash withdrawals through ATMs and a suite of account services through internet and phone banking). They must inspire confidence in the banking public and satisfy investors and regulators that they

Figure 4.2 Strategic importance of capabilities to the firm

can behave as responsible repositories and lenders of funds. Without these baseline features, banks lack recognition in their industry and legitimacy in their wider society, as was graphically illustrated in the failures of many banks in the global financial crisis of 2008–9.

Some writers in the RBV are so focused on the firm that they do not recognise these wider connections. However, it is a strength of the frameworks outlined here that the authors do see the importance of 'table stakes' (Hamel and Prahalad 1994) or 'enabling capabilities' (Leonard 1998). These are features of the business which enable participation in the industry but which do not make the firm distinctive or account for superior performance.

Leonard (1998) makes useful distinctions among three kinds of capabilities: core (which are superior and cannot be easily imitated), supplemental (which add value to core capabilities but can be easily copied) and enabling (which are necessary conditions of being in the industry). These distinctions are shown in Figure 4.2. Both Leonard (1998) and Hamel and Prahalad (1994) note the dynamic nature of capabilities: over time, one company's distinctive or core capability (such as outstanding quality) tends to be emulated by other firms. It then becomes part of the 'table stakes' in the industry and firms that seek superior performance must search for other ways to differentiate themselves. Hamel and Prahalad (1994: 232) note this dynamic in a case most of us can attest to – that of automobile manufacturing:

> in the 1970s and 1980s quality, as measured by defects per vehicle, was undoubtedly a core competence for Japanese car companies. Superior reliability was an important value element for customers and a genuine differentiator for Japanese car producers. It took more than a decade for Western car companies to close the quality gap with their Japanese competitors, but by the mid-1990s quality, in terms of initial defects per vehicle, has become a prerequisite for every car maker. There is a dynamic at work here that is common to other industries. Over long periods of time, what was once a core competence may become a base-line capability.

From an HR perspective, 'table stakes' or 'enabling capabilities' include the minimum HR policies and practices required by each firm to play the competitive game (including similar types of work organisation and employment conditions) (Boxall and Steeneveld 1999, Boxall and Purcell 2000). The types of minimal HR investment needed inevitably vary by industry or, more accurately, strategic groups or customer segments within industries, as we explained in Chapter 3. The key point is that viable firms in a particular industry are *partially* rather than totally idiosyncratic. Valuable resources, therefore, include some elements in common with other firms in the industry and some differences.

Competitive dynamism: the role of knowledge and organisational learning

Standing back from the commentary so far, it should be clear that the management of knowledge plays a key role in resource-based models of the firm. For Hamel and Prahalad (1994), building a focus on knowledge management is much more important than the historical focus of Western firms on product management. For Leonard (1998), understanding the 'wellsprings of knowledge' is the key issue in the long-run renewal of the firm. On a practical level, a lot of interest in the area is directed towards models of knowledge management, of how to identify, protect and enlarge a firm's 'intellectual capital' (see, for example, Edvinsson and Malone 1997, Stewart 1998).

The RBV, therefore, encourages researchers to focus on knowledge and its creation and exploitation within firms (Grant 1991, Hoskisson *et al.* 1999). How to build the organisation's capacity for learning or its *dynamic* capability becomes the fundamental issue (Teece, Pisano and Shuen 1997, Helfat and Peteraf 2003). Some go so far as to talk of a 'knowledge-based view' (KBV) of the firm (for example, Grant 1996) but we think this is generally unwise: knowledge is extremely important to organisational success but access to money, properties and natural resources also continue to be vital. In an energy-strapped world, for example, companies that can access cheap and plentiful energy sources are definitely at an advantage.

Where the KBV comes into its own is in those companies where the knowledge and brain-power of employees is the only substantial source of competitive advantage (Kinnie *et al.* 2006). These are 'professional service companies' in such industries as consultancy practice, media, law and IT. They own very few assets in terms of natural resources and property yet often have a very high market value, like Microsoft. In these firms, professionally qualified employees often have distinctive needs concerned with multiple identities.

Do they, or indeed should they, identify with their employer, their major client, their team or their profession (Swart 2007)? The assumption of the KBV is that the firm is able to leverage this professional knowledge and intellectual capital in a unique way that others cannot copy, to gain competitive advantage and appropriate value. However, rival firms will seek to poach talented staff, often forcing up pay, thus challenging the level of appropriation. And managing talent is not just about pay: it includes ensuring that professionals work on stretching assignments with other talented colleagues in project teams at the forefront of their profession. This, in turn, will have a strong influence on the business strategy of these knowledge-intensive firms since the need to keep talented staff drives the search for innovative and creative work.

It is clearly important that we build an analysis in which we are able to explain why some firms are better at learning and renewal than others. Why do some firms have greater dynamic capability? A large part of the answer must be associated with the people involved and with how they are managed.

HR strategy, competitive parity and sustained advantage

It should be obvious, therefore, that resource-based models of strategic management are replete with references to the human dimensions of resources. A major part of any firm's strengths – and weaknesses – does stem from the calibre of the people employed and the quality of their working relationships.

At the most elementary level, the resource-based view of the firm provides a conceptual basis, if we were ever in any doubt about the matter, for asserting that human resources can be competitively valuable. Taxonomies of valuable resources always incorporate an important category for 'human capital' (Barney 1991, 2000) or 'employee know-how' (Hall 1993) and resource-based theorists stress the value of the complex interrelationships between the firm's human resources and its other resources: physical, financial, legal, informational and so on (for example, Penrose 1959, Grant 1991, Mueller 1996). This much is self-evident: as we emphasised in Chapter 2, a firm is a system of interconnected parts and the firm's human resources form a necessary, though not a sufficient, part of this system.

But this does not get us very far. The key questions raised by the RBV are twofold: *what* is it that can be valuable about human resources and *how* might a firm develop and defend these sources of value? Identifying what is most valuable and protecting it with 'barriers to imitation' is at the heart of resource-based thinking. It helps to remember that the value of human resources can range from forms of human and social capital that are competitively superior, enabling a firm to build and sustain advantages, through to those which are inferior, which actually undermine competitive performance. Outdated skills, excessive levels of employee turnover, and conflict-prone industrial relations are examples of the latter. In between, there are human resources that are competitively neutral or indifferent. As we noted in Chapter 2, all firms need a relevant set of human resources to be viable, in order simply to survive or attain 'competitive parity'. These are competitively valuable but they do not contain the kind of exceptional qualities that help the firm to outperform its competitors.

At a deeper level, then, what has value in HRM? We can certainly rule out the value of formal policy positions in HRM (what top management says the firm should do in managing work and people). These can simply be run off a photocopier or downloaded from the internet. As Mueller (1996) argues, it is hard to see any distinctive and inimitable value in policy positions *per se*. Formal policy statements are, at best, competitively neutral. Furthermore, because they are a set of promises, they actually carry a level of risk: they can turn 'bad' in terms of value. If there are major disconnections between senior management's espoused HR policies and the actual HR practices enacted by line managers, this can be a source of competitive *dis*advantage (Purcell 1999). There is always a danger that gaps between management rhetorics and workplace reality will destroy competitive value through undermining employee trust and commitment (Legge 1995, 2005, Grant 1999), as we shall explain further in Chapters 7 and 8.

Since people vary in their capabilities and cannot work for all firms at once, Wright *et al.* (1994) argue that we are more likely to find value residing in the human resources themselves, in the human capital pool. Human capital is the quality of the individual human talent recruited to the firm and retained in it. All firms need certain kinds of individual talent relevant to implementing the organisation's mission and, if they wish to survive over the long run, capable of helping the organisation to adapt to change or, better still, lead it (Boxall and Steeneveld 1999). Firms which recruit and retain exceptional individuals have the possibility of generating 'human capital advantage' (Boxall 1996, 1998).

Why can individuals be so valuable? The answer lies in Polanyi's (1962) classic distinction between 'tacit' and 'explicit' (or 'articulated') knowledge. Tacit knowledge is 'nonverbalized or even nonverbalizable, intuitive' while explicit or articulated knowledge is 'specified either verbally or in writing, computer programs, patents, drawings or the like' (Hedlund 1994: 75). Table 4.1 illustrates this distinction with examples across four levels of analysis, starting with the individual and moving up to the 'inter-organizational' domain. The

Table 4.1 Types of knowledge

Type	Individual	Group	Organisation	Inter-organisational domain
Explicit knowledge	Knowing calculus	A quality circle's documented analysis of its performance	Organisation chart	A supplier's patents and documented practices
Tacit knowledge	Cross-cultural negotiation skills	Team coordination in complex work	Corporate culture	Customer attitudes to products and expectations

Source: Adapted from Hedlund (1994: 75).

distinction helps to explain why firms are vulnerable to certain kinds of labour turnover (Coff 1997, 1999). They can never entirely capture what individuals know. Some of what and whom we know – including many of our best skills – cannot be reduced to writing or to formulas. When we leave the firm, we take our job know-how and networking knowledge with us. No two individuals are exactly alike and the differences are particularly noticeable in high-skill jobs: as job complexity increases, so does the range of human performance (Hunter, Schmidt and Judiesch 1990). When whole teams of highly talented individuals leave, as was noted earlier in a case from the semiconductor industry, the effect can be devastating.

Moreover, individual human capital is embedded in a social context. The quality of social capital – of human relationships in the firm and with its environment – plays a major role in whether or not firms make outstanding returns from their human capital (see, for example, Ghoshal and Nahapiet 1998, Swart and Kinnie 2003, Collins and Smith 2006). In other words, firms need 'organisational process' or 'social capital' advantages if they are to realise the potential of human capital (Boxall 1996, 1998). This type of advantage is a function of historically evolved, complex *processes* such as team-based learning, and high levels of trust and cooperation, both between management and labour and among co-workers, processes which are very difficult to imitate. Both human capital and social capital can generate exceptional value but they are likely to do so much more powerfully when they reinforce each other. Kay (1993) refers to this as the 'passing game', nicely indicating that teams may have highly talented individuals but their capacity and willingness to play together is vital if they are to achieve outstanding results. Thus, we can say that human resource advantage (HRA) is a product of highly talented people (human capital advantage) and an exceptional working environment (organisational process advantage). In mathematical notation:

$$HRA = f(HCA, OPA)$$

But does the resource-based view imply that all employee groups in a firm generate outstanding value? In a nutshell, no: it suggests that there are some critical, 'core' workers in all firms, while other individuals are less critical or more peripheral (Purcell 1999). As we explained in Chapter 1, some forms of human resource advantage depend more on an elite group of employees than they do on excellence throughout the workforce. Lepak and Snell (1999, 2007) have picked up on this aspect of the RBV, and related economic theories, in developing what they call an 'HR architectural perspective' (Figure 4.3). This framework utilises two dimensions: the extent to which the particular form of human capital represents a valuable resource for the firm and the extent to which it is unique or firm specific. This leads to four types of HR system that fit different sets of human resources.

Lepak and Snell argue that firms need a commitment-oriented HR system for employees whose skills are critical to a firm's core or distinctive capabilities (quadrant 1). Firms should invest heavily in the motivation, empowerment and development of those who hold vital knowledge. Thus, when workers are

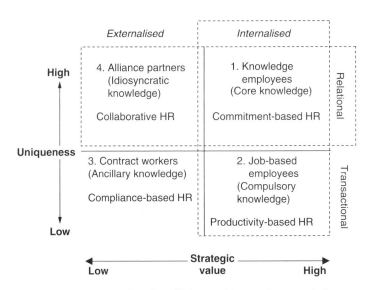

Figure 4.3 Lepak and Snell's 'HR architectural perspective'
Source: Adapted from Lepak, D. and Snell, S., 'Employment sub-systems and the "HR architecture".
In Boxall, P., Purcell, J. and Wright, P. (eds) *The Oxford Handbook of Human Resource Management.*
Oxford: Oxford University Press. © 2007 By permission of Oxford University Press.

perceived as especially valuable to the firm's strategy, the question of how to defend them turns on adopting HR systems which enhance their motivation and retention in the firm. In their analysis of the role of HRM in competitive advantage, Gottschalg and Zollo (2007) underline this point, arguing that firms need the kind of motivational resources that will build strong interest alignment with these types of critical workers. Their model incorporates both intrinsic and extrinsic motivators. The former relate to the extent to which people find their work enjoyable and the degree to which they commit to the company's values and norms while the latter includes rewards such as pay and promotion. Protecting special human resources depends on creating a positive motivational climate and low rates of employee turnover within this core group of workers. The relationship is much more of a long-term, 'relational' kind than a short-term 'transactional' kind (Rousseau 1995). However, firms can adopt a more productivity-based approach to those, such as accounting staff, whose work is valuable in the labour market but not unique (quadrant 2). This means hiring people who can be productive quickly and rewarding them on a more short-term, results-oriented basis. Those whose skills are low in value and generic are prime candidates for contracting out (quadrant 3) while individuals whose skills may be 'unique in some way but not directly instrumental for creating customer value' (Lepak and Snell 1999: 40), such as a firm's attorneys, are likely to be engaged in some form of longer-term alliance (quadrant 4).

This model, then, offers a way of helping firms to distinguish which types of HR system are appropriate for which kinds of human capital. Implementing it is not always easy, however. The debate around who should be considered 'core' in a particular firm has both cognitive and political elements. In reality, managers make different interpretations, as illustrated in the bottled gas market in the UK in the mid 1990s (Purcell 1996). British Oxygen was a long established player in the market with a dominant share. Air Products was a relatively new entrant but with lots of experience in the USA. In 1992, British Oxygen needed to improve delivery, cut costs and get customers to trade up where possible. They had a large existing distribution fleet. Painful negotiations with the drivers' union led to new hours of working, wider job responsibilities including customer relations, more training, and cab-based information technology. Drivers became seen as key staff in direct contact with customers. At the same time, Air Products decided to outsource distribution to a specialist haulage contractor. There was no expectation here that drivers would know anything about gas beyond safety considerations. In the case of British Oxygen, drivers were considered a core part of the firm because they always had been, not because they had typically shown distinctive organisational knowledge or skills. Indeed, this knowledge of the customer and the level of skill relating to gas systems had to be developed once the decision was made to give them customer relations' responsibilities. A similar case in New Zealand involved the privatisation of gas companies. Meters in domestic properties need to be read, but company managers had to ponder the difficult question: are meter readers just 'data harvesters' (carrying out single-task jobs suitable for outsourcing) or are they front-line customer service representatives, who should be trained, and retained, as employees (Peel and Boxall 2005)?

In practice, firms come up with different answers. Some decide that the core should be broadly based and then design the jobs and the employment relationship to fit these core attributes, as in the case of British Oxygen. This seems very explicable: 'many activities in firms . . . are so taken for granted or so strongly endorsed by the firm's prevailing culture and power structure that decision-makers no longer even question the appropriateness or the rationality of these activities' (Oliver 1997: 700). To put it another way, the costs of change, both financial and moral (social legitimacy), can be too high. It can be difficult to overtly differentiate between types of workers within the same organisation, especially where people share the same site and have strong emotional ties.

Baron and Kreps (1999: 460) suggest subtly different criteria in choosing whether to externalise certain jobs or manage them internally that can help with this difficult decision making. First, they suggest that 'the degree to which the task is strategically important for the firm, that is, whether it is a 'core competence' is critical. Here, they are on the same ground as Lepak and Snell (1999) with their emphasis on 'strategic value'. However, Baron and Kreps's second criterion is not the uniqueness of the skill involved but 'the degree to which the activity displays high technical or social interdependence with tasks done by regular employees' (Baron and Kreps 1999: 460). In this regard, Purcell, Purcell and Tailby (2004) studied a call centre where the failure to appreciate the social interdependences of staff – in conditions in which agency 'temps' worked alongside permanent staff – led to escalating labour turnover among both temps and experienced staff.

The real extent of interdependence between employee groups in the work unit is a very important variable that managers should consider before any kind of restructuring. Boxall (1998: 268) makes a distinction between inner- and outer-core workforces. The 'inner core . . . provides the "adaptive capacity" of the firm while the outer core provides it with "credible operational capacity" '. One cannot operate effectively without both capabilities. In Chapters 6 and 8, we draw attention to the firm as a social entity, a community in which management may try to develop a distinctive culture. Too much differentiation between core and periphery can damage the creation of a sense of community through challenging perceptions of fairness. For example, in 2005, an American company in the UK established an employee forum for the first time. One of the first items raised was the fact that management and professional staff were given free health insurance but other staff members were not. This was deemed unfair and at odds with the company's aspiration to be 'an employer of choice' and its emphasis on 'togetherness' (that is, social interdependency). Free health insurance was subsequently extended to all employees.

Despite the point we make here, issues of cost-effectiveness inevitably come into play, as we have seen since the late 1990s in corporate decisions to outsource or offshore large parts of manufacturing and services. Location on a separate site, and performance of technically different tasks from those in the home base, means that both social and technical interdependencies can be minimised. Outsourced sites, especially those offshored to third-world countries, can quickly become 'out of sight and out of mind'. As Lepak and Snell (2007) recognise, many firms now locate operating workers in countries with lower labour costs. In Chapter 1, we considered the case of the British manufacturer, Dyson, which has done exactly this, offshoring its assembly operations to Malaysia. The intention in these situations might be to treat these workers as core resources employed within the firm but management is doing so within a much lower cost structure or is using either a sub-contractor or an alliance partner (quadrant 3 or 4 in Figure 4.3) who does this. The critical core in the firm is thus defined even more sparingly, as the firm's senior executives and the R&D, marketing and other specialists it still employs in its home-country head office.

Leaving aside these labour cost issues, which we will explore in Chapter 5, a key implication of the argument so far must be that carefully enacted *HR systems* can be sources of superior and hard-to-imitate value. Arguably, the scarce and hard-to-imitate value stems from the historically developed, socially complex elements, including the way in which these have formed a variety of important connections over time. Thus, while knowledge of individual HR policies is not rare, the knowledge of how to build and customise appropriate HR systems and create a positively reinforcing blend of HR systems *within* a particular context is likely to be very rare. The value is greater when these astute HR decisions are complemented by a mix of other intangible and tangible assets: senior management commitment, consistent line manager support for critical HR practices over significant time periods, adequate financial resourcing, up-to-date technology, sympathetic management accounting systems, and so on (Boxall 1998, 2003). A commitment-oriented HR strategy, which Lepak and Snell (1999, 2007) argue firms need for their core workforce, depends on a sympathetic social context within the firm (Collins and Smith 2006). We take this argument further in Chapters 8 and 9 in our discussion of the 'mediators' between HR systems and company performance and in our discussion of the role of HR strategy across cycles of change in industries.

In summary, human resource strategy, supported by other sympathetic elements, can enable a firm to build sources of sustained competitive advantage. In any industry, there are likely to be particular firms in which 'human resource advantage' has contributed to this level of success. The evidence discussed by Leonard (1998) certainly implies that Chaparral Steel had built an extensive kind of human resource advantage throughout its workforce, which underpinned outstanding performance in its industry, at least for a reasonable period of time.[4] On the other hand, many forms of competitive advantage hinge more on non-human resources. There are, for example, multidivisional companies achieving high success through skilful financial and outsourcing strategies, as we will explain in Chapter 10. There is no doubt that this depends on the expertise and networks of an elite group of highly skilled executives and specialists but it is not likely to require superior human resources throughout all parts of the company or all of its business units, some of which are only held temporarily and then spun off to other owners. Some element of human resource advantage is clearly desirable for all companies in the long run but the location and extent of this special resource is variable.

Before moving on, let us recall again that there is a problem with thinking about resources only at the level of the firm. Clusters of valuable resources occur at both industry and societal levels. Industry clusters can benefit all firms through providing a skilled labour pool and networking connections across the supply chain, one of the reasons why Dyson found it attractive to locate in Malaysia, as noted in Chapter 1. In addition, countries provide variable resources of infrastructure, politico-economic systems, social order and so on. Some firms have a 'head start' in international competition because they are located in societies which have much better educational and technical infrastructure than others (Porter 1990, Boxall 1995). American, Japanese, German, British and French firms, for example, are all assisted by the existence of long-established traditions of excellence in higher education which enhance

---

[4] Since Leonard's (1998) study, Chaparral Steel became the second largest producer of structural steel products in the USA and was bought in 2007 by Gerdau Ameristeel Corporation for $4.2 billion or $86 per share: http://www.bloomberg.com/apps/news?pid=20601087&sid=aP4iRhmtbjmY&refer=home, accessed 24/3/10

the knowledge-creating capacities of business organizations. The point here is that the potential to develop competitive advantage through human resources does not lie solely in the hands of managers within individual firms.

Conclusions

The resource-based perspective is an important lens for understanding how firms might build competitive advantage. It focuses on the ways in which they can develop valuable resources and erect barriers to imitation of them, so that a superior performance is maintained despite the best efforts of other firms to copy (that is, imitate), or outflank (that is, substitute for), the resources that underpin it. Shareholders benefit when they enjoy better returns from these resources, meaning that the returns are not entirely appropriated by the bargaining activities of well-placed managers and other critical employees.

Resources are valuable when they enable a firm to be successful in its chosen markets, either helping it to grasp competitive opportunities or to counter threats. This includes much more than the type of assets, such as property and cash, that are easily valued in a company's accounts: it includes the more intangible, less-easily valued resources such as a firm's reputation with its customers, its unique production know-how, and the quality of its employees' skills and commitment. RBV theory argues that such resources are built up through astute timing and learning and accumulate in the social complexity that grows as teams of people work together. These can be strong barriers to imitation by other firms, although all resources can be undermined through major, 'Schumpeterian' shocks to an industry or economy. Some element of causal ambiguity is always going to be present in a firm, and can also be a barrier to imitation, but if ambiguity implies confusion and a lack of managerial consensus about how to improve the business, this is usually a bad thing for company performance.

As the name itself implies, the resource-based perspective presents an account of strategic management that is richly laced with *human* resource issues. This is seen in the emphasis on identifying the firm's core or distinctive capabilities, which are inevitably linked to its managerial leadership abilities and its employees' skills. It is seen in the interest in knowledge management and organizational learning. When we take a resource-based perspective on the strategic problem, questions of human resource strategy are going to loom large. A firm's human resource strategy is needed to support its competitive survival or parity but it can also help add exceptional value or destroy it. There is little value to be had in formal HR policies or in highly mobile, 'hit-and-run' managers. In fact, major disjunctures between managerial promises and realities in HRM can undermine employee trust and commitment, contributing to competitive *dis*advantage. A heritage of conflict-prone industrial relations almost always destroys value through alienating customers. On the positive side, a central issue is how to enhance the motivation and development of those individuals whose contribution is core to the firm's mission. Defining who is 'core' is not easy, however. Is it the whole workforce, certain parts of it or a much smaller elite? In answering this question, there are technical and social interdependencies in firms that benefit from careful handling. A second key question is how to build the kind of organisational processes that enable individuals to function effectively or, better still, exceptionally well. What kind of development activities, and what kind of motivational climate, will bring out the best in individuals, moulding them into a high-performing team? It is the interaction of the firm's individual talents (its human capital) with the quality of its collective working environment (its social capital) that is likely to create most value. This means much more than adopting particular HR practices: it is a much more systemic and contextualised question, in which HR models and other systemic features, such as senior management commitment, consistent line-manager implementation, and suitable financing of HR investments, all need to play an appropriate part.

The reader will not be surprised that we regard this line of analysis as extremely important. Our exploration of the resource-based view continues in various parts of the rest of the book. We aim, however, to build on the RBV while staying alert to its weaknesses. We must avoid getting carried away with the notion of idiosyncrasy or heterogeneity. To be sure, all firms are somewhat different and superior firms have valuable differences from others but all firms in an industry or strategic group need a similar resource profile ('table stakes') in order to identify their line of business and to meet typical customer expectations. The RBV, like most of the strategy literature, can become too absorbed with the firm as the unit of analysis, failing to recognise that firms are embedded in a wider context. Competitive resources vary in quality across industries and nations and this variability affects the strengths that firms are capable of building. For example, educational institutions are much stronger in some societies than in others and the knowledge and graduates they produce help to regenerate the research and development capabilities of firms.

part 2

Managing work and people: searching for general principles

5

Work systems and the changing economics of production

As we concluded in Chapter 3, firms fit in with their contexts or they fail. It is not therefore possible to identify a set of best HR practices that will be universally beneficial to firms. Furthermore, as we saw in Chapter 4, the resource-based view of the firm argues that firms have something to gain from being the fittest of the fit, from evolving their HR systems in such a way that they build and exploit valuable differences in human and social capital. On the other hand, both these chapters explain that firms face similar challenges in trying to manage work and people in the industries and societies in which they operate. As long as we recognise the strict limits of prescription at the level of specific practices, there is merit in searching for general or underpinning principles in labour management. This is the concern of this section of the book.

The logical place to begin is with the analysis of work systems. In Chapter 3, we indicated that the HR strategy of a firm typically embraces a number of different HR systems. For example, there are often somewhat different HR systems for managers, core operating workers, and support staff. In complex professional environments, such as hospitals, there can be a different system for each professional group. An organisation's HR strategy is a cluster of such systems. How well HR systems work in their own terms and how well they relate to each other in any firm is a moot point.

There are two key elements to each HR system: the kind of *work* organisation involved and the *employment* practices that are used to hire and manage the people doing the work. The function of this chapter is to analyse work systems while the next two chapters will look at principles underpinning the collective and individual aspects of employing people. Chapter 6 will focus on employee voice, which has traditionally had strong collective elements, while Chapter 7 will examine the management of individual employees. In Chapter 8, we will draw the pieces together, summarising the most common types of HR system, and outlining the key intervening variables that link HR systems to employee and organisational outcomes.

Work systems involve choices about what work needs to be done, about who will do it, and about where and how they will do it. This means work systems vary enormously across industries and occupations: consider the different ways in which work is organised in car plants, schools, call centres, merchant shipping and supermarkets. Not only this, but the same occupations can be organised differently in different countries where, for example, there may be different assumptions about gender and work. Work system choices are fundamental to both operations management and human resource management in an organisation (Cordery and Parker 2007). They are inevitably connected to an organisation's chances of economic survival and its relative performance.

We therefore emphasise in this chapter the way in which work systems are linked to the *economics* of production. Capitalism is a system in which firms need to evolve work systems that will pay. This has always been true but has become graphically apparent over the last thirty years. Since the breakdown in the 1970s of the boom conditions that followed the Second World War, there have been waves of economic reform and restructuring. There has been a process of economic 'globalisation' in which new industrial powerhouses have emerged and challenged the economic elites in Europe and the USA. Japan was the major challenge in the 1970s and 1980s and now market reforms and rapid industrialisation in Brazil, Russia, India and China (the 'BRICs'), among other countries, are changing the old economic order. This is not simply about manufacturing. The growth of cheap computing power and the advent of the internet have made it much more possible to offer services across national boundaries. At the Brookings Institution Trade Forum in 2005 on the 'offshoring' of white collar work, Jensen and Kletzer (2005) reported that over the period from 2001 to 2003, 70 per cent of the US workers displaced by global competition worked in services, not manufacturing.

Massive companies or whole sectors in previously secure national markets have been forced to change the way they operate to meet threats to their financial viability or they have simply failed. Management responses that have involved changing the sales pitch or 're-branding' the same old offering without substantive change to technology, operations management and HRM have been swept aside by firms in newly developing countries that can offer the same quality, or better, but at much lower prices. Companies have been forced to accept the strategic significance of how their work is organised. They have been forced to look internally at all aspects of the way the organisation functions in order to reduce costs while delivering better value. A case in point concerns Aviva, Britain's largest insurer, which owns Norwich Union and RAC, among others. On 14 September 2006, the company announced a cut of 4,000 jobs, made possible by more sales being handled over the internet and a merging of back-office functions. When union leaders protested, Norwich Union's chief executive commented that the company was working in a 'self-service world' and was 'always looking for ways of working smarter with fewer people'.[1] As this example illustrates, the cost-effectiveness of how work is organised does matter to firms and changes in technology and customer habits do alter the economics of work systems over time.

Our intention in this chapter is to look at the economics of work organisation in the major sectors of the modern economy: manufacturing, private sector services, and the public sector. Because it has been the most important source of ideas about work organisation historically, we begin with manufacturing, describing its traditional work patterns in Britain and the USA and then examining social and economic challenges to these patterns. This leads into a fuller discussion of the emergence of 'high-involvement' work systems. Having laid out much of the key terminology through this discussion, we then turn to the impact on both manufacturing and services (private and public) of key contextual changes: globalisation, market reforms and the growth of offshoring. This sets the scene for us to discuss contemporary work systems in private sector services and the public sector. We do not stop at manufacturing but it is the natural place to start.

Work systems in manufacturing

The origins and evolution of the factory system

At the time when Adam Smith was writing his famous text in 1776, *The Wealth of Nations,* with its analysis of the massive efficiency gains to be achieved by the detailed division of labour, factory owners in the emerging British industry of cotton manufacture were taking advantage of new mechanised processes, such as power looms, to create radically new forms of work organisation.

---

[1] As quoted by Phillip Inman, 'Union attacks "brutal" Aviva for 4,000 jobs cut', *The Guardian*, 15 September 2006.

Initially employing large numbers of children, usually taken from the parish work-houses, owners like Samuel Gregg in Styal, just outside Manchester, and Robert Owen in New Lanark near Glasgow, brought to an end the centuries-old system of 'putting-out' whereby merchants would contract home workers using the hand-powered, hand-built looms they owned, to produce bundles of fabric or clothing. In an age of horse-drawn transport, putting-out was slow and inefficient, and at harvest time family members would work in the fields. Families worked to the rhythm of the seasons but exercised greater control over their time as long as they did so. The great advantage of the factory system, then as now, was that it allowed capitalist, or managerial, control to be exerted over the whole work process, gathering workers into a single location around a common power source and enhancing the benefits of job special-isation. New forms of power (water and steam) applied to newly invented machinery like power looms and the spinning jenny made it important and profitable to concentrate workers together at the point of production rather than have them dispersed (Deane 1969: 87, Jones 1994). The technological revolution in power sources and machinery led to a migration of workers from villages into the factory towns and growing cities.

Under the factory system, operators became machine minders working at the pace set by the machines owned by the capitalists and the factory's time clock, not by themselves. They were paid a wage, often linked to output and, working very long hours, undertook a single task or a small number of linked tasks requiring some dexterity but little intellectual skill. Each task took no more than a few seconds or minutes and then had to be repeated again, and again. As Adam Smith understood, workers who specialised at a simple set of tasks learnt to do them quickly and their rate of production would rise. Benevolent owners, such as the two just mentioned, would provide housing, schooling and (compulsory) Sunday worship but little in terms of training or career development. Discipline was strict and power was vested in overseers or foremen. The language at the time, and common throughout the nine-teenth century, and even into the twentieth, of 'the master and his hands', is especially instructive. The implication, as Watson (1986) observes, was that workers were machines using motor not mental skills.

Factories were designed by engineers to function as large engines of cogs and wheels rationally linked together. This metaphor of organisations as ratio-nally coordinated, interlocking parts is still prevalent today and still brings with it a denial of human emotional and social life (see Morgan (1997) for a wonderful analysis of the ways of thinking about or imagining organisation). As work was 'de-skilled' through breaking it down into the simplest tasks, and as workers no longer owned their own means of production, being reliant, as 'wage slaves', on the owner and his management agents, much about the process seemed dehumanising. In a wider sense, this was no more than a reflection of social structures and beliefs in society at the time on the brutish nature of the emerging working class. However, questions were increasingly being asked by British novelists such as Dickens and Mrs Gaskill, and social reformers, for instance, Seebohm Rowntree, about the social consequences of the 'dark satanic mills', as William Blake called them.

The mental models of the early factory owners about the way work should be organised became the standard or 'default' model for the design of work organisation in industrialised societies. In what Cordery and Parker (2007) call the 'mechanistic' model of work design, managers did the thinking and directing while workers were required to obey instructions and mind the machines. As this implies, factories depended on two HR systems operating under different principles: one for workers involving low discretion, low scope and low skill and one for managers involving much higher levels of discretion, responsibility and skill. A pattern of low trust of workers and high trust of managers was born (Fox 1974). Subsequent developments, whether those pioneered by Henry Ford, or turned into a new science of management by F.W. Taylor, continued to rest on these premises.

The key figures we have just mentioned – F.W. Taylor and Henry Ford I – were both Americans. While Britain may have industrialised first, the USA rapidly caught up in the nineteenth century and it was American consultants and business leaders who kick-started the theory of industrial management. What Taylor advocated and Ford put into practice was the application of more rigorous work measurement processes and the ruthless division of responsibility between management and labour (Braverman 1974, Meyer 1981, Warner 1998). Formal processes, such as 'time-and-motion study', were used to investigate the informal methods workers had developed on the job, quantifying how long it took them to carry out their tasks and how they moved within the work space, interacting with materials, tools and machines. Work practices were then redesigned by a management-appointed 'work study' expert to make human activities more efficient and to create a basis for identifying normal output and for linking pay incentives ('bonus systems') to higher levels of output. Under Taylor's concept of 'Scientific Management', the efficiency gains inherent in task specialisation were heightened and incentivised.

While it is wrong to suggest that the Taylorist practice of 'de-skilling' work permeated all manufacturing industries or all manufacturing jobs (Burawoy 1979, Littler 1982), the process of reducing core operating jobs to a set of simple tasks was widespread in the development of the factory system in the nineteenth and early twentieth centuries. Henry Ford's particular contribution came in linking these highly specialised jobs to the *moving* assembly line (Lacey 1986). This minimised the need for operating workers to move around the floor to pick up tools or parts: instead, they remained at their work station and the work came directly to them, creating the basis for 'speed-up' and massive productivity improvements. The Ford Motor Company smashed production records and used these gains to deliver major reductions in the price of cars and thus expand the market, fostering a process in which car ownership eventually spread beyond the upper and middle classes to factory workers themselves. Although these principles had their precursors, the innovations of Taylor and Ford, more than anything, epitomised the American system of 'mass production'.

Political and trade union challenges to the factory system

Work systems matter enormously to workers. The organisation of work deeply affects the level of skill needed, the extent to which individuals can use their abilities, and their levels of job satisfaction and job loyalty (see, for example, Parker 2003, Cordery and Parker 2007). Workers did not necessarily take these new production methods lying down, nor did they meekly accept working conditions where wages were low or work pressures too great. Early factory legislation, bitterly opposed by the owners, outlawed the employment of the youngest children and limited some of the worst excesses of dangerous working conditions. This forced the factory system to adapt and it did so despite the warnings of dire consequences of economic collapse from capitalist leaders. New efficiencies were found, often by replacing people with advances in technology.

However, 'employee voice' became, and remains, a key concern in the governance of the workplace, as we shall explain more fully in Chapter 6. Suffice to say here that from the late nineteenth century onwards, governments, disturbed by threats to social order, began to enact progressive labour legislation supportive of worker rights. This responded to, and was accompanied by, the growth of trade unions. From such beginnings in the nineteenth century, unions grew more strongly in the first part of the twentieth century: at the end of the First World War, throughout the Great Depression of the 1930s, and during the Second World War (see Clegg 1994, Hannan 1995, Kaufman 2004).

Inside the factory, managers responded with steps to shore up the order and stability of the 'labour process' embedded in the factory system. Wherever workplaces were big (and large factories in steel-making, ship-building, textiles and automotive assembly could employ several thousand workers at one site), unions tended to be strong, and senior management moved to appoint labour relations' specialists to their staff. These specialists worked on mechanisms to channel industrial conflict. This meant working with unions through a process of collective bargaining to jointly regulate the terms and conditions of work and employment. It led to the adoption of such bureaucratic control systems as job evaluation, intended as a way of bringing greater order into payment methods by developing a strict hierarchy of jobs and pay grades (see Chapter 7). Through such methods, the role of industrial relations managers was to keep the peace with the unions and help to ensure continuity of production. However, while the accommodations to organised labour that came through this process significantly improved levels of wages and benefits, they rarely challenged the structure of the work itself. What unions with strong shopfloor power did achieve was improvements in pay, employment security, staffing levels and work norms. They helped to build what academic economists call the 'internal labour market' (ILM) (Doeringer and Piore 1971, Jacoby 1984).

This is a strange term because the whole idea of an ILM is to minimise market influences. ILMs are administrative codes, not markets. They are a system of bureaucratic rules for defining jobs, allocating workers to them, enhancing employment security and determining pay. In the most developed systems, recruitment at the bottom levels of the job ladder led into a structure which offered promotion from within and a set of benefits in pay escalation, training, pensions and security which were very hard to obtain working in smaller firms. Unions played a major role in fostering such systems. However, they rarely challenged the division of labour (between managers and workers and between different types of worker) on which the Fordist production regime rested. In many cases, they magnified it through inter-union 'demarcation' disputes in which boundaries between different types of labour (and, thus, union memberships) were contested and policed.

Management was not entirely insensitive to worker reactions to mechanistic work systems and management theory was not entirely moribund. New ideas did emerge on how to boost productivity through enhancing worker autonomy and job scope and thus reducing boredom with repetitive tasks. In the middle decades of the twentieth century, the 'Human Relations School', showed interest in how work and supervisory practices affected employee motivation and in the role of informal groups in the workplace (see Watson (1986) for an excellent analysis). Similarly, in the 1950s, theory developed on 'socio-technical work systems', which aimed to enhance both social and economic outcomes in the workplace (Trist and Bamforth 1951). In the 1960s and 1970s, psychologists laid increasing emphasis on ways of enhancing employee discretion and increasing responsibility through 'job enrichment' (Herzberg 1968, Hackman and Oldham 1980). Job enrichment was seen to improve satisfaction with the work itself and thus employee commitment, an issue whenever labour markets were tight. Parker and Wall (1998) summarise the shape of what Cordery and Parker (2007) call a 'motivational model' of work design based on these innovations (Box 5.1). Most of these ideas, however, made little substantive impact in factories. There were celebrated experiments with work redesign, such as Volvo's attempts to introduce 'semi-autonomous' teamwork at its Uddevalla plant (Berggren 1992), but these were often marginal and short-lived (MacDuffie 1995).

Box 5.1 Recommended strategies to create a more 'motivational model' of work design

1. Arrange work in a way that allows the individual employee to influence his or her own working situation, work methods, and pace. Devise methods to eliminate or minimize pacing.
2. Where possible, combine interdependent tasks into a job.
3. Aim to group tasks into a meaningful job that allows for an overview and understanding of the work process as a whole. Employees should be able to perceive the end product or service as contributing to some part of the organization's objectives.
4. Provide a sufficient variety of tasks within the job, and include tasks that offer some degree of employee responsibility and make use of the skills and knowledge valued by the individual.
5. Arrange work in a way that makes it possible for the individual employee to satisfy time claims from roles and obligations outside work (e.g. family commitments).
6. Provide opportunities for an employee to achieve outcomes that he or she perceives as desirable (e.g. personal advancement in the form of increased salary, scope for development of expertise, improved status within a work group, and a more challenging job).
7. Ensure that employees get feedback on their performance, ideally from the task as well as from the supervisor. Provide internal and external customer feedback directly to employees.
8. Provide employees with the information they need to make decisions.

Source: Parker and Wall (1998: 20).

Competitive challenges to Fordism and Scientific Management

It was not until the 1970s that management thinking about the organisation of factory work really started to change. While the ideas we have just noted had been talked about in management research and education for some time, the impetus for sustained changes to work systems had much more of its origin in serious *competitive* challenges – challenges transmitted through product markets – that started to shake management confidence. The oil shocks of the mid-1970s undermined management complacency by triggering major rises in energy prices and ushering in a period of declining productivity. Alongside this macroeconomic change, Japanese manufacturing firms began to show they had mastered a new form of production which delivered better quality products at lower prices. Japanese factories had adopted ways of manufacturing that reduced wasteful stock levels and involved workers (and not simply managers) in enhancing production quality. Ironically, they had taken American quality gurus, such as Deming (1982), much more seriously than had managers in the West and had used post-war reconstruction to build a manufacturing model which directly challenged Western manufacturers through the way it created higher levels of skill and identification with company goals. Japanese methods of 'lean manufacturing' (Womack, Jones and Roos 1990, Delbridge 2007) and 'total quality management' (Wilkinson and Willmott 1995) began to take their toll, surprising Western manufacturers by the way in which quality improvements could reduce waste and costs. The British motorcycle industry, flatfooted by Japanese production of a range of more reliable, cheaper and more stylish bikes, was one of the early casualties.[2] In the USA, smaller, more fuel-efficient Japanese cars began to gain market share and challenge the hegemony of such household institutions as Ford and General Motors, a process which continues to unfold.

What was painfully realised in the light of Japanese manufacturing success, seen most graphically in the Toyota Production System (Ohno 1988), was that HR systems for operating workers could no longer be ignored by senior managers. Unchanged, the old forms of work organisation could become a source of competitive *dis*advantage. On the other hand, transformed to focus more on quality and on more flexible types of working, new forms of work organisation had the potential to contribute to competitive advantage in a way unimaginable in the 1960s. The implications were well put by the founder

---

[2] For an excellent analysis of the rise and decline of the British motorcycle industry, see Ian Chadwick's website: http://www.ianchadwick.com/motorcycles/britbikes/index.html, accessed 3/5/10.

(Konosuke Matsushita) of one the major Japanese manufacturing companies to a group of visiting western business leaders in 1985:

> Your firms are built on the Taylor model: even worse, so are your heads. With your bosses doing the thinking, while the workers wield the screwdrivers, you are convinced deep down that this is the right way to run a business. For you, the essence of management is getting the ideas out of the heads of the bosses and into the hands of labour. We are beyond the Taylor model: business, we know, is now so complex and difficult, the survival of the firms so hazardous in an environment increasingly unpredictable, competitive and fraught with danger that their continued existence depends on the day-to-day mobilisation of every ounce of intelligence. For us, the core of management is the art of pulling together the intellectual resources of all employees in the service of the firm. Only by drawing on the combined brain power of all its employees can a firm face up to the turbulence and constraints of today's environment.

The development of high-involvement work systems

The threat to Western manufacturing associated with Japanese production systems generated enormous interest in the 1970s and 1980s and forced significant changes in work organisation in key industries (Piore and Sabel 1994, Wallace 1998, Delbridge 2007). In the iconic industry of automobile manufacturing, which deeply concerns public policy makers because its tentacles reach out into a whole host of manufacturers of parts and advanced materials, Western firms made major efforts to reform Fordism, adopting Japanese techniques of 'just-in-time' manufacturing and moving away from low-discretion work systems towards what Lawler (1986) calls 'high-involvement' work systems (HIWSs).

Some use this term synonymously with 'high-performance work systems' (HPWSs), which we discussed in Chapter 3 in our examination of best-practice models of HR systems. While the HPWS terminology has become very prevalent, we think that talking of high involvement is more useful because it is a more descriptive term. There must be multiple routes to high performance, only some of which involve reforms designed to empower workers (Orlitzky and Frenkel 2005, Boxall and Macky 2009). While leading HPWS authorities such as Appelbaum *et al.* (2000) do use the HPWS terminology to signify a change to a more empowering type of work design, we prefer to make the point more plainly by speaking of high-involvement work systems. This clearly signals a shift away from the low-involvement characteristics of traditional Talyorist–Fordist work models.

As emphasised in Chapter 3, it is not possible to argue that HIWSs are generally relevant across all industries or occupations. In high-tech, semi-conductor manufacturing, for example, an industry which has emerged since the Second World War (and especially since the use of silicon chips in personal computers in the 1980s), the role of highly skilled professional engineers, who enjoy high levels of involvement, is very important (Appleyard and Brown 2001). These workers hardly need job enrichment: they already experience it. However, HIWSs do constitute an important part of a reformed production model which has been adopted in those Western manufacturing industries where managers want to move to higher quality production systems and where historical practices of de-skilling and demarcation stand in the way of this.

Management moves to reform production systems in these industries often start with investments in advanced manufacturing technologies, such as robots, computer-aided design (CAD), computer numerical control (CNC) machine tools, and electronic data interchange (EDI) systems. Research shows that advanced manufacturing technologies reach more of their potential when the work of production operators is redesigned and their skills improved to enable them to enhance the operating performance of these technologies (Wall *et al.* 1990, Boyer *et al.* 1997, Challis, Samson and Lawson 2005). Although there can be gains to improved HRM with existing technologies, it is the combination of company investments in new manufacturing and information technologies *and* in the related work practices and employee skills that is likely to bring the greatest productivity benefits (Brynjolfsson and Hitt 2000, Black and Lynch 2001).

As Wall *et al.* (1990, 1992) explain, work redesign and training that enables production operators to solve technical problems as they occur reduces reliance on the need to call in specialist technicians for problem solving and thereby enhances productivity. The productivity benefits come from two sources (Wall *et al.* 1992: 354). The first is simply due to time savings: the more that machine operators are empowered to address routine machinery problems, the quicker the response to these problems and the lower the amount of machine downtime. With highly automated technology, higher levels of error-free machine operation during a worker's shift translate directly into higher output and revenue. The second source is 'anticipatory' or based on more effective use of the capacity of operators for learning: operators who enjoy greater empowerment learn more about the reasons why faults occur in the first place and find ways to reduce their incidence.

In terms of their role in production reforms, it is thus apparent that high-involvement work systems encompass a range of practices that attempt to reverse the Taylorist process of centralising decision making and problem solving in the hands of management and technical specialists. Some elements of decision making and problem solving always remain with management and advanced specialists but high-involvement work practices grant greater autonomy to production workers and enhance their responsibilities, thereby necessitating a greater investment in employee development (Boxall and Macky 2009). As opposed to the traditional Fordist factory, the goal becomes one of making better use of operator skills, capacity for initiative, and potential for learning (Delbridge, Kenney and Lowe 1998, Florida, Jenkins and Smith 1998).

The components of a high-involvement approach to work design are usefully spelt out by Vandenberg, Richardson and Eastman (1999) in the framework shown in Figure 5.1. This is based on Lawler's (1986) 'PIRK' model in which high-involvement work processes encompass workplace power (P), information (I), rewards (R) and knowledge (K). These four variables are seen as mutually reinforcing. In other words, high-involvement work processes empower workers to make more decisions, enhance the information and knowledge they need to do so, and reward them for doing so.

In effect, this parallels the set of lenses in the AMO framework we introduced in Chapter 1: for the high-involvement model to work, it must positively affect employee abilities, motivations, and opportunities to perform. Improvements in knowledge enhance ability while empowerment and information enhance the opportunity to contribute. Rewards are a direct attempt to enhance motivation, which may also be improved through empowerment (enjoying more autonomous work), information (feeling better informed) and knowledge (enjoying a growth in skills).

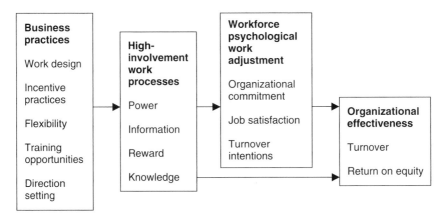

Figure 5.1 Conceptual model of high-involvement work processes
Source: Vandenberg *et al.* (1999: 307).

Figure 5.1 contains two paths (two sets of arrows leading to organisational effectiveness) through which the PIRK variables affect outcomes: a 'cognitive path' in which they take 'greater advantage of the skills and abilities' employees possess and a 'motivational path' in which involvement processes increase 'workers' satisfaction and other affective reactions' (Vandenberg *et al.* (1999: 304). This parallels Batt's (2002) identification of a 'direct' path (enhancing employee skill levels and firm-specific knowledge) and an 'indirect' path (enhancing employee motivation and satisfaction and lowering quit rates). The direct path is important for enabling workers to solve work problems more effectively and the indirect path is important to ensuring they want to do so and continue to take responsibility for doing so. Furthermore, we should not just think about this on the individual level: a successful high-involvement system not only enhances individual human capital but works well on the collective level, improving the social capital of groups inside and across the organisation.

We must, however, avoid thinking there is a best-practice 'silver bullet' here (Boxall and Macky 2009). As underlined in Chapter 3, the specific work practices that will bring about greater employee involvement can be expected to vary across industries, occupations and societies. In some (but not all) situations, HIWSs will involve reforms to create greater teamworking, either on-line (during production) or off-line (away from the production process), as has become increasingly common in automobile manufacturing (Pil and MacDuffie 1996: 438). There are shades of 'teamness' but moving to a situation where a group of workers agrees their own roles and helps each other with problem solving when quality problems occur constitutes a major change in philosophy after years of highly individualised jobs and supervisor control. Such a process encourages something of a reintegration of mental (traditionally, management-dominated) and manual (traditionally, worker-dominated) work. A very good example of this type of integration was the Toyota–GM joint venture factory (the 'NUMMI' plant) in California where performance in efficiency and flexibility was well above average (Adler, Goldoftas and Levine 1999). The plant lasted from 1984 to 2010 when it was closed in the light of differences about future plans and severe difficulties facing both parties in the global financial crisis.[3]

Reintegration of work in HIWSs often encompasses more than the vertical (management–worker) dimension. A second form of integration comes from the efficiency improvements associated with combining specialist work

_____

[3] For a history of the plant, see http://en.wikipedia.org/wiki/NUMMI, accessed 3/5/10.

roles within operational teams. This means, for example, that responsibility for maintenance and quality inspection, previously carried out by specialists in different departments is brought within the ambit of the team as far as the members have technical competence to do so. In some cases, individuals with special skills will work as team members. A third form of integration can build social capital across organisational boundaries when manufacturing workers are linked to suppliers and customers. In some car assembly plants, for example, assembly workers are members of teams that meet with suppliers to discuss problems and improvements. Electronic data interchange and the internet, accessed by computer-literate workers, can facilitate these networks. A fourth kind of reintegration occurs when there are attempts to better integrate workers into the cultural or organisational fabric of the firm, rather than treat them as outsiders or lesser citizens. At a trivial, yet symbolic level, this is seen in the adoption of the language of inclusion: in some companies, senior managers start to talk of employees as 'associates' or 'members'. They attempt to blur the old rigid distinction between managers and workers. More significantly, some managerial tasks are devolved to team leaders who usually work alongside and with their team members, compared to traditional foremen, for example, who often sat in glass-fronted offices on the shop floor. In this way, front-line management is less remote and the task of front-line managers and team leaders changes to give more emphasis to training, coaching and encouraging better performance.

As explained in Chapter 3, the evidence suggests there are industries in which a transition to HIWSs helps to significantly improve operating performance. Assessments of the pay-off are much more believable when they are associated with in-depth, industry-based studies. On this basis, some of the best evidence we have is based on high-involvement changes in US steel making (Arthur 1994, 1999, Ichniowski *et al.* 1997, Ichniowski and Shaw 1999, Appelbaum *et al.* 2000), in US medical electronics manufacturing (Appelbaum *et al.* 2000) and in the worldwide automobile assembly industry (MacDuffie 1995).

In thinking about the strategic value of HIWSs, it is helpful here to return to the notion of 'table stakes', a concept we introduced in Chapters 2 and 4. It is likely that in the automobile industry, for example, customer demand for higher quality standards means that nearly all car manufacturers now require higher employee involvement as part of industry 'table stakes'. In other words, such work systems have become part of the price of being in the game: survival depends on having them, along with other key investments in new technologies. This is not, however, true in all industries and whether HIWSs offer gains more generally is still a moot point. As mentioned in Chapter 3, the best assessment we have, a very careful longitudinal study of US manufacturing by Cappelli and Neumark (2001), concludes that the effects of HIWSs on profitability are unclear. A study of some 3,000 small US firms (less than 100 employees) by Sean Way (2002) also calls for caution. It indicates that the costs may not outweigh the benefits in small organisations.

Where there is potential to make HIWSs pay off, however, we should not imagine that top results can be easily achieved. An important part of what brings these new systems alive is the behaviour of managers, especially the immediate managers or team leaders. Many of the HR policies designed to suit high-involvement work systems can only be applied by line managers. Studies of lean methods of working, however, frequently cite growing levels of stress among team leaders, who feel caught in the middle as both team worker (one of 'us') and as manager (one of 'them') (Hutchinson *et al.* 1996, 1998). The ability of front-line managers to enact change is an outcome of the way these managers are themselves selected, developed, monitored and rewarded. An environment that also includes cost cutting and downsizing can put intense pressure on line managers.

Furthermore, as Figure 5.1 makes plain, HIWSs hinge on the responses of employees. Survey evidence suggests that HIWSs can bring improvements in employee autonomy, greater development and use of their skills, and greater financial rewards, which appeal strongly to workers, significantly lifting their job satisfaction (Berg 1999, Vandenberg *et al.* 1999, Macky and Boxall 2008). However, studies indicate that the gains to workers are most likely to occur when increases in their responsibilities do not come with excessive work pressure (Mackie, Holahan and Gottlieb 2001, Macky and Boxall 2008). Case studies often point to a 'dark side' of lean manufacturing, including increases in stress (Delbridge 2005), and a survey conducted in 15 European countries indicates that while lean production systems enhance autonomy they come with 'tight quantitative production norms to control employee effort' (Lorenz and Valeyre 2005: 429).

There can, for example, be a problem with inappropriate applications of teamwork. Research by Sprigg, Jackson and Parker (2000) illustrates how greater use of teamworking is much more likely to appeal to workers when they are working in a highly interdependent production process, where they must interact at a high level to improve how things are done. In situations where workers are largely independent of each other, however, imposing teamworking can undermine individual autonomy and job satisfaction. In Appelbaum *et al.*'s (2000: 113–14, 180) study of high-involvement work reforms in three manufacturing industries, the job satisfaction and commitment of workers in US apparel firms was actually lower among those in self-directed teams. Thus, we repeat again the caution that it is important to avoid over-generalising about *particular* work practices, such as teamworking. Some workers undoubtedly feel that some forms of teamwork undermine, rather than enhance, their personal autonomy (Berg 1999, Harley 2001, Bauer 2004).

All of this underlines the fact that success with work reforms is far from assured. The quality of implementation is extremely variable. Parker's (2003) longitudinal study of the effects on workers of lean production in a UK vehicle manufacturer indicates how much care needs to be taken with specific implementations if they are to improve the quality of the work for different types of worker involved in the production process (in this case, assembly-line, technical support and lean-team workers). This means, however, returning to the resource-based view of the firm discussed in Chapter 4, that well-designed, well-implemented HIWSs can be competitively valuable. Where management does successfully build an HIWS with operating workers, Lepak and Snell (1999, 2007) argue this will merit protection through a high-commitment HR system (see Figure 4.3). The need to protect HIWSs through higher levels of employee loyalty is underlined in Guthrie's (2001) study of 164 New Zealand firms. This survey shows that when firms pursue high-involvement work practices, lower employee turnover is associated with higher productivity. Conversely, when firms pursue more control-oriented (Taylorist) forms of work organization, higher employee turnover is associated with higher productivity. In other words, firms which make the costly investment in high-involvement work processes, and the related skills, will have better economic performance in conditions of low labour turnover. Worker loyalty might be taken for granted when the introduction of HIWSs occurs alongside major lay-offs, as happened in the steel industry in the 1990s (Bacon and Blyton 2001), but when labour markets are tight, employers who have invested in HIWSs will need to take measures to improve employee commitment if they are to achieve low labour turnover.

We must note here, however, that Guthrie's (2001) study gives us no basis for arguing that HIWSs are generally good for productivity. His study shows *two* paths to higher productivity, one of which works through HIWSs and the other through low involvement and high employee turnover (see also Siebert and Zubanov (2009) for a parallel case within a large British retail chain). This is a key point because it is now apparent that many firms, faced with insurmountable pressures from low-cost producers, have given up on the idea of HIWSs in high-wage countries, if they ever entertained it (see, for example, Konzelmann, Forrant and Wilkinson 2004). They have decided instead to *offshore* their production.

Globalisation, market reform and production offshoring

'Globalisation' of production was strong in the nineteenth century under the 'Pax Victoriana', when Britain ruled the waves (Krugman 1997), and under the continuing impetus of industrial innovations, including the growth from the 1820s of steam shipping (Solar 2006). International trade, however, suffered major setbacks in the first half of the twentieth century as a result of the two world wars and the Great Depression. Globalisation is not a new phenomenon but is something that has reasserted itself since the Second World War through a process of significant reduction in tariffs and other trade barriers between countries and regions. This has been a fraught, imperfect process but other factors, such as the liberalisation of financial markets, the collapse of Communism as an alternative economic system, the growth of improved modes of transport (better air travel and containerised shipping) and higher speed and more comprehensive communications through the internet, have all played their part in opening up the world to higher levels of trade in goods, services and ideas. Globalisation has also been associated with the growth in the number of mergers and strategic alliances stretching across national borders, for example in pharmaceuticals, motor cars and management consultancy companies (see Chapter 10).

Globalisation has made a major impact in those manufacturing industries where technology has been less successful in automating production and, thus, the ratio of labour costs to total cost remains fairly high. This is the case, for example, in clothing, footwear, consumer electronics, and toy manufacture. In these sorts of industries, as Table 5.1 indicates, operations in high-wage countries are extremely vulnerable to differences in labour costs. The USA and Canada have relatively similar levels of labour costs, somewhat more competitive than some of the higher-cost European countries such as the UK, the Netherlands and Germany. However, hourly compensation costs in Korea are currently around half of those in the USA and western Europe, while those in Taiwan are around 22 per cent of UK levels and those in Mexico and the Philippines are around 10 per cent and 4 per cent of UK levels, respectively.

These are national labour cost figures and do not necessarily give an accurate picture on comparative labour costs in an industry. This information is readily available on the internet, making comparisons much easier than in the past, and thus informing company strategies on offshoring, or reacting to competitive threats. For example, steel industry data for labour costs in the production of crude steel show that the unit cost in the USA in 2005 was

Table 5.1 Hourly compensation costs in US dollars for production workers in manufacturing, 2007: selected countries

Country	US$ p/hr, 2007
Germany	50.73
Netherlands	39.47
United Kingdom	36.66
Australia	34.75
Canada	31.91
United States	30.56
Japan	23.95
New Zealand	19.19
Korea	18.36
Taiwan	8.15
Mexico	3.91
Philippines	1.37

Note: Hourly compensation costs include total hourly pay before tax (including pay for time worked, holiday pay and any wage premia and bonuses regularly paid) plus employer social insurance expenditures and other labour taxes.
Source: US Department of Labor, Bureau of Labor Statistics, March 2009, http://www.bls.gov/news.release/ichcc.t02.htm, accessed 3/5/10.

US$23.80. It was US$26 in the UK but as low as US$0.90 in India and US$1.10 in China. This very low level of labour cost is not just a far eastern phenomenon. Costs in the Ukraine were US$0.80 while in the Czech Republic they were US$6.10. Meanwhile, Mexico, a member of NAFTA (the North America Free Trade Association) and thus in a tariff-free zone, can produce steel for US$2.50, roughly a tenth of the cost in its northern neighbour, the USA.[4]

These numbers speak for themselves. Such marked differences in labour costs place intense pressure on the cost structures of labour-intensive operations in the advanced industrial nations. These pressures are by no means restricted to manufacturing. Governments and regional economic areas such as the European Union have dismantled regulations that protected service industries in the past, whether the abolition of retail price maintenance, or the deregulation of particular sectors such as banking and airlines. In airline deregulation, which took place in the USA in the 1980s and in Europe was

---

[4] http://www.steelonthenet.com/labour_cost.html, accessed 3/5/10.

begun in the 1990s, the effect was that the protected routes 'owned' by a national airline or a favoured few were opened up to competition. Now labour cost increases could no longer be passed on automatically to the captive customer. New, low-cost airlines, which we discussed in Chapter 2, entered the market, like Southwest Airlines in the 1970s in the USA and easyJet and Ryanair in Britain and Ireland ten to fifteen years later (Gittell and Bamber 2010, Harvey and Turnbull 2010). As labour costs are the largest component of variable costs in the airline industry, huge pressure was placed on finding means of achieving cost reduction (Batt 2005). Farrell (2005: 679) notes how one airline carrier gained US$75 million 'in previously lost receivables on top of the $50 million it saves every year by operating its accounts-receivable department in India'.

The pattern of low-cost, new-entrant firms rapidly taking market share from long-established companies repeated itself in many service industries like telecommunications, information systems, and banking, insurance and finance. In each case, established players found that the rules of the competitive game had changed. Now they, too, had to find ways of rapidly introducing new technologies or systems in order to reduce costs drastically while improving quality and the speed of customer service. This had to be done by finding better ways of managing operations and people, and here offshoring can be important. Farrell (2005) cites figures from a study in 2003 indicating that US companies saved $0.58 for every dollar of spending on jobs they shifted to India. In a financial services' case, this saving made it profitable for the firm to provide poorer customers with some of the services previously reserved only for high-net-worth individuals, 'thus opening up large new customer segments in its home markets' (Farrell 2005: 679). It is no wonder that the managerial preoccupations of the 1990s included 'benchmarking', 'business process re-engineering' and 'change management'.

Similar forces have been at work in the public sector. Pressures to reduce government expenditure as a proportion of gross domestic product and to reduce government debt were associated with the large-scale privatisation of government-owned industries in the 1980s (Bach and Kessler 2007). Pioneered by Mrs Thatcher's government in the UK, this approach to minimise the role of the state quickly spread around the globe and was enthusiastically supported by the International Monetary Fund and the World Bank. New forms of government action came in the form of state-sponsored regulators and auditors whose jobs were to ensure that privatised firms were not exploiting 'captive' customers. Regulators had the power to order significant reductions in prices, as they did, for example, in British water companies in 2000. This had dramatic consequences for jobs in the industry. Governments, whether national or supra-national like the European Union, ordered the opening up of sheltered service markets to competition, as for example in telecommunications. Utilising the latest technologies and building on the changing nature of customer preferences with the growth of mobile phone and internet access, new companies were able to enter the market. They had significantly lower cost structures compared to the existing, long-established firms which were burdened with sunk costs. Pressure to reduce these costs while improving quality and adopting new technologies was, and remains, intense.

The force of change was experienced, too, in those parts of the public sector that could not be privatised. This is the sphere of public hospitals, state schools and other central and local government services which have few independent sources of revenue beyond taxes. Here the import of the 'new public management' (Hood 1991, Ferlie, Ashburner, Fitzgerald and Pettigrew 1996) sought to replicate private-sector competitive strategies. This could involve compulsory competitive tendering of service provision, such as school meals, refuse disposal or hospital facilities' management, or the creation of proxy markets to force competition. This was achieved in health care through the artificial splitting of 'purchasers' from the 'providers' of services.

The initial response of many organisations affected by these cost pressures was often to lay off workers. Downsizing, one of the dark sides of HRM, is now a prevalent strategy (Baron and Kreps 1999, Batt 2005). Unless technology is improved at the same time or client demand falls, downsizing leaves a smaller workforce which works longer hours or works the same hours under a greater sense of pressure. The first half of the 1990s, in fact, witnessed a general rise in work intensity in many European countries (Green and McIntosh 2001). In an extensive study using a variety of data sources, Green (2001) noted that in 1986 some 37 per cent of employees in the UK said they were subject to work pressure from clients or customers but by 1997 this had risen to 54 per cent. In the same period, the proportion who reported that they were subject to work pressure from fellow workers or colleagues rose remarkably from 29 to 57 per cent. 'It seems that peer pressure has come into its own as a source of labour intensification' (Green 2001: 70). This is strongly confirmed by the University of Bath *People and Performance* study (Purcell, Kinnie, Hutchinson, Swart and Rayton 2003). Many of those interviewed said that 'they could not let their mates down'. This type of 'concertive' control by team members over themselves is, suggests Barker (1993), more powerful than other, more traditional methods of control to gain worker compliance with management's requirements.

However, while there are major variations in working hours and work pressure across countries, with Britain and Ireland and other neo-liberal economies exhibiting relatively high levels, working hours generally declined in European countries in the late 1990s (Clark 2005, Gallie 2005). Certainly, this masks variations across the labour market. There are high stress levels in public-sector professional services and, in the private sector, high-income, highly skilled workers often find themselves in companies with long working hours' cultures where they eventually experience problems of work–life imbalance. But the fact that we have now entered a period in which working hours seem to have stabilized suggests that work intensification has peaked for the time being.

There may be an important clue here as to how companies have increasingly reacted to low-cost competition. In the private sector, work intensification is a limited strategy which will rarely bridge the gulf in costs we have talked about. In globalised manufacturing and service industries, firms either downsize their workforces, but in tandem with advanced technologies and work reforms which drive a productivity revolution (Brynjolffson and Hitt 2000), or they transfer their operations to attractive low-cost countries. Offshoring production to countries in which labour costs are markedly lower, and labour regulations are less demanding, has become one of the preferred HR strategies of multinational companies (Cooke 2001, 2007b). Multinational companies with factories and offices in diverse countries have often been able to play one location off against another, rewarding the efficient with new investment and new model work (as in the motor industry), and bargaining with governments for development grants as an inducement to keep existing plants open (Mueller and Purcell 1992). In many cases, established firms have ceased manufacturing altogether in high-wage countries. We saw this in the case of Dyson, referred to in Chapter 1, which shifted its assembly operations to Malaysia while another iconic British case is that of the shoe company, Clarks, which closed its last factory in Weston-super-Mare in 2001, moving production to Taiwan. A recent high-profile case concerns the US food multinational, Kraft, which, after its takeover of Cadbury in 2009, continued with Cadbury's major investment in its new Polish factory and its decision to close one of the two remaining UK plants (the 75-year old Somerdale factory near Bristol).[5]

---

[5] For comments on the political repercussions of this decision, see the report of the relevant House of Commons' committee: http://www.publications.parliament.uk/pa/cm200910/cmselect/cmbis/234/23405.htm, accessed 5/5/10.

We thus see a range of strategies playing out as firms in advanced economies respond to a globalising economic order. Some have adopted new technologies, including, quite critically, an escalation of investment in new information technologies, and made companion investments in high-involvement work systems. This is easiest in capital-intensive or high-tech industries where workforce numbers and labour cost levels are already relatively low. For example, BMW, in its Oxford UK plant, making the highly successful Mini, announced the move of engine production from Brazil to its engine plant nearby in Ham Hall in 2006 despite labour costs in Brazil being two thirds of British costs.[6] BMW Oxford, the old Cowley works of Morris Motors and British Leyland, was notorious for poor industrial relations in the 1960s and 70s. It is now a classic case of successful HIWSs. This probably contributed to the decision. More important was the fact that labour costs only contributed 15–20 per cent to total costs and, by getting major suppliers within one hour of Oxford, significantly reduced transportation costs and increased flexibility, for example in engine choice.

Others, in industries more limited in their technological options, may have initially tried to downsize and intensify work. However, this is a much more limited strategy which can rarely bridge the cost gap that exists in such labour-intensive industries as clothing manufacturing and call centres between the high-wage economies of North America and Western Europe and the industrialising economies of Southern Asia, Central and South America and Africa. Here the unfolding story is that we see large-scale offshoring to sites where labour costs are so much lower that traditional Taylorist–Fordist work systems can be used without much difficulty.

Work systems in services and the public sector

Our discussion of the origin and evolution of work systems in manufacturing has given us much of the terminology and theory we need to discuss work systems in services, both private and public. Moreover, our discussion of the effects of globalisation and market reforms has underlined issues that are critical to analysing trends in service industries. It is vital that we pay proper regard to work systems in services. Services, after all, commonly account for three-quarters of all employment in advanced economies (Segal-Horn 2003).

---

[6] *The Guardian*, 14 September 2006.

Services, however, differ from manufacturing in a number of important ways, as noted by a variety of commentators (for example, Segal-Horn 2003, Batt 2005, 2007, Lovelock *et al.* 2007). First, they are typically much more labour intensive than manufacturing, with ratios of labour to total costs that typically exceed 50 per cent and are often around 60 to 70 per cent, including in the public sector (Bach and Kessler 2007). There are still labour-intensive parts of manufacturing but services are nearly always labour intensive. Second, the balance between tangibility and intangibility in the 'product' is different. In a rental-car company, for example, the tangible parts of the service offer include the cars available for hire and the branch sites owned by the company while the intangibles concern the human-provided customer services, such as the level of staff efficiency and friendliness, the quality of car cleaning, and the possibility of home delivery of the car. Services generally have a higher level of intangibles than manufacturing and thus a greater range of quality levels ('heterogeneity') to which customer satisfaction can be sensitive. While large service firms often try to standardise the service encounter (as, for example, in fast-food chains and in cinema complexes), services are inevitably affected by the skills, personalities and moods of those who provide them. Third, services are typically produced and consumed as and when customers demand them ('simultaneous production and consumption') while manufactured goods can generally be stored, sometimes for very long periods of time. Simultaneous production and consumption means that firms need flexible staffing systems to cope with peaks and troughs in customer demand, as in the retail sector (Siebert and Zubanov 2009). Fourth, customer self-service now plays a large role in routine or low-cost services. While people generally can't make their own motor car, they can put the petrol in it and adjust the tyre pressure and oil levels. Such self-service activities are now more or less compulsory and help to reduce labour costs and keep prices down. Self-service is not uniform, however, in services. It is very limited in higher quality and more esoteric, knowledge-intensive services. Conducting one's own divorce case is rarely done, as is one's own root-canal treatment or heart surgery!

To broaden our discussion into services, it helps to refer to a typology of work systems developed by Herzenberg, Alic and Wial (1998: 41) (see also Batt 2000 and Frenkel, Korczynski, Shire and Tam 1999). This typology is shown in Table 5.2. It has the value of summarising four readily discernible categories of work. Typologies can never recognise all the complexity or nuances that exist in work organisation but the framework in Table 5.2 usefully stretches from Taylorist work design, first developed in manufacturing, to high-discretion systems, such as high-skill professional services where Taylorism has rarely intruded. In between are two other categories. One category recognises the

Table 5.2 Herzenberg *et al.*'s (1998) typology of work systems

Work systems	Tightly constrained	Unrationalized labour intensive	Semiautonomous	High-skill autonomous
Examples	Telephone operators, fast-food workers, cheque proofers	Some nurses' aides, hotel maids, domestics, long-distance truck drivers, child care workers, clerical home workers	Clerical and administrative jobs with relatively broad responsibilities, low-level managers, some sales workers, UPS truck drivers	Physicians, high-level managers, laboratory technicians, electricians, engineers
Markets served	High volume, low cost; standardised quality	Low cost, low volume; often low or uneven quality	Volume and quality vary	Low volume (each job may differ); quality often in the eye of the beholder
Task supervision	Tight	Loose	Moderate	Little
Formal education of workers	Low to moderate	Low to moderate (skill often unrecognised)	Moderate	High
On-the-job training	Limited	Some informal, unrecognised learning from other workers	Limited to moderate	Substantial

Source: Abridged from Herzenberg *et al.* (1998: 42–3).

large amount of work which is labour intensive, less skilled and largely 'unrationalised' by management systems. Many personal services are very informal and have remained this way: examples include a host of jobs in small shops, in family-owned restaurants, in nurse aiding, and in services offered directly to households including childcare and gardening. These jobs may draw heavily on the interpersonal skills and physical stamina of the individuals involved but they have not required the high levels of educational and experiential preparation that are associated with professional services in such spheres as education, accountancy, engineering, medicine and the law. The other intermediate category recognises semi-autonomous work which requires mid-range skills and is neither high in discretion nor highly constrained. This latter category covers sales, clerical and associate–professional work. It is very prevalent in large, private sector bureaucracies, such as the major banks and insurance companies, and in the administrative cadres of central and local government.

We will turn our attention first of all to private sector services. Boxall (2003) draws on the work of Herzenberg et al. (1998) and on economic and strategic management theory to define three broad types of competition and work organisation in private sector services (Table 5.3). Where the interaction between technology and people is typically critical to the choice of work systems in manufacturing, the interaction with customers, and the level of knowledge needed for this encounter, is critical in services.

Table 5.3 Types of work design in private sector service

Service market type	Competitive dynamics	Knowledge content of service	Typical work design
Type One: Mass service markets (e.g. petrol stations, fast food, supermarkets)	Cost-based competition except to the extent limited by unions and state regulation; substitution of labour for technology and self-service	Low: key managers or franchisees have critical knowledge but general labour uses limited, mostly generic know-how	Low discretion; may be highly 'Taylorised' in international franchises or major chains; otherwise unrationalized, low-skill work
Type Two: A mix of mass markets and higher value-added segments (e.g. elder care, hotels, call centres)	A mix of cost and quality-based competition; greater profit opportunities for firms that identify higher value-added segments	Low to moderate knowledge levels; mix of skill levels needed in the workforce	Traditionally low to moderate discretion but potential for HIWSs
Type Three: Highly differentiated markets (e.g. high-level professional services)	Expertise and quality-based competition but with some anchors on relative pricing; some services may be routinised and migrate back to Type Two competition	High knowledge intensity except where some professional services become rountinised	Generally high discretion; the natural home of HIWSs

Source: adapted from Boxall (2003).

Mass service markets

In mass service markets, such as petrol stations, fast-food outlets, and super-markets, customers tend to have choice in where to buy and quality differences are either non-existent or not that important. Customers are therefore very price sensitive. As noted above, because this is the low-skill end of services, customers will often *co-produce* the service, one of the defining features of basic, everyday services. This may include pumping their own fuel, queuing at a counter and then carrying their food to a table at a fast-food outlet, and weighing their own fruit and vegetables in the supermarket. The more firms engage customers in co-production and the more they automate ser-vices or offshore 'back-office' functions to lower-cost countries, the lower their unit costs will be (Farrell 2005). Once one firm in an industry pioneers a major cost-saving innovation, virtually everyone has to follow to stay in busi-ness. The key managers or franchisees who run operations must have critical knowledge to establish, maintain and renew their business model as competi-tion unfolds but general labour in these services uses limited, mostly generic know-how.

Work design here typically involves one of two types in the Herzenberg *et al.* (1998) framework. Some mass-service firms adopt Taylorism. We see this, for example, in the high-volume, in-bound call centre industry where manage-ment may rationalize work practices by measuring such variables as call length against prescribed time, the calls waiting to be answered, the abandoned call rate, and the time taken to 'wrap up'. In addition, there will frequently be recording of calls and remote monitoring where managers listen in to ensure that 'scripts' are used properly and efficiently, creating a kind of 'customer-oriented bureaucracy' (Korczynski 2001). In these situations, an equivalent of the manufacturing 'speed-up' occurs, and stress levels and employee turnover can rise (Deery, Iverson and Walsh 2002, Cordery and Parker 2007). On the other hand, scripting of interactions can bring a welcome order into the chaos of high-demand services and the taping of calls can actually protect employees from ill-founded customer complaints or management criticism (Rosenthal 2004). We see similar work formalisation strategies in the large-scale retailing sector, including the national or regional chain stores. These organisations often use surveillance via closed-circuit TV and video cam-eras and may use 'mystery shoppers', who secretly score sales assistants on their willingness to smile and be helpful (Guy 2003). Training in the chain stores and supermarkets often includes 'scripting' in an attempt to ensure that customers are greeted in a standard way and handled in preferred ways when problems arise. These attempts to prescribe and enlist 'emotional labour'

(Hochschild 1986) can be stressful, especially when customers are rude or abusive (Korczynski 2001).

Alongside the mass service providers are many smaller organisations which try to make a living by keeping out of the way of the 'big boys' and offering more localised and personal services. This includes many small shops, service agencies, regional taxi services and a host of local bars and restaurants. The owners of these businesses have hardly ever used the bureaucratic, rationalised practices that the big players need for their large workforces, relying instead on the personal contacts and control of the owner or a 'hands-on' manager (Marchington *et al.* 2003). This can actually be a much more enjoyable working environment because people are not alienated by huge layers between them and the owners. The owner is a real individual who may well engage in a certain degree of 'give-and-take' over working conditions to build the loyalty of the people he or she trusts (Edwards and Ram 2006).

As our discussion indicates, cost pressures in basic services mean that work systems that involve higher levels of employee discretion and skill are rare in this sector. This does not rule out creative responses by individual firms but high levels of competitive pressure do constrain management behaviour. They mean that large firms offering low-priced services to a mass market are continually looking for ways to take out labour costs through self-service, offshoring and labour-saving technology. Small firms competing at the fringes of these markets may be able to 'keep their heads down', at least until a large trader threatens their patch, but they are often working with low margins and with their personal wealth at stake. When labour markets are hot, high levels of employee turnover can undermine even basic service levels and firms are forced to raise wages and improve conditions to hold the higher-performing, better experienced workers. However, the general pressure of cost cutting tends to reassert itself over time in mass services and this means that state regulation of pay levels and working conditions, and trade union activity, are very important to creating a floor of rights and more dignified conditions for workers.

Mass service markets with some quality differentiation

There is an important shift in the economics of production when firms find segments of mass markets where customers will pay a premium for a better quality of service (Boxall 2003, Batt 2005, 2007). We see this in such service markets as elder care, hotels, and call centres, where there is major variation in customer preferences and higher value-added customers can be targeted for better service (Batt 2000, Eaton 2000, Hunter 2000). A study by Haynes

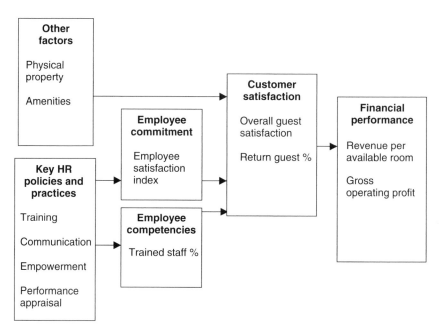

Figure 5.2 Competitive differentiation through HR strategy in a luxury hotel
Source: Haynes and Fryer (2000).

and Fryer (2000) of a five-star hotel located in a large New Zealand city illustrates the point (Figure 5.2). Like all luxury hotels, physical amenities and the refurbishment of properties drive one aspect of the hotel's strategy but tend to fall into the category of 'table stakes'. With enough money, hotel owners can create the kind of opulent surroundings that position them in the luxury hotel segment. However, the bricks and mortar (or, in this case, the marble and polished wood) do not confer any form of advantage in the segment. Superior returns also turn on the way staff deal with customers in the context of these surroundings. This includes the way in which guest preferences are discovered and catered for in successive visits. It means that there is a role for investments in the more intangible variables: in broader, more empowering job design, in development reviews and more comprehensive training, and in staff committees and surveys through which management learns about employee motivators.

When firms aim for higher value-added segments in services, then, investments in creating HIWSs are more likely to be economically justified. At this point, however, it is vital to underline a key distinction between the economics of higher quality production in manufacturing and in services. As we saw earlier, Japanese manufacturers in such spheres as automobiles and motorbikes showed that it was possible to create improvements in quality and reductions in price at the same time. This process has now unfolded in many capital-intensive manufacturing industries (for example, consumer electronics) where customers have become used to buying better models as they are released at lower prices. There are many service industries, however, where improvements in quality will *only* come at a higher price. This is the case when the larger part of the service is geographically fixed. For example, if you want to stay in a good hotel in Paris, the hotel will be in Paris and, despite the internet and outsourcing, the bulk of the service provision will take place with staff working in Paris and being paid Parisian wages. While companies in differentiated services continue to apply new technologies and offshoring wherever they can to reduce costs, higher quality service in the geographically fixed components of services translates into higher costs and prices.

Highly differentiated service markets

We now come to another major point of contrast with work design in manufacturing. In high-level, professional services and other knowledge-intensive services, work organisation has traditionally involved high levels of employee discretion. Workers in high-skill services typically have advanced educational qualifications. How they work depends much more on how these professions educate and train their own people (Combs *et al.* 2006). We are not therefore talking about a situation where work practices have traditionally been imposed by managers but one in which managers are typically senior professionals themselves. They have to deal with major performance differences among professionals but their effectiveness typically depends on working in a way that is sympathetic to professional discretion. Managerial attempts to increase control over professional behaviour often meet with professional resistance.

Recent research by Kalleberg *et al.* (2006) in the USA underlines key differences between work practices in professional services and those in manufacturing and less skilled services. While professional organisations, such as schools and healthcare services, are big users of team meetings, where professionals collectively discuss goals and problems, they are significantly less likely to use job rotation: you simply cannot rotate professionals across jobs unless they have the relevant professional qualifications. Employee growth in professional services tends to come as individuals deepen and extend the experience they have in their particular specialisation.

In the private sector, we therefore see a conjunction of high discretion, high quality and high pay in advanced, complex services. This implies, as just noted in our discussion of quality differentiation, that customers or clients have to pay higher prices if they want the service in question. Access to the top lawyers and financial advisers, for example, depends on being able to pay their 'professional fees'. To be sure, some advanced services become 'routinised'. This happens where consulting firms roll out standardised solutions to more common business problems and use more junior professionals to deliver them (Dooreward and Meihuizen 2000). There is also a growth now of 'knowledge-processing offshoring' where aspects of such services as insurance underwriting and legal and financial research are conducted in low-wage countries, most notably in India.[7] However, the more complex or esoteric the knowledge, requiring a high level of adaptation to each client's needs, the higher the control exercised by the professional and the higher the price that will be charged.

Public sector services

We have already said a great deal about the public sector, which has been affected by the same sort of cost pressures as the private sector. Downsizing and budget constraints have been applied while client demands, as in public education and health, have risen. These pressures have often been as intense as anything in the private sector or worse (Green 2001, Smith 2001, Kersley *et al.* 2006). Many public services are geographically fixed and work intensification pressures, unless effectively resisted by trade unions or undermined by high levels of employee turnover, can operate for long periods of time.

Two broad patterns of work organisation are important in the public sector. One occurs in the public service ministries and local government departments, which are typically much larger and much older than private sector establishments (Kalleberg *et al.* 2006). They have therefore relied heavily on tall hierarchies and such bureaucratic devices as job descriptions, job evaluation and performance appraisal systems. The public service has historically rivalled the largest manufacturers and the high-street banks in growing huge 'internal labour markets'. To ensure governments can account to taxpayers for how public funds are spent, pressures for standardisation of conditions have been strong, as have procedures which help to show equity of treatment across different grades of workers and across different individuals (Bach and Kessler 2007). As in large-scale manufacturing, but arriving somewhat later, the public sector has been, and remains, a strong site of unionisation. As there, unions have had the effect of increasing the number of work rules adopted in the

---

[7] Randeep Ramesh, 'Analyse this: Wall Street looks to India', *The Guardian*, 6 November 2006, p. 26.

internal labour market. Given these large organisations and pressures for joint regulation, government clerical and administrative work has been closest to the 'semi-autonomous' pattern shown in Table 5.2. It often involves a degree of discretionary judgement (for example: Should a sole parent receive a benefit or not? Should this taxpayer be granted this exemption? Should this child be granted entry to this school?) but this is typically exercised within a prescribed policy framework and a set of operating rules.

The other major pattern in the public sector is the existence of a high degree of highly skilled professional work, which we have just discussed in talking about highly differentiated service markets. In the USA, six out of ten public sector establishments operate in professional services (Kalleberg *et al.* 2006: 282). Being in the public sector, where there are large organisations with tall hierarchies, this means a higher level of bureaucracy than one finds in private-sector professional firms but it also means a high level of independent action by professionals, both acting as individuals and working through trade unions.

Bach and Kessler (2007) outline the way in which these traditional models of public sector work have been challenged by the 'new public management', referred to above. Governments from the Thatcher era have sought to con-strain the growth of, and get greater control over, the huge amount of public money that is invested in public sector workforces. This has included attempts to split 'purchasers' from 'providers' in the public sector in order to create organisational contracts which promise a certain level of services for a given amount of public money and which enable regular audits of performance. On the individual level, it includes greater mechanisms for accountability such as individual performance plans and performance-related pay. The use of performance targets is now, in fact, ubiquitous, whether goals for hospital waiting times, for exam performance in schools or for financial performance in local authorities, all increasing the pressure on public sector management teams to reduce costs and improve performance. There is little doubt that the target/audit culture has brought work intensification of a kind that has antagonised public sector professionals, lowering levels of trust in the public sector (Guest and Conway 2002) and exacerbating problems of recruitment and retention (Audit Commission 2002). In the British health service, it has actually led to an explosion in the number of people who are categorized as managers (Kirkpatrick, Ackroyd and Walker 2005).

Governments may now be starting to appreciate the limits to the 'new pub-lic management' but this does not predicate a return to the public sector of old. Increasingly, governments have sought to separate the provision of a ser-vice free at the point of delivery from the ownership of the service provider. Increasingly, we see privately run prisons, hospitals and schools alongside, and to a growing degree competing with, the traditional public sector, much to the fury of the unions. This has strong parallels with multidivisional companies, as we discuss in Chapter 10, where performance comparisons are linked to investment decisions. Any idea that the public sector is immune from job cuts and efficiency comparisons has been almost completely removed with the arrival of private sector competitors subject to less stringent rules governing work organisation.

Controversy over HRM looks set to continue in the public sector. Pressures are currently growing as governments take action to deal with the 'hole in the public finances' brought about by heavy expenditures to stave off banking collapses in the global financial crisis of 2008–9. The Coalition government elected in the UK in 2010 has announced its plans for various cuts: for example, a cut of a third in the administration of the national health service and a cut of £6 billion in non-frontline public services in 2010–11.[8] How this will be achieved is unclear and, in the heavily unionised public sector, it will not be easy. Outsourcing of services and the development of 'shared service centres' (for example, for HR support) are widely expected. With much about all this that is highly contentious, the public sector continues to provide an important case study of what can go wrong in the HR strategies of large organisations, as we will argue more fully in Chapter 8.

Conclusions

Work systems – choices about what work needs to be done, about who will do it, and about where and how they will do it – are fundamental to both operations management and human resource management in organisations. The appropriateness of a firm's work systems are inevitably connected to its chances of economic survival and to its relative performance. And they matter enormously to workers, being a principal source of job satisfaction or dissatisfaction and a major factor in employee turnover.

Many of our ideas in work design have originated in manufacturing. The growth of manufacturing in Britain and the USA in the nineteenth century depended heavily on highly specialised work systems in which operating work was characterised by low discretion, low scope and low skill. This kind of work design emerged in the early factories and was reinforced by Taylorist principles of 'Scientific Management' and Henry Ford's moving assembly line. Political

---

[8] http://www.guardianpublic.co.uk/coalition-programme-for-government-proposals, accessed 26/5/10.

and trade union challenges forced the model to adapt, leading to better incorporation of worker interests, including higher pay levels and better conditions, and encouraging the growth of 'internal labour markets' in which employee security and promotion prospects were enhanced.

It was not until Japanese competition exposed the weaknesses of Western manufacturing that principles of work design began to be seriously reformed. High-involvement work systems (HIWSs) now constitute an important alternative to traditional Taylorism–Fordism. These systems, which enhance employee discretion and skills, have been adopted in various parts of Western manufacturing where firms had become vulnerable to higher quality and lower-priced competition. In certain industries, including steel manufacturing and automobile assembly, a transition to HIWSs and greater investments in computerised technologies, has enhanced the chances of survival or significantly lifted performance. There is also evidence to indicate that HIWSs can bring improvements in employee autonomy, greater development and use of their skills, and greater financial rewards, significantly lifting job satisfaction. However, in the case of both firms and workers, the relative costs and benefits of HIWSs depend heavily on the context in which they are attempted and how they are implemented.

In terms of the context facing firms, industry deregulation, tariff reductions, new information technologies and the growth of the internet have opened up greater competition from new producers and from newly industrialising countries with much lower labour costs. These forces have had major impacts in those industries where the ratio of labour costs to total cost remains fairly high. This is not simply an issue in labour-intensive parts of manufacturing but applies to many services given their high labour content. Strategies of downsizing and work intensification have played their part in industry restructuring but tend to be limited. In some globalised industries, the dramatic improvement in labour costs needed can only be achieved by offshoring operations or those parts of service production which do not need to be geographically fixed.

Mass services are subject to major pressures for cost reductions, which are increasingly pursued through strategies of customer self-service, offshoring of 'back-room' functions and new technologies, such as internet shopping. Large firms often adopt Taylorist work design in mass services while smaller firms, operating at the fringes, rely on more informal methods of control. There is less scope in basic services for the kinds of work reform seen in high-tech or capital-intensive manufacturing. In higher quality segments of service markets, however, there are possibilities for firms to offer higher quality at a higher price, thus making investments in work redesign and higher skill more worthwhile. In professional services, Taylorism has rarely intruded and high discretion, high quality and high pay are typical, though even here there are some service activities which are not geographically sensitive and thus have offshoring potential. The public sector embraces a mix of bureaucratic work systems in which workers exercise moderate levels of discretion and a host of professional jobs. In recent years, budget constraints, workforce downsizing and a rise in bureaucratic controls have met with a very mixed response from the public sector workforce, a theme to which we will return.

6

Managing employee voice

In our discussion of the rise of the factory system in Chapter 5, we explained how employee voice became a controversial area for management. We are concerned with underpinning principles of HRM in this part of the book and the fundamental question here is how much influence do, and should, employees have over decisions that affect them at work. What forms of employee voice prevail in organisations and why? And how should management develop strategy in this area? Answering the latter question is not simply a matter of management considering the economic value of different voice options because this aspect of HRM is deeply embedded in notions of social legitimacy. The voice dimension of HRM raises the question of what sort of limits should be placed on managerial power in a democratic society. The answer does not lie solely within management's control. Employees are deeply affected by how managers exercise their power and typically react to managerial approaches that threaten their interests while nearly all governments around the world regulate managerial power in the wider interests of society. Furthermore, supranational bodies like the International Labour Organisation (ILO) and the European Union (EU) have major policy agendas in the arena of employee voice: the former is committed to an international baseline of employee rights, including rights to freely associate in trade unions and negotiate with employers through collective bargaining, while the latter is fostering higher levels of employee information and consultation. Thus, the chapter must begin by discussing the contested, essentially political nature of employee voice. The first section therefore enters into a review of contemporary trends in voice, including the growth of individual forms of employee involvement, the increasing influence of the European Union's approach to collective consultation, and the decline of trade unions, particularly in the private sector. We then review evidence on the impacts of employee voice systems within organisations, examining how they affect employee well-being, productivity and the ability of management to bring about change. With the backdrop of research on the impacts of employee voice, the chapter concludes with a framework enabling managers to reflect on the 'should' question: what should be their underpinning styles in employee relations as they respond to the demand for voice in their organisation?

The contested nature and changing contours of employee voice

'Employee voice' is a relatively new term designed to cover all types of opportunities where employees can have their say and exert some influence over workplace decisions that affect their interests. But even the definitions of employee voice are controversial. As George Strauss comments, 'voice is meaningless if the message is ignored' (2006: 803). He much prefers the term 'participation'. Participation is 'a process that allows employees to exercise some influence over their work and the conditions under which they work' (Heller *et al.* 1998: 15). Strauss adds, 'that for me, it is actual influence, not a feeling of influence that is important' (Strauss 2006: 778). Others take a softer approach. In the same journal where Strauss's stringent definition is found, the editors define participation 'to encompass the range of mechanisms used to involve the workforce in decisions at all levels of the organization – whether direct or indirect – conducted with employees or through their representatives' (Gollan, Poutsma and Veersma 2006: 499).

While cost-effectiveness is the primary goal of management in HRM, it is not possible simply to look at questions of employee voice through an economic lens. Rather, issues of social legitimacy are involved and these can clash with managerial power, as we explained in Chapters 1 and 3. Marchington (2007) expresses the dilemma neatly: 'voice is probably the area of HRM where tensions between organisational and worker goals, and between shareholder and stakeholder views, are most apparent because it connects with the question of managerial prerogatives and social legitimacy'. Few nation states leave this area to the owners of capital to resolve themselves, unfettered by legislation. The issue for the state to determine is how much restriction should be placed on the 'right to manage'. If modern democracies are based upon political citizenship, how far should there also be a concept of industrial or employment citizenship? If the exercise of arbitrary power by those in authority in government is constrained by laws giving rights to citizens, and enforced by the judiciary, how far should equivalent rights be applied in the world of paid employment and how far can they be enforced in workplaces?

Ultimately, the justification for employee voice is as an end in its own right in a society committed to democratic values and in a world-order, or international trading environment, in which the ILO and various governments have an interest in baseline labour standards (Hughes 2002, Haworth and Hughes 2003). As such, it is always contentious and subject to reinterpretation as different generations of power-holders in enterprises and the wider world of politics debate the ethics of employment relations and reform the law to reflect their ideologies. Social democratic governments, which often have historical links to the trade union movement, typically see it as their role to nurture the opportunities for worker participation and representation. As we shall see, however, these old alliances can wear thin. Conservative governments tend to opt for a position which believes it is up to managements to evolve their own voice arrangements directly with workers. Sometimes they will seek to roll back trade union rights, although doing so can back-fire at the ballot box, because the majority of electors in any society are workers.

It has often been noted that the 'fashion' for worker participation tends to come in waves or what Ramsay (1977) called 'cycles of control', a point also noted by Fox (1974) in his ground-breaking analysis of management styles and beliefs in industrial relations. The pressure to adopt more participative styles of management is greatest during periods of strong economic growth, when people have good job opportunities, and management raises wages, improves working conditions and enhances channels for worker voice in order to recruit, motivate and retain. If trade unions are well organised in such upswings, managers will tend to introduce various forms of participation that share greater control with workers in order to hold the enterprise together. This need to accommodate labour power tends to recede during economic downturns when jobs are scarce and the voice of organised labour is more muted. We think it useful to recognise that a 'demand for voice' is always present among employees in organisations, but it is evident that the degree of pressure that workers can bring to bear in their employment relationships tends to vary across different economic and political contexts.

What types of voice are there and who adopts them?

Since they come in a plethora of forms, we need some way of analysing voice mechanisms and what is going on below the surface. It helps to distinguish two main types. The first type gives employees a direct say in how to do their jobs, including how to choose among different working methods or ways of meeting a customer's needs, or allows them to influence their working conditions, such as their daily start-and-finish times or weekly roster. This form of voice is worked out in the relationship between the individual and their supervisor or it may be based around decision making in the work team: team briefing, problem-solving groups and self-managing teams are all examples of groups of workers exercising more say in decisions about the work itself and the conditions that immediately impact on it. This kind of voice is largely informal, although various forms of training may support it. It is undertaken at managerial discretion or with the blessing of the first-line manager, and located at the point of production or the work station. Direct voice tends to grow as employees become more experienced and require less supervision. British research shows that workers who are more committed and more highly skilled enjoy greater discretion in how to handle their work tasks: there is both 'leeway for the loyal' and greater autonomy in managerial and professional jobs (Green 2008).

The major contrast to direct voice lies in those forms of voice which rely on some kind of indirect or representative system. In this second type of voice, managers inform, consult, and/or negotiate with representatives elected by employees or appointed by trade unions in the workplace. Senior managers are often drawn into the process, as are specialist HR managers who may manage the process on behalf of the management team. The distinctive characteristics of this type of voice are that it is more formal, typically involves collective representation, takes place in meeting rooms away from the point of production, and is underpinned by societal regulation. Most countries have employment statutes that uphold the requirements of the International Labour Organisation (ILO), which sees union recognition and collective bargaining as fundamental worker rights, although the extent of the regulation, and the quality of its enforcement, vary enormously. In the European Union (EU), supranational regulation is more powerful than in most other parts of the world: for example, considerable attention has been given to the development of collective consultation on business changes. This includes consultation when large-scale redundancies are proposed. As we will explore later, there are now numerous EU Directives covering information sharing and consultation with workers that apply to all but the smallest employers across the 28 countries in the EU or associated with it.

Senior managers often, but not invariably, find the management of formal rights to information, consultation and negotiation less appealing that individual employee involvement and more difficult to deal with. Such rights involve a sharing of power or, at the least, a requirement to discuss business proposals before a final decision is taken. Consultation does not mean having to reach an agreement, as is the case with collective bargaining with trade unions, but it does imply entering into a meaningful dialogue with employee representatives on proposals and responding to suggestions made, even if the final decision is for management to take. This makes the management process more time consuming and makes senior managers more widely accountable in society than simply to shareholders.

With these two broad types of voice in mind, we can now turn to a more nuanced classification of the forms that voice practices can take and a review of how they are changing. In any analysis of voice systems allowing for, or encouraging, employees to have a say, and thus, influence in decision making, five linked questions need to be addressed:

1. How much say/involvement/participation is envisaged in the scheme?
2. Over what sort of decisions?
3. Taken at what level in the enterprise, or beyond, in the wider political economy?
4. Who is participating and, if a representative, how are they elected or selected?
5. What are the enforcement mechanisms, both to keep the system going and to ensure that action follows?

The first question, how much say, is the most important since it will strongly influence the form of voice system adopted and the answers to subsequent questions. In the German co-determination and consultation legal framework, there is a clear delineation of degrees of influence (information to be provided, topics subject to consultation and so on). Elsewhere, especially in Anglo-American societies, there is much more ambiguity but it is still possible to suggest a scale based on the extent of influence allowed or expected. This is shown in Figure 6.1. Marchington and Wilkinson (2000: 343) display this diagrammatically as an 'escalator' of participation (Figure 6.2).

The types of decision and their location in the managerial hierarchy attract different degrees of participation. For example, decisions on health and safety will often (and, in many countries, must, by law) involve employee representatives in an evaluation of risks and their avoidance in current operations and in the purchase of new technology. In some extreme cases, safety representatives have the right to delay or to veto a decision if they consider there is a danger to life and limb. In the same firm, it would be most unusual for employees to have the same degree of voice, or any voice at all, over product marketing or distribution decisions. In a thriving system of collective consultation, however, it may be that management will explain and account for these commercial decisions and gain employee views. Examples of such joint discussions in recent

None:	Unilateral management
A little:	Information provided
Downward:	Right to be told
Some:	Opportunity to make some suggestions
Two-way:	Consulted/opinion sought during decision making
:	Consultation/opinion sought at all stages of decision-taking implementation
A lot:	The right to delay a decision
Power to affect outcomes:	The right (or power) to veto a decision
Substantial:	Equality or co-determination in decision making
Complete:	Employee self-management and ownership

Figure 6.1 Scale of participation allowed to employees and their representatives

years have included consideration of declining quality in a car manufacturer and exploring means to correct it (Purcell *et al.* 2003), the pricing and shelf display of a biscuit maker's products concerning the relationship with a dominant supermarket (Purcell and Ahlstrand 1994), and a major plant location and investment decision in a multinational company (*ibid.*). More recent examples come from the way in which extensive information sharing and consultation took place in the recession of 2008–9. In an American-owned manufacturing site in Wales, which reduced headcount from 450 to 110, this involved consideration of the jobs, skills and deployment of every employee, undertaken jointly by management, the works council and the union (Hall, Hutchinson, Purcell, Terry and Parker 2009). In all of these examples of collective consultation, the 'right of last say' still rested with management but the desire to

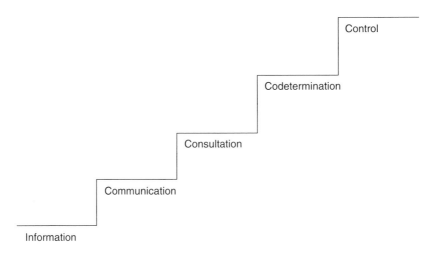

Figure 6.2 Marchington and Wilkinson's escalator of participation
Source: Marchington and Wilkinson (2000: 343).

justify decisions, and the subsequent discussions, did influence management's approach.

The importance of effective consultation is not just in the way management decisions can be influenced. It helps shape employees' views about their employer and the senior management team. The extent to which employees believe their views are listened to, and have influence, affects the way employees evaluate voice systems and judge management effectiveness. The quality of the underlying relationship in terms of levels of trust is crucial if the exchange is to be anything more than 'white knuckle' adversarial posturing (Walton and McKersie 1965, Purcell 1974, Marchington 1989). If the underlying relationship is positive, this can increase job satisfaction, organisational commitment and employee engagement (Guest and Conway 1997, Appelbaum *et al.* 2000, MacLeod and Clarke 2009).

If the scale of involvement varies by type of decision, and by its location, then these variables, in turn, strongly influence the structure of the voice system. Some types of employee voice, in all but the smallest companies, can best be undertaken by collective consultation or negotiation with a few employees elected or selected to represent their co-workers to meet with senior management. In these indirect forms of participation, questions are posed on how the tenor and outcome of joint meetings is communicated among 'constituents', and how, and to what extent, representatives take soundings before meetings, especially when dealing with confidential information.

Despite ongoing ambivalence among employers, there is some evidence of growth in collective consultation in Anglophone countries, apart from the USA, in recent years (Boxall, Freeman and Haynes 2007). The UK provides comprehensive data from the most recent WERS survey (Kersley *et al.* 2006: 126–32). While they are unusual in small firms (and small firms make up a growing proportion of British firms (*ibid.*:19), two thirds of workplaces with between 100 and 199 workers have an employee forum either at the workplace itself or through access to one at a higher corporate level. This figure rises to 72 per cent in respect of workplaces with between 200 and 500 workers and 82 per cent in workplaces with 500 or more employees.

One of the most significant features of collective consultation bodies is their composition since, as we discuss later in the chapter, management's response to dealing with these consultation forums varies significantly if they are based on union representation or are non-union committees. Overall, in 2004, 11 per cent of the collective consultation bodies were composed exclusively of union representatives, 67 per cent of them were non-union, and a further 22 per cent were mixed, with both union and non-union representatives sitting alongside each other in discussions with management (Kersley *et al.*

2006: 131). These are usually referred to as hybrid bodies and mark a significant development in employee voice.

This kind of preference for representative voice is not, however, recognised in some companies, especially those employing professional workers, each with their own personal computer. Here the use of the intranet and forms of interactive reply-and-response methods may be preferred, and many employers are wary of collective voice since it can mean, they believe, a form of power sharing on business decisions.

As we have noted, various voice practices provide individual employees with opportunities for direct involvement. This can happen through their membership of semi-autonomous or 'self-managing' teams, through problem-solving groups like quality circles, through the way their jobs are designed to give them more autonomy, through attitude surveys, and through their involvement as individual shareholders. Most individual involvement methods are designed to provide opportunities at the level of the task in 'on-line' and/or 'off-line' arrangements for worker involvement. In on-line voice, workers have greater influence over deciding how the work is done. In off-line voice, workers take part in problem-solving groups like quality circles and continuous-improvement or 'kaizen' teams. These types of voice practices can be central to high-involvement work systems, as discussed in Chapter 5. Such practices help to secure worker cooperation in improving the productivity and competitive flexibility of the firm.

The evidence is clear that individual involvement types of employee voice have grown since the 1980s across the industrialised world, both in Anglo-American countries (Boxall, Freeman and Haynes 2007) and in continental Europe (Poutsma, Ligthart and Veersma 2006). In the UK, forms of direct communication between management and employees are widely used with 91 per cent of workplaces having face-to-face meetings, 83 per cent using one form or another of downward communication, like an intranet (34 per cent) or communication chains (sometimes called cascade briefing) (64 per cent), and with written two-way communication methods like e-mail or suggestion schemes evident in two thirds of workplaces (Kersley *et al.* 2006: 135). Some form of team working is also widespread in Britain (72 per cent of workplaces) although in only half of these establishments are all employees in teams. The evidence suggests that the adoption of higher levels of employee involvement is more likely where there is a strategic need for worker cooperation and a reliance on skilled human capital (Benson and Lawler 2005: 166), especially since a major investment in high-involvement work systems will significantly raise labour costs (Cappelli and Neumark 2001, Boxall and Macky 2009). Poutsma *et al.* (2006: 523) report that in Europe 'collaborative practices' appear to be 'more often practiced in innovative workplaces facing intense competition, with highly qualified personnel, where management considers direct participation a competitive advantage'.

Other factors influencing the type of voice system, and rates of adoption, include being a foreign-owned firm, making more extensive use of information technology, and the size of the company and the workplace. Large enterprises are much more likely to have formal voice systems in place (Kersley *et al.* 2006). We know that in small firms the perception of employees of the 'influence gap' is lower (Boxall, Freeman and Haynes 2007). In small organisations, formal systems of worker voice are rare, yet worker satisfaction with communication is often relatively high (Forth, Bewley and Bryson 2006). The reason, of course, is that there is likely to be much more personal, face-to-face contact between senior management and workers, something which fades rapidly once the workplace gets above 50 employees. This rather forcibly makes the point that big firms tend to be more impersonal, bureaucratic and rule-driven. The social and power distance between the managed and top decision makers is much greater. Formal systems of worker voice can be imagined as antidotes to these tendencies, but it must be doubted how successful they can be unless management gives support and brings them to life.

Table 6.1 combines direct and indirect forms of employee voice systems with the location of decisions. We use the terms 'power-centred', 'ownership-centred' and 'task-centred' to categorise voice practices. For example, power-centred types of schemes will usually involve collective consultation and/or negotiation through high-level dialogue at meetings with senior and specialist managers. Besides collective bargaining with unions, these meetings will be held with works councils or with 'employee forums' or 'voice committees' of some kind. In companies with recognised trade unions, the long-established name is a joint consultative committee (JCC).

Power-centred schemes can also involve employees directly, such as taking part in an employee attitude survey or what are increasingly called 'engagement surveys'. Such employee attitude surveys are growing in popularity and in 2004 had occurred in around two-fifths of British workplaces (Kersley *et al.* 2006: 68). We call these 'power-centred' because the results are usually reported to senior managers, if not to the board of directors, and can lead to changes where low levels of satisfaction or engagement are revealed. In one British bank, the first time the board of directors had considered HRM on the agenda was to receive the results of the new employee satisfaction survey. They were shocked by the results as they showed widespread criticism of their leadership style. Employee engagement surveys are of particular value when linked with other company data, as we explain in Chapter 11. There is often a strong

Table 6.1 Types of employee voice mechanisms

Power-centred

Indirect	Worker directors
	Collective bargaining
	Works councils/employee forums/joint consultative committees (JCCs)
	Joint partnership committees
Direct	Attitude surveys
	Newsletters/e-mail/intranet
	'Town hall' meetings

Ownership-centred

Indirect	ESOP (employee share ownership plans) where shares are held by trustees directly elected by employees
	Worker cooperatives
	Share option (purchase schemes) giving employees 'votes' as shareholders
Direct	Employee representatives meeting local/department management

Task-centred

Indirect	Job enrichment (voice in how the job is done)
Direct	Semi-autonomous teams
	Team briefing
	Problem-solving groups (quality circles/kaizen teams, continuous improvement groups)
	Suggestion schemes

connection between employee engagement, customer satisfaction and financial performance (Fulmer, Gerhart, and Scott 2003, Gelade and Ivery 2003, Van de Voorde, Paauwe and Van Veldhoven 2010), as this bank subsequently discovered. Another form of power-centred, direct involvement involves meetings of all employees on site addressed by top management, often called 'town hall meetings' in the USA. These are now very common, happening in 79 per cent of UK workplaces (Kersley *et al.* 2006: 134). A generation ago, such workforce meetings only took place in a third of workplaces (Millward and Stevens 1986: 152).

Ownership-centred forms of employee voice are much less well developed, if only because they involve shareholder approval. From time to time, governments seek to encourage financial participation by providing tax incentives for employee shareholding (Pendleton, Kaarsemaker and Poutsma 2010). As shareholders, employees have a vote alongside traditional owners of capital, albeit a tiny one. Employee share ownership plans (ESOPs) are more common in the USA than in Europe and usually involve shares held in a trust with some trustees being employee representatives (Rosen, Case and Staubus 2005). Worker cooperatives, where all of the equity is owned by employees, remain rare despite their emotional appeal to those seeking alternative forms of ownership (Bradley and Gelb 1983, Oakeshot 2000). Much more interest is shown in 'employee partnerships' such as the well-known, and very successful, John Lewis Partnership in the UK where employees, the partners, own all the equity and profits are redistributed to them.[1] This type of ownership participation is sometimes seen by politicians in the UK as a new model for public sector organisations coming out of the recession, sometimes called 'social enterprises'.[2]

Types of voice system are not mutually exclusive. In some large organisations, it is common to find that task-centred and power-centred forms operate alongside each other in quite a complex web of voice arrangements covering a wide use of communication media, individual involvement systems centred on the line manager, annual workforce meetings and regular meetings of the collective consultation forum between senior managers and employee representatives (Hall *et al.* 2009). The evidence is that the outcome effects can be more powerful when these systems operate in tandem.

The European Union's agenda for information and consultation

Forms of collective consultation with non-union or joint union/non-union employee forums take place in many advanced economies in the larger enterprises – with the notable exception of the USA where legal prohibitions against 'company unions' greatly diminish innovation in collective consultation (Kaufman 2001, Boxall, Freeman and Haynes 2007). In Europe, the policy focus of the European Union over the last 40 years on the promotion of information and collective consultation has changed the political landscape in employee relations and led to a degree of convergence in systems of employee voice across Europe. With it has come a new language of 'partnership' and a search for more effective ways of incorporating employee opinion into company decision making (see, for example, Haynes and Allen 2000, Belanger, Giles and Murray 2002).

---

[1] On the John Lewis Partnership, see http://news.bbc.co.uk/1/hi/magazine/8441108.stm, accessed 03/03/10.
[2] See www.socialenterprise.org.uk.

The right of employees to be informed about company decisions and to be consulted when proposed changes affect jobs and the organisation of work is a fundamental tenet of EU policy. Two of the early Directives (the EU term for legal requirements which must be turned into national legislation) provided a requirement for representatives of employees to be consulted at times of major organisational change: in large-scale redundancies and in mergers between organisations. The requirements for collective consultation are tough. For example, in the case of large-scale redundancies, defined as when over 20 employees are to be made redundant in a three-month period, senior management must consult employee representatives once the redundancies are contemplated (that is, *before* the final decision has been made), give time for employee representatives to formulate alternatives, and attempt to reach an agreement on the final proposals.[3]

Similar regulations apply to company mergers and some member states have provided strong enforcement methods in their courts. An example comes from France. In the summer of 2009, a government-induced amalgamation of 20 'people's banks' (Banque Populaire) with 17 savings banks (Caisses d'Epargne) was announced, with a probable loss of 10,000 jobs. The national works council of the savings bank asked for information but management refused to supply this. An application to the court led to a provisional prohibition on implementation measures as long as the information and consultation process with the works council on the consequences of the merger had not been correctly accomplished. This ban was lifted three months later once discussions had taken place.[4]

Not every country allows the courts to postpone management plans but quite stiff financial penalties can be imposed. These rights to information and consultation in mergers and large-scale redundancies apply whether or not a trade union is recognised and can be seen as universal employee rights. In the UK, in the recession of 2008–9, the number of complaints heard by employment tribunals, the local labour courts, that employers had failed to consult properly and in good time rose by over 100 per cent compared with previous years.

The EU has produced Directives on European Works Councils (EWCs) applying to multinational companies over a certain size.[5] Roughly a third of

---

[3] See Acas discussion paper (2009) 'Collective Consultation in Redundancies', http://acas. ecgroup.net/Publications/Policydiscussionpapers.aspx, accessed 1/6/10.
[4] EWC News issue no. 4, 2009, http://www.ewc-news.com/en042009.htm, accessed 26/3/10.
[5] http://ec.europa.eu/social/main.jsp?catId=707&langId=en&intPageId=211, accessed 1/6/10.

MNCs covered by the Directives have chosen to create an EWC although some doubt how effective it is in promoting collective consultation (Marginson *et al.* 2004; Waddington 2006). In 2002, a potentially far-reaching Directive was issued concerning 'national' information and consultation arrangements covering all enterprises with 50 or more employees, known as 'information and consultation of employees' (ICE).[6] This may seem a radical step in those countries where the government does not promote collective consultation but in practice it is much less important than originally envisaged. This is because, following extensive lobbying from employers, the hard definition of consultation seen in the earlier Directives was substantially modified. Now an employer can choose to do nothing until, or unless, 10 per cent of employees indicate in writing that they want a works council. The definition of consultation is very vague, being 'the exchange of views and establishment of a dialogue'.

Different countries in the EU have chosen to implement the ICE Directive in varying ways. Countries such as Germany, the Netherlands and France, where there are long-established legal requirements for collective consultation, and even for worker directors on company boards, already had reasonably effective consultation systems through works councils. In these counties, there is a form of 'embedded collectivism' (Paawue 2004, Gumbrell-McCormick and Hyman 2006). The ICE Directive did nothing to add to long-established country practice.

In those countries with no tradition of state-induced collective consultation, such as the new member states from Eastern Europe, and the UK and Ireland. where the tradition of voluntarism meant that the state leaves it to management and unions to sort things out, the ICE arrangements were modified, leaving management largely with a free hand over how they organised collective consultation (Carley and Hall 2008). This reveals a political dimension to the role of management in HRM, that of lobbying at national level. The British employers' aim in lobbying was to minimise, or even stave off, legislation by promoting the productivity agenda and emphasising individual involvement over the preservation of collective, especially union, rights. This 'business agenda' has dominated UK governments since 1997, when what had historically been the pro-union Labour Party came to power. It rapidly changed its view on the role of the state to one of promoting business interests over collective relations (Davies and Freedland 2007).

In practice, in the UK, trade unions have not, with a very few exceptions, sought to use the ICE regulations to promote their interests as some employers

---

[6] http://ec.europa.eu/social/main.jsp?catId=707&langId=en&intPageId=210, accessed 1/6/10.

had feared – what was known as the 'Trojan horse' effect. And very few employees have clubbed together to collect 10 per cent of signatures to negotiate an ICE collective consultation system under the regulations. The way has been open for managements to do as they wish. The response tells us a lot about the ambivalent views of employers toward collective consultation. Up-to-date data on the proportion of companies creating collective consultation systems through works councils or employee forums will not be known until 2012 (see Hall 2010 for a summary of current data). Large firms are more likely than those with between 50 and 100 employees (the smallest category covered by the law) to have an employee forum. MNCs have been at the forefront in creating non-union collective consultation bodies. This has led some researchers to conclude that, prompted by the ICE legislation, 'MNCs are a leading force in the changing contours of representation and voice practice in Britain' (Marginson, Edwards, Edwards, Ferner and Tregaskis 2010: 174). They note that 'both direct and indirect channels were present in the great majority of MNCs' (*ibid.*: 175), confirming the complementarities between individual involvement and collective consultation.

A longitudinal study in the period 2006–9 of 13 private sector companies with employee forums, many founded in response to the ICE legislation, is revealing since it throws light on what consultation really means (Hall *et al.* 2009). In five of the firms studied, there was an 'active forum for consultation' where senior management was proactive in taking proposals for workforce changes on a confidential basis to the consultative forum before they were announced. In two of these, there was an attempt to reach agreement with time given for the employee representatives to formulate a response. This type of active consultation can only happen if the employee side is organised and has a means of consulting the employees and formulating a response. This required management to provide facilities, allow for pre-meetings for the representatives to formulate their response, and organise training for the representatives. In six other cases, management's view was that the consultative body was primarily a forum for communication, allowing representatives to raise matters that concerned them. Management rarely gave information in advance of major changes and, where a strategic change was announced, the representatives were expected to communicate this to the workforce and bring back any concerns. It was unusual for pre-meetings of representatives to take place and many expressed frustration with this restricted role and resigned. It was hard to find replacements. In two cases, the employee forum had collapsed after two years. Management had done nothing to promote it or attempt to make it an authoritative body, preferring instead to use individual involvement as the only means for employees to have a voice.

The critical difference between these cases of collective consultation in practice was the degree to which management was prepared to share plans in advance with employee representatives. Despite all the employee forums having written constitutions which referred to active consultation, when it came to the practice of consultation management, in eight of the companies, managers held on to their preconceptions of their prerogative and the need for unilateral freedom of action. It is only when the law unambiguously requires consultation 'in contemplation' of change, as in large-scale redundancy and mergers according to EU law, that this type of active consultation becomes more widespread (Hall and Edwards 1999).

The decline and changing role of trade unions

Our review so far highlights two 'mega-trends' in employee voice that pose substantial challenges to trade unions: one is the growth in individual forms of employee involvement in workplaces and the other is the advent of non-union and hybrid (union/non-union) forms of representation. Union membership has been undergoing a long period of decline and far fewer employees have their terms and conditions of employment determined by collective bargaining than a generation ago. The decline in union influence is most marked in the private sector in industrialised countries and it is here that the growth of non-union collective consultation has been most evident alongside a rapid growth in individual involvement activities (Boxall, Freeman and Haynes 2007). Surveys of worker attitudes in the Anglophone world suggest that 'while some worker groups need and want traditional union representation, others have moved on to a more developmental orientation to work based on self-help and personal growth' (Boxall 2008: 221).

The dilemmas for the unions crowd in. There is some evidence that unions are not as effective as non-union consultative bodies. Bryson (2004a: 234) observes that 'in general, non-union voice is more effective than union voice in eliciting managerial responsiveness in British workplaces, and direct voice is more effective than representative voice (whether union or non-union)'. He notes that the combination of non-union representative voice with direct voice is 'more effective (in delivering benefits to employees) than any other voice regime' (*ibid.*).

The better success rate of non-union employee forums in dealing with worker needs is explained in a number of interlocking ways. There is clear evidence in Britain that union members report more needs and problems than non-union employees and that 'on-site union representation engenders greater critical awareness on the part of workers and perhaps increases voice-inducing complaining' (Bryson 2004a: 235). Union members can be more critical of voice arrangements than non-members even when collective consultation and collective bargaining is undertaken by the union (Benson and Brown 2010). Union representatives have much lower levels of trust in management than non-union representatives and this tends to be reciprocated by management (Kersley *et al.* 2006: 172). Managers tend to discuss a much wider range of issues, such as production issues and future plans, with non-union representatives than they do with union reps (*ibid.*: 165). One of the reasons for this may be that employee forums made up of directly elected representatives usually cover the whole workforce, representing everyone. Union representatives are naturally concerned to look after the interests of *their* members and negotiate on their behalf in collective bargaining.

Despite these problems, it would be folly for management to ignore trade unions in countries like the UK where just under half of employees work in places where a union is recognised (Kersley *et al.* 2006: 120). In the public sector, this is true for 92 per cent of employees while, in the private sector, one-third are covered by collective bargaining (*ibid.*). In general, public sector unionisation is much higher than in the private sector, and large firms are more likely to recognise trade unions for collective bargaining.

The attitude of management toward unions is a crucial dimension in explaining how successful unions are in recruiting members (Heery and Simms 2010). Kersley *et al.* (2006: 113) show that 60 per cent of the managers they interviewed were neutral about union membership while just under a quarter were either in favour or actively encouraged membership. Only 3 per cent actively discouraged union membership. Where managers were in favour, or proactively supportive of union membership, around 60 per cent of employees belonged to the union. Where membership was discouraged, membership was around the 5 per cent mark (*ibid.*: 114).

A difficult management problem nowadays is how far it wishes to support the recognised union when membership is falling. One option some managers take is to create a collective consultation body for all employees while preserving collective bargaining on pay and conditions with the union: in effect, side-lining the union. An alternative is to persuade the union to join a hybrid consultative forum working alongside non-union representatives, but some unions object to this (Hall, Hutchinson, Parker, Purcell and Terry 2007). Or, more draconically, de-recognise the union, but this step is rarely taken. An option that does not undermine the union's legitimacy is to seek a new form of working relationship with the recognised union based on 'partnership'. This is where discussion focuses on possible mutual gains and exploration of a much wider range of topics, including business strategies that affect the workforce. This, after all, is what top-level collective consultative bodies do.

'Partnership' has become widely accepted in the lexicon of industrial relations (Samuel and Bacon 2010). As a rhetoric, it is very powerful, implying a markedly new role for trade unions, both with employers and with union members, potential and actual (Haynes and Allen 2000). In its idealised form it is (Tailby and Winchester 2000: 365):

> a qualitatively different form of indirect participation or employee representation . . . and offers each of the parties significant gains: employers are able to secure a greater degree of job flexibility and stronger commitment of employees and union representatives to organisational goals; trade unions are offered a more cooperative form of involvement in enterprise-level employment regulation; and employees are promised greater employment security and the opportunity to participate in new forms of consultation.

One of the reasons for a shift to partnership working is that the traditional union roles of job protection through restrictive work rules and gaining above-average pay rises through collective bargaining have been eroded by intense international product-market competition (Brown 2009). What is left is what Freeman and Medoff (1984) call 'voice-response interaction': that is, dialogue and discussion with management about the operation of the firm in general and the management of people in particular. These union roles are depicted in Figure 6.3.

The ability of unions to gain 'monopoly' power in wage bargaining (the top line in Figure 6.3) has been reduced as the coverage of collective bargaining has shrunk and more contracts of employment have been individualised (Brown, Deakin, Hudson, Pratten and Ryan 1998). The dilemma, too, as the model makes clear, is that there is often a trade-off between pay and jobs. Higher labour costs, unless these can be passed on to the customer, make it more attractive to move work overseas or invest in labour-saving technologies and work methods that increase productivity. The middle line in Figure 6.3, showing restricted work practices and 'featherbedding', was common in the 1960s and 70s in established manufacturing firms and in whole sectors like the UK newspaper industry (Martin 1981). This was the case, too, in the British docks where 'custom and practice', or what were rather oddly called 'Spanish customs', controlled actual hours of work, who did what job, and restricted the adoption of new technology (Turnbull, Woolfson and Kelly 1992). Many of these practices have been swept away in the last 30 years, either because of the virtual collapse of the industry, as in ship-building, or by new entrants to the market able to utilise the opportunities of greenfield sites, as we explained in

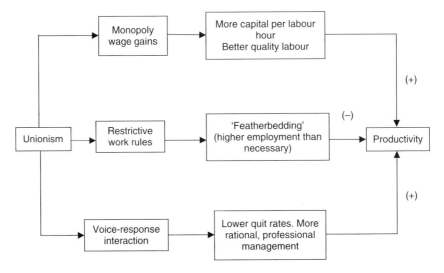

Figure 6.3 What unions do
Source: adapted from Freeman and Medoff (1984).

Chapter 5. In other cases, change has been imposed on the workforce, as in the UK Royal Mail in 2010. In Britain, there are relatively few places left where such controls remain.

The type of transformational change required to sweep away restrictive practices has sometimes been achieved by union de-recognition, for example by the Murdoch newspapers. More often, it has been the outcome of painful and protracted negotiations with trade unions leading to agreements establishing 'full flexibility' with management. These agreements have achieved or regained management the right to design jobs and allocate labour: in other words, a rediscovery of the management prerogative. This process is particularly evident in sectors where global competitive pressures have intensified. The public sectors in many countries have not been immune to these pressures where 'marketisation' has been implemented (Brown 2009).

The bottom line of Figure 6.3 is more diffuse and ambiguous and is centred on the union role in having a positive voice, responding to management proposals in consultative forums, and working with management on change agendas. In effect, with the collapse of unions' traditional roles in many, but not all industries, they are left with a difficult choice of either being marginalised and continuing to lose members, or of seeking new forms of relationship based on cooperation and joint problem solving. This presupposes that management is willing to accept a joint philosophy and work to make it meaningful (Haynes and Allen 2000). It is management's response which is critical here. It is extremely difficult for unions to insist on a high level of cooperation or a climate of 'partnership' (Boxall and Haynes 1997).

All of the partnership deals analysed by Haynes and Allen (2000), Tailby and Winchester (2000), Marks, Findlay, Hine, McKinlay and Thompson (1998) and Martinez Lucio and Stuart (2004) have been about the management of major change. Both unions and managements dealing with major change have to choose between what Walton, Cutcher-Gershenfeld and McKersie (1994) call 'fostering' and 'forcing' strategies or a subtle mixture of both (Table 6.2).

Fostering and forcing as strategies are not simply about the nature of union–management relations but cover management's relationships with individual employees, with different degrees of emphasis placed on obtaining behavioural compliance and generating employee commitment. Walton *et al.* (1994) call the patterns that emerge from these choices 'social contracts' and suggest that, when management want a social contract based on high individual commitment and strong labour–management cooperation, they will be likely to emphasise fostering in industrial relations, although there may be elements of forcing, such as a 10 per cent cut in staffing levels, in

Table 6.2   Conditions that affect choices to force and foster: Walton *et al.*'s propositions

	Conditions that promote:	
	Forcing	Fostering
Objectives of initiating party (management)		
Priority for and ambitiousness of substantive change?	High*	Low
Priority for improvement in social contract?	Low*	High
Expected responses (labour)		
Labour expected to be persuaded by business rationale?	Unpersuaded*	Persuaded
Labour believed to be receptive to social contract changes sought by management?	Unreceptive*	Receptive
Power equation		
Management confident it can force substantive change?	Confident*+	—‡

* The more strongly these conditions are fulfilled, the more likely *unrestrained* forcing.
+ When labour and management are both confident of their power, *unrestrained* forcing becomes even more likely.
‡ No hypothesis for this power condition and fostering.
Source: Walton, Cutcher-Gershenfeld and McKersie (1994: 57).

order to kick start the change process. Fostering strategies will typically require investment in extensive individual involvement and employee communication programmes as well as union-based collective consultation and collective bargaining based on mutual gains.

Walton *et al.* (1994) suggest that an employer will be likely to adopt a forcing strategy when major, dramatic changes are required and when they believe there is no point in extended dialogue with the unions (Table 6.2). A good example is the dispute with cabin crew at British Airways in 2009–10 in which management was prepared to face down a major strike by members of the union. For this strategy to work, management has to believe it can win, or has the resources to survive a long, drawn-out battle to destroy labour resistance. Fostering strategies, on the other hand, typically focus on the need for a move to new ways of working that require, or are predicated on, employees embracing high-involvement work practices, as described in Chapter 5. Here the presumed union role is one of helping the management of change. The union stands to gain in terms of greater institutional security, better consultation and a greater role in supporting skill formation. It may gain some guarantees of employment security although this is now much less likely. In forcing, the union is seen to be the blocker of change while, in fostering, its role is legitimised by management as an ally in the process of change.

Overall, this kind of framework is useful in considering how to manage major change affecting employee interests. It recognises that much of the positive long-term change in companies depends on fostering strategies which build employee involvement and commitment but it also recognises, very realistically, that there are times when company survival depends on job losses or a major restructuring of labour costs. These are win/lose scenarios and management will be forced, as it were, into forcing strategies. The alternative is that management abdicates its responsibility to shareholders by continuing to lose their capital, but this is a basis for sacking the senior executives and for company liquidation.

What are the impacts of employee voice systems?

There is plenty of evidence that voice arrangements can be no more than 'bolt-ons' which become an additional burden on line managers who fail to provide the necessary support to make them effective (Marchington 1989, 1995; Danford, Durbin, Richardson, Tailby and Stewart 2009). This is particularly clear in the chequered history of problem-solving groups like quality circles (Collard and Dale 1989, Hill 1991). Here, developing and encouraging employee voice in problem solving can be a fashionable fad, or worse, a sop, with little expected or experienced from its introduction. Not surprisingly, voice systems which are disconnected from organisational decision making, and are irritants to line managers, have a short life. However, when linked to wider changes in work organisation, as we discussed in Chapter 5, these systems very much form part of the capital O in AMO: the opportunity to participate. We know that employee perceptions of the extent to which they are provided with information by their manager, the degree to which the manager provides a chance to comment and responds to suggestions, are associated with higher levels of job satisfaction and employee engagement, and these variables are linked to performance (Appelbaum *et al.* 2000). Millward, Bryson and Forth (2000: 130) show how positive responses in employee attitude surveys on these variables are strongly associated with the existence of individual involvement arrangements. Gallie and White (1993: 44), in their large-scale survey of employees in the UK, conclude that:

> Participation is of fundamental importance for employees' attitude to the organisation for which they work. It is strongly related to the way they respond to changes in work organisation and with their perception of the quality of the overall relationship between management and employees.

What Cox, Zagelmeyer and Marchington (2006) call 'embedded' voice systems, where the majority of employees take part in direct schemes and where employee forum meetings are held regularly, often lead managers in these firms to assert that they produce positive outcomes (Marchington *et al.* 2001). It is more difficult, however, to find hard evidence on the financial performance of voice systems.

The crucial variable in success is *how*, and *to what extent*, line managers support and activate employee involvement as a process. Research which asks if a practice exists, or even what proportion of the workforce is covered by a practice, is not particularly helpful. Structure does not equate with process (Purcell 1999). In the area of voice arrangements, the supporting organisational climate, especially the level of trust, is crucial in providing the seed-bed for effective participation to germinate (Ichniowski, Shaw and Prennushi 1997).

There are often hard-to-measure changes over time in the effectiveness of voice processes. While employee financial participation is often associated with positive performance outcomes (see Pendleton 2000 and 2006 and Hyman 2000 for reviews of the evidence), Bhargava (1994) suggests that, in respect of profit sharing (which can be a form of voice mechanism if linked to firm ownership), there may be an effect, but it is one-off at the point of implementation and not subsequently. Thus, positive effects can be transitory and restricted to employees who are able to compare the new arrangements with what took place before. New starters can see these developments in a different light and memories have a habit of fading.

Despite the difficulties in evaluating performance effects, we do have some clues. Coyle-Shapiro (1999: 45), in a careful time-series study, found that 'the extent of employee involvement is positively related to the assessment of the benefits of total quality management (TQM)'. In particular, and echoing earlier comments on the crucial role of line managers, she found that 'supervisors have a positive role in getting employees involved in TQM' (*ibid.*). Kessler and Purcell (1996) in a study of joint working parties, where managers and employee representatives jointly deal with workplace problems, found that trust between them increased markedly. This was especially the case where employee representatives, and the employees themselves, were actively involved in all stages of the change process, overseen by a joint working party. Where this happened, well over half of the managers considered that their organisation had benefited 'a lot' from this form of involvement. Similarly, Vandenberg, Richardson and Eastman (1999) found in the insurance industry in North America that employees' perceptions of the quality of involvement processes was related to their job satisfaction and commitment and to the organisation's level of employee turnover and return on equity (see Chapter 5).

Research by Sako (1998), on the impact of employee voice in the European car components industry, is particularly interesting. She showed how the combination of individual involvement and collective consultation had the strongest effect in this industry. Thus, rather than these two forms of voice being alternatives, it was the combination of the two which improved performance. The outcome effect of combined types of voice arrangements was also clear in a large-scale European survey of participation in the mid-1990s. The greater the types of voice systems used, the more likely it was that managers reported benefits from increased output through to declining absenteeism (Sisson 2000). Similarly, Purcell and Georgiades (2007) show that well-embedded, combined voice systems are strongly associated with higher levels of organisational commitment, job satisfaction and the amount of discretion workers say they have in their job. This makes a lot of sense since the two forms of involvement play different roles. While collective consultation can provide employee participation with senior management on strategic issues, individual involvement with the line manager can have a more direct influence on everyday work and working lives (Delbridge and Whitfield 2001).

These findings are repeated when the question of worker needs or problems is assessed. Here researchers ask what needs employees have and whether they are resolved. This approach was adopted in comparative research in the Anglo-American world studying what workers want and what they experience in voice practices (Freeman, Boxall and Haynes 2007). For example, Bryson and Freeman (2007) show that a combination of collective consultation and 'open door' policies, where employees can raise issues with managers, reduces the number of needs reported by British employees. The combination of open-door policies, meetings with the workforce, problem-solving groups and collective consultation seems particularly effective. Interestingly, these authors find that the mere existence of an HR department has no effect in reducing worker needs or problems. It is those HR departments that foster effective systems of employee voice that add greater value.

Surveys of employee perceptions of management responsiveness are similarly revealing. In these, the focus is on the extent to which managers seek the views of employees, respond to suggestions, share information, and treat employees fairly. Both Purcell and Georgiades (2007) and Bryson, Charlwood and Forth (2006) find that the experience of individual involvement is closely associated with positive worker evaluations of management responsiveness. Bryson *et al.* (2006: 448–9) relate responsiveness to productivity. Their research shows very clearly that firms reporting labour productivity much higher than that of their competitors are more likely to have employees who say that their managers are responsive to worker voice.

One of the justifications for the development of voice regimes is that they can contribute to the successful management of change. The facilitation of change is sometimes strategically more important than a fixation with bottom-line financial outcomes (Purcell 1999). In Chapter 1, we referred to the achievement of organisational flexibility as one of the key goals of employers alongside cost-effective labour, social legitimacy and management power. Employee involvement is clearly critical to the achievement of social legitimacy but there is evidence, too, of its role in the pursuit of flexibility or responsiveness to change. We see this at various levels in the organisational hierarchy. Giangreco and Peccei (2005: 1825) looked at middle managers and their responsiveness to change, reminding us that managers are employees too. They concluded that 'the more deeply involved . . . middle managers were in the various aspects of the development and implementation of the change programme [in the Italian firm they studied], the more positive they were about the change and the lower the level of resistance to change that they exhibited'.

Overall, employee voice has a number of critical impacts and we affirm here one of the key themes of this book: HRM needs to serve multiple goals.

Employee voice institutions are important for reasons of social legitimacy. They help to ensure that companies serve a wider public of 'stakeholders' and not only the economic interests of shareholders. But well-implemented, well-embedded voice practices also have economic value, both in the short term through reducing problems in the workplace and, in the long run, through helping to facilitate the management of change. The evidence suggests, however, that the economic benefits of extensive voice systems are more important in those firms seeking to compete through higher levels of employee skill, creativity and commitment. Managers in firms operating in industries where skills are lower, and employee turnover levels higher, are not likely to be persuaded by the 'posh arguments' retailed here. In these contexts, voice practices are likely to remain fairly basic and reflect the beliefs of particular managers as they come and go.

Management style in employee relations

As our review of trends in employee voice indicates, union influence has receded in the Anglophone world and management now has a greater impact on the shape of voice regimes inside organisations, choosing what type of involvement to pursue with individuals and how to respond to societal regulations on collective consultation and negotiation. How do, and should, senior managers think the issues through? What sort of management style does the company want with its employees? Management style can be defined as 'a distinctive set of guiding principles, written or otherwise, which set parameters to, and signposts for, management action regarding the way employees are treated and how particular events are handled' (Purcell and Ahlstrand 1994: 177).

A highly consistent management style is an attribute of 'strong' HRM systems (Bowen and Ostroff 2004). It includes the role of line managers in engaging in supportive behaviour and being responsive to employees in the 'leader–member exchange' (Uhl-Bien, Graen, and Scandura 2000). It cannot be assumed that what top management seek in terms of management style in employee voice will necessarily be enacted by middle and line managers. The fundamental role of such managers in 'bringing policies to life' is increasingly recognised (Purcell and Hutchinson 2007), as we will explore further in Chapter 8.

It is top management, however, who make the critical design choices on what sort of relationships they want with employees directly through individual involvement, and with trade unions and/or elected employee representatives in collective bodies. That is, choices in voice arrangements, while to a greater or lesser extent constrained by legislation, employee expectations and societal beliefs on legitimacy, need to be taken by senior management. Do they wish to avoid, live with, or embrace forms of partnership with representatives and with employees directly? The way these systems of participation are designed and operated is at the heart of management style. Relationships with unions and non-union or hybrid collective consultation bodies range along a continuum from avoidance to high levels of cooperation (Boxall and Haynes 1997). Some, often American firms, seek to avoid all forms of collective worker representation. Others have to come to terms with the union since it has gained recognition and has a significant membership in the firm. Yet others may reluctantly accept the collective consultation imposed by law, but choose to do so with a minimal level of interaction: a 'hands-off' approach. Another group is more positive, seeking collaborative working with employee representatives, providing strategic information, discussing major proposals for workforce change and valuing employee opinion.

These choices are strongly mediated by the type of line-manager behaviour expressed in the way individual workers are managed. In crude terms, the choice is between a 'command-and-control' style and a commitment-oriented one. It is here that the extent of individual involvement comes into play. We have noted that this is more likely to be extensive where workers are highly skilled and where their cooperation is critical to the achievement of strategic objectives. Here, high-involvement, high-commitment management is more likely to be found. In contrast, where labour is easily recruited, where investment in terms of training and skill formation is low, and where work is repetitive with short job-cycle times, a command-and-control style of managing individual workers may predominate.

Figure 6.4 shows the main choices. Choices in such countries as the Netherlands or Sweden, with long traditions, and acceptance of, collective worker representation, may well be different from those taken by the same type of firm in the USA or the UK. While Figure 6.4 stylistically describes six distinctive management styles, in practice each of the axes is a continuum and all styles are the outcome of the complex interplay of tensions and choices between conflicting demands.

Organisations operating with an avoidance strategy, seeking to prevent trade unionism and trivialise voice systems, do so either by forceful opposition (box 1) or by competition in the sense of preferring to provide competitive conditions of employment and extensive use of direct voice arrangements (box 2). The former, described by Guest (1995) as 'black hole' firms, have neither high-commitment policies in their relationship with their employees,

Relationship with employees	Avoidance	Adversarial	Cooperative
Commitment-involvement	Individual-based high-commitment management Extensive direct voice systems *Box 2*	Emphasis on high-commitment management and direct voice Hands-off relationship with representatives Low trust of external unions *Box 4*	High-commitment management Partnership with unions or non-union representatives Extensive direct and indirect voice systems High trust *Box 6*
Command-control	Low trust No voice *Box 1*	Low trust Restricted voice Conflict *Box 3*	Emasculated representatives No real voice 'Sweetheart unionism' *Box 5*

Relationship with trade unions and elected works councils/JCCs

Figure 6.4 Voice systems and management style

nor any positive industrial relations policies of working with trade unions. These firms will tend to utilise low-skill employees and minimise investment in people, as seen in low pay, little training and little job discretion. Box 2 firms, such as management consultancy organisations or software houses, place emphasis on human capital and knowledge management, seeking to get the best out of their core employees and emphasising policies that encourage high performance and retention of the best. They eschew any form of collective representation but emphasise individual involvement through e-mail, intranet, employee surveys and management meetings.

Boxes 3 and 4 include companies caught in adversarial, hands-off relationships with trade unions. Traditional patterns of conflict, and scientific management control systems, are found in box 3. These still exist in some manufacturing companies (especially in developing countries), in parts of the public sector and in parts of the service economy like routine, short-transaction call centres. While formal methods of consultation may exist at corporate and workplace levels, they are generally seen to be ineffective, being marked by distrust and posturing and come to be relegated as 'communication only' bodies.

Box 4 organisations are usually in transition. While formal relationships with trade unions or works councils are marked with distrust and a failure by each party to communicate effectively with the other, direct forms of voice are used, often to bypass and undermine the unions while work organisation places emphasis on high levels of individual involvement. It is here that non-union collective consultation bodies may be created as a union substitution device in the hope that union membership will fade away.

Box 5 is where work organisation is traditionally 'command and control' and relationships with unions or works councils exist more for show than for substance. They do not function as robust participation channels but employee leaders enjoy personal favours and benefits from management. This is sometimes called 'sweetheart unionism' and can occur where the union representatives are more concerned with their own pay and careers than with fighting for their members' interests. While examples are rare, they are sometimes found where company unions or staff associations exist, in part to keep out external unions.

Box 6 firms exhibit strong voice arrangements, combining both direct and indirect arrangements. It is likely that a variety of schemes operate in tandem and are embedded in a bundle of HR practices which encourage high involvement and employee well-being. The leading HIWS adopters, described in Chapter 5, have these types of voice arrangements, especially those that recognise trade unions and where union-management 'partnership' is accepted as appropriate.

Management styles, like the organisational culture of which they are a part, evolve over time but, once established, become difficult to change. It is hard to eradicate embedded assumptions and values held by key groups such as middle managers (Martin 1992, Legge 1995, Batt 2004). These assumptions and mental maps set the parameters of 'how we do things here'. Studies in supermarkets by Rosenthal, Hill and Peccei (1997) and Ogbonna and Harris (1998) show the difficulties that planned cultural change programmes can run into. The assumption that senior management has the power to change workplace culture easily is severely challenged in such studies.

Conclusions

A critical choice at the heart of HR strategy in any firm concerns the extent to which employees are offered a voice in job, workplace and company-level decisions. Particular employee voice arrangements are deeply influenced by senior management's values and by what line managers actually do in practice. They may include direct means of individual involvement or indirect consultation and negotiation through employee representatives or both. The more central are employees to competitive success, the more likely systems to encourage employee voice will be developed. Employee voice practices are naturally critical in those firms in which managers see employee initiative and commitment as central to a business strategy built around innovation or high levels of quality. On the other hand, where employees are less critical to competitive success, which may hinge more on financial and outsourcing strategies, voice activities may be minimal.

However, a key principle we have emphasised in this chapter is that it is important not to create the impression that choices in voice arrangements are solely about the economic performance of firms. The beliefs and values of employees, and of the society of which they are part, provide a crucial extra dimension. Few voice systems and positive union–management relations will exist, or exist for long, unless they are valued in their own right as morally necessary activities in a democratic society *irrespective* of economic outcomes. They are there for reasons of social legitimacy.

The politics surrounding social legitimacy in employee voice varies from one generation to another and from one society to another. The move to market individualism or neo-liberalism in the last two decades of the previous century, especially in Anglo-American societies, has challenged traditional notions of legitimacy, especially in regard to the role of trade unions. On the other hand, in Europe, the EU has increasingly emphasised the rights of employees, including the right to a voice in the affairs of the company for which they work. Regulation, to be effective, needs to have a catalytic effect on beliefs and values, especially on managers who are required to share power and to be accountable to their subordinates, as in the more formal, representative voice systems. The growth in partnership arrangements may be one clue to a change in perspective in some British and Irish companies but, in general, it is much too early to say whether underlying changes in values and beliefs are occurring among managers or what form they might take.

The development of voice systems giving employees access to, and involvement in, management decisions is dependent, therefore, on strategic choices at organisational, national and supranational levels. Historically, many employers have opposed new regulation constraining their prerogatives, yet adapted to it as a political expedient. Taken in isolation, and grudgingly accommodated, voice systems may have little impact, or can become a focus for negative adversarial relationships between management and labour. Seen as an important ingredient in high-involvement models of human resource management, or in its own right, employee voice can positively influence the way people are managed and impact on their sense of commitment. There is evidence in various countries of a growth in voice practices, especially direct forms, partly stimulated by the growing awareness that higher levels of employee engagement are necessary for higher levels of customer satisfaction or product quality.

In terms of HRM, much is at stake here, which is why this domain merits its own chapter. Questions of employee voice are ethical choices with profound implications for every other aspect of HR policy. There are many ways in which they can be approached, as we have reviewed, but let us look at the principle that underpins them all. Trust is the critical underlying variable and it is this, or rather the lack of it, which limits the effectiveness of systems of worker voice. This principle is relevant in any size of organisation: it is not so much the particular voice practices that matter but the level of managerial sincerity and degree of responsiveness that comes through them. If there is an owner-manager or CEO with a strong belief in valuing employees, healthy trust levels are easier to achieve in a small organisation. Higher trust levels are much harder to achieve in larger, more layered organisations in which there is greater managerial turnover and greater potential for slippage between management intentions and management actions. For such organisations seeking to compete through a high level of employee skill and commitment, evidence points to the way in which well-integrated, highly embedded dual channels of employee voice (using direct and indirect practices) can bring positive outcomes for both the organisation and its members. To achieve this, senior executives need to be clear on the fundamental management style that should be adopted in their firm and ensure high levels of consistency within the whole management team across time, as we shall argue further in Chapter 8.

7

Managing individual
employment relationships

Chapters five and six explored principles associated with the organisation of work and with the management of employee voice. These two chapters deal with much that is inherently collective in the workplace or sets the context into which individuals are hired. We turn now to issues associated with managing *individual* employment relationships within this framework. Without compromising the importance of the specific contexts in which the organisation is located, what guiding principles might inform the management of individual employees in the firm?

The disciplines of industrial psychology and 'micro' HRM (Boxall, Purcell and Wright 2007) have always been concerned with managing individuals within the given structure of the firm's work systems and its employee relations style. The focus has been on how to use individually oriented HR practices, such as particular selection, appraisal or training techniques, in order to recruit, motivate, develop and retain individual employees. Textbooks in this tradition typically cover a huge range of practices across the 'individual human resource cycle', a framework based on the idea that most employment relationships are intended to be more than short-term (Figure 7.1). This is typically true, at the very least, for those employees management deems to hold core, strategic value, as discussed in Chapter 4. The cycle of employing such individuals includes a trail of techniques stretching from the staffing process through performance appraisal to training, remuneration, and to other forms of reward, such as promotion. However, in some cases, managers will identify the sort of poor individual performance or misconduct that leads to discipline and, in some cases, dismissal.

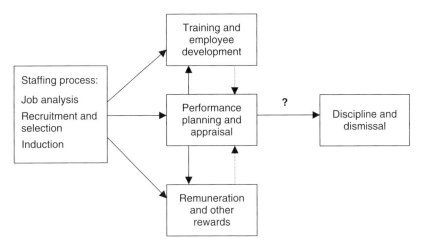

Figure 7.1 The individual human resource cycle

Our concern, however, is with highlighting the underpinning principles that can help managers make sense of this detail. Our interest lies in the important theoretical principles that underpin the welter of HR practices available to managers. In order to highlight these principles, we use the AMO model of individual performance as an important organising framework but, in so doing, we bring 'relationship analysis' into the picture. In other words, we aim to look at the employment relationship from both perspectives: the employer's and the employee's. A relationship will only last if it works, at some baseline level, for both parties. Terms such as 'balance', 'mutuality', 'reciprocity', 'equity' and 'matching' of interests will recur throughout the chapter because stable employment relationships are those in which *both* parties feel relatively satisfied.

The performance equation

We must start with some thinking about the kind of human performances that employers expect. What constitutes a performance? Some performances can be described very objectively (for example, the train did or did not arrive on time) while other performances (for example, how well a public relations manager handles the media or how effectively a teacher handles demotivated teenagers) are much more subjective. In organisations, performance expectations are not always explicitly expressed by management: if they were, there would be far fewer misunderstandings. When they are, however, managers typically define them either in terms of job *outputs* or job *behaviours* or in a mix of the two. Job outputs, such as targets for production and quality levels may be used with individuals or with their teams in manufacturing environments. Output targets, such as a particular level of monthly revenue, are also common with sales representatives, both in territory-based roles and in call centres. Goals are also frequently used with managers themselves (for example, goals for profitability or return on investment) and with business professionals such as lawyers, professional engineers and chartered accountants (for example, billing targets for revenue or chargeable hours). When output standards are hard to define or lie well outside individual control, there is a tendency to use job or task behaviours. These typically involve expectations around how other people, such as customers, employees and suppliers, should be treated in the human interactions that are central to the job. They are common in service roles, in the caring professions, and in the human side of managerial roles. For example, a restaurant manager may have a behavioural script for how a waiter should greet customers in a restaurant and take their orders. Behavioural standards may also be used for how a nurse interacts with a patient or how a manager expresses themselves as a team leader.

However it is defined, the effective management of individual performance depends on some understanding of the factors that drive it. In Chapter one, we referred to the 'AMO' framework. This argues that performance in any kind of role is some function of the individual's abilities, motivation, and their opportunity to perform in the specific context:

$$P = f(A, M, O)$$

On the colloquial level, this model has been around for a long time. Academically, a more formal version of AMO theory can be found in the work of the industrial psychologists, Campbell, McCloy, Oppler and Sager (1993) (Figure 7.2). In their formulation, ability is broken down into 'declarative' knowledge (what we know about things) and 'procedural knowledge and skill' (how we actually go about things). The elements of motivation are also usefully identified. They include the choice to perform, the level of effort applied, and the degree of persistence. However, the role of 'opportunity' is not acknowledged. Like Blumberg and Pringle (1982), we think it is important to have an O factor in the equation because this helps to make the point that individual performance is embedded in a context. To be sure, individual attributes have a huge impact but even the most able and motivated people cannot perform well if they lack adequate equipment or

P = f {Declarative knowledge} × {Procedural Knowledge and Skill} × {Motivation}		
Facts	Cognitive skill	Choice to perform
Principles	Psychomotor skill	Level of effort
Goals	Physical skill	Persistence of effort
Self-knowledge	Self-management skill	
	Interpersonal skill	

Figure 7.2   Determinants of job performance
Source: Reprinted with permission of John Wiley & Son, Inc. From Campbell *et al.* (1993).

technologies – 'the tools to finish the job'[1] – or work in an unsupportive social environment.

What, then, are the implications of the performance equation? For one thing, it clearly reminds us that firms should aim to hire 'motivated capability': people who have the *can do* (ability or capability) and the *will do* (motivational) factors relevant to the job. Both factors are essential. From this basic premise, some authors have developed broad-brush typologies of human performance to assist employee development and succession management activities. One such model, which we have evolved from Odiorne's (1985) 'human resources portfolio', is shown in Table 7.1. The implicit argument here is that performance management needs to be adjusted to handle different individual types effectively. All firms need some blend of 'stars' and 'solid citizens' while aiming to minimise the numbers who fall into the problematic categories – 'marginal performers' and 'chronic under-achievers'. Star employees have the sort of qualities that are important for innovation and path-finding. In knowledge-intensive industries, such individuals can make disproportionate impact, as is recognised in what some call the global 'war for talent' (Wooldridge 2006). It thus pays to think very carefully about their rewards, development and retention. Solid citizens are also vital: they make things happen reliably once direction has been decided. This should never be underestimated because customers want to deal with companies that deliver on promises. The idea of an 'all star' company is therefore impractical. Firms need to manage *both* change and stability: they need to find a way forward while also reaping the profits to be made in a given context (Boxall 1998). A high performing team is much more likely to exhibit a blend of team roles, as Belbin (1981, 1993) demonstrated (see Chapter 2).

---

[1] One of war-time Prime Minister Winston Churchill's most famous pleas was: 'give us the tools and we'll finish the job'. British motivation was not in question but resources were certainly scarce.

Table 7.1 A typology of performance types

Stars	*Ability*: advanced, highly respected technical experts, very capable general managers or highly creative business winners; over time, perceived as having star abilities by most people in the workplace and possibly the industry.
	Motivation: always operate with the necessary motivation; often capable of several periods of outstanding achievement in a single year; but may be vulnerable to 'burnout' and 'workaholism'.
Solid citizens	*Ability*: possess valued technical or managerial know-how related to established business operations; help to ensure the organisation can reliably deliver what it has promised its customers.
	Motivation: always operate with the necessary motivation; generally capable of sustaining performance through some periods of high pressure in a single year.
Marginal performers	*Ability*: could be generally adequate but not able to handle high pressure situations or weak in a couple of critical performance domains; or slightly below most performance standards but capable of improvement through greater personal efforts to improve know-how.
	Motivation: may be inconsistent in motivation ('blowing hot and cold'); or generally motivated but occasionally depressed.
Chronic under-achievers	*Ability*: may have misrepresented their abilities at recruitment; or may be carrying major intellectual or emotional weaknesses which have never been appropriately dealt with; or may be an example of the 'Peter Principle' (promoted to the level of their incompetence).
	Motivation: may be seriously depressed; or annoyingly inconsistent in motivation; or perversely motivated; or may be highly motivated but unable to bridge major gaps in their experience and abilities.

The sort of model shown in Table 7.1 is sometimes used by firms to map the talent they have in particular teams, and plan their employee development and retention strategies accordingly. Table 7.1 is not, however, a precise framework. It is simply a loose approximation to reality. Reality is always more complex.

While recognising the important role of ability and motivation, we ought to base our conceptions of how to manage individuals on a more secure footing. Our concern in the rest of the chapter is to outline theory and research that can assist.

Managing employee ability

Levels and types of ability vary enormously across the human population. At any point in time, a person's ability – their capacity to perform – reflects the knowledge and skills they have acquired through education, on the one hand, and through their experience of work and of 'real life', on the other. Education is a necessary stepping stone for most modern forms of work, which rely less on physical strength and more on the foundational or generic skills of literacy and numeracy taught in basic education and on the various bodies of specialist theory taught in secondary and higher education. These academic skills and theoretical understandings provide a launching pad for learning through work experience. On-the-job learning enables us to apply, critically evaluate, and extend our academic learning. It provides insights and confidence that education, alone, cannot. Both education and experience therefore have a vital role to play in building our abilities. Those who simply have 'book learning' are limited until they can extend their know-how in the workplace while those who simply have experiential learning may be held back from positions that require a higher level of theoretical knowledge.

There are two underpinning factors that affect our potential to acquire knowledge and skills. The first of these, quite obviously, is the state of our physical and mental health. Good health enables us to participate in the kind of activities that build our abilities. Poor physical or mental health will affect our ability to attend work or sustain the concentration needed in the work. A second key underlying factor is our intelligence. Research consistently demonstrates the impact of intelligence or 'general cognitive ability' on our performance (Hunter and Hunter 1984, Judge, Higgins, Thoresen and Barrick 1999, Hunter, Schmidt, Rauschenberger and Jayne 2000). Except in cases of very deprived or traumatised backgrounds, more intelligent people typically secure a better education and gravitate towards more demanding work (Baumeister and Bacharach 2000). The process of tackling more challenging work then develops their abilities further, increasing their value to potential employers and further enhancing their advantages over others. It is not surprising that more intelligent people earn more and get promoted more often (Baumeister and Bacharach 2000, Judge *et al.* 1999). They may not be happier with the intrinsic dimensions of their work or less stressed, something we shall explore further, but they typically get employed in more complex and better paid work.

The crucial role of recruitment and selection

When one looks at the size of the recruitment industry around the world, it seems that practitioners act as if recruitment and selection is the most important human resource function. The research on the critical role of ability in explaining performance suggests they are right to do so. Failure to recruit workers with appropriate competencies will doom the firm to failure or, at the very least, to stunted growth. Firms need to attract and nurture people with the kind of abilities that will make the organisation productive in its chosen industry.

While firms should aim to recruit effectively at all levels of ability, the need to recruit astutely is particularly important where higher levels of discretion or specialised blends of skills are required in the work. As job complexity increases, so does the range of human performance (Eysenck 1953, Hunter *et al.* 1990). Thus, as we move up from low complexity work (such as routine clerical work) to jobs where greater ambiguity is involved in decision making, differences in skills and judgement become more pronounced and are more consequential for the organisation. It is quite possible for one professional, such as a lawyer or an IT consultant, to be several times better than another at the same task. The phenomenon of large performance variation is also commonly recognised in sales work, such as insurance sales (Hunter *et al.* 1990). Some people simply lack the blend of cognitive abilities and personality traits needed (such as a friendly manner plus the ability to pursue the sales deal and not be deterred by rejections) and should not be recruited at all. Among those who do have the threshold abilities, the performance range will still be enormous. In Anglo-American countries, at least, firms commonly find they need 'sales compensation packages' which allow high achievers to earn a higher pay packet better linked to their personal productivity.

Recognising the crucial role of ability in performance, the literature on recruitment and selection is vast. Our concern is not to summarise it but to point to underlying principles. In terms of highlighting the key messages in this literature, it is important to make a distinction between selection practices and recruitment strategies. Selection is about choosing among job candidates. It is about how to make fair and relevant assessments of the strengths and weaknesses of applicants. It is concerned with the value of particular selection techniques. Recruitment strategy is best understood as the way in which a firm tries to source or attract the people among whom it will ultimately make selections. Recruitment strategies include attempts to make the organisation an attractive place to work and attempts to reach better pools of candidates.

As has been noted before in this book (Chapter 3), the literature on selection is an area where concepts of 'best practice' do have a logical place, as long as we bear in mind that such concepts are embedded in a cultural context. In the Anglo-American context, the fundamental issue is how to make selection more 'valid': how to define performance appropriately and how to use techniques that improve the ability of firms to predict which individuals will be good performers (see, for example, Rynes, Barber and Varma 2000, Schmitt and Kim 2007). Hardly anyone would recommend unstructured interviews over interviews where questions have been based on a careful job analysis or over the use of work sample or cognitive ability tests. Across a variety of jobs, the selection literature offers valuable insights into how the process can be made more effective for employers and fairer for job candidates.

The focus of the recruitment literature is somewhat different. The literature here has many more gaps (for comprehensive reviews, see Taylor and Collins 2000, Orlitzky 2007) and the notion of 'recruitment strategy' needs further development. One of the few papers in the area which is useful for considering the strategic questions was written by Windolf (1986). Windolf identifies the task of profiling the ideal kind of candidate and the choice of recruitment channels (among 'headhunting', advertisements, networking and so on) as key dimensions of recruitment strategy. We would add a third dimension to these: the quantity and quality of inducements offered to job candidates. Some firms are powerful recruiters because they are sufficiently well-resourced to be able to pay wage premia which increases their ability to pick and choose in the labour market (Guthrie 2007). The capacity to offer better pay and greater internal development makes it easier for firms to build high-involvement work systems and out-compete under-capitalised firms (see Chapters 5 and 9). Some firms competing for scarce talent develop an 'employment value proposition': a formal statement of the particular benefits they can offer potential recruits (Wooldridge 2006: 16). This may include superior pay, training and career opportunities but can also extend to such factors as the company's reputation for work-life balance or social responsibility (Orlitzky 2007).

Recognising the need to identify what the firm offers by way of inducements, we find the typology of recruitment strategies developed by Windolf (1986: 238–46) a useful framework. An adapted version is shown in Figure 7.3. Firms vary in their labour market power (the vertical axis). They also vary in the extent to which management is creative and proactive in forming

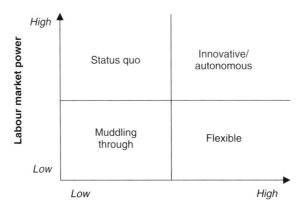

High

Labour market power

| Status quo | Innovative/ autonomous |

| Muddling through | Flexible |

Low

Low   High

**Management creativity and proactivity
in recruitment activities**

Figure 7.3 A typology of recruitment strategies
Source: Windolf (1986: 239).

and reviewing recruitment strategies (the horizontal axis). This framework usefully makes the point that some firms ('status quo' recruiters) have resource advantages but do not use them thoughtfully. Their recruitment practices tend to be conservative, often recruiting from the same social strata and age groups without challenging the way this can discriminate against certain kinds of job seekers. One the other hand, 'innovative' firms attempt to recruit talented people who can help them develop a stream of new products and processes. They therefore use all possible channels to generate a 'heterogenous group of applicants'. Another proactive type, the 'autonomous' firm, plans very carefully for all types of recruitment and aims to 'cream off' the best candidates whatever the condition of the labour market. Most firms classified as 'muddling through' or 'flexible' are small or medium-sized and cannot offer above-average conditions. They do gain some power in slack labour markets but face serious difficulties when labour markets are tight. The two types of firm are differentiated on the basis of the HR expertise they bring to their problems. Flexible firms are more thoughtful: they make more astute use of what little power they have.

The key implication of Windolf's (1986) framework is that firms have something to gain from more creative use of their resources. This is particularly so for small firms competing against much better resourced rivals. As a general rule, more proactive employers do better in tight labour markets: for example, by dropping 'ageist' assumptions and opening up channels for workers over the age of 50. A lot of companies, including many which are well-resourced, still imagine recruitment to be about attracting young workers, fresh from colleges, or after only a few years in the labour market. Such conservatism is out-of-step with the rise in the average age of the workforce and with the fact that age discrimination is increasingly illegal in developed economies. Similarly, the more creative companies have become better at sourcing talent internationally. This includes outsourcing activities to countries such as India – for example, in software engineering – and opening branches internationally to build the firm's human capital pool in growth markets (Wooldridge 2006).

It is also outdated to think that firms can always recruit exactly the employment experience they want in individuals. Sometimes they can, especially when a recession throws lots of highly experienced workers onto the job market, but this should not always be the primary focus of the recruiter. Providing candidates have the truly necessary, base-line qualifications and experience needed in the role, and there ought to be some sharp thinking about what these really are, a more creative approach is to focus on hiring the *underlying potential* of individuals. For example, someone returning to the workforce after raising children may have much better ability to handle conflicting demands in a service role than someone who technically has much more 'work experience'. It may not be conventional to treat life experience as equivalent to specific employment or industry experience but it often makes a lot of sense because individuals hired this way may be more reliable and have better long-term adaptability. A good example comes from a British bank when it opened a call centre. It was rationalising the branch structure and moved 'tellers' who look after customer accounts to the call centre. They were experts in banking but, as it turned out, did not have the 'wow' factor in dealing with customers on the phone. Replacements were sought from people with good interactive skills, used to dealing with personal problems. Taxi drivers, nurses and teachers were found to be ideal because of these underlying abilities. They also knew when to ask for help and soon learnt what they needed to know about banking.

The complementary role of training and development

This discussion of the crucial role of recruitment and selection (which we might call 'buy') helps to put training and development (which we might call 'make') in its context. As our discussion indicates, 'make' cannot be a total alternative to 'buy'. This is obviously true on quantitative grounds: at some point, there has to be an inflow of talent even in large companies with extensive 'internal labour markets'. More importantly, it is true on qualitative grounds. Given the fact of major ability differences in the population, for which companies can rarely compensate, training should be seen as a complement to, rather than a substitute for, careful recruitment.

Having said this, all companies have a lot to gain from encouraging informal and incidental learning on the job (Marsick and Watkins 1990, Hendry, Arthur and Jones 1995). Besides encouraging individuals to try new things and thus learn by trial-and-error, it is typical to expose new workers to the skills of experienced performers. This approach is sometimes colloquially referred to as a 'buddy' or 'SBN' system – 'sit by Nellie' (with the sub-text: 'and do what she does').[2] Alternatively, the direct line manager may play the crucial role of job coach (Purcell and Hutchinson 2007). This may be complemented by some formal on- and/or off-the-job training in technical skills where the expense can be justified by the fact that such skills are needed for acceptable job performance. Much training in the use of new computer software is of this nature.

Informal learning and short-term training are probably the most common approach among small firms in English-speaking countries. The expense is kept down and the costs of losing good workers through 'poaching' – an ever-present risk in tight labour markets – is minimised. The overall approach is often described as a 'deficit model' (simply based on bridging obvious performance gaps). It is wrong, however, to criticise small firms for this kind of pragmatic attitude to training investment. They are acting in an economically rational manner and the problem of under-investing in employee development lies in wider national and industry institutions over which they have no control (Lane 1990, Winterton 2007).

The opportunity to use education and training more powerfully really arises where firms have invested more comprehensively in recruitment, and thus built a labour pool with greater long-term potential (and consequently greater aspirations). Such firms would be wise to maximise their greater investment in human resources. In this context, training and development offers the kind of complementary potential recognised in models of high-involvement work systems (see Chapter 5). Such firms are well placed to consider more ambitious training strategies which involve moving beyond immediate demands in jobs to longer-term employee development. The key principle here is that, in the context of a superior investment in work and employment practices, employee development should not be restricted to a deficit model. Rather, it should aim to build employee potential and the firm's agility over the long run (Dyer and Shafer 1999, see Chapter 9).

---

[2] For a historical reference to the role of 'Nellie' in employee training, see Crichton 1968: 33–4.

Unlike short-term training, long-term development plans involve a more balanced mix of formal training and education (typically off-the-job) and informal coaching and team-building (typically on-the-job). Formal learning can be important to enhance the individual's grasp of relevant theory (the template through which they understand their experience) and their ability to tackle abstract problem solving. This kind of development becomes more powerful when individuals also, or subsequently, face a more challenging work environment in which their informal learning is extended (Marsick and Watkins 1990). There are stages in careers when a mix of abstract, theory-based learning and more difficult assignments help to extend individual abilities and open up more satisfying work.

Deploying ability and developing a career: the employee perspective

This brings us naturally to the point where we should turn the tables and think about ability from the employee's perspective. How do employees think about their capacities and their development over time? Our discussion so far has been driven by the employer's perspective but relying only on one side is unsatisfactory in a relationship analysis.

Research suggests that employees are generally keen to ensure that their knowledge and skills are fully deployed in the work they do. Employees are drawn to work that makes use of their potential. A key contribution to our understanding of how employees think about their skills is contained in a major study of social change and economic life (SCELI) in Britain, conducted in the late 1980s. This study contains a survey of some 4,000 employees (Penn, Rose and Rubery 1994).[3] Through the SCELI study, Michael Rose (1994) has developed the theory that people are more satisfied in their jobs (and more loyal to their employers) when the skills they use in the job ('job-skill') match the skills they actually have ('own-skill'). His work is backed up by a study of 2,460 workers in the Netherlands which finds that those who feel their skills are under-utilised have lower job satisfaction and a greater propensity to look for another job (Allen and van der Velden 2001). These findings are quite a refreshing argument because they imply that most people can be happy in their work, irrespective of how intelligent they are or how many talents they

---

[3] The SCELI sample was drawn from 6 localities – Aberdeen, Coventry, Kirkaldy, Northampton, Rochdale and Swindon – but very closely matches the 'class composition' of Britain as a whole.

have. The key factor for the individual is finding a job that uses the talents *they do* have.

In this respect, Rose (1994) defines three categories. The first are the 'under-utilised' whose talents are not fully engaged (own-skill greater than job-skill). University students doing low-skilled jobs while studying often fall into this category but so too does anyone working in a job which does not make good use of their talents. The second group are 'matched' (own-skill approximates job-skill) while the third category are 'under-qualified' (own-skill less than job-skill). These categories are refined somewhat further in Rose's (1994) analysis of the satisfaction levels of the three groups, shown in Table 7.2. The satisfaction levels in the right-hand column of Table 7.2 indicate how people in these categories feel, on balance, about their work. The study indicates that people who feel their talents are under-employed at work are the most unhappy while those where talents needed and possessed are equivalent are generally satisfied with their work. The findings on the under-qualified represent an amusing, but dangerous, story. People whose talents are inadequate for their work feel quite happy. Not surprisingly, they are the group which is best pleased with management (Rose 1994: 258). After all, management's failure to deal with their incompetence has been very rewarding!

The key point to be taken from Rose's (1994) work, however, is the value to employees of a job in which they can fully deploy their abilities. If the

Table 7.2 Types of skill-matching and satisfaction levels

Skill situation of subgroup	Satisfaction level
Under-utilised	
Low job-skill, moderate own-skill	−27
Moderate job-skill, high own-skill	−15
Low job skill, high own-skill	−13
Matched	
Low job-skill, low own-skill	+1
Moderate job-skill, moderate own-skill	+5
High job-skill, high own-skill	+4
Under-qualified	
Moderate job-skill, low own-skill	+12
High job-skill, moderate own-skill	+13
High job-skill, low own-skill	+33

Source: Rose, M. 'Job satisfaction, job skills, and personal skills', in Penn, R., Rose, M. and Rubery, J. (eds) *Skill and Occupational Change*. Oxford: Oxford University Press. © 1994. By permission of Oxford University Press.

employer wants the employment relationship to last beyond the short term, it is important to get a good match between people's skills and the demands of the jobs in which they are employed. This is captured in the old notion of 'person-job' fit (see, for example, Kristof 1996, Carless 2005).

We need to understand it in a dynamic way, however: people's knowledge and skills typically grow over time and lead to a demand for new challenges. In time, a job that once matched our talents may become boring. Unless the organisation can find a bigger job for us, one that uses our expanded capacities, we are likely to seek 'greener pastures'. Studies in adult life-cycle theory, based on in-depth biographies of middle-aged and older adults, help us to understand this process (Sheehy 1977, Levinson 1978, Levinson and Levinson 1996). They suggest that there will be several times over a person's adult life when they will seek major developmental challenges. According to life-cycle theorists, the adult life-cycle consists of alternating periods of *stability* (structure-building) and *transition* (structure-changing). In each stable period, the emphasis is on pursuing one's goals and values *within* a given structure of key choices. In the transitional periods, one 'questions and reappraises the existing structure, to explore various possibilities for change in self and world, and to move toward commitment to the crucial choices that form the basis for a new life structure in the ensuing stable period' (Levinson 1978: 49). At the transitional points, some people 'externalise' their inner turmoil more than others: changing their job, their address, their spouse, perhaps even their country of domicile.

Research indicates that up to about the age of thirty, most men and women are experimenting with the workplace, finding out what kind of work they do or do not like. Labour turnover rates are generally much higher among the under-thirties than other age groups (Burgess and Rees 1998, Boxall *et al.* 2003). The pattern of stability alternating with change across the life cycle is likely to be similar for both sexes (Sheehy 1977, Levinson and Levinson 1996). There is greater variety, however, in women's patterns (Gilligan 1982). Women who focus on being mothers, and have no paid (or very incidental) employment after their first child is born, have a life pattern which is obviously very different from that of the typical male. On the other hand, women who are not, or chose not to be parents, may have very similar career orientations to men. Paid employment is a very central life interest, if not the most important. A third pattern includes those women who try to balance family and employment (Buxton 1998), either on the basis of part or full-time employment.

Where paid employment makes up a significant element of the life, we can expect both men and women to seek some regular growth opportunity (such as acquiring new skills in the latest technology or extending skills from one career context to another or shifting from employee to self-employed or from part-time to full-time). Periods of reflection and change will naturally occur throughout the lifespan. As a rule of thumb, people seek some kind of significant opportunity to grow every three to four years.[4] The challenge of retaining high performers over the long-term, therefore, becomes one of providing a setting in which developmental challenges can be navigated in-house.

This analysis puts an interesting spin on the issue of change in the workplace. We are frequently told that employees are resistant to change. However, research on job satisfaction and life-cycle theory suggests that people leave firms because their employer cannot offer them *enough* stimulating change (Boxall *et al.* 2003). Generally speaking, firms can do better at designing career opportunities for individuals because more people nowadays are looking to the workplace to find avenues for personal growth. This is the rise of 'expressivism', as Rose (2000, 2003) explains, or what Bryson (2004b: 22) calls the 'aspirational agenda'. One use of performance appraisal systems, which we will discuss further below, lies in fostering a dialogue around personal growth opportunities (Latham and Latham 2000). It often makes sense to use the annual 'appraisal' interview as a vehicle for encouraging the employee to discuss their development interests and use it as a forum for planning ways to match these with opportunities in the firm.

In summary, we have looked at ability from both sides of the coin: the perspective of the employer and that of the employee. In a free labour market, both parties are seeking to meet certain needs, and these evolve over time. The firm is looking to attract and develop the abilities it needs to compete in its chosen industry. This works well for the firm's workers when the jobs the firm offers enable them to deploy their knowledge and skills effectively. When the firm does not offer a good match with an employee's skills and their rate of development, we can expect them to look outside for personal growth. How to balance or match these sets of needs is an issue we will now take further in thinking about motivation and commitment.

Managing employee motivation

As the AMO framework makes clear, ability is not the only factor explaining individual performance. In order for performance to occur, workers must also

---

[4] There is an old adage that 'it takes one year to learn a job, a second year to master it, and a third year to become bored with it'.

choose to apply their capabilities with some level of effort and consistency. *Motivated* capability is the quality that firms most need from individuals: they need people who have the ability to implement the firm's mission and who *want* to do so. One can admire people's abilities all day long but unless the employer can attract such people to work, and to work well, their ability is irrelevant. This means that firms must offer workers sufficient incentives to join the organisation and to do at least an adequate job. And this is simply to survive. As explained in Chapter 4, strong levels of alignment with talented individuals and teams can lead to much better results, helping firms generate competitive advantage. The current surge of interest in employee 'engagement' is a contemporary manifestation of this point. The value that can be generated when employees are highly motivated and committed is being empathised in a range of practitioner and policy publications around the world, including in the influential report to government by MacLeod and Clarke in the UK.[5] However, all of this relies on understanding employee interests and knowing how to align them with those of the firm. Like the employer, the employee is motivated to enter an employment relationship when the benefits in terms of their interests outweigh the costs. For an employee this typically means that the rewards such as the wage level, the intrinsic enjoyment, and the social standing of the job exceed the mental, physical and emotional effort that the work implies and are worthwhile in the light of alternative job offers or simply staying at home. In other words, there must be a relatively balanced relationship or sufficient levels of mutuality in the relationship if employment is to be stable (Barnard 1938, Watson 1986, Boxall 1998, Shore *et al.* 2004, Hom *et al.* 2009).

Aligning interests in employment relationships: the principle of balance

The extent to which employment relationships are balanced is, of course, variable. Both parties make investments in employment relationships and the stability of the relationship hinges on the extent to which these are matched. There is a range of possibilities (Figure 7.4). Both may perceive that they are making high investments, which they consider balanced, but moderate and low levels of investment can also be stable when they are mutual. For example, a great deal of part-time labour in restaurants and shops, often used in peak trading periods, does not involve much investment by employers in

---

[5] http://www.berr.gov.uk/policies/employment-matters/strategies/employee-engagement, accessed 2/6/10.

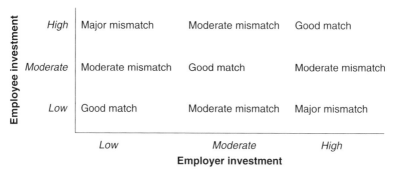

Figure 7.4 Balanced and imbalanced employment relationships

wages, which tend to be at or close to the legal minimum, or in training, because many of these jobs rely more on general social skills and personal reliability than on technical knowledge. However, nor does the relationship involve much investment on the part of the workers who are often students gaining some work experience and passing through such jobs while completing their education. When such workers launch themselves into the full-time workforce, seeking jobs that use their educational investments, their attitudes will naturally be different.

The problem cases in Figure 7.4 are all those relationships which are mismatched because one party is contributing significantly more than the other. There can be various levels of mismatch but it is the moderate to major levels of mismatch that are likely to cause problems. There is now a large literature in occupational health on 'effort/reward imbalance' from the employee perspective, much of it driven by Siegrist's (1996) model, which argues that a combination of high effort and low rewards at work (for example, low pay, low security, and few chances of promotion) generates stress and negative health outcomes. The now famous Whitehall II study of over 10,000 British civil servants found strong support for the effort-reward imbalance model (Bosma *et al.* 1997, 1998). However, imbalance can cut both ways. In some cases, under-qualified, incompetent or low-performing workers are taking advantage of an employer's over-investment in them, as indicated in Rose's (1994) research discussed above. Both parties can fail to reciprocate.

Intrinsic and extrinsic motivators

It is standard to distinguish between intrinsic and extrinsic sources of employee motivation. Intrinsic sources are associated with the work itself. Work is intrinsically motivating when the individual finds it enjoyable and interesting, and naturally wants to get involved in it. It is boring, distasteful or a 'turn-off' when they don't. When we take on any kind of new job, the intrinsic interest we find in the job – how it feels to do it – makes a large impact on us, as we explained in our discussion of work systems in Chapter 5. Extrinsic factors cover the material and social rewards that holding the job delivers, such as the level of pay, the status accorded the role, and the degree of employment security.

Which of these sets of factors looms larger in employee motivation? The answer is that both matter. Table 7.3 lists the results from a survey of some 7,000 British workers conducted in 1999–2000, showing the top factors they rated as their priorities in searching for a job (Rose 2003). The nature of the work itself is clearly very important to whether someone is motivated to do a job. This is chosen first by 27 per cent of people and adding the two columns in Table 7.3 shows that some 45 per cent of people give it as either their first or their second priority, a finding backed up by other major surveys of worker opinion (for example, Clark 2005). There is little doubt that intrinsic enjoyment of a job matters enormously to employees. Many people will rule out certain kinds of job that just don't appeal to them on this basis. Some jobs are a good fit with our personalities and tastes and others are not.

However, intrinsic factors are not all that matters. Pay and job security are also highly valued, rated either first or second priority by 48 per cent and 43 per cent respectively. Such extrinsic motivators should not be underestimated, including what some people would now regard as old fashioned: the desire for job security. But this desire is hardly old fashioned. Employment security remains highly important to most people (Clark 2005). In effect, it overlaps with the pay factor because secure employment generates stable levels of pay and regular income is essential for taking on life's commitments, such as home-ownership and child support. Anyone who has faced a bank manager seeking a loan knows this.

Table 7.3 Job facet priorities of British workers

Job facet priorities	Chosen first %	Chosen second %
The actual work	27	18
Job security	25	18
Pay	22	26
Using initiative	10	13
Good relations with manager	8	13

Source: Adapted from Rose (2003).

In terms of the intrinsic factor, the nature of the work, what then makes a person happy? First, people like jobs they personally find interesting because they deploy their particular skills effectively and offer them opportunities to grow, as noted above in our discussion of employee ability. This means that the happiest people in the workplace are not necessarily those with the highest academic qualifications but those with the best fit between their personal capacities and what they do for a living. Hairdressers, for example, who have good opportunities for personal expression in a sociable job context, come out very highly in British job satisfaction studies while solicitors, who have much higher academic qualifications, are among the least satisfied.[6]

Second, research in most European contexts argues that people like jobs in which they enjoy a good degree of autonomy in *how* they do the work (see, for example, Bauer 2004, Kinnie, Hutchinson, Purcell, Rayton and Swart 2005). Karasek's (1979) landmark analysis of Swedish and US workers concluded that strain and dissatisfaction is greatest in jobs with high work demands but low opportunities for employees to exercise control (that is, low levels of decision authority and discretion). As Karasek (1979: 303) puts it, 'the working individual with few opportunities to make job decisions in the face of output pressure is most subject to job strain'.

Better-quality jobs therefore have a fair level of work demand while using the individual's capacity for decision making and learning as much as possible (Gallie 2005, Mackie *et al.* 2001). There can be problems with both the level of pressure and the degree of decision-making power. Both are important to analyse when job holders report low satisfaction. What might be undermining the job satisfaction of lawyers, for example, could be excessive work pressure.[7] It is possible that lawyers might generally like the work, and be well paid for it, but there is simply too much of it and this eventually undermines their satisfaction and compromises their work–life balance. This is likely to be particularly problematic in the law firms in which the partners have inherited, and collectively perpetuate, a culture of high work expectations.

Originally known as the 'demand-control' model, this theory has now been extended to include managerial support, becoming the 'demand-control-support' (DCS) model (Karasek and Theorell 1990, Wood 2008). This extension of the theory argues that higher levels of employer and/or peer support to

---

[6] http://www.dailymail.co.uk/news/article-473331/Why-hairdressers-fulfilled-jobs.html, accessed 22/4/10. http://www.esrcsocietytoday.ac.uk/ESRCInfoCentre/about/CI/CP/the_edge/issue2/howtofind.aspx, accessed 22/4/10.
[7] http://www.thenewlawyer.com.au/article/can-t-get-no-job-satisfaction/510825.aspx, accessed 2/6/10

individuals may soften the effects of stressful work environments. There can, however, be problems in situations where jobs are intrinsically interesting and empowering, and where the company's managers are supportive, but an individual's personality means they take on much more work than is good for their health. 'Workaholism' of this kind is potentially a killer for the individual as well as posing problems for colleagues and family members, who must somehow cope with an individual whose life is out of balance. Such workers are difficult for supervisors to handle but can sometimes find help in organizations that are well enough resourced to have access to a confidential 'employee assistance programme' (EAP)[8].

Pay systems: purposes and perversities

Although personal expression has grown as a workforce value, the main reason for working is still the need to earn money to live – sometimes called the 'provisioning motive' (Rose 2000, 2003). This should never be underestimated. We all have material needs and a primary motive for changing jobs is to get higher levels of income. This is naturally a critical factor among the low paid and among those who, for whatever reason, feel they are currently underpaid relative to their skills or performance (Griffeth, Hom and Gaertner 2000, Boxall *et al.* 2003, Guthrie 2007).

Pay is the most important extrinsic motivator. It is an essential part of securing an employee's services and a major investment from an employer's perspective. Total labour costs can get out of control and require major restructuring during a recession or a company downturn, as happened in the global financial crisis of 2008–9 in which tens of millions of people were laid off around the world. It is therefore critical to think clearly about what employers should aim to achieve in their pay systems. A discussion of objectives in pay systems is also useful in terms of starting an analysis of the equity or fairness issues that concern employees.

There are three objectives that pay theorists have traditionally advocated for employers in the Anglo-American world (see, for example, Bergman and Scarpello 2001, Milkovich and Newman 2004). The first is the goal of ensuring that the pay system supports the recruitment and retention of suitably qualified people: that is, people who can serve the firm's interests in its chosen industry. If such people accept the firm's pay offers, and do not leave because of pay dissatisfaction, the firm is fundamentally succeeding on this

---

[8] There is an employee assistance professionals' association operating in the USA, the UK and various other countries: http://www.eapa.org.uk/, accessed 4/5/10.

criterion. Achieving this recruitment and retention goal depends, then, on 'external equity' or 'external relativity': in other words, the employer's pay offers are competitive in relation to alternative job offers in the relevant labour market.

Firms that fail on this primary criterion struggle to survive in a capitalist economy. Concern with this fundamental problem is what generates interest in salary surveys conducted by remuneration consultancies and wage-trend data published by government agencies. Remuneration firms will typically advocate that employers pay at or near the market median. Lagging behind the market too much is obviously dangerous but *how far* an employer needs to go to 'meet the market' is a moot point. As Guthrie (2007: 357) explains, there are 'diminishing returns to increases in market pay position'. Firms that systematically pay near the top of the market ('upper and top quartile payers') definitely attract job candidates and do have a better chance of retaining people. However, they run the risk of creating 'honey traps' where people can't afford to leave. This will apply just as much, if not more, to the incompetent employees in the workforce.

The second goal advanced by pay theorists is associated with 'internal equity'. There is a pay hierarchy of some kind in virtually every organisation and employees typically judge the fairness of this hierarchy. The idea, then, is that the employer's pay system should be perceived by employees as fair in terms of rewarding jobs that involve greater demands with higher pay. Job evaluation systems, such as the well-known Hay system[9], were historically developed to foster a sense of internal pay equity (Rock 1984). A job evaluation or 'job-sizing' process typically looks at three (and occasionally four) dimensions of job difficulty:

1. *skill* (the extent of education and prior experience needed to do the job)
2. *effort* (the extent of cognitive complexity involved in the job)
3. *responsibility* (in classical job evaluation, this boils down to the extent of control over people and money)
4. *working conditions* (relevant only in physically dangerous jobs and often not used at all in executive job evaluation).

Measuring and summing these factors in some appropriate way leads to a set of pay brackets into which jobs of different difficulty can be placed after a careful job analysis (for a good explanation, see Armstrong and Baron 1995 or Kilgour 2008). Job evaluation systems constitute a huge part of the work carried out by remuneration consultancies. It is unusual to see them used in

---

[9] http://www.haygroup.com/ww/services/index.aspx?ID=111, accessed 2/6/10.

small firms, which rely much more on their sense of the 'going rate' or low-cost advice on a suitable pay offer from an employers' association. However, they are often found in large, bureaucratic firms with a plethora of managerial and specialist roles and in those public sector bureaucracies, such as the policy ministries, the police and the armed forces, where there is a real difficulty in making job comparisons to an external labour market. They can also be used to help organisations respond to questions about gender neutrality in pay. When men and women largely fall into different occupational groups in an organisation, there can be a question around whether there is 'comparable worth' or 'equal pay for work of equal value' (see, for example, Bowey 1989, Armstrong and Baron 1995, Chicha 2009). Job evaluation can be a way of formally responding to this concern by defining job values and analysing the underlying qualities of the work that make up the different jobs in the organisation.

The law can be very important here. Many countries require that there be equal pay for work of equal value between men and women. Determining 'equal value' requires some form of job evaluation and the courts can look closely at its scientific merit since it is very easy for biases to creep in. It is then necessary to pay jobs equally well that are deemed of 'equal value' and, thus, placed in the same grade but this should include all pay, including bonuses, if they are job-related. Birmingham City Council, one of the largest local authorities in the UK came seriously unstuck when, in 2010, it was ruled that some 5,000, mainly women, workers had been underpaid for at least 10 years.[10] The council had been paying bonuses to workers in some male-dominated jobs, such as garbage collectors, but not to workers in female-dominated jobs, such as school cooks, but now deemed of 'equal value'. One estimate puts the cost of correcting these 'anomalies' at £600 million! One of the solicitors representing the women workers said 'the fact that Birmingham City Council simply failed to acknowledge it had a problem should be a warning to other (employers) who continue to deny their female employees their basic rights'.

Issues of internal equity can generate strong feelings. However, it should be apparent at this point that the goals of external and internal equity can come into serious conflict. The external labour market is hardly ever under the control of an individual organisation, and strongly held views of an internal pay hierarchy can easily be disturbed by movements in the external labour market for particular occupations. For example, while executives in other functions

---

[10] http://news.bbc.co.uk/2/hi/uk_news/england/west_midlands/8647072.stm, accessed 2/6/10.

may not think that IT specialists are worth more in terms of job size, if there are major shortages of IT skills in the labour market, firms are well advised to favour external competitiveness over outdated perceptions of internal equity. The risk is that the firm's pay offers will fail to motivate good IT people to join and will only retain those existing IT employees who are less competent. It is therefore unwise to run a firm's pay system in a free labour market simply, or primarily, on historical notions of internal equity. Job evaluation experts explain that firms need to periodically relate their internal job distinctions to the external labour market (Armstrong and Baron 1995, Kilgour 2008) and it is clearly important to retain the flexibility to respond to changing conditions for different occupations if one wishes to recruit and retain suitable people. It is important, therefore, to take care that the goal of internal equity works within the fundamental priority for the business of recruiting and retaining talented employees effectively.

The third goal typically espoused by pay experts in the Anglophone world is that of 'performance equity'. As noted earlier, within any given job, some people will perform at a much higher level than others and this variation grows as jobs become more complex. Some form of variable or performance-related pay (PRP) is therefore attractive to higher performing employees and lack of opportunity to be recognised for their higher productivity can demor-alise them or induce them to go elsewhere (Trevor, Gerhart and Boudreau 1997, Boxall *et al.* 2003). Some form of PRP is also common when manage-ment wants to incentivise certain kinds of behaviour and is not constrained by rules negotiated in collective bargaining. Instead of having a single 'rate-for-the-job', many organisations now have a salary range or 'range of rates'. PRP can take the form of 'merit pay' where an increase based on performance is permanently added into the pay packet, typically following an annual pro-cess of performance appraisal or review. Higher performing employees are thus advanced up the salary range for their role. It can also take the form of some kind of bonus (not permanently added into the pay packet), either on an individual, team or company-wide basis. These forms of PRP are not mutually exclusive. Some firms have layers of PRP, especially for their senior executives.

What kind of effects can such systems achieve? An interesting analysis in this regard is contained in a study of individual bonuses conducted by Lazear (1999), who gained access to the records of the Safelite company, a firm which installs automobile window glass, and which changed in 1994 from time-based to piece-based pay (with a minimum hourly wage guarantee). Full data was available on worker output before and after the change in the pay system. The data revealed that overall productivity increased by 44 per cent after the change to performance-related pay. Lazear was able to show that the firm benefited in two ways: high-potential workers increased their output (an 'incentive effect'). But he was also able to show a 'sorting effect': the rate of labour turnover of higher performers dropped and more workers of high potential were attracted to the firm. At the same time, lower performers tended to leave in search of more secure payment regimes elsewhere. This is functional, not dysfunctional labour turnover. By the end of 1995, Safelite's workforce was on average much more productive than it had been when associated with time-based wages alone.

The study is valuable because Lazear (1999) notes some of the critical contingencies which make it a case where individual bonuses will work well: the work is highly individualised, it is quite observable, and cooperation in teams (for which group bonuses may be more appropriate) is not important in this company's business. Based on this and other studies (O'Neill 1995, Campbell *et al.* 1998), we summarise the factors that favour individual PRP and those that favour team-based PRP in Box 7.1.

Box 7.1   Supporting conditions for performance-related pay

Good conditions for individual performance-related pay:

1. Individuals have high job control
2. There is high performance variation among individuals due to individual abilities or efforts, not primarily due to their context
3. Management can make fair individual performance attributions and will reward for them
4. High-performing individuals expect the firm to reward them, by pay and/or promotion, for their individual productivity (or will leave or reduce effort)

Good conditions for team-based performance-related pay:

1. There is a high level of interdependence among team members
2. There are only minor performance differences among team members (i.e. there is little 'social loafing' or 'free riding' in the team)
3. Management can, and will, work with the team to create a fair system of team goals (with good 'line-of-sight' from team efforts to them)
4. Management can, and will, work with the team to create good team development and ongoing support (many people will need greater training and coaching to become better team workers)

Box 7.1   (Continued)

5. Performance rewards are not overly diluted by large numbers of recipients
6. High-performing team members see performance rewards as fairer at the team-level than at any individual level

Most pay researchers validate the importance of these conditions and argue that various contingent factors will affect choices of pay systems over time (for example, Kessler 1998, Guthrie 2007). Wood's (1996) study of pay systems in a sample of British manufacturing firms pursuing 'high-commitment management' is instructive. Many 'best-practice' models of HRM would advise such firms to adopt a serious element of variable remuneration but Wood finds that UK manufacturers pursuing higher employee commitment are circumspect about bonuses. If using any form of PRP, they are more likely to add merit pay permanently into the salary, so it is not 'at risk' from year to year. When one reflects on Wood's findings there is an intuitive logic to them. Employers may well avoid individual bonus systems if they discourage the kind of flexible attitude the firm seeks (Wood 1996: 65, 72). If wanting higher production quality, it can be safer to use the supervision process to brief employees on a regular basis and to change their focus when necessary. The advantage of time-based pay systems (either an hourly wage or an annual salary) is that they are actually more flexible in terms of managing priorities as they change. The company is not locked into a specific set of targets linked to pay and can more readily shift its goals without undermining confidence in the pay system.

It is, in fact, far from essential to manage employee behaviour through variable pay. Time-based payment in the context of instructions and feedback from a supervisor ('direct supervision') is actually a much more common method of managing employee behaviour. One of the risks in PRP systems is that they will create 'perverse incentives': for example, when goals linked to pay channel the employee's actions too narrowly or towards a misguided target (Kessler and Purcell 1992). All pay systems contain perversities and have the potential to become demoralised. This can happen, for example, where there is an initial incentive effect but changes in the business context that employees cannot control – such as a downturn in the economy or the entry of a powerful, new rival firm – mean that the bonuses disappear or fall to a level that is no longer significant enough to motivate.

The greatest concern currently with PRP schemes relates to the growth of such schemes and the related inflation in executive pay that took place in the 1990s and continued throughout the first decade of the twenty-first century (Bartol and Durham 2000, Sisson and Purcell 2010). Along with senior executives, strategically placed staff in financial services and investment banking enjoyed a spectacular bonus boom, as we noted in Chapter 1. In 2006, it was estimated that some 4,200 individuals in the City of London would earn an annual bonus of over one million pounds.[11] With this enormous largesse came an expansion of expectations: some 93 per cent of financial sector staff in London then expected a bigger bonus than the previous year. Given the amount of money allocated to these schemes and the escalation of expectations, it is less obvious that shareholders are benefiting: recalling Chapter 3, one would hardly call this a 'best practice' but, potentially, a serious problem with conflicting interests over the appropriation of profits, as noted in Chapter 4. Elite PRP schemes have created more, rather than less, shareholder concern with appropriation problems in companies (Bruce and Buck 1997, Conyon 1997), while also fuelling concerns about the legitimacy of extreme pay inequalities within society and across sectors of the economy (Kochan 2007).

The worst fears about PRP schemes did, in fact, materialise in the global financial crisis of 2008–9. In the banking sector, particularly in the USA, it was common practice for mortgage brokers, retail bank staff and investment bankers to receive a bonus based on their roles in selling mortgages and financing them through mortgage securities. This went along swimmingly for several years as the property market boomed. Unfortunately, these performance bonuses were based on short-term targets and faulty assumptions about the property market (Stiglitz 2010). Many loans were sold to people at great risk of not repaying them ('sub-prime' loans) and then repackaged via investment banks to pension funds and other investors around the world who were ill-informed about the true risks. Tragedy struck when the property bubble burst, to the disillusionment of those who thought that property inflation would go on forever. Tragedy turned to farce when many bankers profited not only from the bonus-generating financial instruments that helped to fuel the boom, but also from the government bail-outs of the banks afterwards, while shareholders were losing capital and a range of workers were being laid off, not only in banking but well beyond it (Stiglitz 2010). In an attack on the perversities of this kind of bonus culture, the British Labour government instituted a

---

[11] Teather, D., 'The bonus bonanza', *The Guardian*, 4 November 2006, 27–8.

'bank payroll tax' on bonuses of more than £25,000 paid to employees between 9 December 2009 and 5 April 2010.[12] In the USA, the outrage was, if anything, greater. The Obama administration appointed a 'Pay Czar' to regulate the remuneration of top executives in US companies bailed out by public money in the crisis.[13]

This huge public interest in executive pay does seem to have prompted some re-thinking about executive PRP. While the bonus culture has quickly re-emerged, there are now more promises to take care in building a link between employee bonuses and *longer-term* measures of a company's performance. Excessive levels of bonus pay linked to short-term sales of highly risky, and poorly understood, financial products not only tripped up financial institutions but contributed to a wide-ranging economic and social disaster. If ever one needed an example of the power of ill-conceived approaches to HRM to do more harm than good, this was it.

What can companies do, then, to minimise the potential for such PRP schemes to become so perverse? In one US study, Martell and Carroll (1995) obtained detailed responses on HR practices for managing top management members, as well as assessments of business performance, in a sample of 115 strategic business units based in 89 Fortune 500 companies. The study found that the practices associated with better management performance were:

- very selective recruitment (but whether executives were hired from within or outside the group did not have an impact)
- high external relativity in pay (implying that firms should try to pay executives well in terms of the labour market)
- rigorous use of performance planning and appraisal (while there were no relationships between the bonus systems used in these firms and business performance).

Martell and Carroll's study reinforces the argument in this chapter about the crucial role of recruiting for good ability in the first instance. It also produces interesting evidence that having ongoing dialogue around desirable objectives for executives (a well-led, well-implemented performance appraisal system) is more important in fostering good performance than having bonus systems. Of course, this does not invalidate the need to pay them well in terms of the external labour market, something which correlates with hiring the best candidates.

---

[12] http://www.guardian.co.uk/business/2009/dec/09/bank-bonus-super-tax, accessed 22/4/10.
[13] http://www.reuters.com/article/idUSN2220981520100322, accessed 22/4/10.

What the study suggests is that the desired results of bonus systems (getting managers to focus on the right things) can be achieved more effectively (and, almost certainly, more cheaply) by strong attention to performance planning and feedback, a subject which we will discuss further below.

All of this underlines the point that the question of the best way in which to align employer–employee interests through pay needs very careful handling (Kessler 1998, Guthrie 2007). As a general rule, pay systems should be designed to recruit and retain the kind of people the firm needs ('external equity'). This requires competitive (but not necessarily excessively generous) pay ranges and implies some way of fostering 'performance equity' within the structure in order to retain high achievers. Serving 'internal equity' is important, too, but not in a way that undermines the firm's ability to recruit and retain. However, there is a need for great care whenever the goal of performance equity is expressed through schemes that aim to incentivise particular kinds of behaviour: such schemes work best when certain key conditions are met and when they do not create perverse incentives. If major perversities are possible, as has recently happened with bank bonuses, other forms of performance management are desirable or bonuses need to be linked much more closely to the firm's long-term performance. Among operating-level workers, individual bonuses are only sensible when team effects are not important, when workers are able to reach high performance through their own discretionary efforts, and without limited resources, management politics or other factors limiting them. In field-based sales work, these conditions can quite often be achieved and sustained for serious amounts of time. If, however, such conditions cannot be carefully orchestrated or are not desirable (because high levels of team cooperation are wanted), firms should tread warily or consider more group-based options (such as team or company-wide incentives). The sort of difficulties that can arise mean that careful firms ensure that full consultation with the parties concerned is undertaken in any new form of pay-system design (Bowey and Thorpe 1986, Purcell 1999). The area of pay incentives is one of those dimensions of HRM that is extremely sensitive to the 'how' of implementation: many a bright idea has come to grief because of failure to study the potential for interest conflicts in the particular context and consult the stakeholders, including both the target employee group and their direct managers.

The 'performance of performance appraisal'

The argument so far has referred, in passing, to the issue of performance planning and appraisal systems (typically shortened to 'performance appraisal'

(PA) systems). Such systems are formal methods of planning and evaluating employee performance that involve employee interviewing (typically annually) to discuss work goals or behavioural standards and the individual's achievement in terms of them. In goal-based systems, new goals can then be agreed for the next year or period. But PA systems are not just about performance planning and feedback. They frequently require the line manager to make a recommendation about pay (for example, a merit-pay increase within the salary range) and may provide input into decisions about promotion to a higher position. They also very often include some form of planning for employee development, including training, coaching and task-assignment actions, although some organisations separate these activities in case the 'developmental' discussion is impeded by the 'evaluative' discussion going on around the individual's performance.

PA systems, then, are among the most complex kinds of HR practice. They are not actually a single HR practice but a nexus of various HR practices (as implied in Figure 7.1). Surveys of HR practices that treat PA as a single practice are, thus, making a fundamental error. The complexity of PA systems means that their design and quality of implementation varies enormously. A lot can go wrong with them, which can undermine employee motivation and trust rather than enhancing these underlying variables. The notion that 'performance appraisal improves performance' because the 'performance' word is embedded in it should be treated circumspectly, as with any HR technique containing the word 'performance'. Each element in a PA system requires advanced skills of the line manager and carries risks. Reviews of research on PA systems stress that they can play a productive role, but only if they are managed astutely (Latham and Latham 2000, Marshall and Wood 2000, Bradley and Ashkanasy 2001, Latham, Sulsky and MacDonald 2007).

Despite the formidable challenges, executives have long been able to see a valid and important role for formal performance appraisal, particularly in large organisations with major numbers of salaried staff (Huber and Fuller 1998). Research in Britain shows that PA systems are growing as a way of managing individual performance, particularly in managerial and professional work (Gallie, White, Cheng and Tomlinson 1998, Kersley *et al.* 2006). As noted above, the spread of performances in work with higher levels of discretion is vast and it seems only logical to manage each 'human asset' in an individualised manner. From the employee's perspective, there is also potentially something to gain from a PA system. PA systems can form a basis for discussing the individual's job and their career development in a way that only otherwise occurs at their recruitment interview. This means that employees are often keen to have an annual review: it is frequently their best chance to talk back. PA systems provide a one-to-one forum for employee voice which at least the more assertive type of individual finds useful.

The problem we must wrestle with is that good intentions in the PA area have often been associated with disappointing outcomes (Latham *et al.* 2007). As well as huge variability in how (or even whether) managers conduct formal interviews, research has long confirmed the existence of 'rater bias', stemming from use of invalid performance criteria and lack of representative data on performance (amongst other things). As a result, some industrial psychologists now routinely distinguish between 'objective' and 'rated' performance in organisations (Hunter *et al.* 2000). The implication of this distinction is that good performers may be under-recognised while poor performers may be over-recognised.

Let us take this further. Like any other performance, carrying out a performance appraisal can be analysed through the AMO framework. There are, first of all, ability or 'can do' factors. Can managers set appropriate goals or performance standards? Can they do so consultatively with people who need, or want, this kind of involvement? Can they then accurately discern performance differences and give performance feedback that is fair? Can they identify the factors that contribute to an individual's performance and recommend good ways of developing their capacities and enhancing their motivation and opportunity to perform? Can they see how to have the kind of conversation that will retain high performers? Just listing this string of questions suggests we have a very tall order here, which makes a high demand on the planning, analytical and people-management skills of managers. These are often called the 'cognitive problems' of PA systems and management training can be useful in dealing with them, especially if it actually involves practice, with feedback, at better techniques (Latham and Latham 2000). The need to develop managerial skills in these difficult tasks is now widely recognised as important in implementing a PA system.

However, it is also now very clear that the performance of managers in PA systems is not simply about the 'can do' factor, their knowledge and skills. Key writers have recognised that the problem of PA-performance is not simply cognitive. It is also concerned with managerial motivations (the 'will do factor') and with their opportunity to perform. The work of writers such as Murphy and Cleveland (1991) and Huber and Fuller (1998) points out that managers act in a political context. As Longenecker, Sims and Gioia (1987: 190) put it, 'few [performance] ratings are determined without some political consideration'. Managers have goals of their own that include personal survival and advancement and that may not include giving accurate appraisals. In any organisation where people 'rub shoulders' daily, a common syndrome is conflict avoidance, leading to inflated appraisals (Longenecker *et al.* 1987). Managers who must continue to work with the people they appraise tend to avoid actions that involve confrontation or conflict escalation. They are therefore often prepared to give soft appraisals that 'don't rock the boat'. They take care what they commit to writing. This typically means that poorer performers will drift up the rating scale and will thus gravitate to higher pay levels, making them less likely to leave (a 'honey trap'). On top of this, when higher-level managers do not support lower-level managers who wish to challenge poor performance, there is very little chance of building an organisational culture in which it is appropriately managed. Addressing poor performance is a risky personal strategy in such an organisation: better to leave the problems alone and pass them on to the next manager.

Soft appraisal ratings are probably the most common political syndrome in PA systems but, at the other extreme of the political spectrum, there are the managers who are motivated to 'do down' talented individuals or 'rising stars' who threaten them. There is a 'dark side' to personality which can affect leadership behaviour (Burch and Anderson 2008). Some managers, as Kets de Vries and Miller (1984) argue, have dysfunctional personality syndromes including 'powerholic' problems and infantile jealousies of more productive people. Politically shrewd managers may use the PA system to exact their revenge on political rivals or to hobble an individual's chances of advancement.

Admitting the possibility of motivational/political problems implies that senior managers must improve accountability mechanisms around PA systems – for example, requiring lower-level managers to summarise and justify all proposed evaluations in advance of interviewing any employees (Marshall and Wood 2000). This means the higher-level manager can form a sense of how rational the proposed ratings are, based on their knowledge of the people involved and the unit's results. If they are all being rated highly, but the team, as a whole, is doing poorly, something is probably wrong. Similarly, if some people are being rated harshly when other evidence suggests they are high achievers, who also happen to speak their mind, something is probably wrong. Senior managers can also improve systems by spending better time clarifying their purposes and how key linkages to rewards and development will actually be achieved consistently in practice (Marshall and Wood 2000), including through ongoing training and coaching of managers. All of this is hard work and senior managerial commitment to doing it sets the opportunity–context for effectiveness in the 'performance of performance appraisal'.

It seems, then, that PA systems can be used effectively when they are well led and well resourced. In this light, small firms might be well advised to stick with good informal performance management and some 'golden rules' (such as aiming to hire as well as they can, intervening early in any case of poor performance, and doing what they can to recognise and retain their best performers). In large organisations, however, such as public companies and government ministries, the scale of the problems associated with planning work and rewarding performance is simply too great to rely on informal methods, as we see in the fact that the use of PA systems continues to grow in large organisations (Kersley *et al.* 2006). It is hard to see how multinational firms, involved in time-consuming expatriate management, can operate without a formal PA system for assessing performance (Dowling *et al.* 2008). The challenge in these contexts remains one of making formal PA systems reach more of their potential.

Psychological contracting and employee commitment

As this discussion implies, there is often much more going on below the surface of HRM than meets the eye. Our analysis of employment relationships should never to limited to the surface layer of HR practices – or a simple counting of which ones exist in a firm – but needs to examine the nature, and the quality, of the underpinning processes (Purcell 1999). The theory of 'psychological contracting' represents an attempt to analyse the attitudinal variables that need careful management if a positive motivational climate is to be built, and sustained, in an organisation over time. This is not so much about 'what' rewards are attractive, but about 'how' the reward system should be managed. There are important lessons here in terms of the relationship analysis that is central to this chapter.

As various writers have noted, early sources on the notion of psychological contract placed their emphasis on shared expectations between the employer and the employee (Wolfe Morrison and Robinson 1997, Coyle-Shapiro and Kessler 2000, Shore *et al.* 2004). Schein (1978: 48) defined the psychological contract as 'a set of unwritten *reciprocal expectations* between an individual employee and the organization'. He developed a simple model which argued that successful employment relationships involve *matching* organisational needs with individual needs (Schein 1977, 1978), as we emphasised above. Individual needs are seen to be changing across early career, mid-career and late career phases, again as emphasised earlier. On the other hand, Denise Rousseau (1995), a prominent writer on psychological contracting, defines the psychological contract as an individual's beliefs about the terms of their relationship with the organisation that employs them. Spot or 'transactional' contracts have very little psychological content but the standard, open-ended employment relationship has lots of 'relational' content (MacNeil 1985, McLean Parks and Kidder 1994). The distinction between the two is particularly relevant to the consideration of differences between core and more peripheral types of employees, as discussed in Chapter 4. A range of contrasts is usually made between transactional and relational contracting (Table 7.4). These types are best understood as located at the ends of a continuum, rather than as absolute categories.

An example of how a psychological contract is formed is shown in Figure 7.5. For Rousseau, the employment contract is 'fundamentally psychological – agreement exists in the eye of the beholder' (1995: 6). The rectangular boxes indicate the individual's thinking and work orientations while the words in the ovals indicate processes from the organisational side. The formation of the individual's psychological contract is shaped by recruitment claims and company policies but also by social cues in the work environment. The diagram helps to illustrate how difficulties can arise. The individual in this case forms the view that they are being promised early promotion in exchange for hard work. They come to rely on this as a kind of promise but it is really a false assumption. People often conflate 'hard work' with performance, concepts which may overlap but which do not perfectly coincide because of ability

Table 7.4 The continuum from transactional to relational contracting

Transactional contracts	Relational contracts
Specific economic conditions (e.g. wage rate) as primary incentive	Emotional attachment as well as economic exchange
Limited personal involvement in the job (e.g. working relatively few hours, low emotional attachment)	Whole person relations (e.g. growth, development)
Close-ended timeframe (e.g. seasonal employment, 2 to 3 years on the job at most)	Open-ended time frames (i.e. indefinitely)
Commitments linked to well-specified conditions	Both written and unwritten terms (e.g. some terms emerge over time)
Little flexibility (change requires renegotiation of contract)	Dynamic and subject to change during the life of the contract
Use of existing skills	Pervasive conditions (e.g. affects personal and family life)
Unambiguous terms readily understood by outsiders	Subjective and implicitly understood (i.e. conditions difficult for third party to understand)

Source: Rousseau (1995: 91–2).

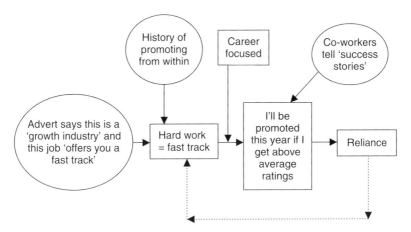

Figure 7.5 An illustration of the formation of a psychological contract
Source: Rousseau (1995: 34).

and resourcing differences. Their personal assumption that they can be promoted in a single year is just that: a personal assumption. It may have been encouraged by the recruitment rhetoric but it is not grounded in anything the employer has specifically promised. In actual fact, something like 2 per cent of individuals are promoted in this organisation in a single year (Rousseau 1995: 34), so the individual is more than likely heading for disappointment and disillusionment.

Given the prevalence of scenarios like that depicted in Figure 7.5, it is not surprising that research on psychological contracting finds that psychological contracts are frequently 'violated' (Wolfe Morrison and Robinson 1997). A study by Robinson and Rousseau (1994) argues that violation of the psychological contract is the norm rather than the exception. The study tracked 128 MBA graduates two years after their graduation. Some 55 per cent said their psychological contract had been violated over this short timeframe. Robinson and Rousseau (1994) inject a sense of proportion into this: there are obviously degrees of violation. Some aspects of an employee's psychological contract are more significant than others. It is therefore helpful, as Wolfe Morrison and Robinson (1997) suggest, to make a distinction between 'violation' and a less damaging kind of 'breach'. It is also helpful to recognise that some violations are owned up to and explained by management. In certain situations, employees do accept as credible the explanations they are given for violations (Rousseau 1995: 127).

The risk, however, with more serious violations of psychological contracts is that they undermine employee commitment and valuable employees leave prematurely (before the employer has had a good payback) or stay and adjust what Organ (1988) calls their 'organisational citizenship behaviours' (OCBs). OCBs include a range of cooperative and caring behaviours that can be very valuable to collegial relations, teamwork and client service in a firm. If an employee who has tried to work hard feels violated in some important aspect of their psychological contract, the argument runs that they are less likely to work sacrificially in future. They become less 'engaged', to use the current terminology. Much as predicted by Adams' (1965) famous 'equity theory', they adjust their work inputs (effort) to take account of the lowered outputs (rewards) they are actually experiencing at work.

There are, however, problems with the approach that Rousseau (1995) takes to the notion of psychological contract. As Guest (1998) argues, Rousseau's model makes the psychological contract entirely subjective, something only in the head of the employee. This means that it cannot be seen in any meaningful way as 'contractual'. If one cares about the plain meaning of words, a psychological contract must mean, surely, that employer and employee *share* some common understandings that go beyond what was written in their employment agreement, as earlier writers on psychological contracting argued.

Guest (1998) also points to the huge difficulty that multiple agency presents in large organisations. Given the fact that so many managerial actors can be involved in the recruitment and then the ongoing performance management of an individual, it is hard to see how management can ever maintain a consistent set of psychological messages. Breach and violation are virtually inevitable and perhaps employees come to realise and accept this. While these are serious difficulties, Guest (1998) still sees some value in the notion of psychological contract as a way of analysing the variety of individual employment relationships that exist in today's labour market. As suggested in Chapter 4, it can be used in the analysis of core-periphery employment models in firms. In core-periphery models, management is often trying to send a different set of messages to different groups which vary in their centrality to the firm's mission (Lepak and Snell 1999, 2007). The notion of psychological contracting is also important for the way in which it helps us to understand the dynamics of employment relationships.

Expectations and trust dynamics

A key paper which underlines the dynamic nature of psychological contracting has been written by David Grant (1998). Grant points out that concepts of psychological contracting really stem from expectancy theories of motivation. The key dimensions of expectancy theory are shown in Figure 7.6. The text boxes with borders are the elements of the pure theory of expectancy while the

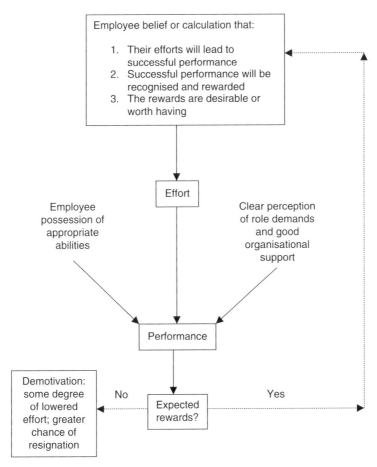

Figure 7.6 The expectancy theory of motivation and performance (with added
factors to recognise the full 'performance equation')
Source: Adapted from Watson (1986: 119).

other parts of the diagram have been inserted to build a more comprehensive
model of individual performance. We have done this by drawing on the work
of Tony Watson (1986), whose concept of the implicit contract is synonymous
with the psychological contract, and by drawing on the performance equation
which is fundamental to this chapter.

Expectancy theories of motivation do not tell us about the content of
human motivations (about pay, security and intrinsic job satisfaction, for
example) but make the fundamental point that our *ongoing* motivation at
work is affected by the expectations we form *and* our experience of whether
these are met over time. On a practical level, expectancy theory tells us
three quite important things. First, impossible goals will frustrate rather than

motivate. Most of us see little point in putting forth effort if we expect to fail. We might try once or twice but, over time, we need to believe that our efforts can achieve the results desired. It is better if goals are challenging but not impossible, as long recognised in goal-setting research (Locke and Latham 1990, Latham and Pinder 2005). Second, employees are reward seekers, as the problem with bonus cultures in the banking sector amply illustrates. They may simply ignore unrewarded goals. Third, employees are reward critics. This means that firms cannot motivate good performers at all unless people believe they will receive rewards they value. It is impossible to employ some people, for example, unless the work interests them and the pay meets at least their threshold expectations. Over time, to keep people motivated, the firm needs a virtuous cycle in which the rewards that people value do come to them when they perform.

Expectancy theory implies that faith in the management process is something that needs to be built and maintained over time. Those writing on psychological contracting increasingly draw on the notion of 'social exchange' (Gouldner 1960, Blau 1964) to argue that employees reciprocate the kind of treatment they receive from management as the employment relationship unfolds (see, for example, Whitener, Brodt, Korsgaard and Werner 1998, Whitener 2001, Shore *et al.* 2004, Hom *et al.* 2009).

The critical principle at stake here is that employee trust and commitment tend to be based on their perceptions of fairness and trustworthiness in management decision making (Guest 2007). If firms are only interested in a short-term exchange (for example, so much money for a small task or a very finite project), this is not so much of an issue. Where, however, management wants a particular employee to stay over the long term because their skills and experience are of ongoing value, there is an important issue with trust dynamics. Eisenberger *et al.* (1986, 2002) use the notion of 'perceived organizational support' in this connection. The argument is that employees who perceive good organisational support in their employment relationship respond with increased trust in management and greater commitment to the organisation. They are more 'engaged'. As Chapter 4 on the resource-based view of the firm argues, the trust and commitment of core employees can be very valuable 'intangible assets' for organisations. Higher levels of trust foster greater collaboration and can facilitate change management while greater commitment can bring benefits in retaining valuable experience in the business (Whitener 2001, Macky and Boxall 2007). In service firms, for example, this greater experience can help to win and hold important customers who are unimpressed by firms where employees lack the expertise to solve their problems or do not recall their preferences.

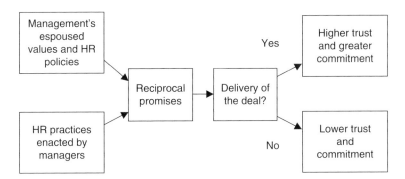

Figure 7.7 Promises, trust and commitment in the psychological contract

Source: Modified from Guest, D., 'Human resource management and the worker: towards a new psychological contract?'. In Boxall, P., Purcell, J. and Wright, P. (eds) *The Oxford Handbook of Human Resource Mangement*, Oxford: Oxford University Press. © (2007) By permission of Oxford University Press.

Figure 7.7, modified from the work of Guest (2007), underlines the key insights involved here. Where employee commitment is valuable to the firm, employee trust in management matters and this trust is sensitive to the state of the psychological contract: to whether the employee perceives management to have made and have kept important promises in their employment relationship. As we shall argue further in Chapter 8, employee perceptions of management values, policies and practices are critical in the chain of variables that link HRM to company performance.

Conclusions

This chapter has been concerned with the important principles that underpin individual employment relationships. From the employer's perspective, we have used the performance equation (P = f(a,m,o)) to emphasise that firms need people who have the *can do* (ability) and the *will do* (motivational) factors that will serve the organisation's interests. Both elements are essential and reach more of their potential when there is a supportive context in which to perform (the 'opportunity' factor). There is a vast range of abilities in the working population and the range of individual performance is greater in the more complex jobs, where people can add more value or do more harm. This gives recruitment and selection a particularly crucial role in any kind of approach to HRM. The more proactive employers, who are not saddled with outdated assumptions, do better in tight labour markets in which workers have good choices.

It thus pays to think about the employment relationship not simply from an employer-dominated perspective. Successful employment relationships depend on mutuality or reciprocity, and this means thinking about what employees find attractive at work. Research suggests that individuals are keen to deploy their talents effectively. They typically look for a good match between the skills they possess and the skills needed in the job. Furthermore, there is a dynamic element to this. While 'provisioning' is still the main motive for working, research points to the rise of 'expressivism' in the workforce, to the drive of many employees to find greater avenues for personal fulfilment as they develop over their working life. Where firms are concerned about improving the long-term retention of valuable employees, therefore, attention should be given to ways of opening up regular opportunities for their personal growth. Firms that cannot provide growth opportunities are likely to lose many of their more talented workers.

The functions of recruitment and selection and training and development can generate human potential but this will be wasted if motivational strategies are neglected. Employment relationships involve investments by both parties. They are more stable when these are well matched. For employees, this means a good balance between their efforts and the rewards they receive ('effort–reward balance'). Both intrinsic and extrinsic rewards matter in this respect. Finding the work interesting and enjoying good levels of control over how to carry it out are very important factors, as are the economic and social rewards that accrue to the jobholder. For the employer, therefore, it is important to ensure that the firm's reward practices enable it to recruit and retain talented individuals. As a general rule, within the Anglo-American context, employees will expect to be paid close to their productivity. Ensuring that they are, however, takes some very careful management because good pay-system design depends on a range of contingent factors and pay systems always carry the potential for perverse incentives. Careful consultation and critical examination of interest conflicts are essential if the 'loaded gun' of performance-related pay is to be handled safely. The global financial crisis of 2008–9 illustrated the ways in which bonus systems can reward the kind of short-term risk-taking behaviour that severely damages shareholder interests and those of the wider community.

Managing employment relationships effectively means thinking about the underlying processes they involve rather than fixating on the HR practices that appear on the surface. The theory of psychological contracting brings in an understanding of how management promises and behaviour affect employee trust over time. Where management is concerned to enhance employee commitment, it implies that faith in the trustworthiness of management is something that should be strived for. An organisation in which management is seen to treat employees fairly in reward decisions, and delivers on its promises to individuals, will generally enjoy greater employee loyalty. Some level of commitment makes any business work better but it is particularly valuable wherever firms need experienced employees to handle complex operating systems, to drive innovation or to retain valued customers.

8

Linking HR systems to organisational performance

We have been searching in this section for general principles underpinning better HRM. In this chapter, we draw our ideas together to enable readers to form an overview of HR strategy, to see overall patterns in how work and people are managed and not just parts of the picture. We do so through the concept of HR systems, examining the notion of 'bundling' or 'internal fit' among the practices in such systems, and outlining a typology of common HR systems and the contexts in which they are typically found. This over-simplifies reality but helps us to summarise the huge variation we see in the way firms approach HRM. Models of HRM range from the familial and informal ones found in small firms through to the complex mixes of diverse HR systems prevalent in large, bureaucratic and multinational firms. We then review theory linking any kind of HR system to performance. While the characteristics of HR systems are highly variable, all are intended, in some way, to reach valued organisational outcomes. What mediating links are important in this 'black box'? The chapter examines the problem of gaps between the espoused intentions of senior managers and their actions, underlines the crucial role of first-line managers in bringing HR policies to life, and emphasises the importance of employee perceptions and responses. Managing these links is a tall order, especially in the larger organisations in which the problems of broken promises, managerial politics, and misperceptions of motives are that much greater.

HR systems and organisational patterns in HR strategy

As explained in Chapter 3, a firm's HR strategy is typically 'variegated': it incorporates a mix of HR systems or models. HR systems are clusters of work and employment practices that have evolved to manage major hierarchical or occupational groups in the firm. In some contexts, firms even have different HR systems within occupational groups, as can happen in those retail organisations where a small group of permanent sales assistants works in close association with a much larger group of more transient part-time ones (Siebert and Zubanov 2009). HR systems help management to build the human and social capital the firm needs to reach its overall goals in HRM.

In our discussion of the research on 'best fit' and 'best practice' in Chapter 3, we underlined the way in which managers generally try to ensure that HR systems fit in with their environment. We emphasised three levels of fit: 'societal', 'industry' and 'organisational'. These involve the need to adapt to social factors such as laws and cultural norms, industry factors, such as production technologies and dominant business models, and organisational factors, such as the firm's size, its stage of development and its operating strategy. In Chapter 4, which draws on the resource-based view, we explained that such a process of adaptation to context does not rule out idiosyncrasies in the firm: management ideologies, competencies, personalities and power struggles will inevitably put particular twists on HR systems. Thinking about this more positively, there is an opportunity for viable firms to create a unique form of fit in HRM: some management teams tailor and nurture HR systems which create 'human resource advantage' for the firm. A companion notion that has been emphasised in the strategic HRM literature alongside these ideas of societal, industry and organisational fits is the concept of 'internal fit'. Internal fit is often seen as critical to a high-quality performance in HRM (Kepes and Delery 2007).

HR systems and the problem of 'internal fit'

The theory of 'internal fit' is concerned with the way in which HR practices are 'bundled' or interact *within* a particular HR system (MacDuffie 1995, Gerhart 2007b). Which HR practices go together best when we want to achieve certain goals (Lepak, Liao, Chung, Harden 2006)? Let's say we want to achieve high-quality production in a manufacturing team or we want to achieve a high level of safety in a road-repair gang. Some theorists seem to have in mind the idea that practitioners can stand back from the action and decide whether to add HR practices into the mix one by one. In reality, all employment relationships rely on some minimal level of bundling of HR practices. When someone starts a job, at least four sets of HR practices have already coalesced into a bundle: some set of recruitment and selection practices, some process for negotiation of, or at least acceptance of, employment conditions, including the rate of pay, some kind of deployment to a work role or allocation to a set of duties, and some kind of supervision. There may also be some training, if only a brief familiarization with the place of work and with co-workers. Some form of bundling of HR practices is therefore inevitable in employment relationships. This said, there are questions for managers around how to make any bundle more effective and more efficient.

Those who talk of internal fit are usually making an argument for a high level of *coherence* among the HR practices that make up an employment relationship or an HR system. MacDuffie (1995) talks of the need for positive bundling in the HR practices used to support work reform in automobile assembly plants. In his terms, this means adopting the skill development and incentive practices that will support more participative styles of working among core operating workers in such plants, as discussed in Chapter 5. Positive bundling is a search for 'powerful combinations' among practices (Becker, Huselid, Pickus and Spratt 1997). The corollary is that managers should avoid 'deadly combinations' (Becker *et al.* 1997, Delery 1998): policies which work in directly opposite directions such as strong training for teamwork but appraisal which only rewards highly individualistic behaviour. Coherence in HRM implies designing policies that pull in the same direction.

Delery (1998) also warns against the costly duplication of practices, such as over-designed selection systems where extra hurdles add no further predictive power to the process and are not therefore an efficient use of time and money. Consider the example of the firm that would benefit from structured interviewing and reference checking of job applicants but decides instead to design an 'assessment centre' with five or six kinds of test involved. Chances are that much of the assessment centre is an expensive white elephant. Little of value has been added for the considerable extra expense involved. This is not so much a point about coherence as about cost-effectiveness, which should always be borne in mind.

The notion of *consistency*, which overlaps with coherence, is also used in discussions of internal fit. One of the more useful summaries is provided by Baron and Kreps (1999: 39) who define three types of desirable consistency in HRM. The first type is 'complementary' fit or what they call 'single employee consistency': for example, ensuring that where firms use expensive selection approaches they also invest in training and promotion policies that aim to reduce labour turnover (thus increasing the chances of reaping rewards from their investment in individuals, as we explained in Chapter 7). In effect, this is about coherence in HR policy design and entails the search for 'powerful' rather than 'deadly combinations'. The second type of fit Baron and Kreps (1999) argue for is consistency across employees doing the same kind of work ('among employee consistency' but better known in everyday usage as 'standardisation' of employment conditions). There are often strong normative or ethical pressures for standardisation in HR policies in firms, at least for the same class of labour: one of the main ways employers argue they are treating people equitably is by treating them all the same when it comes to employment conditions (for example, standard working times and leave policies). The third kind of consistency is what Baron and Kreps call 'temporal consistency': consistency of employee treatment across a reasonable period of time. 'In general, how employee A is treated today should not differ radically from how she was treated yesterday' (Baron and Kreps 1999: 39). Again, and assuming employee A has not done something radically different in the last 24 hours, this principle makes good sense: employees like to be able to predict an employer's behaviour and can be seriously demotivated by violation of their 'psychological contract', as argued in Chapter 7.

As far as it goes, this kind of advice seems very reasonable. Is there anything wrong with it? Unfortunately, there is: it is somewhat over-simplified. While rightly emphasising the value of various forms of coherence and consistency, which help to build stability and trust, the notion of 'internal fit' tends to be discussed in a way that overlooks the paradoxical elements involved in managing work and people. The problem stems from the fact that, as emphasised in Chapter 1, there are multiple goals in HRM and these bring a range of strategic tensions. There are, for example, tensions between economic goals and the need for social legitimacy. There are also tensions between economic performance in the short term and preparation for the long term. The reality of these tensions means that mixed messages will often be transmitted to employees within the firm's HR systems.

As an illustration, consider work by Pil and MacDuffie (1996) on automobile manufacturing, important research we have discussed previously. Pil and MacDuffie (1996) find a general increase in the use of high-involvement practices in the industry around the world. As we noted in Chapter 5, these are practices that foster higher skill and solicit greater commitment to, and creativity in, problem solving. However, at the same time, firms have had to pursue downsizing, often of major proportions. The same picture is described by Bacon and Blyton (2001) in the international iron and steel industry: new work systems designed to increase employee involvement in decision making have been introduced at the same time as firms have introduced more contingent employment contracts (fixed-term contracts and subcontracting of jobs) and have continued to carry out redundancy programmes. As anyone with experience of downsizing and sub-contracting processes knows, these sorts of actions typically raise suspicions, reduce trust in management and undermine employee commitment to the firm (Zatzick and Iverson 2006). This climate of insecurity, however, has not prevented management in these firms from seeking higher involvement from the remaining workforce. Here, then, is a critical tension: between needing more skilful, more creative work while not being able to hold traditional staffing levels and offer traditional levels of employment security. It seems that management often needs a blend of 'forcing' and 'fostering' behaviour as it wrestles with the problem of renewing the firm (Walton, Cutcher-Gershenfeld and McKersie 1994), as we noted in Chapter 6.

We must be careful, then, with the concept of 'internal fit'. It rightly underlines the importance of seeking coherence among the HR policies aimed at a particular group of employees and consistency in their application. Where, for example, management aims to introduce a new style of working for a major occupational group, such as one that implies higher levels of skill and creativity, striving for reinforcement across the HR policies needed, and their consistent application, is obviously important. However, striving for 'internal fit' in this sense will never rule out the fact that there are competing interests in the workplace or the fact that management may have to change its HR strategy to adapt more effectively to change.

A typology of HR systems

HR systems, therefore, are clusters of related HR practices for particular workforce groups, which benefit from coherence in their design and consistency in their application, but which may still contain paradoxical elements. We are now in a position to consider the main HR systems we observe across firms. Our typology of HR systems or models is shown in Table 8.1. The typology cannot be presented as something which is culture free. It mainly reflects sources which are based on studies in the Anglo-American world. However, it does recognise patterns – such as the familial model – that surface in many cultures and the typology specifically incorporates an awareness of the process of globalisation.

We begin with the 'familial' model. Family firms are important nearly everywhere in capitalism. In the UK, they make up 76 per cent of all firms while they constitute 75 per cent in Italy and 80 per cent in Germany (Colli, Fernández Pérez and Rose 2003). They are rare, of course, in industries where operations require large workforces or high levels of physical capital and account for lower percentages of total employment. In the UK, family firms currently make up 40 per cent of all firms with at least 10 employees and account for 31 per cent of private sector employment in this category (Kersley *et al.* 2006: 19).

Table 8.1   A typology of HR systems

Type of HR system	Defining characteristics	Typical context and goals
Familial model	Family members, among whom trust levels are high, provide the core labour resources and control decision making.	Common among small businesses (e.g. in agriculture, retail, construction, transport) where owners want strategy and succession under family control. High-trust relations and preferential employment conditions may be extended to key long-term employees if the firm expands.
Informal model	Workers are managed personally by owners or supervisors. Wages and skill levels are often relatively low and trade unions are rare. Temporary and part-time forms of employment are common and levels of employee turnover tend to be high.	Common in the early stages of industrialisation; remains common in low-skill services and in various types of small business for groups of labour which are outside the core. The goal of cost-effectiveness is paramount and legitimacy is typically secondary.
Industrial model	Highly specialised, low-discretion ('Taylorised') jobs, set within a hierarchy of management authority but linked to bureaucratic rules that bring standardisation and various career features ('internal labour markets'). Trade unions are common.	Developed in the late nineteenth century and in the early to mid decades of the twentieth century to support efficiency-oriented mass production with greater workplace stability and higher levels of social legitimacy.
Salaried model	Managers and white collar specialists are employed in jobs which enjoy higher levels of discretion, responsibility, pay and security than other employees. Their career development is actively fostered within the firm.	The necessary, more trusting corollary of the industrial model designed to build strong identification with the company. Provides the authority and decision-making structure that enables the industrial model to function.

Table 8.1 (Continued)

Type of HR system	Defining characteristics	Typical context and goals
High-involvement model	Work organisation is reformed to break down Taylorism. Specific practices vary but employee empowerment, higher levels of skill and better incentives are core dimensions. Managerial roles change to facilitate greater employee participation.	Common in capital-intensive or high-tech firms where it is often accompanied by high levels of mechanisation and computerisation. Also used in service firms targeting higher quality market segments. Intended to enhance cost-effectiveness through greater worker involvement, skills and commitment.
Craft-professional models	Work practices reflect roots in 'craft' control and long periods of professional education and socialisation. Employee skills, discretion and pay levels are all high. Professionals may work in teams but cannot rotate across their specialisations. Democratic decision-making is often practised among the partners although this tends to become representative rather than direct as organisations get larger.	Craft models survived in high-skill parts of manufacturing where Taylorist practices would not work or were successfully resisted. Professional models are the natural approach in private sector professional services where employee ownership is the norm and in those parts of the public sector which depend on professional work (e.g. public health and education). Craft or professional autonomy and high economic rewards are typical goals.
Outsourcing model	The work concerned is outsourced to a specialist provider in the country of domicile or is off-shored to a lower-cost country. This implies nothing about the nature of the outsourcer's HR system which could be any one of familial, informal, industrial, salaried, craft or professional types in their various cultural and regulatory guises.	Common in globalised and electronically connected production environments where firms seek quantum improvements in labour cost. Better quality and customer service may also be desired but is not always achieved.

Their incidence, however, is growing and the familial HR system is something that should be recognised and better understood in HRM.

The defining characteristic of the familial model is that family members, among whom trust levels are generally high, provide the core labour resources the firm needs (often sacrificially) and control decision making. The family patriarchs and/or matriarchs at the head of these firms are highly motivated to retain their control. This is not surprising: they typically have their personal wealth, including the family home, at stake. Retaining wealth, employment opportunities and leadership succession in the family can be more important than making the highest rate of return (Colli *et al.* 2003, Marchington *et al.* 2003). A key advantage of established family firms is that they can remain viable at lower rates of financial return without shareholders kicking up a fuss. Small, specialist businesses can sometimes survive at the edge of markets where it is sub-economic for the dominant, public companies to reach them, as argued by organisational ecologists in the theory of 'resource partitioning' (Carroll and Hannan 1995: 215–21). While the familial model is family-oriented, familial conditions and trust are often extended to key 'outsiders' (non-family members) if the firm grows to the extent that this becomes necessary (Colli *et al.* 2003).

Our second HR system is the informal model. This is sometimes called a 'low-wage' HR system (Katz and Darbishire 2000: 10). We prefer to describe it as informal because its defining characteristic is that workers are managed personally and informally by owners or supervisors. This was the main way individuals were managed in the early stages of industrialisation when an overseer hired and supervised their own workers, as we described in our discussion of work systems in Chapter 5. Speaking of nineteenth-century factories in the USA, when foremen (and they were usually men) had high levels of autonomy in hiring and firing, Jacoby (2004: 15) calls the informal model the 'drive system'.

This era has largely passed (at least in the developed countries) but the informal model is still commonly used in small firms for those who are not in the family or core workforce. As noted in Chapter 3, lower levels of formalization and standardization are common in small organisations. Quite simply, there are fewer HR policies: much less is written down. For small service firms operating in mass service markets where margins are tight, cost-effectiveness matters enormously, as explained in Chapter 5. Wages and skill levels are often relatively low. Trade unions are rare and standards of social legitimacy can also be low: the more established firms are typically compliant with their obligations under labour law but some owners are unaware of them or non-compliant (Edwards and Ram 2006). In terms of the employee relations styles discussed in Chapter 6, the preference is often for union avoidance. Temporary and part-time forms of employment are common with jobs not generally linked into a longer-term career structure (Osterman 1987). Workforces often have disproportionate numbers of less experienced and more vulnerable groups: student workers, new migrants and women returning to the workforce after child-rearing. Whenever labour markets are tight, levels of employee turnover tend to be high. However, informal models can include situations where critical workers are offered significant discretion and flexibility in order to retain them (Edwards and Ram 2006). They also include situations where workers make high wages, as in the construction sector and in home maintenance when skills are in short supply.

Our third type, which Osterman (1987) calls the 'industrial model', grew out of the informal type, as explained in Chapter 5. As workers were gathered into factories around a common power source (first water, then steam, then electrical power) in the nineteenth century, a process of specialised working was reinforced. Jobs low in discretion, responsibility and scope were created ('Taylorised' jobs) and workers were subservient to a hierarchy of management authority. Trade union and government challenges to these work systems, however, reinforced and expanded bureaucratic rules that brought standardisation and career features ('internal labour markets') to employment conditions. Workers were not insulated from lay-offs but seniority rules negotiated by unions often protected those with longer tenure (Osterman 1987, Jacoby 2004).

The industrial model was built to foster the efficiency advantages of high degrees of specialisation and economies of scale in mass production. However, reformers within management and, more importantly, pressure from trade unions and governments helped to ensure that wages and employment conditions, including levels of job security and scope for internal promotion, were improved (Jacoby 2004). While many firms continued to adopt a style of limiting union influence or keeping the unions at 'arms-length' (Chapter 6), the overall result was greater workplace stability and higher levels of social legitimacy. The industrial model was enormously influential. Its core features of specialised jobs embedded in strong 'internal labour markets' spread into large service firms and the public sector and across the world.

The necessary corollary of the industrial model is the 'salaried' system (Osterman 1987, Pinfield and Berner 1994). This was developed to manage the managers and 'white collar' specialists who were also essential to factories and to other large-scale organisations, such as large service firms and government departments. Under the salaried system, the individual is paid an annual salary rather than a wage calculated on the actual hours worked.

This in itself conveys a lot more trust and suggests a lot more flexibility is desired of managers in the way they carry out their roles. Managers and specialists employed in this way enjoy higher levels of discretion, responsibility, pay and security than other employees (Fox 1974). Jobs are more open to interpretation and lateral thinking. Career development within the firm is fostered. While such bureaucratic practices as job descriptions, job evaluation and performance appraisal are prevalent in large organisations, there is often scope to recognise individual strengths through merit-based pay. At the highest levels of management, reward levels, including bonuses and share options, are extremely attractive. Identification with the employer is assumed to be high and unions are rare (except in the public sector and in the finance and insurance sector).

As we explained in Chapter 5, the economic and technological context has changed very significantly over the last 30 years. One outcome of the changes is that various firms have made a move from the industrial HR model to a high-involvement one. This grew among manufacturers in high-wage countries who needed to respond more effectively to competitors delivering better quality at lower unit cost. As Chapter 5 shows, leading examples of HIWSs have emerged in such industries as automobile assembly and steel manufacturing (MacDuffie 1995, Appelbaum *et al.* 2000). Under the high-involvement model, work organisation is reformed to reverse the dysfunctional aspects of Taylorism. Specific practices vary across occupations, industries and societies but the underpinning aims are to enhance employee discretion and expand skill formation and employee incentives. Managerial roles must change to facilitate greater employee participation or the model will not work well.

The high-involvement model represents an attempt by management to reform earlier management strategies. It has features in common with craft or professional HR systems. Craft models have their genesis in 'craft' control: in direct control of work practices by highly skilled, often mobile workers whose critical skills in the production process give them greater labour market power (Osterman 1987). Taylorism did not affect all manufacturing workers: some successfully resisted it or occupied jobs which were much less amenable to it. Maintenance workers in factories, for example, who had completed apprenticeships and were responsible for machine performance, often formed an 'aristocracy of labour' (MacKenzie 1973) who were able to distance themselves from the work practices imposed on less-skilled operating workers.

In a similar way, the professions, such as law, medicine, accountancy and professional engineering, have developed their own work practices through long periods of professional education and socialisation (Combs *et al.* 2006).

Professionals may work together in teams but cannot rotate across their specialisations without the requisite qualifications (Kalleberg *et al.* 2006). Professionals form organisations serving their own ends. Autonomy and high economic rewards are typical goals and customers who want advanced professional services must pay a premium, as Chapter 5 explains. Professional models are the natural approach in private sector professional services where firms are based on an elite form of employee ownership, one in which partners, who remain working members of the firm, own the firm's shares (see, for example, Boxall and Steeneveld 1999, Malos and Campion 2000). Democratic decision making is practised among the partners in the professional HR system although this tends to become representative rather than direct as organisations get larger. Professional HR systems are also prevalent in those parts of the public sector which depend on professional work (for example, public health and education). However, in these contexts, unionisation tends to be high and struggles between professional groups and between professionals and managers tend to be common (Bach and Kessler 2007).

We call our final HR system the 'outsourcing model'. As explained in Chapter 5, globalisation, deregulation, new technologies and public sector reforms have exposed more organisations to lower-cost competitors, both domestically and internationally. The outsourcing of work has grown: sometimes to firms which specialise in high-volume, back-office functions (such as, aspects of accounting, IT and HR work) and sometimes off-shore where whole operations can be performed much more cheaply. Parcelling out of non-core activities to make major cost savings is a trend with major implications for HR systems. In our typology, we use the term, 'outsourcing model', to indicate an HR system which is thus very much driven by the cost side of cost-effectiveness. However, we are implying nothing beyond this about the nature of the outsourcer's HR system. The outsourcer could adopt any one or more of the familial, informal, industrial, salaried, craft or professional models in their various cultural and regulatory guises. There are clearly major cost differences when an industrial model is adopted in China as opposed to the UK or the USA.[1] But there are also major cost differences when highly educated professionals are employed in India as opposed to Europe or North America.[2]

---

[1] See, for example, the outsourcing survey in *Business Week*, 30 January 2006: http://www.businessweek.com/magazine/content/06_05/b3969401.htm
[2] See, for example, Randeep Ramesh, 'Analyse this: Wall Street looks to India', *The Guardian*, 6 November 2006, p. 26.

HR systems and organisational patterns

Having defined the most common HR systems, we now come back to the point that HR strategies in organisations typically incorporate a range of HR systems. Organisations and HR systems are rarely equivalent. It is very unusual to have a 'single status' HR system covering all employees in a firm. It is therefore helpful to use another typology, shown in Table 8.2, which identifies the common *mixes* of HR systems across major types of organisation.

We begin with two types which do not typically have external shareholders and which are generally managed by the owners rather than by career managers. The first type is the family firm in which workplaces are small and trade

Table 8.2 A typology of organisational types and their HR systems

Organisational types	Typical HR systems used	Contextual factors and major variations
Family firms	Familial and informal systems	Familial models dominate in family-owned small enterprises in agriculture, manufacturing and less-skilled services. Workplaces are small, unions are rare and informal models are used for non-family members.
Professional service firms	Professional and salaried systems	In high-skill, private-sector services, professional models dominate. Unions are rare. Professionals own and jointly manage the firm while employing lower-level professionals, managerial and support staff on salaried systems. Large professional-service firms use more representative modes of partner democracy.
Classical bureaucracies	Salaried, industrial and craft systems	Classical bureaucracies include the large private and public sector organisations that grew strongly in the early to middle decades of the twentieth century. Salaried career managers lead large workforces which are predominantly managed through an industrial model (while some groups are employed on craft models). Trade unions are commonly involved and tend to heighten bureaucratic standardisation and restrain management power. There are three main variants: the industrial bureaucracy (typical in large manufacturers), the service bureaucracy (e.g. in the large banks and insurance companies) and the public sector bureaucracy (standard in public service departments and local authorities).

Table 8.2 (Continued)

Organisational types	Typical HR systems used	Contextual factors and major variations
Participatory bureaucracies	Salaried and high-involvement systems; salaried and professional systems	A mix of salaried and high-involvement HR systems is common in capital-intensive or high-tech firms seeking to respond to high-quality competition through higher skills, learning and innovation and in service firms trying to serve higher-quality, more lucrative market segments. The main variants in the private sector concern whether employee involvement is driven by non-union practices or is built around a union-management 'partnership'. Participatory bureaucracies can also be found in the public sector for professional services (e.g. in public health and education). In these situations, unions are common and employment practices are prone to ongoing tensions between professional disciplines and struggles between professional and managerial control.
Flexible bureaucracies	Salaried and outsourced systems	Typical in large organisations where a salaried hierarchy remains but where it has become legitimate to out-source operations and specialist functions, downsize workforces and weaken long-term commitments to employees. Where trade unions exist, they may extract relatively high wage levels for slimmer workforces but cannot protect jobs against rounds of restructuring. Common among organisations which now see the need for a better balance between short-run efficiency and long-run agility, including multinational firms which are responding to heightened cost pressures in international markets, large service firms in deregulated industries (e.g. airlines, telecommunications) and public sector organisations which have been required to adopt the greater emphasis on flexibility and financial control in the 'new public management'.

unions are rare. In agriculture, in small manufacturing firms and in the less-skilled service sector, family firms typically aim to use a cost-effective blend of familial and informal HR systems. The family members and their trusted associates are employed under the familial model, providing the 'backbone' to the firm, while other workers are employed under the informal model. How far the familial model is extended to non-family members is a variable. It is more likely to be extended when employees have critical skills or can affect sensitive customer relations. Thus, in a regional trucking firm, loyal, skilled and trusted drivers are likely to be 'looked after' by the family (Marchington *et al.* 2003) while student workers or new migrants picking fruit and vegetables in summer for a contracting firm are likely to be treated in a much more disposable way.

In the second type, professional service firms (PSFs), ownership resides in the hands of a group of partner-professionals. This amounts, in effect, to a restricted system of employee ownership: the partners are simultaneously owners, workers and managers (Greenwood, Hinings and Brown 1990, Boxall and Steeneveld 1999). In small PSFs, partners work closely together and try to manage the firm in a direct, highly democratic kind of way. This does not mean that things will work out well. How long such a firm will last depends very much on the quality of relations within the partnership group. In large professional service firms, formalisation increases with staffing levels and partnership democracy tends to be more representative. The partners employ lower-level professionals and non-professional staff (for example, clerical workers, practice managers, accounting, marketing and HR specialists) on salaried conditions. In PSFs, therefore, managerial specialists are subservient to the professional partners, not the other way round.

The other three types of organisation are all best understood as management-driven forms of bureaucracy. We use the term 'classical bureaucracies' to describe the large organisations that emerged in the nineteenth century and the early and middle decades of the twentieth century. In these organisations, shareholders were remote and salaried, career-oriented managers took charge of large workforces. Trade unions were common. As Chapter 5 explains, unions did not stop high levels of job specialisation but did help to lift wages, restrain management power and foster 'internal labour markets'. In the 'industrial bureaucracy' typical in large manufacturers, Taylorist and Fordist philosophies made their marks and the main HR systems were therefore industrial models for waged workers and salaried models for line managers and management specialists. Some groups of workers, however, retained craft models (for example, highly skilled maintenance workers and design engineers).

In the service bureaucracies that grew in the private sector (such as in the large banks and insurance companies), job specialisation was also prevalent, creating a kind of 'office factory'. Salaried systems were common but were fairly basic in terms of pay levels and discretion at entry and lower levels in the hierarchy. Salaried systems became progressively more empowering and generous as individuals were promoted to higher-level, managerial cadres. This 'office factory' was also typical of public sector bureaucracies. However, unionisation became stronger and more extensive in public service departments and local authorities than in private sector services.

The final two organisational types both represent attempts to reform the classical bureaucracy. Rather than bureaucracies disappearing among large organisations, what has happened is more akin to a reform of bureaucracy (Jacoby 2004). We see two major trends here. One is the 'participatory bureaucracy' (Kelley 2000), a reform of the industrial bureaucracy designed to foster high-involvement HR systems. Managerial and specialist staff remain on salaried systems but need to adjust their relationships with core operating staff if the model is to succeed. The participatory bureaucracy is common in capital-intensive or high-tech firms seeking to respond to high-quality competition through higher skills, learning and innovation, as noted in Chapter 5. As explained there, it is also a feature of large service firms, such as hotels, banks and rest homes, trying to target higher-quality, more lucrative market segments. The main variants in the private sector concern whether employee involvement is supported by non-union voice practices or is built around a union-management 'partnership', as discussed in Chapter 6.

Participatory bureaucracies are also common in the public sector for professional services (such as, in public health and education). It is fair to say, however, that the bureaucratic features are stronger in the public sector than in the private. Employee ownership is not possible and unions remain common, fighting for professional autonomy and income levels. Employment practices are prone to ongoing tensions between professional disciplines (for example, between medical and nursing professions in hospitals). In recent times, conflict levels have been high due to major struggles between professional and managerial groups (for example, over cost cutting and an escalation of bureaucratic controls under the 'new public management', as discussed in Chapter 5).

Finally, we see the emergence of what we call the 'flexible bureaucracy'. We use this term to recognise what Grimshaw, Marchington, Willmott and Rubery (2005) describe as a growth of fragmentation in large organisations. Like Jacoby (2004) and Grimshaw *et al.* (2005), we do not see this type of organisation as a repudiation of bureaucracy but, rather, a reform of it in which it is more legitimate to downsize workforces, to weaken long-term commitments to employees and to consider all sorts of outsourcing and offshoring. The flexible bureaucracy combines an inner core of salaried managerial and specialist staff, whose own contracts have often been heightened in terms of performance expectations and rewards, with outsourced

HR systems. The outsourced models adopted can include any number of types, including those which foster high levels of involvement but do so with lower-cost workers. Where trade unions exist, they may extract relatively high wage levels for slimmer workforces in the developed countries but cannot protect jobs against rounds of restructuring. The flexible bureaucracy is common among organisations in which senior managers now see the need for a better balance between short-term efficiency and long-term agility. This includes multinational firms which are responding to heightened cost pressures in international markets, large service firms in deregulated industries (for example, airlines, telecommunications) and, once again, public sector organisations which have been required to adopt the greater emphasis on financial control in the 'new public management' (Bach and Kessler 2007).

The 'black box' problem: links between HRM and performance

As we have indicated, the quality of the investment made in people varies across the models we have described. In family firms, for example, those managed informally are clearly not offered the same trust and employment terms as those managed under the familial model. Similarly, in the flexible bureaucracy, there is a core of highly paid salaried staff who provide leadership and networking coordination. However, these individuals are responsible for finding outsourced arrangements in which the whole idea is to employ people around the world who are treated more contingently and paid at much lower levels. HR systems vary in the messages they send: some are more oriented to achieving low labour costs with adequate levels of effectiveness than they are to achieving high levels of employee commitment and expert performance.

Having said this, are there some commonalities in how HR systems should operate? Are there some key links that all HR models need if they are to reach their intended outcomes? This is what HR researchers have called the 'black box' problem (Purcell *et al.* 2003, Wright and Gardner 2004): what chain of links leads from HR policies through to whatever notion of organisational performance is desired? Despite the variation in the goals of HR systems, there are some important principles here that we need to understand. These are of particular relevance to large, bureaucratic organisations where tall hierarchies, changes in ownership, and swings in ideology threaten coherence and consistency in HR strategy. Although they are much more resource-constrained, coherence and consistency are easier to achieve in small firms, as we shall explain.

The centrality of employee attitudes and behaviour

Virtually all scholars who specify a causal chain between HR policy and organisation performance see employee attitudes and behaviour as the fulcrum or critical linking mechanism. This is true on both the individual and the collective (workforce) levels, as noted in Chapters 6 and 7. To bring about valued organisational outcomes, management needs to influence individual employee ability, motivation and opportunity to perform. On the collective level, to make individual performances possible, management needs to build a sufficient degree of workforce organisation, capabilities and positive attitudes.

However, these employee variables will not move in a positive direction if things go badly wrong within the management process itself. One of the most elaborated models linking HRM and performance is that proposed by Wright and Nishii (2004). Their causal chain proposes, (1) *intended* HR practices, leading to (2) *actual* HR practices, leading to (3) *perceived* HR practices, leading to (4) employee reactions, and leading, finally, to (5) organisational performance.

The problem of gaps between espoused intentions and actions

Wright and Nishii's (2004) model underlines the fact that there can be major gaps between management intention and management action that are damaging to employee attitudes and behaviour and ultimately to performance outcomes. Other scholars have made the same point in talking about a gap between management rhetoric and reality (for example, Legge 2005). We live in a time when it has become common for senior managers to espouse a certain kind of 'culture' in their organisations: a desired way of working with employees, customers and suppliers. Some publish on the web their statements of 'vision and values'.[3] The problem is that the workforce will typically treat such statements as rhetoric and look for the extent to which high-sounding cultural statements are manifested in reality.

Grant (1999) explores the issues involved through the theory of psychological contracting, which we discussed in terms of individual employment relationships in Chapter 7. However, he raises the level of analysis to the collective level, defining four types of psychological contract between management and its workforce:

- The 'congruent contract' (where management's 'rhetoric' in HRM appeals to employees and 'coincides with their perceptions of reality'). Previous experiences 'tally with the content of the rhetoric'.

---

[3] For example: http://www.pfizer.ca/en/about_pfizer/vision_and_values/, accessed 7/5/10.

- The 'mismatched contract' (where 'the rhetoric fails because it has no appeal to the employee and does not match the perceived reality'). This can happen, for example, when past experience tells employees management cannot deliver on its rhetoric.
- The 'partial contract' (where 'parts of the rhetoric appeal to the employees and parts do not'). 'For example, the employee may feel that rhetoric promising personal development reflects reality, while at the same time they may feel that rhetoric linking personal development to increased levels of pay does not.'
- The 'trial contract' (where 'rhetoric is given a chance to prove itself and become reality'). This can happen where employees are prepared 'to "buy in" to the rhetoric on a "wait-and-see basis" ' (Grant 1999: 331).

Grant (1999) reports a case in the UK consumer electronics sector ('Renco') where data was obtained through two periods of data gathering on employee attitudes, some 18 months apart. Renco, a Japanese-owned company, opened a greenfield site at which Japanese practices of shopfloor participation and a cooperative approach to industrial relations were promised (in effect, a shift to a participatory bureaucracy). Workers were keen to give this approach a chance (a trial psychological contract). After 18 months, however, management practice had diverged significantly from the initial rhetoric. Japanese-style consultative practices were allowed to decay. Employees did not experience consistent opportunities for involvement. The trial contract passed away as employees revised their effort (for example, lowering the quality of work) in a quid-pro-quo for a disappointing management performance. The psychological contract shifted back to a mismatched one. The case illustrates the danger of raising expectations which are then subsequently dashed because management does not care about follow-through or because the internal politics within management de-rail top management's espoused values. Cynicism is bred in this kind of environment and any future change management programmes will have serious credibility issues.

Case study research of this nature frequently underlines the importance of bringing senior management's espoused values – or cultural signals – closer into alignment with the collective actions of both senior managers and the various layers of line and specialist managers who report to them. Large organisations in which there are high levels of inconsistency in management values and, thus, in the HRM process, do not have strongly positive workplace cultures (Gordon and DiTomaso 1992). Stronger cultures are more readily built in small, owner-managed organisations where trust levels tend to be higher (Macky and Boxall 2007). Because those who own the firm directly manage employees, there is much less chance for miscommunication to occur and for debilitating internal politics to take root. Where small business owners retain control for long periods of time, they are able to bring a high degree of consistency into the way the firm is managed. This does not mean that small business owners will give employees everything they want – far from it, because they usually lack the resources to do so – but they are in a much better position to follow through on any promises they make.

Such consistency is much harder to achieve when organisations are large and subject to frequent changes in ownership or in senior management leadership. Public sector organisations have become a paradigm case of how much can go wrong with HRM within the management process. A large part of the difficulties experienced in the quality of employee relations in the public sector occurs because governments (in effect, the owners) change frequently, introducing new philosophies, policy requirements and senior leaders. In addition, the public sector is characterised by high-level policy groups, which can 'dream up' new bureaucratic initiatives, often from elegant theory, but without in-depth managerial experience and at a great distance from the people who actually deliver public services. On the positive side, governments have often had very valid reasons for wanting to control taxation and get better value for the public from government spending. However, a rhetoric of 'partnership' with the public sector unions sits uncomfortably with processes that involve workforce downsizing, privatisation, and contracting out of services, on the one hand, and increased bureaucratic controls through performance targets and audits, on the other (Bach and Kessler 2007). Rather than feeling like partners with government in reforms, public sector workers typically feel under greater stress and less trusted than previously. A common complaint is having too much bureaucratic work to do to get the real job done. Work intensification is particularly noticeable in Britain among professionals coping with the higher levels of client demand and escalating social problems that characterise contemporary health, education and social work (Kersley *et al.* 2006: 101).

The crucial role of line managers

The possibility for gaps between rhetoric and reality underlines the need not only for senior managers in large organisations to figure carefully what they want to achieve and then follow through on their pledges – achieving greater consistency in their own behaviour – but also indicates how dependent they are on lower-level line managers to achieve the results they seek.

While this includes both staff specialists, such as HR specialists, and line managers, the latter are particularly important if consistency is going to be high in HRM. Line managers are not ciphers or simple conduits. Line manager action or inaction is often responsible for the difference between espoused HR policies and their enactment. Many HR policies can only be converted to practice by line managers. Their behaviour often reflects the 'informal' or 'real' culture of the firm rather than the values articulated by top management (Truss 2001). In their interpretations of official policy, line managers are not necessarily trying to be perverse. They are often trying to make the organisation function more effectively. If the firm's executives are simply financiers rather than people with deep industry experience, the role of line managers in making things work on a daily level becomes even more important. Firms that are being spun off from larger ones, and in which financiers may be holding temporary ownership positions, can be at risk of operational collapse. Loyal supervisors and middle managers may be all that stands between viability and ruin.

Thus, at times, line managers help to keep a sinking ship afloat. At other times, they may be letting a policy die that they think is unworkable or against their interests. This can happen if senior managers or HR specialists have introduced a policy without consultation with those who must implement it. The relationships between HR departments and line managers are important and often contested (Hope-Hailey *et al.* 1997, McGovern *et al.* 1997). There are numerous examples of line manager adjustment of HR policies to make them more suitable for specific work settings or, on the 'dark side', for their own personal or political ends (McGovern *et al.* 1997, Whittaker and Marchington 2003, Batt 2004). These include policies in performance appraisal (Chapter 7) and in involvement and communication (Chapter 6), to name two of the most obvious areas which rely on line managers for their success.

The quality of the relationships between line managers and their team members is starting to receive greater attention in the analysis of HRM (Purcell and Hutchinson 2007, Purcell *et al.* 2009). Uhl-Bien, Graen and Scandura (2000:138) adopt the term 'leader–member exchange' (LMX) to argue that 'one critical element of HR systems that has not been well addressed . . . is the role of interpersonal relationships'. Research on managers and their subordinates, they suggest, 'shows that more effectively developed relationships are beneficial for individual and work unit functioning and have many positive outcomes related to firm performance' (*ibid.*: 143).

There is no doubt that ties within a work team can be much stronger than those with remote senior executives. It is much easier to trust someone you know, especially if you share their values and find them to be a person of competence and integrity (Macky and Boxall 2007). Becker, Billings, Eveleth and Gilbert (1996) find a stronger relationship between commitment to supervisors and performance than that found between commitment to the organization and performance. As Liden, Bauer and Erdogan (2004) comment, the 'immediate supervisor plays a critical role as a key agent of the organization through which members form their perceptions of the organization'. And, as Redman and Snape argue (2005: 304), 'there may . . . be a general tendency for the more cognitively proximal focus (i.e. supervisor or team) to exert greater influence over employee behaviour'.

Thus, research on the links between HRM and performance needs to take account of the mediating role of line managers since the HR practices that employees perceive and experience will be heavily influenced by the quality of their relationship with their direct manager. The quality of this relationship is, in turn, heavily shaped by the extent to which senior leaders in the firm invest in the selection, coaching, appraisal and reward of lower-level managers (Purcell and Hutchinson 2007). Like other employees, managers benefit from a supportive relationship with their immediate supervisor and from development programmes that help them with the challenges involved in managing people.

Variety in employee perceptions and responses

Employees, therefore, are going to be influenced not simply by top management values and formal policies but by the reality of what they perceive and experience on a daily basis. Some formal HR policies (such as their base rate of pay and the details of their pension) can be directly transmitted from policy to practice without slippage but much else is filtered through line managers, positively or negatively. In addition to the signals coming through the HR system, employees gain experience of the quality of material and financial resourcing in their organisation. High-sounding policies for employee rewards and development that are not met with good financial allocations are unlikely to be very convincing after a while.

All of this means that employees are receiving signals on various levels in a large organisation, with the potential for conflict among them. Not only this, but there is a question around whether they hear the same thing in relation to any one signal. In a sophisticated study of employees in a supermarket chain, Nishii, Lepak and Schneider (2008) show that employees can make quite different 'attributions' about management's purposes in implementing what seem to be the same HR practices. One employee can perceive a performance-related pay scheme as fostering service quality and employee well-being while another perceives it as an attempt to control costs and intensify their work. Different attributions then connect to different levels of satisfaction and commitment: predictably, those who interpret management's motives more positively are happier. Such variability in the attributions that employees make about managerial motives reinforces the importance of studying employee experiences of, and responses to, HR practices, rather than relying solely on management reports of a company's HR practices (Nishii *et al.* 2008: 528–9). Any one individual manager who is asked to respond to a survey about an organisation's HR practices can only reliably report their own perception of what the HR practices are supposed to be and their own experience of them in practice. They cannot authentically describe whether *other* individuals, including the vast bulk of employees, perceive the firm to have these HR practices in reality and how they affect their interests.

For each employee, then, there is a 'psychological climate' in the workplace: their own, individual sense of what is happening in their employment relationship and how it affects their well-being, which will then affect their individual attitudes and behaviour (James and James 1989). When employees, however, form a relatively common perception of management's intentions and actions, we can also talk meaningfully of a 'social' or 'organisational' climate in the workplace (James *et al.* 2008), which then becomes a collective mediator, or intervening variable, in the links between HRM and organisational performance. In stronger climates, with high levels of coherence and consistency, there is 'a shared perception of what the organisation is like in terms of practices, policies, procedures, routines and rewards – what is important and what behaviours are expected and rewarded' (Bowen and Ostroff 2004: 205). When management is seeking high levels of commitment, this shared perception needs to be as positive as possible with management deemed trustworthy. This does not rule out the need for difficult decisions at times – such as an unavoidable period of downsizing – but workforces are likely to adjust to these more quickly when the overall pattern of management style is deemed ethical and is as consistent as possible across time (Zatzick and Iverson 2006).

The role of shared perceptions in HRM is demonstrated in McKay, Avery and Morris's (2009) study of the 'diversity climate' in 654 stores in a large US-based retail organisation. They define a work context as 'pro-diversity when, consensually, employees feel they have an equal opportunity to succeed on the job and are made to feel like integral members of the organization' (McKay *et al.* 2009: 771). This means, for example, that both men and women, and people of different ethnicity feel treated fairly and respected for their views. What McKay *et al.* (2009) find is that the link between diversity climate and organisational performance is greater in those stores where both employees and their managers perceive there to be a highly pro-diversity climate. Performance is lowest in the stores where both report a less hospitable approach to diversity. The higher-performing stores, therefore, have a high level of positive consensus about the climate for diversity: this, clearly, is a 'strong' climate in Bowen and Ostroff's (2004) terms. Consequently, the point, is that organisations will vary in the extent to which individual psychological perceptions are shared across the group. Where they are, they can have strongly positive implications when management's motives are welcomed and management is trusted. However, it must be said, strongly shared negative perceptions of managerial motives and behaviour can do major damage, creating a legacy of low trust, as studies such as Grant's (1999) demonstrate.

A model of the 'black box'

We are now in a position to look at an expanded model of the mediating links that influence the effectiveness of HR systems. This model, shown in Figure 8.1, tracks intentions, actions, perceptions and responses and aims to integrate the individual and collective levels of analysis we talked about in Chapter 1 (Figures 1.1 and 1.2) and have fleshed out in the three preceding chapters in this section of the book. HRM involves attempts to build individual abilities, motivations and opportunities to perform (AMO) but this is set within a collective context in which management is trying to build relevant types of workforce capability and work organisation and a reasonably positive set of social attitudes.

At the far left of Figure 8.1 is the box containing the intended elements in HRM – such things as top management's espoused values and employee relations style and the organisation's formal HR policies, both for individuals and for larger groups. Alongside these intentions for how the firm will conduct its HRM are other relevant organisational policies, including those that structure operations and establish resource levels. What we are emphasising here is that the experience of work is not simply about policies that are explicitly called HR policies or are obviously to do with people. Much that is done in marketing, finance and operations management affects what people experience at work and the possibilities they have to express themselves.

The next key box in Figure 8.1 is the one where we represent management actions. There are three aspects here. First, senior managers not only form intentions but they also take direct actions, such as deciding actual budget levels and deciding what they will say in an important team briefing when financial results are disappointing. There are also direct actions by HR specialists in those parts of HRM, such as collective negotiations, which depend on their expertise and networks. How senior managers and HR specialists actually behave in carrying out the organisation's espoused voice practices is a key

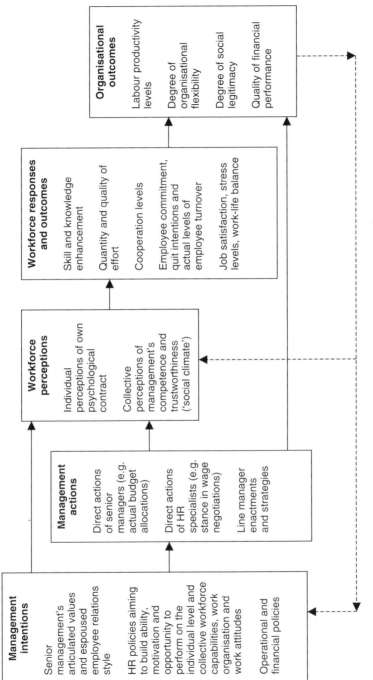

Figure 8.1 HR systems and the links to organisational performance

issue, as Chapter 6 explained. Then, very importantly, there is the behaviour of line managers as they enact HR policies – to the extent that they need to and want to – and also express their own personalities in the way they do things. Line managers are responsible for converting much of HR policy into actual HR practice, given the resources they are allowed to work with and their judgement about what will work or what serves their interests. We are emphasising here that HR practice is rarely a 'straight line'. It is more useful to think of HR practice as a 'curve' or a range of actual managerial behaviour around a notional policy line.

The next box in the figure represents employee perceptions and attributions, both individual and collective. On the individual level, where there is a gap between what management promises and delivers, people are likely to feel their psychological contract has been violated and are therefore likely to work less effectively and to look for other options, as explained in Chapter 7. Individual perceptions and attributions are always going to affect individual feelings and actions but they can feed into, and are influenced by, the larger social climate. This consists of collective perceptions of management's competence and trustworthiness, built up over time. As explained in this chapter, there is variability in the strength of this collective level of climate.

Perceptions and attributions lead on to workforce responses and outcomes: to growth in skills and knowledge, to particular kinds and levels of effort in individual and group working, to degrees of cooperation between management and labour and among peers, and to individual feelings of commitment, levels of employee turnover, job satisfaction, stress and so on. As we have been at pains to emphasise, these employee attitudinal and behavioural variables are key mediators which then feed into organisational performance, along with other factors in the way the organisation is resourced and managed. The figure is completed with feedback loops. This helps to make the point that more successful organisations are likely to be able to build better human and social capital over time: success often breeds success.

We are not saying through Figure 8.1 that all organisations should be aiming to achieve high levels of consistency across these links or outstanding levels of employee skill, trust, effort and commitment. This is not what all organisations are aiming for, as our discussion of HR systems should have indicated. In the informal model of HRM and in many types of outsourced HRM, for example, managers will often settle for adequate levels of employee performance at low costs. In low-skill services, where customers value low prices and are willing to take part in self-service, such an approach may be perfectly workable. However, the strategy will break down if the labour market tightens and managers have to worry about high levels of employee turnover.

Weak links in the HRM performance chain are also a strategic risk when prices are higher and customers expect careful attention from knowledgeable and accommodating staff. They are a risk whenever companies are trying to compete through higher quality and this depends on employees exercising high levels of skill and discretion.

The value in a diagram like Figure 8.1 lies in helping large organisations, in particular, identify weak links in the HRM-performance chain. Larger organisations are much more prone to internal contradictions, confusions and power struggles. This makes it more difficult to build the kind of idiosyncratic value in human and social capital that can underpin competitive advantage, as discussed in Chapter 4. A first step to building such a level of competitive performance lies in opening up more comprehensive ('dual') channels of employee voice, including employee opinion surveys, in order to provide the data that will help management to strengthen the links in the chain, as we explained in Chapter 6. This is a very practical idea to which we will return in the final chapter.

Conclusions

The HR strategies of firms are usefully thought of as clusters of HR systems. Each HR system is a set of work and employment practices that has evolved to manage a major hierarchical or occupational group in the firm. Over time, managers inevitably put their own twists on HR systems, both positive and negative. Small firms typically depend on a blend of familial and informal models while craft-professional models are critical to professional service firms, to large parts of the public sector and to various niches in manufacturing. Industrial and salaried models emerged first in large-scale manufacturing and then spread to the large 'office factories' of the private sector and the public sector bureaucracy.

The economic and technological context has changed significantly over the last 30 years and this has led to some major adaptations in HR systems. In various industries, firms based in high-wage countries are now seeking to compete through high skill and quality and have therefore moved from the industrial model to one which fosters higher employee involvement. Others have been seeking greater flexibility through lowering their labour cost structures and weakening their commitments to employees. They have used the opportunities presented by new information technologies, by globalisation and by weaker institutional constraints to outsource various functions and non-core parts of their operations.

The concept of 'internal fit' places a premium on achieving high levels of coherence and consistency in HR systems. Coherence is concerned with the extent to which HR policies are designed to reinforce each other while consistency is mainly to do with the strengthening the links from policy to practice within the management process and over time. We should never underestimate the value of coherence and consistency but they do not rule out the possibility that at times there will be trade-offs between organisational and employee interests or that management may need to change HR systems to cope with threatening change. A management team with a high reputation for competence and integrity will negotiate these difficulties more effectively, doing less damage to the social climate in the firm.

Firms that want to enhance the quality of their HRM need to think carefully about the 'black box' of links within HRM. There are fragile links between what is intended, what is enacted and what is perceived in HRM that lead on to important employee attitudes and behaviours and thence to organisational outcomes. While they hold resource advantages over small firms, these links are more difficult to manage in large firms, where there can be major slippage between intentions and outcomes. This includes the highly politicised organisations in the public sector where mixed messages in HRM have contributed to low morale and ongoing problems of effectiveness. The key links in the HRM-performance chain are also important in any firm which seeks to compete through high quality or in which the satisfaction levels of customers are sensitive to the interactions they experience with the company's staff.

part 3

Managing people in dynamic and complex business contexts

Human resource strategy
and the dynamics
of industry-based competition

In this section of the book, we move from our discussion of general principles underpinning HRM to an analysis of HR strategy in dynamic and complex contexts. In Chapter 10, we examine the twin complexities of HR strategy in multidivisional and multinational firms. In this chapter, we pick up an idea first advanced by Baird and Meshoulam (1988) – that HR strategy should somehow fit with the firm's stage of development.

Our goal in the chapter is to ask: how can HR strategy support business viability and how might it help firms to develop sustained advantage as they grapple with change in their industries? Readers will recall the argument in Chapter 2 that all firms face strategic problems. The primary problem is how to become and remain a viable player in the chosen industry. Various aspects of management – marketing, operations management, finance, and HRM – have a critical role to play in this. The fundamental priority of HR strategy in a firm is to secure and maintain the kind of human resources that are necessary for the firm's viability. To use mathematical terminology, a reasonably effective HR strategy is a necessary, but not sufficient, condition of firm viability. The 'second order' – or higher level – strategic problem is that of how to develop sources of sustained competitive advantage. In theory, there exists opportunity for any firm which remains viable in its industry to build some relatively enduring source of superior performance. This may depend more heavily on non-human than human resources while in other cases the reverse is true. In both scenarios, HRM needs to support the firm's efforts to build superior performance, either by nurturing an elite core of employees or by building a more extensive form of human resource advantage. How it might do so is something that is usefully analysed across cycles of stability and change in industries (Boxall 1998).

Industry dynamics: cycles of stability and change

We begin with the basic observation that firms are located in industries (Carroll and Hannan 1995). Even when we look at firms that have grown by unrelated diversification, we find that their constituent parts – their business units – can be located in particular industries. Individual business units do not compete with every other kind of business: they compete with those who seek to serve the same set of customer needs in much the same kind of way – or in a better way. This does not mean that business units compete with every other business in their industry. As we explained in Chapter 3, it is more accurate to identify the 'strategic group' in the industry with which they associate them-selves – a cluster of rivals who take significant interest in each other's products, technologies, executives, workforce skills and so on – without overlooking the fact that new competitors can come in 'from left field'. This is why it is useful to speak of *industry-based* rivalry.

It is important to note that the concept of rivalry does not mean that firms are constantly competing. The leaders of firms have a common inter-est in the health of their industry (Miles, Snow and Sharfman 1993, Nalebuff and Brandenburger 1996). They are certainly engaged in competition for survival and profitability but they also cooperate when it is helpful. Firms are frequently observed in collaborative efforts to develop foreign markets. Australian and New Zealand wine exporters benefit from the joint market-ing of 'New World' wines by their national trade organisations in Europe, for example.[1] They also have interests in collaborating in the labour market. The need to build a labour market on which all can draw is often a reason for co-location of firms (Levinthal and Myatt 1994). Good institutions for skill formation and labour supply benefit all firms in the sector. All Australian and New Zealand wine-makers, for example, benefit from supporting the excellent educational and research institutions, such as the School of Agriculture, Food and Wine at the University of Adelaide,[2] that help to ensure a good supply of graduates for the expanding Antipodean industry.

---

[1] http://www.wineaustralia.com/uk/, accessed 12/5/10; http://www.newzealandwineevents. co.uk/, accessed 12/5/10.
[2] http://www.sciences.adelaide.edu.au/wine/, accessed 12/5/10.

A focus on industry-based rivalry emphasises the point that history matters, a key argument in the resource-based view of strategic management discussed in Chapter 4. Industries emerge at particular points in time and evolve through periods of crisis – in which there are winners and losers – and periods of relatively stable growth (Schumpeter 1950, Miller and Friesen 1980, Tushman, Newman and Romanelli 1986). This understanding of industry evolution is analogous to the well-known biological concept of 'punctuated equilibrium': the idea that the life forms we find around us are not simply the product of incredibly long periods of time, as originally argued by Charles Darwin, but result from alternating periods of intense change and periods of gradual adaptation (Gersick 1991). For convenience in the argument that follows about the nature of industry evolution, the words 'business' and 'firm' are used interchangeably.

Phases of industry evolution

At the outset of industry formation, pioneering firms introduce product or service innovations that create new competitive space. They are typically joined by others who seek to exploit profit opportunities by imitating the pioneers (Carroll and Hannan 1995, Freeman and Boeker 1984). To get established at all, firms must either be successful leaders or successful followers. All industries, in effect, demonstrate a dynamic interplay between innovation and imitation (Schnaars 1994). Over the long haul, resilient firms exhibit an astute blend of the two processes, something than can be difficult for those business leaders who cannot accept emotionally anything 'not invented here' – NIH syndrome.

The microcomputer industry provides an interesting example of the dynamics of innovation and imitation. The legendary innovators, Apple Computer, and about a dozen other firms, entered the industry in 1976 (Carroll and Hannan 1995). Apple produced the first personal computer that could display colour graphics and which could operate with floppy disks. IBM, the industry behemoth, entered five years later, in 1981. For quite a while, David thrashed Goliath. Apple enjoyed the fruits of successful leadership through its various innovations (including the ability of Apple 11 to run spreadsheeting software.) However, as we all now know, IBM showed an extraordinary ability to execute an astute 'fast follower' strategy (Utterback 1994, Carroll and Hannan 1995).

The mature context arrives when the industry settles into a period of stable growth based around one or two 'dominant designs' for products or services and the organisations that provide them. The development of a

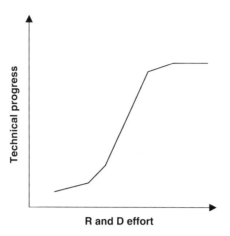

Figure 9.1   The S-curve
Source: Foster (1986).

dominant design in manufacturing industries enables firms to move quickly up what technology strategists call the S-curve (Foster 1986, Utterback 1994, Henderson 1995), depicted in Figure 9.1. High levels of R and D effort achieve slow progress to begin with but breakthroughs associated with the dominant design create the basis for rapid improvements. Ultimately, the potential of existing technology reaches some kind of performance limit or asymptote.

In the case of personal computers, the IBM PC brought together the defining features that shaped the industry standard: 'a TV monitor, standard disk drive, QWERTY keyboard, the Intel 8088 chip, open architecture, and MS DOS operating system' (Utterback 1994: 25). Dominant designs represent the strategic configurations that have proved more successful than rival models of strategic management in the establishment phase. As Mueller (1997: 827–8) puts it:

> At some point the market begins to select its favourite model designs, producers begin to concentrate upon the best production techniques. Those firms that have selected the 'right' product designs or production processes survive, the others depart. Following this 'shake-out' period, the industry stabilizes and enters a mature phase in which the number of sellers and industry concentration do not change dramatically.

In the mature context, those who remain credible members of the industry enter a period of relative stability in which the emphasis is on continuous improvement within the prevailing business paradigm. They vary, however, in their profitability and in their readiness for change. Stable growth is punctuated by the next crisis which calls for renewal or leads to decline. Renewal crises may be the result of a new round of technological or organisational innovation within the sector – not necessarily by the original pioneers – or may be introduced by a general threat external to all firms – such as a national or global economic recession, the decline of tariff protection, or a technological revolution in a different field which has dramatic implications across industry boundaries. In the case of technological challenges, particular technologies tend to reach limits (the flat top of the S-curve) and firms must move to new technologies (with their own S-curves) or fail if they cling to an obsolete technology (Foster 1986).

The renewal context challenges the continuities built up over the establishment and mature phases, threatening to turn previous strengths into weaknesses. It is very hard to change the 'core features' of organisations – such as their fundamental mission, their basic technologies and their marketing strategies – so the difficulty of change in the renewal context should never be underestimated (Carroll and Hannan 1995: 26–8). Two kinds of mature firms manage to survive (Baden-Fuller 1995). One is the firm that succeeds in dominating the direction of industry change: the ultimate level of economic achievement for any firm. The other is the firm that manages to adapt to the direction of change. This kind of firm incurs serious costs of adjustment but retains its viability by making the necessary changes without insolvency or loss of investor confidence. It imitates key changes by the new innovators quickly enough to stay afloat. All other firms fail. New entrants may, of course, appear at this point and may hold a winning advantage if they can add new sources of value and behave as nimble entrepreneurial firms which out-manoeuvre the more inertial mature organisations around them.

Successful weathering of the renewal crisis ushers in another opportunity for stable growth. In effect, the cycle of stability and crisis continues for as long as the industry remains relevant to a profitable set of customer needs. If it does not, the industry enters terminal decline and firms must find something else to do or disappear altogether from the corporate landscape. With the advent of free internet-based news services, the daily and weekly newspapers have been facing just such a challenge in the early twenty-first century. Their business model, which relies on a mix of advertising and a high volume of paying subscribers, is now heavily compromised. Many have closed, others are making major losses and some are consolidating their local market as their rivals collapse.[3]

---

[3] See, for example, http://www.digitaljournal.com/article/281092, accessed 12/5/10.

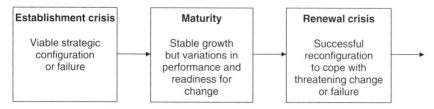

Establishment crisis	Maturity	Renewal crisis
Viable strategic configuration or failure	Stable growth but variations in performance and readiness for change	Successful reconfiguration to cope with threatening change or failure

Figure 9.2 Phases of industry evolution

The framework shown in Figure 9.2 has been drawn to encompass both goods and service industries. As noted, the S-curve is essentially a concept that relates to manufacturing or to service industries which depend heavily on manufactured technologies for customer service (such as air travel which depends greatly on aircraft technology as well as computerised reservation and passenger management systems). However, all industries – service, manufacturing, public sector and so forth – can be thought of as facing alternating periods of change and stability. Change need not stem from technological breakthroughs: it may stem from ecological, social or political change as well as general economic trends (such as the global financial crisis of 2008–9).

It is also important to note that Figure 9.2 does not imply that all industries change at the same rate across the contexts of establishment, maturity and renewal. Some, like the profession of law, in which precedent and personal service are so engrained, seem to change only in a slow, stately manner. New information technologies have been adopted in law offices but the fundamental nature of legal research and representation has changed very little over the last 100 years or more. Others, such as consumer electronics, seem characterised by what some consultants call 'permanent white water'.

A useful typology of differences in rates of industry change has been developed by Jeffrey Williams (1992). He distinguishes between slow-cycle, standard-cycle and fast-cycle industries (Table 9.1). One might usefully imagine a dental practice. The dentistry itself (extraction of teeth, filings and so on) is an example of a slow-cycle industry. Little has changed in the fundamental nature of dental work for a long period of time. On the other hand, the toothpaste used by the dentist and his/her clients is an example of a standard-cycle industry. The product is mature, controlled by huge oligopolists, and advertising budgets jostle to hold and enlarge market share. Finally, the accounting and client management software on the computer in the dentist's office may be an example of a fast-cycle industry. New upgrades, new versions are almost constantly available.

Despite variations in rates of change, the three-phase model of industry evolution – establishment, maturity and renewal/decline – is well supported by

Table 9.1 Three types of industry

	Class 1: slow cycle	Class 2: standard cycle	Class 3: fast cycle
Competitive analogue	Local monopoly	Traditional oligopoly	Schumpeterian
Rivalry	Relaxed: sheltered markets, isolated competition	Extended market share battles, competition on scale	Dynamic: intense rivalry, focus on innovation
Market scope	Narrow: company markets localized	Defined broadly: national or global mass markets and advertising	Varies: overlaps traditional markets, in state of redefinition

Source: Williams (1992).

research in industrial economics (Mueller 1997) and provides a useful basis for our analysis. Similar models are commonly used to analyse firm and industry evolution in strategic management textbooks (for example, Walker 2003).

HR strategy and industry dynamics

With this understanding of industry dynamics, we are now in a position to explore the challenges facing HR strategy in each phase or context. Much more research needs to be conducted on the dynamics of HR strategy. Where they are available, key studies are cited but the discussion is necessarily tentative and suggestive of further lines of enquiry. Our concern in each context is with what HR strategy needs to do to help secure the viability of the firm and, secondly, with what it might do to help create some form of sustained advantage.

The establishment context

Any serious search of the HRM literature will confirm that the establishment or founding phase of industry is the least studied of all by HRM researchers. Apart from the work of Hendry, Arthur and Jones (1995) on the role of human resources in the formation of small firms, the typical HRM text-book assumes a ready-made, large scale, bureaucratic corporation with an HR department whose staff are concerned with choosing and improving an appropriate set of human resource policies. Few HR researchers have studied small, entrepreneurial start-ups or even new ventures spawned by large corporations. Yet if we are to take the point seriously that history matters to competitive advantage, we must try to understand the roles human resources play in the establishment phase. Strategic management research indicates that that key decisions taken at founding have profound consequences, establishing a pattern of behaviour that is difficult (though not impossible) to change (Freeman and Boeker 1984, Boeker 1989, Eisenhart and Bird Schoonhovern 1990).

The need for talented entrepreneurs

We must begin with the obvious point that all firms depend on appropriate human capital to make any sort of beginning. At the outset, the fundamental kind of human talent needed is entrepreneurial. Firms are established by entrepreneurs or by 'intrapreneurial' teams in existing corporations (Schumpeter 1950, Porter 1985, Schnaars 1994, Freeman 1995, Mueller 1997). They are founded by people who create new sources of value ('pioneers') or by others who perceive that new value is being created and successfully join the industry ('followers'). It is possible to fail at both leading and at following. As noted earlier, success depends on being good at one or the other or at demonstrating an astute blend of the two over time. The resource-based view, discussed in Chapter 4, argues that pioneers can build strength through better timing and learning, moving more quickly up the 'experience curve'. This means that those following them tend to perform better if they are 'fast followers', capitalising on the market growth opened up by the leaders while astutely avoiding some of the mistakes that leaders can make.

What, then, do we know about the qualities of successful entrepreneurs? In a major US study of 'entrepreneurial human capital inputs and small business longevity', Bates (1990) finds that more highly educated entrepreneurs have a better chance of succeeding and of raising finance capital. The likelihood of business failure is lower for high school graduates and for university graduates than it is for those who did not complete high school. The rate of failure drops markedly if entrepreneurs have four or more years of university education. Better-educated business founders make fewer mistakes, it seems. This result has been supported by a study of top management teams in the UK which finds that these teams perform better when the individuals in them are better educated (West, Patterson and Dawson 1999). In a comparison of 50 rapid-growth and 50 slow-growth US companies, Barringer, Jones and Neubaum (2005) also conclude that education matters. It is likely, for example, that those educated in science or engineering disciplines benefit from the technological insights gained from their specialist education, which enable them to launch new products or develop new processes. In addition, Barringer *et al.*

(2005: 678) find that more successful founders tend to have greater industry experience, which provides them with 'critical knowledge plus the advantage of access to a network of contacts that can help'. This makes a lot of sense: a fairly common way of losing money is to buy a business in an industry in which one has no experience. Not only is the seller likely to take advantage of an ignorant buyer but the new owner simply lacks the critical know-how and network needed in the industry. Barringer *et al.* (2005) also suggest that some entrepreneurs are more highly motivated, more determined to make a go of it than others. Overall, then, research suggests that both ability and motivational factors make a difference to entrepreneurial success.

The need to stabilise a competent and well-coordinated workforce

While entrepreneurial talent is a necessary element, it is not, however, sufficient to ensure successful navigation of the establishment phase. Firms need to be able to secure the kind of 'stable and committed labour force' (Rubery 1994: 47) that will enable them to deliver on their promises to customers. They need to be able to recruit and retain a wider group of employees who work together effectively in expanding the founder's or the founding team's concept of the business. Otherwise, the business will simply not grow. As a study of 122 start-up companies in the USA emphasises, an ability to recruit employees is strategic to business growth, along with an ability to win customers and attract finance (Alpander, Carter and Forsgren 1990). Marketing ability, adequate money, and the people needed to handle the firm's operations come in as the three biggest factors explaining success.

Lack of growth potential is fine in those businesses, such as small professional-service firms, that can remain viable as permanently small firms (Storey 1985), but it does not work in other contexts. In many industries, firms need to meet a threshold for 'critical mass'. Viability depends on establishing credible operational capacity in the industry, on recruiting and retaining a pool of people with industry-relevant abilities. Whether firms can do this depends on the degree of labour scarcity in their industry and their ability to make competitive job offers. When labour markets are tight, it is often hard to attract talented people to employment 'in a relatively obscure company' (Alpander, Carter and Forsgren 1990: 14).

A classic example of an attempt to create a viable labour pool in the establishment phase comes from the automobile industry. Henry Ford 1 began production of the Model T in 1908, the same year in which General Motors was founded (Carroll and Hannan 1995). The Ford Motor Company experienced 370 per cent labour turnover in 1913, a level that was not uncommon in manufacturing at the time (Meyer 1981). In a context of massive product market growth, Henry Ford set out to create a large, competent and stable workforce with a highly innovative 'bundle' of HR policies. This included a rational system of job grading and promotion based on skill differences, along with the 'Five Dollar Day', an early example of 'efficiency wages' (Meyer 1981, Lacey 1986, Main 1990).[4] Facing a major problem with literacy levels, it also included a schooling system for workforce education. Ford's spectacular and controversial adoption of profit sharing (coupled with a highly demanding pace of work on the moving assembly line) ensured that he attracted and retained much of the best labour then available in the industry. Workers queued to get in. Once recruited, those who could not cope with the pace dropped out. Ford built a workforce which was at least equal to that of his rivals, a critical achievement at a time of labour transience in the USA. (His subsequent attempt to fight union organisation is not offered here as a model.)

It is wrong to assume that a good workforce is readily available when the skill requirements of the firm are advanced and specialised. High-skill industries can only survive in particular countries if that society generates sufficient numbers of people educated in the relevant science and technology. The great economic historian, David Landes (1998), cites the case of the chemical dye industry which grew phenomenally prior to the First World War. Germany trained far more chemists than anyone else, enabling the foundation and growth of the German chemical giants: Hoechst, BASF, Bayer and Agfa, all 'equipped with well-fitted house laboratories and closely tied to the universities' (Landes 1998: 290). When key German chemists teaching in Britain were 'drawn back home by attractive offers, the British organic chemical industry shrivelled' (*ibid.*: 290). In an illustration of the role of tacit knowledge (discussed in Chapter 4), the confiscation of German industrial patents during the war did not help American firms to emulate German chemical success. Not to be out-done, they turned to the recruitment of German chemists in the 1920s (Landes 1998: 291).

Our argument, therefore, is that stabilising a competent workforce of the appropriate size for the industry and for the firm's competitive goals is critical to viability in the establishment phase. This should not be thought about simply in terms of individualistic recruitment and retention. As Chapter 2 argued,

---

[4] Introduced in 1914. The effect was to roughly double the income of automotive workers employed by Ford. The length of work shifts was reduced at the same time: from 9 to 8 hours. 'Efficiency wages', in this case, means that there can be value in certain circumstances in paying a wage premium (well above the going rate) to improve the recruitment pool and reduce undesirable turnover of highly trained workers (McConnell and Brue 1995: 214).

effective teamwork is also needed. There needs to be reasonably good teamwork among top managers as well as throughout the organisation. Research on the establishment of the semi-conductor industry in the 1950s helps to illustrate these principles (Holbrook, Chen, Hounshell and Klepper 2000). One of the early leaders, Fairchild Semiconductor, combined a good mix of research and production skills in its core group of executives – the so-called 'traitorous eight' who broke away from the Shockley company (as noted in Chapter 4). Not only did this group work together well as a team but they worked hard to ensure that R&D activities were closely coordinated with the firm's production. When the ability of Fairchild to coordinate R&D and production was undermined in the mid-1960s, a subsequent breakaway formed Intel (Holbrook *et al.* 2000: 1027).

Sources of human resource advantage?

How, then, can firms use HRM not only to support their viability at this stage of development but to build some form of enduring advantage? This is clearly going to be difficult for new firms which start small. Large firms that have the ability to pay wage premia (significantly higher wages), and the capacity to offer superior internal development, are hard to compete against in the establishment phase. This certainly seems the case with long-established firms such as IBM that enter new markets and helps to explain why so many new businesses fail to expand successfully or remain small, tenuous organisations with ongoing recruitment and retention stresses (Storey 1985, Hendry *et al.* 1995). The bigger and more established firms operating in the same labour market have better financial resources and more developed 'internal labour markets' (Rubery 1994: 48–51). Large, established firms enjoy superior legitimacy with investors and bankers in the capital markets and with would-be employees in the labour market (Storey 1985). This enables them to offer greater training and career development possibilities to talented employees, something which many people want, as noted in Chapter 7. By comparison, many new firms suffer from what Stinchcombe (1965) calls the 'liability of newness'.

What possible routes are available for the very small new venture, founded by an under-capitalised individual rather than a well-known, multidivisional corporation? Arguably, this often means clever use of personal networking (Hendry *et al.* 1995, Leung, Zhang, Wong and Foo 2006) at a strategic moment in the industry's development. We might consider the example of a young, and very successful, entrepreneurial software engineer (Boxall 1998). This young entrepreneur used their network from Engineering School to recruit highly intelligent individuals willing to work outside large organisations (perhaps because they preferred an informal, 'can do' environment) and swiftly offered those who generated outstanding value an ownership stake in the firm to align their interests over the longer term. Having worked with them at university, the young entrepreneur had special knowledge about the abilities and predispositions of classmates as well as personal or social ties based on friendship and trust. This created an edge over corporate recruiters forced to rely on formal screening processes and more opaque forms of information (such as university grades) rather than personal knowledge and close connections. In terms of resource-based theory, the young entrepreneur lacked superior financial clout and market reputation but used personal background and social networks to out-manoeuvre recruiters from large, established organisations.

Our knowledge about sources of human resource advantage in the establishment phase is still very limited. It seems likely, however, that *early alignment* of interests among highly talented people plays a decisive role (as was the case at Fairchild Semiconductor). This means that history – being there at the right time – matters enormously in the creation of positions of strength in industries, as argued in the resource-based view. It also implies that clever use of personal knowledge – such as an ability to network among likeminded and similarly gifted people – is needed to overcome the formidable resource barriers associated with firms that are more established in labour and capital markets.

The mature context

We can be somewhat more confident about the priorities of HR strategy in the mature context. This is the familiar terrain of the HRM textbook. Writers typically assume that a viable business has been handed on from the establishment phase. To be fair, it is usually the firms which have grown beyond about 100 employees that employ HR specialists. This means that the vast majority of HR specialists are working in the mature context or in the renewal context into which it typically leads (see below).

Enduring principles but greater sophistication

Growth beyond the establishment phase into the mature context *does* introduce problems that require a different style of management. It is still vital to hire, coordinate and retain a sufficient pool of motivated labour with appropriate industry know-how. This principle is hardly likely to vary with time in the industry. However, the challenges of size, increasing workforce complexity, the need to comply with various employment regulations, and the possibility of unionisation, all mean that HR systems need to become more comprehensive and more formalised, as explained in Chapters 3 and 8. Reliance on the implicit philosophies and informal practices of the small, entrepreneurial firm becomes much less realistic. When recruited into a larger organisation, workers typically expect some formalisation of their role requirements in a written job description. They tend to expect some formal orientation which will introduce them, *inter alia*, to the firm's policies for training, development, pay, promotion and so on. Properly handled, formalisation eases the process of socialisation and psychological contracting by reducing uncertainty and limiting arbitrariness in management practice. Standardisation of policies also makes the management of staff more efficient because it reduces the transaction costs of employing large numbers of people.

On the other hand, the maturing of organisational structure can alienate the very people who have helped to make the firm successful so far. The trend to bureaucratisation may antagonise those who revelled in the informality and adrenalin-pumping riskiness of the firm's founding years. These individuals may experience a sense of loss, a sense that the company will never again be driven by the same white-hot creativity and sense of fun. Thus, growth can generate a tension around the desirability of bureaucratisation: on the one hand, it is needed to manage size and complexity and, on the other, it threatens the intimacy and flexibility of earlier times.

Supposing this tension does not get out of hand, firms that successfully survive the establishment crisis will have reasonably competent executive leadership and will have built an adequate operating workforce. They will typically have created a sound reputation as a source of respectable employment and have laid the basis of trustworthy employee relations. In terms of the HRM challenges facing the business, they should at least aim to retain 'competitive parity': their HR strategy may not be the best in the industry but it has not so far undermined the firm's growth. Arguably, this situation should persist providing there are no major reversals in the quality of HR strategy. At the very least, the firm's leaders should avoid turning their competitive parity in HRM into a form of competitive *dis*advantage (Purcell 1999: 241).

Figure 9.3 summarises the key dimensions of what is required in HRM to help secure a firm's viability. As indicated in our discussion, firms need talented and functioning leadership teams, along with a motivated and capable workforce which can reliably execute its work processes and deliver on promises to customers. These critical human resources are developed through an appropriate mix of HR systems and through supportive non-human resources, including adequate levels of finance. The arrows in the diagram are double-headed because of the interaction among these elements. For example,

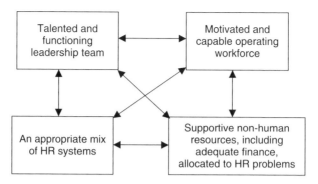

Figure 9.3 HRM and the viability of the firm: key elements

good HR systems and adequate funding will help the firm to recruit (or develop internally) good leadership teams. However, it is also true that good leadership teams will, over time, improve the quality of HR systems in the firm and make the kind of financial allocation decisions that enable it to attract and develop other people. Similarly, a motivated and capable workforce will help the firm to generate profits, part of which can be reinvested in HR systems.

Potential sources of HR advantage?

What, however, might a firm do if it wishes to develop some form of 'human resource advantage' in the mature context? What argument can be built from the resource-based view discussed in Chapter 4? Very little theory is available on this question but one argument is based on the value of improving the quality of management perception in HRM, the quality of HR planning, and improvements in the consistency of HR practice (Boxall 1998).

The quality of management perception in HRM
Firms vary in the quality of management's perception of the firm's strengths and weaknesses in HRM in relation to the strengths and weaknesses of rival employers. Specialised knowledge about individual HR practices is widespread (for example, the knowledge developed by recruitment consultants about selection tests or the knowledge developed by remuneration consultants about pay packages) but the ability to discern the *patterns* embedded in the firm's unfolding HR practices is more likely to be rare. The ability to perceive ways of minimising critical trade-offs in labour management (such as the trade-off between short-run employment flexibility and long-run employee commitment) is also likely to be rare (Boxall 1999).

Research suggests that few managers have a superior understanding of how to 'bundle' or integrate HR practices into HR systems that fit the firm's specific context and its unfolding strategies (MacDuffie 1995, Barney and Wright 1998). If, however, a firm employs individuals with this kind of rare knowledge and perception, and the opportunity to exercise it, what might prevent it being lost to rival firms? If much of the knowledge remains tacit, or associated with executive teamwork, it may be difficult for rivals to discern what it is or who has it (causal ambiguity and social complexity). There is little doubt, however, that this sort of skill will eventually become visible to good search consultants ('head-hunters') and therefore vulnerable to mobility. Individual perception remains, in effect, individual property.

The quality of HR planning

To build human resource advantage in the mature context, the firm needs to develop attributes that are more deeply institutionalised (Mueller 1996). A superior system of human resource planning, which identifies and integrates key human variables with other strategic concerns, is one way of institutionalising the perceptual insights of key HR strategists (either specialists or general managers) who may decide to resign from the firm. The kind of human resource planning which encourages firms to manage 'key value generators' proactively and plan to improve key processes (such as learning across intra-firm boundaries) is both valuable and rare (Koch and McGrath 1996). Human resource planning for concerns that transcend the short-term business context helps to avoid the all-too-common situation where financial targets, reinforced in the annual budget cycle, crowd out longer-term strategic issues in management planning (Goold 1991), a theme we take further in Chapters 10 and 11.

Even very large firms have problems developing sophisticated strategic planning systems which incorporate a framework of strategic HR objectives capable of structuring internal debate and decision making (Purcell and Ahlstrand 1994, Boxall 1999). How might such a discipline be developed and defended? Clearly it depends on the recruitment and retention of leaders who have exceptional HR insight, as discussed above. But this is not sufficient because so much of strategic management depends on good teamwork, as argued in Chapter 2. At some point, a powerful coalition of managers must evolve the conceptual framework and generate the consensus for its ongoing application. At a minimum, a shared understanding between the firm's most influential general managers and its top HR specialists, which persuades other key managers, seems essential. Any firm that achieves this has accomplished an unusual feat in the management process given the political conflicts and paradigmatic disputes that typically afflict the management teams of large organisations. The difficulty of overcoming these internal conflicts is a powerful barrier to imitation. It is not, of course, perfect: the loss of key individuals who act as process champions can compromise the quality of any planning system.

The consistency of HR practice

The possibility of developing HR advantage will be greater to the extent that intelligent HR planning is linked to superior consistency of enlightened practice (Benkhoff 1997, Mueller 1996). This is an argument we developed in Chapter 8 where the problem of major gaps between management intentions and actions in HRM was discussed. Significant gaps between management rhetoric and the reality of management practice can be particularly damaging, as illustrated in the work of Grant (1999).

As mentioned in Chapter 8, there is no such thing as the single HR practice of the firm. HR practice in large firms typically includes all sorts of variation around the formal HR policy position. Some of this variation is good because line managers can be trying to make poorly designed policies work better in practice. Other variations are negative, stemming from personal politics or from the difficult job line managers face in reconciling HR aspirations with the resources made available to them. In those multidivisional firms where HR strategy is very devolved, for example, but managers are only rewarded in terms of short-term financial results, long-term HR priorities can suffer, as we will explain in Chapter 10. While there is value in enhancing the ability of divisional or business-unit managers to make decisions that fit their circumstances, short-term performance incentives discourage long-term processes like management succession planning and development. This is not a problem if the firm's main rivals are equally weak at developing plans for long-term human resource development but it is not a recipe for building sustained advantage or undermining a more positively 'planful' competitor.

In summary, the argument here is that the possibility of creating HR advantages for a firm is greater when exceptional perception about HR strategy is embedded in sophisticated planning systems which are connected to consistent practice. The level of insight, and the degree of internal consensus, required to achieve this kind of superiority should not be underestimated. It is likely to be very rare.

The renewal context

The renewal context challenges the continuities built up over the establishment and mature phases. It threatens to turn previous strengths into weaknesses through technological (or other) shocks which call for a reconfiguration of the strategic paradigm in the firm (Schumpeter 1950, Tushman *et al.*

1986, Barney 1991, Mueller 1997). As noted earlier, two kinds of mature firms manage to survive (Baden-Fuller 1995). One is the firm that succeeds in dominating the direction of industry change. The other is the firm that manages to adapt to the direction of change. All other firms fail. New entrants may, of course, appear at this point and may hold a winning advantage if they can behave as clever and nimble entrepreneurial firms. They needn't necessarily be small firms: they may, for example, be special business units operating within very powerful multidivisional firms.

What, then, are the implications for human resource strategy? Rather than assuming that firms are privileged by their past, we must now regard history as a double-edged sword.

Conditions for securing viability

There are, arguably, three conditions firms must meet to retain their viability during this kind of industry upheaval (Boxall 1998). Two of these conditions are primarily concerned with HR strategy but the third is not.

The first is political. The renewal context threatens the patterns of mutuality – of interest alignment – that have solidified over the establishment and mature phases. The renewing firm needs the kind of mandate from its core staff which enables it to bring about major change without enormous resistance. Here the impact of the established hierarchy is important. To begin with, the key players in senior management must be able to form a new political consensus. As noted in Chapter 2, significant, unresolved conflict in the senior management team over the need for change (possibly linked to personal career ambitions and historical power bases) will disrupt renewal efforts at the outset (Hambrick 1987, 1995).

Having said this, the ability to open the political gateway at the senior level is necessary but not sufficient for successful renewal in the industry. It is also essential to achieve the necessary change to business capabilities while maintaining an adequate motivational climate throughout the core of the firm's workforce, thus ensuring wider political acceptability for the desired changes. Or, if a large part of the changes are to be formulated from the bottom-up, it involves achieving a culture of change acceptability which fosters a willing acceptance of new learning trajectories as a matter of course. In general terms, as we outlined in Chapter 8, HR systems have evolved in the last 30 years to accommodate higher levels of change. Some business leaders have been seeking to evolve their organisations into 'flexible bureaucracies', which have a core workforce but also use high levels of outsourcing for non-core functions that can be obtained much more cheaply elsewhere. Others have moved to a 'participatory bureaucracy', which embraces higher levels of employee involvement as a way of building better learning and resilience.

The second condition is perceptual. The firm needs leaders who can see what competencies will retain their relevance in the future while perceiving what capabilities have already become liabilities. Where, in effect, should the firm consolidate its learning and what should it 'unlearn' and to what extent (Miller and Friesen 1980, Leonard 1992, 1998, Snell, Youndt and Wright 1996)? And when, and in what order, should it make the desirable changes: how should it shape its 'strategic staircase' (Baden-Fuller and Stopford 1994)? Senior management faces a complex cognitive problem in discerning the kind, extent and timing of the change that is needed to enable the firm to survive. As noted in Chapter 2, this has been called the problem of forming a new 'mental model' (Barr *et al.* 1992). It is highly likely, of course, that senior management does not have all the answers in which case the firm's leadership must perceive how to design the sort of participative processes that will generate the necessary learning. The cognitive problem leaders face in renewal is not simply about content: it is also about process. It is altogether more complex than the perceptual problems associated with the mature phase.

The third condition is concerned with related resources. The firm must actually have the access to the financial resources it needs to make the necessary changes. As ever, human and non-human resources are interdependent (Mueller 1996). When renewal means radical change, it requires more than human willingness and cleverness. It requires the cash box to make things happen. Lots of firms fail at the renewal phase simply because they are under-capitalised, rather like the establishment phase. Despite great ideas and the best of intentions, no one will lend them any more money.

Opportunities for human resource advantage?

If these are the conditions for retaining viability in the renewal context, where do the opportunities lie for building sustained advantage through human resources? One argument is that it is simply a case of hanging on, of still being there once restructuring and rightsizing strategies – both good and bad – have made their mark on the industry landscape (Boxall 1998). Some rivals will have been fatally weakened in the process – perhaps because they divested the wrong bits – and will go into bankruptcy or suffer the sort of share-price collapse that makes them easy takeover targets. The firms with the bigger cash boxes then acquire their weaker rivals, retaining the branches or plants (and people) they really want and divesting or shutting down the rest. The industry concentrates around the strongest survivors. This process may not be pleasant – and rarely, if ever, discussed in HRM textbooks – but it does suggest that superior human capital will tend to concentrate in the dominant firms despite a prevailing climate of employment insecurity in the industry. On the other hand, the dominant firms cannot afford to be complacent because processes of concentration allow some clever teams to split away from the major firms and occupy specialist market niches (Carroll and Hannan 1995: 215–21).

Human resource strategy and organisational agility

An alternative argument is more proactive, asserting that the surest way to achieve human resource advantage in the renewal context lies in preparing for it more effectively in the mature context (Boxall 1998). Abell (1993) argues that the outstanding firm manages with 'dual strategies': 'mastering the present and pre-empting the future'. Duality implies superior perceptual and planning abilities in all contexts: the firm must not become locked into the inertia of a single strategy at any point in time. Providing the firm's industry does not collapse by becoming technologically irrelevant, this scenario is plausible in theory.

Based on exploratory case studies in the USA, Dyer and Shafer (1999) have developed a model of how HR strategy might support organisational agility. In their definition, agile organisations aim 'to develop a built-in capacity to shift, flex, and adjust, either alone or with alliance partners, as circumstances change, and do so as a matter of course' (Dyer and Shafer 1999: 148). In effect, they aim 'to optimise adaptability and efficiency simultaneously' (Figure 9.4). Recalling our discussion of HR objectives in Chapter 1, agile organisations can

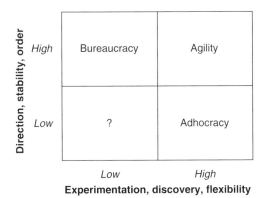

Figure 9.4 A definition of organisational agility
Source: Dyer and Shafer (1999).

be thought of as firms that aim for high levels of cost-effectiveness (in the current context) and high levels of organisational flexibility (to cope with future contexts). In terms of technology strategy, they are firms that can maximise the gains from their current S-curve while moving when desirable to the next one and reaping its benefits. It might be worthwhile to inject a note of caution here, however. In terms of Jeffrey Williams' framework (Table 9.1 above), it is firms in fast-cycle industries that most need this capacity. The idea that all industries demand this level of change readiness is exaggerated in popular accounts.

Dyer and Shafer (1999) note that organisational theorists tend to write about organisational agility with little regard for the people elements involved. To help fill this void, their model starts by defining the characteristics of agile organisations and works back through employee behaviours and competencies to desirable HR practices. We have paraphrased and summarised this model in Figure 9.5.

Dyer and Shafer incorporate resource-based thinking in their model: achievement of an agile organisation is very likely to be valuable and hard to imitate. The concept of an agile organisation is fleshed out to mean one that can read markets well (both current and emerging), can create a culture which welcomes change, and one that readily embeds organisational learning. Like Schuler and Jackson (1987), they then specify certain kinds of desirable employee behaviours and link these to HR practices (see Chapter 3). Much of this thinking is tentative and exploratory but flexible work design is central to Dyer and Shafer's model (fluid job assignments rather than fixed jobs or positions). They then suggest certain kinds of employment practice which should accompany fluid work organisation. The ideas here resonate with much that we described as a high-involvement HR system in Chapters 5 and 8.

As Dyer and Shafer (1999) advise, we need much more research on the nature of 'organizational agility', and the kind of HR strategies that might support it. One critical question must surround the problem of incentives or mutuality. Why would talented workers want to join an agile organisation if very little security is being offered and if, as a relatively flat organisation, little career development is possible? One can imagine that some people will want to buy into the culture for the sheer thrill, the joy of learning, and quite probably, the high pay level if the firm does well. However, as Dyer and Shafer (1999: 169) imply, it is likely that an agile firm will need a stable core of long-term, talented employees if it is to be able to sustain committed learning over time:

> Most agile organisations, contrary to what might be expected, lean toward a so-called closed internal staffing system ... They go to great lengths to retain core

employees who continue to contribute; most have relatively low voluntary turnover rates and, despite having little reluctance to part company with non-performers, most make every effort to avoid lay-offs because...they have rather extensive investments in their core employees.

Clearly, the design of agile organisations is a 'frontier area' in strategic HRM and more work will need to be done, particularly on the management of the strategic tensions involved (Evans and Genadry 1999). The contemporary environment contains major tensions between corporate needs for flexibility,

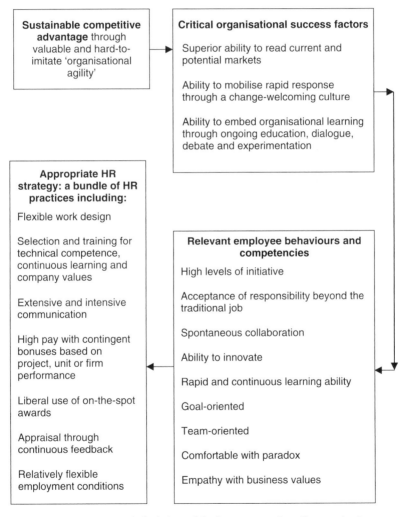

Figure 9.5 Dyer and Shafer's model of HR strategy in agile organisations
Source: Paraphrased and summarised from Dyer and Shafer (1999).

on the one hand, and typical employee needs for certain base-line elements of stability, on the other. Talented, versatile employees have good choices in the international labour market, so the need for compromise and adjustment is not one-way. Further work on how these tensions can be better reconciled is vital.

Conclusions

This chapter has built on resource-based concepts discussed earlier in the book and examined an area that is rarely thought about in HRM texts: the ways in which HR strategy might need to adapt across cycles of change and stability in industries. Not all industries change at the same rate but change pressures are universal.

Drawing on the distinction made in Chapter 2, priorities for HR strategy were considered from two angles: what is needed for viability in the industry and what might contribute to sustained competitive advantage? To achieve viability in the establishment context, firms need talented entrepreneurial leaders and need to be able to stabilise a competent workforce. Viability depends on establishing credible operational capacity. Whether firms can do this depends on the degree of labour scarcity in their industry and their ability to make competitive job offers. Firms cannot afford to assume that all the advanced or specialised skills they require will be readily available. Large, well-funded firms are obviously at an advantage when it comes to making offers of good pay and strong internal development to talented individuals. The small, under-capitalised business has great difficulty competing against better funded rivals but astute use of personal networking, and early alignment of interests, may help them to out-manoeuvre more bureaucratic organisations.

In the mature context, it remains important to create, coordinate and retain a sufficient pool of motivated labour with appropriate industry know-how. Firms that survive from the establishment context will have something close to competitive parity in HRM and should aim, at the least, to maintain it. However, they will find that the challenges of growth indicate that the style of management will need to change: size, diversity, regulation and the likelihood of employee representation will mean that HR systems need to become more comprehensive and more formalised. Arguably, sources of advantage can be created by firms whose management teams exhibit high levels of perception in HR strategy. Talented HR strategists can be lured away, so it is better if these insights are embedded in excellent HR planning systems and consistent HR practice. This combination of strengths is likely to be very rare. It is not unusual to find ways in which the HR performance of mature firms can be enhanced.

All bets are off in the renewal context. History could now be as much a source of 'core rigidity' as 'core competence' (Leonard 1992, 1998). Simply managing the perceptual, political and funding problems associated with survival is a major achievement. One of the most interesting questions in strategic HRM concerns the characteristics of 'agile organisations', firms that anticipate the need for renewal and are well prepared to take advantage of it (Dyer and Shafer 1999). Arguably, this is more important in fast-cycle industries. Existing work is exploratory and research in this area needs to consider ways in which tensions between company and employee goals can be managed more effectively. There is no doubt that agile organisations need greater flexibility but they are unlikely to reach high performance levels without stabilising at least a critical core of highly talented individuals and teams who work in a highly participative way. In working out the tension between stable harvesting of the current environment and preparation for radical change, firms are likely to find that at least some strong commitments need to be made to fair, interesting and reliable employment relationships if they are to attract and hold talented staff.

10

Human resource strategy in multidivisional and multinational firms

Most models of strategic HRM start with the premise that the firm is an independent entity engaged in a single kind of activity. With this assumption in place, it is possible to model the behaviour of the firm, as we did in Chapter 9, examining the role of HRM within business strategy as the firm and its industry evolve over time. All models need to reduce the infinite complexity of organisational life through a process of variable reduction, enabling us to make some sense of what is going on and extrapolate trends. Sensible though this is, it can reduce complexity too far. We aim in this chapter to take account of the effect on HR strategy of being a multidivisional, and often a multinational, firm and we discuss the ways in which these firms frequently use mergers and acquisitions to grow. These are the most complex contexts in which HRM takes place and they are critically important for the quality of HRM and organisational performance in advanced economies.

A chapter like this recognises that multidivisional firms are widespread. It is common in developed economies for many workplaces to be part of larger organisations where top management is geographically remote, either domestically or internationally. For example, in 2004, in the UK, 58 per cent of all workplaces with at least 10 employees were branches of multi-site organisations (Kersley *et al.* 2006: 20). This was true for nearly every workplace in the public sector and around one in two private-sector workplaces.

We treat multidivisional and multinational firms as companion topics in this chapter because foreign direct investment (FDI) is a major driver of the growth of multi-site organisations. Foreign ownership in the UK more than doubled between 1980 and 1998 (Millward, Bryson and Forth 2000: 32) and grew again in the period to 2004. By then, 31 per cent of private sector workplaces were wholly or partly controlled by foreign companies, compared with 23 per cent in 1998 (Kersley *et al.* 2006: 19). The largest proportion were US-owned (37 per cent), followed by other European multinationals (23 per cent) (*ibid.*: 19). Much of this development has been through mergers and acquisitions 'which constitute around three quarters of FDI. In 2006 alone, over 600 British firms were acquired by a foreign multinational, more than a quarter of the EU total and more than 10 per cent of the global total' (Edwards and Walsh 2009: 285). The proportion of shares listed on the UK stock exchange owned by investors outside the UK rose from 4 per cent to 36 per cent between 1981 and 2004: a ninefold increase. The UK has one of the most open, or least regulated, economies when it comes to company mergers and takeovers. This is often a matter of some controversy, recently seen in the acquisition of the iconic British company, Cadbury, by the US multinational, Kraft, as mentioned in our discussion of the globalisation of production in Chapter 5.

The inexorable rise of the multinational company (MNC) is having a major impact on strategy and HR practice in multi-site organisations. This is not just in those workplaces now owned by an MNC. There is also an indirect effect on suppliers through the use of procurement requirements, which often have implications for HRM. A form of 'regime competition' is evident as nation states seek to attract foreign investment. A good example is the announcement in 2010 that Nissan will build its new electric car (the 'Leaf') in the northeast of England and nowhere else in Europe. The quality of the workforce there certainly helped the decision, but so too did a government grant of £20.7 million[1].

The rise of MNCs has, in fact, been a major feature of the last 20 years. By 2007, global FDI had reached $1,833 billion, ten times its value in 1990 (UNCTAD 2008: 3). There are now estimated to be 79,000 MNCs worldwide, more than double the total in 1990 (*ibid.*: p. 9). Multinationals employ increasing numbers of workers: employment in their overseas operations totalled 82 million in 2007, up from 25 million in 1990 (*ibid.*: p. 9). Amongst the OECD (advanced industrialised) countries, one in five employees work for an MNC and a further one in five is employed in companies supplying MNCs (Marginson and Meardi 2010: 207). The ownership and leadership of MNCs is heavily based in the richest countries, in 'the Triad' of the United States, Western Europe and Japan (Ohmae 1985). In 2005, all but four of the top 50 multinationals were headquartered in the Triad (Croucher and Cotton 2009:16). However, MNCs are now developing strongly in the

---

[1] http://news.bbc.co.uk/2/hi/8573724.stm, accessed 8/6/10.

BRICs (Brazil, Russia, India and China). The expansion of Chinese MNCs is set to become one of the biggest business stories of the twenty-first century.

The task of this chapter is to assess the implications of multi-business and transnational firms, and the way they grow, for strategic HRM. We do so by first examining the structural arrangements of multidivisional organisations, paying particular attention to philosophies of corporate control and how these affect HR strategy. Attention is then turned to the particular challenges of strategy in MNCs and how HRM is an important aspect of them. This is followed by an analysis of mergers and acquisitions, which are an important strategy for growth, both in divisionalised firms and in MNCs. These growth strategies, however, need very careful handling. They have major implications for HRM and can easily destroy corporate value when the HR issues are poorly managed.

Structure, control and HRM in multidivisional firms

To get to grips with the ways in which HRM is a strategic issue in the management of large, diverse firms, we need to look at trends in their structure and control. This takes us into an understanding of the dynamics of the multidivisional company (the 'M-form' company) and the way it has spread to a dominant position worldwide. Some argue that we are now seeing the emergence of a new type of M-form based around networks: the 'N-form' (Hedlund 1994). The evolution of the N-form company has major implications in the way that critical resources of human and social capital, including managers and expert workers, are developed and interact across boundaries, whether organisational or political-geographic.

In so doing, we need to look at the impact of ownership and control on workplace HR systems. Our concern first of all is with dilemmas in structural configuration and with the forms of control exercised from headquarters, the corporate office. To what extent do multidivisional firms centralise or decentralise their decision making and with what implications? And should corporations seek to integrate the different businesses they own, or treat them as separate entities but try to manage them better than if they were wholly independent? The crucial question is how does the centre add value, how does it develop what has been called 'parenting advantage' (Goold, Campbell and Alexander 1994)? And what contribution, if any, does HRM make to parenting advantage?

Most firms start as single businesses. As they grow and mature, and as the market they serve changes, a number of critical choices must be faced. Will the firm's competitive position in its current markets be sustainable once new entrants arrive, is there sufficient capital available from revenue to fund future investment needs, is the market maturing such that growth potential and margins are likely to be eroded? Another type of question faced is whether there are opportunities to use distinctive technologies or know-how to enter other markets. What is certain is that doing nothing is rarely viable and, for many business leaders, rather boring too. One route to growth is to branch away from the traditional market: in other words, to diversify. This could be to do the same thing in a new market, as British retailer, Tesco, did by expanding into Central and Eastern Europe and the Far East, especially China, and into the USA with the acquisition of Fresh & Easy. By 2010, two thirds of its floor space was outside the UK.[2] Another route is by vertical integration, seeking both to protect the supply chain and to enter new markets where there is growth potential or to make life more difficult for competitors by cornering a market position. It may also be that another firm possesses knowledge of a technology or market that the single-business firm lacks or, indeed, they may feel the lack of general management expertise. Whatever the reason, the critical choice that follows is how far to pursue diversification and how best to manage a diversified business.

To begin with, the traditional firm adopts a functional or unified form ('U-form') where specialists in marketing, operations, finance and HRM each coordinate their own areas, linked to the board of directors through the chief executive (CEO) and, usually, a separate chairman. The board will most likely contain non-executive directors drawn from 'the great and the good' in the business world to provide oversight, advice and access to networks. As firms diversify, this structure is placed under severe strain. Policy and operating decisions become increasingly difficult when managers have responsibility for multiple sites and markets, which each require some unique adaptation to their particular situation.

As a result, a common organisational form for the multi-business company is the holding company where the corporate office owns the various companies in the portfolio but allows each to manage its own affairs as a separate business and to retain a proportion of the profits that they generate. In effect, the holding company is a type of institutional shareholder or friendly banker. A common criticism, however, is that the holding company may do little to add value and may, in fact, destroy value by protecting the inefficient

---

[2] http://www.guardian.co.uk/business/2010/jun/08/tesco-terry-leahy-profile, accessed 14/6/10.

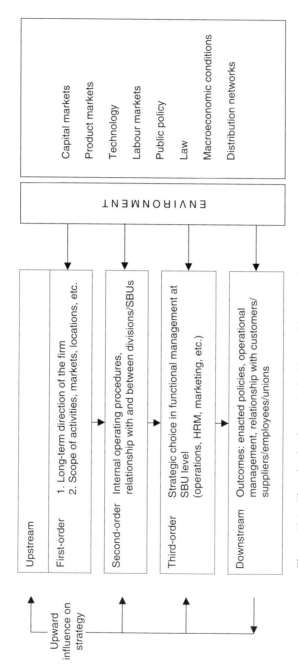

Figure 10.1 Three levels of strategic decision making in Anglo-American multidivisional firms
Source: Purcell (1989).

Upstream

First-order
1. Long-term direction of the firm
2. Scope of activities, markets, locations, etc.

Second-order
Internal operating procedures, relationship with and between divisions/SBUs

Third-order
Strategic choice in functional management at SBU level (operations, HRM, marketing, etc.)

Downstream
Outcomes: enacted policies, operational management, relationship with customers/ suppliers/employees/unions

Upward influence on strategy

ENVIRONMENT

Capital markets
Product markets
Technology
Labour markets
Public policy
Law
Macroeconomic conditions
Distribution networks

businesses or preventing the good from gaining access to the capital market to fund further expansion.

The American solution to the problem of how best to manage diverse businesses was the adoption of the M-form structure. In a famous book in the early 1960s, Chandler (1962) extrapolated from the experience of General Motors under Alfred Sloan to assert that 'structure follows strategy'. This meant that decisions on the long-term direction of the firm and the scope of its activities (its 'corporate strategy') should be the dominant factor in decisions on the structure of the corporation. These 'second-order' decisions on internal operating procedures, and, especially for our purposes, the relationship between parts of the organisation, flowed from 'first-order' corporate strategy. This has a profound influence on the location of decision making in HRM, both directly, and indirectly (seen in how corporate control is exercised over operating decisions and activities). HR strategies in operating units are then best seen as a 'third-order' activity or 'downstream' process, which is deeply influenced by first- and second-order strategy (Figure 10.1).

Thus, the distinctive feature of the M-form organisation is a clear separation of 'operational management' from 'strategy makers' in the corporate office. All profits are returned to the corporate office and frequent reports are required on performance, such as rate-of-return on sales (ROS) or rate-of-return on investment (ROI). In effect, the M-form company is composed of a number of U-form profit centres or, to use the preferred term, 'strategic business units' (SBUs). These SBUs are often limited liability companies in their own legal status. Between SBUs, which often face distinct, narrowly defined markets, and the corporate office, divisional structures may exist to coordinate whole sectors or geographic areas (for example, a European division, an American division and a Middle East division). In the rational minds of industrial economists, M-form companies have five advantages over other forms of corporate control. Williamson (1970: 120–1) argues that these are:

1. The responsibility for operating decisions is assigned to (essentially, self-contained) operating divisions.
2. The elite staff attached to the general office performs both advisory and auditing functions. Both activities have the effect of securing greater control over operating division behaviour.
3. The general office is principally concerned with strategic decisions involving planning, appraisal and control, including the allocation of resources among the (competing) operating divisions.
4. The separation of the general staff from operations provides general office executives with the psychological commitment concerned with overall

performance rather than becoming absorbed in the affairs of the functional parts.

5. The resulting structure displays both rationality and synergy: the whole is greater (more effective, more efficient) than the sum of the parts.

Whittington and Mayer (2000: 67), following the work of Jelinek (1979), note the similarity with the scientific management of F.W. Taylor, described in Chapter 5:

> The separation of strategy and operations ... was the analogue of Taylor's own separation of conception from execution on the shopfloor. Divisionalisation was the scientific management of the corporation.

Seen in this way, the M-form becomes less of a structure than a process of managing or a basic philosophy of corporate management that could be applied anywhere. It grew first in the US private sector and then spread throughout the Anglo-American world. In a copy-cat way, the 'marketisation' of the public sector, which we discussed in Chapter 5, was built on the principle of the separation of strategy from operations, adopted with new performance reporting requirements and with the single-minded pursuit of efficiency or, to use the language of the private sector, 'shareholder value'.

The ultimate logic of the M-form structure or process of control is that an increasing number of firms will move from being single businesses through a process of gradual diversification and divisionalisation into a collection of related businesses, each serving different markets. The next logical step is further diversification so that the corporation is composed of unrelated businesses, usually called 'conglomerates'. At this final stage, no one business dominates the portfolio by having 70 per cent or more of corporate turnover and there are little or no market or technological relationships among businesses. This seems to be the logic of the 'private-equity' firms which rose to prominence, if not notoriety, at the time of the boom which preceded the global financial crisis of 2008–9. Private-equity firms took the leveraging of debt – buying and selling companies through borrowed money – to new heights to acquire often unrelated, mature businesses. They then sought to extract value through a focus on efficiencies, including the shedding of labour, at least initially (Folkman *et al.* 2009). As private companies, not traded on the stock exchange, relatively little is known about how these firms operate in the strategy-structure sense beyond that managers in the acquired firms are heavily incentivised through performance-related pay with the source of gains, at least before the crash, often coming from financial dealings.

In recent years, the attractiveness of conglomerates has waned and many have divested some of their businesses in order to refocus the corporation around a few related businesses, known colloquially as 'sticking to the knitting'. In a sense, the high point of the M-form was reached in the last quarter of the last century, when it was seen as superior in terms of profitability and shareholder value (Rumelt 1982, Hill and Pickering 1986), but it still remains the dominant logic for organising and controlling multi-business firms. There is clear evidence of a growth in diversification and a move to M-form structures beyond the Anglo-American environment to cover parts of continental Europe (Whittington and Mayer 2000) and well beyond. 'Country differences have been erased as most major corporations have learned to dance to the same drum beat of divisionalisation and decentralisation' (Kidruff 2001).

What happens to HR strategy in the divisionalised company?

The critical question for HRM is how the corporate office seeks to manage the SBUs or operating units. Here, there are two fundamental approaches. One is to emphasise financial controls, keeping the units at arm's length from the centre and often from each other. The other is to build synergies, to emphasise collaboration and knowledge sharing. This is a rather exaggerated dichotomy and reality is less clear-cut but it is hard for the corporation to do both equally well since one is premised on the separation of units and the other favours a kind of integration.

In most cases, the divisionalisation of companies tends to heighten the emphasis on profit accountability. Corporate executives focus on the setting and monitoring of financial targets for SBUs while minimising administrative controls on other areas of management. As Goold and Campbell (1987) note, this can be liberating for SBU managers and the use of high-value performance-related pay, where bonuses can easily constitute one third or one half of an executive's remuneration, and sometimes more, can be a real incentive, as private-equity companies have found.

In the typical Anglo-American model, budgets are negotiated or imposed annually, planning horizons are short, and performance targets are monitored frequently: 'these companies are willing to act speedily to exit from the businesses that are not performing or do not fit... and are quicker to replace managers, fiercer in applying pressure through the monitoring process and more effective in recognising and acclaiming good performance' (Goold and Campbell 1987: 126, 132). This decentralisation of operating decisions, but strong, centralised control over budgets, has important implications for work and people. It means that the general managers of operating units are given much greater autonomy over many aspects of HRM, such as how many people to employ, the types of pay systems to use, and decisions on recruitment, training and development (Marginson *et al.* 1993). There are, however, some important exceptions: few organisations, for example, give *carte blanche* to SBUs on questions of trade union recognition. The corporation will often have firm views on such matters, with US-owned corporations being notorious for favouring union avoidance wherever they can.

In this model, therefore, investment decisions are made by the corporate office and the SBU operating budgets, as approved, usually have no reserved area for HR priorities, such as a particular level of investment in employee training and development. Such issues are devolved to the SBU general manager. The problem is that management by short-term financial targets tends to render desirable long-term HR goals difficult to achieve (McGovern *et al.,* 1997). Since human resourcing is an indirect cost, SBU managers will often look for ways to reduce 'HR overheads', including through outsourcing. Devolving HRM to SBU control is as much about budgetary constraint as it is about progressive policies to encourage line managers to be responsible for the management of their own people.

In addition, strong decentralisation and separation of businesses to expose profit responsibility renders it difficult to emphasise or build on relationships between business units. Each is treated as an atomised unit. Additionally, in some multidivisional firms, managers beyond head office simply have contracts of employment with the operating company, not with the corporation. This means they are not considered as a corporate resource and management development across the group can suffer.

As noted, the predominance of organising the control of SBUs through the use of financial economies is a particular feature of Anglo-American corporations. It is explained in large measure by the dominance of short-term capital markets emphasising shareholder returns, which may even have become more pronounced in the recent era of 'financialization' (Sisson and Purcell 2010: 91, 98). It is not, however, a model of capitalist management that enjoys universal support. Jacoby's (2005) careful analysis of US and Japanese corporations shows how, despite facing common competitive pressures unleashed by globalisation, Japanese firms still retain a more stakeholder-oriented perspective, which gives employees a greater role in corporate strategy and governance. Human resource departments are much more influential than in their US or British counterparts. This draws attention to the debate on 'varieties of capitalism', which we noted in Chapters 1 and 6.

An alternative form of corporate control, therefore, places more emphasis on 'synergy'. Where M-form companies organise around related businesses, there are likely to be knowledge or technological links between divisions. The corporation's leaders can, if they wish, manage these linkages to add value. For example, this may be through vertical integration along the supply chain, requiring integrated production and distribution, although nowadays vertical integration is often combined with, or superseded by, outsourcing and strategic alliances. Alternatively, synergy may be pursued through a process of building and spreading product or process innovations. Inter-business relationships may be designed to achieve 'scope' economies through the exploitation of a common-root technology, as we explained in our discussion of core competencies in Chapter 4. Here, organisational practices which focus on knowledge creation and sharing are crucial (Volberda 1998), meaning that managers will be encouraged to communicate more frequently and assist one another without simply thinking of their own territorial interest.

The critical point of this search for synergies is that corporate management cannot simultaneously achieve the financial economies of separation and decentralisation and those of synergy. Choices have to be made, structural models have to shift, and HRM needs to come into some kind of alignment. After the logic of separation in the M-form, some argue that firms seeking synergies have moved towards the N-form, organised around networks (Hedlund 1994). 'The N-form works best with the Eastern appreciation of the tacit, the embedded and the ambiguous, rather than the explicit, tightly specified knowledge systems of the West' (Whittington and Mayer 2000: 81). An apt metaphor is between the masculinity of the M-form and the femininity of the N-form. An example of what this might mean comes from the transformation of General Electric (GE) from a financially controlled corporation to a more synergistic one under the leadership of Jack Welch (who retired in 2001):

> By 1990, Jack Welch had formulated his notions of coordination and integration within his view of the 'boundaryless company'. A key element of this concept was a blurring of internal divisions so that people could work together across functions and business boundaries. Welch aimed at 'integrated diversity' – the ability to transfer the best ideas, most developed knowledge, and most valuable people freely and easily between businesses. (Grant 1998: 415)

This kind of highly networked approach to knowledge and people is what we termed the 'participatory bureaucracy' in Chapter 8. To achieve cross-business synergies, it draws on high levels of sharing and trust and, underpinning this, high levels of commitment to employees and suppliers. This means it requires higher levels of investment in the workforce and, inevitably, in teams of HR specialists to support this. HR departments need to be more generously staffed, giving them time to pay attention to management and employee development and be concerned with the transmission of innovative practices across the group. In reality, many Anglo-American firms are not taking this option. Instead, they are more concerned with cost levels and have adopted outsourcing and offshoring of non-core operations when they consider it delivers acceptable or superior performance. This is the 'flexible bureaucracy', as explained in Chapter 8, and it implies a much more restricted or 'focused' investment in the workforce. If the divisionalised firm is to be astutely led, an elite core of managers and specialists does need to be nurtured but there are typically fewer HR specialists in the corporate head office, employee and supplier contracts are more contingent, and there is a more restricted investment in employee and managerial development throughout the group.

Strategy and HRM in multinational firms

Any discussion of the management philosophies of multidivisional firms leads naturally into a discussion of multinationals, which typically have some kind of divisionalised structure. The distinguishing feature of multinationals is the fact that they have internationalised: they have developed operations in at least two, and typically more, countries. They often start by adding an international division to their existing multi-business structure. However, coordinating international operations can be very difficult unless the company establishes offices in its foreign markets. The management environment is different in the three broad regions of 'the Triad' – Europe, with its extensive legal frameworks in the EU social chapter, North America, with its emphasis on market individualism, and the Far East, with its concern for group relationships (Li and Cropanzano 2009). Recent large-scale research on MNCs in the UK reveals that three quarters of MNCs standardise a product or service across Europe or globally and around 80 per cent integrate operations across borders by supplying to, or receiving, components and services from other plants in other countries (Edwards *et al.* 2006). This is reflected in organisational structures with 82 per cent having a regional structure, 68 per cent having a global business function and two thirds having an international product division. These complex, overlapping structures reflect the need to integrate global corporate direction with regional and national management as well as extract efficiencies through cross-border product divisions.

The MNC, then, is a more complex version of the M-form company, one in which structure and strategy are both more complicated because they have transnational dimensions. To understand them better, we need to ask why some companies adopt internationalisation as a growth strategy. Dunning (1993) suggests that the decision to internationalise depends on three conditions. First, the firm must have an ownership advantage that firms in other countries do not have. Its source of competitive advantage may stem from brand reputation, from the control of supplies and materials or from special know-how. Second, it must be advantageous for the firm to keep these advantages to itself rather than seek alliances or other forms of production and distribution that might dilute them. This is particularly the case where it is necessary to preserve exclusive knowledge. Finally, the firm must stand to benefit from 'location-specific advantages', such as access to local markets, raw materials or a competitive labour force. This does not necessarily mean the cheapest labour available in the world but a workforce which has the productive skills and will work at a competitive cost. Although multinationals increasingly seek out cheaper labour, as we shall emphasise below, they will typically rule out workforces that lack the level of educational attainment or skill that is needed to be productive (Marginson and Meardi 2010). As emphasised in Chapter 1, labour is only supportive of a firm's performance when it is both cost competitive and effective (that is, cost-effective).

However, Dunning's (1993) analysis is largely based on economic theory and tends to overlook the political dimensions that come into multinationals' decision making. For example, the 'geographical scope of a multinational's operations [may give] it a powerful position in its dealings with nationality-based institutions . . . able to negotiate tax breaks and aid packages with governments' (Edwards and Rees 2006: 56). A firm may also internationalise in order to put political pressure on its home-base workforces to accept changes in work practices, a form of *reverse* diffusion where the MNC learns from overseas experience and imports it back into its home country. Setting up international operations can be a 'forcing' strategy, as explained in Chapter 6.

In thinking about the decision to internationalise, it can be helpful to use Bartlett and Ghoshal's (1989) distinction between 'multinational' and 'global' industries. In the former, responsiveness to local conditions is critical since each local market has unique characteristics. This distinction is expressed a little differently by Porter (1990) who calls multinational industries 'multi-domestic'. In service industries, such as life insurance and retailing, 'competition takes place on a country by country basis' (Porter 1990: 53). Firms in global industries, in contrast, such as the automobile industry, often attempt to achieve 'economies of scope' through standardisation. While the prime aim of FDI in multi-domestic firms is 'market seeking', for those in global industries, it is 'efficiency seeking' (Marginson and Meardi 2010: 212). MNCs seeking efficiency savings are increasingly using high levels of offshoring to gain quantum improvements in cost structures. For example, we made reference in Chapter 1 to the decision by the electric appliance manufacturer, Dyson, to relocate production to Malaysia for cost reasons while keeping R&D in the UK.

The choice of where to locate is influenced by considerations such as 'market size, proximity to customers, infrastructure, investment incentives, taxation, ease of divestment and labour costs' (Cooke 2007b: 493). It is quite likely that some countries are ruled out simply because they lack political stability and are unsafe or lack an adequate infrastructure of ports, roading and electricity or an adequate level of basic education. However, when these sorts of factors stack up, it is likely that labour costs loom large in the calculation, along with the degree to which management has power to manage. Cooke (2007b: 493) summarises several studies which 'yield strong and highly consistent evidence that MNCs typically (but not always) invest less than they would otherwise in those countries in which industrial relations systems are characterised by factors viewed by employers as driving up unit labour costs; either directly or indirectly by restricting the freedom of employers to manage human resources'. Among these factors, beyond just unit-labour cost considerations, are restrictive workplace policies and regulations, collective bargaining conditions, notably a dislike of multi-employer bargaining, and a history of strikes.

In effect, some countries have a kind of regime advantage, which attracts foreign investment. The UK and Ireland are good examples of what this means in terms of competition for plant locations in Europe. Government ministers in the UK often point to the UK's relatively 'flexible labour market' as attractive to MNC investment. What this euphemism really means is that, compared with continental Europe, it is easier to make workers redundant in the UK: there are fewer employment rights given to workers, especially temporary and agency workers. MNCs in the UK use agency workers more than domestic firms and have done so consistently over many years (Edwards and Walsh 2009: 298) In effect, the costs of exiting the business in the UK are significantly lower than, say, in France or Germany, a matter of bitter complaint from trade union leaders. Much the same applies in Ireland where FDI has been crucial in expanding the economy. Over the last twenty years, and helped by very low corporate tax rates (another dimension of regime competition), this enabled Ireland to become 'the Celtic tiger'. Now, however, the withdrawal of major firms, such as Dell Computer, in the global recession of 2008–9, has been a body-blow to the economy. Dell came to Ireland in 1990 and became the country's biggest exporter with revenues amounting to 5 per cent of GDP.

In January 2009, it announced that production would move to Poland with the loss of 1,900 jobs[3], a move paralleling that being carried out by Kraft, after its takeover of Cadbury in the UK, as noted in Chapter 5.

As is often observed, MNCs that seek efficiency gains in their international locations can be 'foot loose and fancy free'. Multinational firms, after all, are international companies that aim to serve their shareholders, not the governments or workforces of particular countries. They often have strong roots in a particular country (French MNCs retain a lot about them that is French, for example) but their interests are not necessarily those of nation states. They do not necessarily aim to retain plants or service centres in a particular country 'come hell or high water'. All this underlines the fact that human resourcing issues are very central to the strategies of multinational firms and can bring both competitive opportunities and political controversies.

HR strategy in the multinational firm

To become an MNC, then, is to face a whole new layer of management complexity. Many of the challenges are about the management of work and people, as we underlined in Chapter 3 in our analysis of the importance of 'societal fit' in HRM. Is it possible, or desirable, to export the favoured HR systems developed in the home country and, if so, does this mean a reliance on expatriate managers sent out from the corporate office? Managing expatriates effectively has traditionally been one of the major concerns in international HRM (for example, Dowling, Festing and Eagle 2008). So, too, is the tension between global policy and local adaptation (for example, De Cieri 2007). How far is management choice constrained by the different laws and institutions in the host country? How should management decisions, and the way they are implemented, be influenced by differences in cultures between nations? In MNCs, the problem is magnified whenever there are language differences and, underneath them, different cultural values and expectations. Local managers can be expected to know a lot more about these factors but will this knowledge lead them to play a political game to favour their own interests? Management decision making is political, as explained in Chapter 2.

Some countries, it must be said, offer greater scope for the MNC to carry over its pre-existing management philosophies. The UK is one of these, given its relatively flexible labour market. In their study of MNCs in the UK, Marginson *et al.* (2010) note the preference of US multinationals for direct

---

[3] http://www.industryweek.com/articles/dell_closing_ireland_plant_18157.aspx, accessed 3/6/10.

forms of communication and involvement, but in a context of non-unionism, as we discussed in Chapter 6. By contrast, German MNCs are more likely than their US counterparts to recognise unions while also pursuing direct voice arrangements, and Japanese-owned MNCs tend to emphasise representative consultation through employee forums, given their strong heritage of participative management. A particular influence on the type of choices made in employee voice systems is whether the MNC is long established in the UK, like Ford, or a more recent arrival. It is the newer firms which, in the main, try to avoid unions or opt for a dual system of employee voice.

In general terms, there is always a need for local adaptation in employment practices, as Chapter 3 explained. This is illustrated in a fascinating study of Japanese retail firms opening stores in China, in which Gamble (2010) shows how a high level of customer service, which flourished in Japan, was nurtured in China, leading Chinese-owned retailers to try to copy it. Like most Japanese MNCs, the firms placed a heavy reliance on expatriates to manage the Chinese operations. One way of improving customer service standards in China was to recruit staff with no work experience 'because you need them to do as they are told', as one manager put it (Gamble 2010: 718). On the other hand, cultural expectations about the promotion of women, which is rare in Japan but common in China, led the firms to adopt the local practice, partly because many talented people would otherwise leave. Some of the firms used seniority-based pay as in Japan, while others did not because this is not necessarily helpful in the Chinese labour market in which experienced performers expect higher pay more quickly. Labour retention is a big issue in Chinese cities whereas in Japan loyalty and long service to the corporation remain cultural norms. One small illustration of cultural differences is that in Japan employees' bags are checked when they leave the store. This was done at first in China but stopped after a week as expatriate managers felt constrained from exercising harsh discipline outside their home country (*ibid.*: 721).

Overall, therefore, sensitive local adaptation of HR practices is usually required. Even if they were inclined to, how far MNCs can impose a standard set of HR policies in all operating units is limited. There is no doubt that some multinationals want to ensure that certain key practices are widely used but a common approach is to let key policies in HRM 'take the form of frameworks or "global footprints" which lay down the main principles and parameters, but leave detailed implementation to the individual businesses and countries in the light of local regulation, conventions and practice' (Marginson and Meardi 2010: 217). The framework principles are mandatory but it makes much more sense if implementation can be varied to local conditions. As Gamble (2010) emphasises, subsidiary managers, including expatriates, soon come to appreciate the need to adapt to local labour markets and attitudes to employment practices, which can vary both within and between countries.

We should not really imagine that MNCs are somehow desperate to export the specific HR practices used in their home country and disappointed if they can't. As we explained in Chapter 3, citing the work of Edwards and Kuruvilla (2005), the literature in international HRM often makes the faulty assumption that multinational firms somehow want to export the way they manage people from the richer countries to the less developed ones. In contrast, research on the 'international division of labour' often reveals the reverse: many firms go offshore to take advantage of lower labour costs and less demanding labour regulations. This is definitely the case when MNCs move to newly industrialising, low-wage countries, but it can also be observed within the rich, developed world. There is evidence, for example, that 'the opportunity to escape perceived constraints at home and/or to experiment with Anglo-American practice may . . . be attractive to some Swedish MNCs' (Marginson *et al.* 2010: 157; see also Meardi *et al.* 2009). This, in turn, can come to be reflected back to the home country with pressure from MNCs to relax employment constraints at home. This is seen, for example, when MNC executives push for plant-based collective bargaining, using comparisons with lower-cost plants in other countries as part of their bargaining stance. Comparative or 'best-practice' performance monitoring can play a big part in regional or global management, supported by regular meetings among operations and HR managers (Marginson *et al.* 2010: 218). In those MNCs where efficiency saving is a corporate objective, there is always the potential to reward and punish SBU managers in the allocation of investment through the use of such 'coercive comparisons' (Mueller and Purcell 1992).

Comparisons of production and service performance – benchmarking – are typically very important in the multinational world (Farndale and Pauuwe 2007). Analysis of comparative statistics on business performance leads into strategies to improve plants or sites with under-performing production systems, supply-chain or labour problems. An example of this comes from ArcelorMittal, the world's largest steel manufacturer, head-quartered in Luxemburg. The company has grown very rapidly through acquisitions since it was founded in 1989 by the Indian entrepreneur, Lakshmi N. Mittal. It claims to have 'proven expertise in turning around under-performing assets and . . . integrating its previous key acquisitions by implementing a "best practice" approach in operations and management to enhance profitability . . . The combined company has achieved operational integration . . . consolidated support functions, optimised its supply chain and procurement structure and leveraged research and development across a wider base, thereby achieving cost savings and revenue synergies, as well as other synergistic benefits.'[4]

As this example illustrates, multinationals, like multidivisional firms generally, require their different plants/sites to meet performance benchmarks. The business priority is to achieve certain performance outcomes rather than to export or import HR practices *for their own sake*. Managers whose plants/sites have a low-productivity performance will get help through the transfer of technologies or know-how developed elsewhere or their subsidiaries will be sold off. As Cooke (2007b: 501) explains, multinationals tend to emphasise the transfer of 'technological capabilities over HR capabilities'. This means that change in under-performing sites is most likely to be led by operations managers, who may, for example, push for total quality management or lean methods of working or, alternatively, for outsourcing and reconfiguration of the supply chain. They tend to be the innovators in workplace change with HR specialists following their lead (Wood and Bryson 2009, Guest and Bryson 2010). There are, thus, important 'downstream' impacts on the management of people but these, as Chapter 3 explained, will involve a large measure of adaptation to the local social and political context. ArcelorMittal, for example, has a European Works Council and regular meetings are held between very senior management and union leaders to discuss issues of mutual concern such as health and safety and environmental concerns, both especially important in steel production. Employee relations specialists from Europe and North America meet regularly in London to share knowledge, coordinate initiatives and ensure that collective bargaining remains at the plant or local company level.

Being a downstream activity does not, however, mean that the work of HR specialists is unimportant or that it is totally circumscribed. Local HR professionals are important for their knowledge of national and regional cultures, labour markets and regulation, which is vital for effective integration of the MNC into the local economies and societies. In any large multinational company, HR departments are critical for dealing with regional bodies such as European Works Councils and for negotiating with trade unions seeking to establish standards of employee treatment. These are areas that depend on specialist HR expertise and on trust-building in networks that include counterparts in the public bureaucracy and in works councils and trade unions. MNCs run into major problems, as we explained in Chapters 1 and 6, when

---

[4] http://www.arcelormittal.com?index.php?lang=en&page=15, accessed 31/5/10.

their local practices are allowed to breach prevailing employment ethics and notions of social legitimacy. There can be consumer boycotts of multinational firms reported to exploit local labour in low-skill operations, like clothing manufacturing in Bangladesh or toy-making in China[5]. To counter this, many MNCs now subscribe to codes of conduct, as explained in Chapter 1. Some of these are issued at a world level, like the OECD Guidelines on Multinational Enterprises or the UN Global Compact (Seifert 2008). Yet others are voluntary codes issued on a sectoral level. Within Europe, the regulation of MNCs has been taken much further through the creation of European Works Councils, as explained in Chapter 6. Trade unions also have a strong interest in MNCs and around sixty-five International Framework Agreements have been signed between the, predominantly, continental European MNCs and international trade-union federations (Croucher and Cotton 2009: 58–60). The influence of these agreements has so far been weak with the creation of a dialogue but with little sign of collective bargaining or active coordination of terms and conditions of employment. This is left to workplace activities and it is extraordinary difficult to organise concerted union action across national boundaries if this is premised on strike action.

The importance of management development

Where a multinational has a strong commitment to developing synergies, corporate and regional HR staff also play a critical role in management development. This includes the selection and management of staff to serve abroad as expatriates, the development and career management of indigenous managers from host countries and the provision of training and development programmes. As MNCs increasingly organise themselves across national boundaries, the labour market for managerial and expert workers has increasingly become global and the search for exceptional talent more intense (Wooldridge 2006). In this context, HR specialists may foster the use of strategic performance-management processes, develop global capability or competency-based HR systems, pursue global talent-management strategies, and help develop corporate 'employer brands' (Sparrow *et al.* 2004). Hird, Marsh and Sparrow (2009: 25) give an example of Vodafone. The company has a European HR director and there is an HR director in each of the nine European operating companies. There are specialists in reward and organisational development in 'centres of expertise' with business-partner HR staff at the operating companies. The HR director explains that 'on an annual

---

[5] http://www.ethicalconsumer.org/home.aspx, accessed 11/6/10.

basis we get the operating company HR directors together with the centres of expertise to discuss and debate internal and external factors which drive the people agenda for the coming year. During the session we jointly prioritise and plan the initiative list for the year. It is a very powerful way of creating mutual buy-in and a shared agenda' (Hird *et al.* 2009: 25).

In Unilever, the Anglo-Dutch, long-established, food, detergent, personal products and speciality chemicals MNC, the management of the management cadre is of fundamental importance. Although it is heavily decentralised, there is a strong culture of coordination and linkages between businesses. This is achieved by building elaborate networks and lateral relationships between managers in different businesses and retaining tight control over career management and promotion decisions. All managers worldwide are considered a corporate resource. The process starts with recruitment. 'The greatest challenge of recruiting is to find the best and the brightest who will fit into the company.... For international careers in our current operating company, we look for people who can work in teams and understand the value of cooperation and consensus' (Floris Maljers, then joint chairman of Unilever, quoted in Goold *et al.* 1994: 154). Around 1,000 graduate management trainees are recruited each year. Thereafter, career movement for the best takes on a triple spiral: between functions, between divisions, and between countries. An elaborate, knowledge-based information system for careers is widely used to aid this process. Looking at Unilever's 'parenting advantage' in the way the centre adds value, strategy analysts conclude that 'Unilever's system for managing its human resources creates a direct linkage benefit by providing the businesses with a larger pool of suitable management talent to draw on. It is also a mechanism that promotes other linkages. By fostering a common culture, promoting networks, and exposing managers to a broad range of experiences, the Unilever system speeds up the circulation of product knowledge and best practice' (Goold *et al.* 1994: 155).

This example of Unilever shows how some MNCs build social capital through organisational processes that foster networks and generate trust across boundaries. Lengnick-Hall and Lengnick-Hall (2005: 477) define social capital in an international context as 'the intangible resource of structural connections, interpersonal interactions and cognitive understanding that enables a firm to (a) capitalize on diversity and (b) reconcile differences'. Social capital helps MNCs to manage the tension between pressures for integration on a global scale and pressures for local adaptation: to cope with the challenges that arise from diverse national value systems, economic systems, and workplace conditions (Sparrow and Braun 2007). MNCs vary, however, in the extent to which they wish to build this kind of social capital. Some level of investment in an elite core of leaders and experts is needed in all large firms but, as noted above in our analysis of multidivisional firms, it is the ones that are seeking knowledge-based synergies that are much more likely to invest in extensive forms of management and employee development.

The HR implications of mergers and acquisitions

We noted at start of the chapter that three-quarters of FDI into the UK had been via mergers and acquisitions. This means, of course, that when the new owners arrive to pick up the keys, there are already HR systems in place and some modes of behaviour are deeply embedded. The problem of integration or embedding practice from other parts of the MNC outside the host country is likely to be especially difficult. It is regularly argued in the literature on mergers and acquisitions that a half or more are failures in the sense of either an inability to provide shareholder value greater than the sum of the previous two companies or an inability to maintain market dominance, achieve promised cost reductions or manage synergies between the new firms effectively. Difficulties in achieving organisational fit, especially the meshing of cultures or management styles, are often identified (Buono, Bowditch and Lewis 1985, Datta and Grant 1990). This can be exacerbated in MNCs. 'Cross-border M&As frequently fail to deliver the synergistic or other benefits strived for, lead to human resource and cultural problems, result in power plays, and often produce problematic consequences for various internal and external stakeholders' (Soderberg and Vaara 2003:11).

Most often, the failure of M&As occurs not at the negotiation or purchase stages, although this can be important if a firm pays excessively for a purchase, but at the implementation stage when the two firms come together. Hunt, Lees, Grümber and Vivian (1987) find a positive correlation between the success of implementation and the overall perceived success of an acquisition in 83 per cent of cases, making it the 'most decisive variable in success and failure'. KPMG (1999) distinguishes between 'hard keys' to successful mergers which need to happen at the start of the process, such as synergy evaluation, integration project planning and due diligence, and 'soft keys'. These soft keys include classical HR issues such as the selection of the management team, the resolution of cultural issues, and communication inside the two companies (which needs to be compatible with communication externally to shareholders and the business press). Thus, 'human factors' loom large in M&As from the beginning, but become especially acute during the post-acquisition implementation phase, and beyond that in what is sometimes called the stabilisation period (Hubbard and Purcell 2001). Taking account of all of the research on the performance of M&As, Schmidt (2002: 8) finds that the top seven difficulties all 'directly or indirectly relate to the management of people'. Mergers and acquisitions, especially in the post-merger rationalisation stage, involve highly political processes.

In a study of international mergers, including the period of post-merger rationalisation, Rees and Edwards (2009) show how political and institutional factors in host countries slowed or significantly modified the integration process. In one company, SnackCo, the plan involved a move to a standardised individual incentive plan but 'in many European countries HR managers argued that they needed works council approval. The reaction from corporate and European HQ was pragmatic, reluctantly accepting that many pre-existing practices should be left in place' (*ibid.*: 32). Similar resistance was experienced in EuroFuel through a combination of labour law and collective bargaining. Two years after the merger it was 'admitted that there was little hope of meaningful integration across sites and that a "patchwork quilt" of different sets and conditions would persist indefinitely' (*ibid.*: 32). The authors conclude that 'the rationalisation process in the post-merger period is not simply determined by market and institutional factors but is also an intensely political process in which the interests of many actors are challenged, leading them to respond with whatever resources they have at their disposal to influence outcomes' (Rees and Edwards (2009: 36). This echoes our analysis in Chapter 2 of the political nature of strategy making.

A crucial element is the uncertainty generated by the acquisition process and the response of employees to it. It is hardly surprising to find that employees suffer from uncertainty in acquisitions (Buono and Bowditch 1989) and this is linked to perceived violations of their psychological contracts with the employer, especially the new employer (recall Chapter 7). Such violations typically lead to a withdrawal of support for the organisation and a reduction in discretionary behaviour and motivation (Robinson 1990). In an acquisition, this psychological process can occur on a large scale, covering groups of employees and leading to damaging consequences for the acquirer through the withdrawal of trust and commitment. In practice, the political, and politicised, environment of an acquisition severely reduces the opportunities to participate. People often feel powerless and suffer from anomie. They may ask their direct managers what is happening but it is rare for them to know any more than they do. Trade unions may be informed one or two days before the public announcement but are generally unable, at that time, to raise issues of concern about the acquisition's consequences, unless provided with legal rights to do so, as in the EU under the Transfer of Undertaking Protection of Employees (TUPE) regulations (see Chapter 6).

Beyond this, there can be a profound sense of loss – a form of bereavement (Cartwright and Cooper 1992) – when a long-established company is swallowed up and effectively dies. Mergers and acquisitions frequently lead to a round (or rounds) of job cuts. They can also lead to a substantial increase in voluntary labour turnover, to reductions in effort and cooperation, and to resistance to integration moves, which thus take longer and cost more in terms of performance dips than anticipated. Maguire and Phillips' (2008) analysis of the merger in 1998 between Citicorp and Travelers Group is a case in point. Citicorp, whose core business unit was 'Citibank', had grown organically since its founding in 1812. By contrast, Travelers, a diversified financial services company involved in a range of activities including lending, brokerage and insurance, had grown rapidly through acquisitions. Their merger resulted in the massive Citigroup, which naturally lacked a commonly understood or shared culture. Maguire and Phillips (2008) argue that immediately following the merger, institutional trust suffered because of ambiguity surrounding the identity of the newly merged organisation. This was compounded when 'Citibankers' came to the view that, in effect, it was not a merger of equals but a takeover by Travelers' executives whose style of organisation and management became dominant. As a result, Citibankers, who had closely identified with 'their' company, experienced low institutional trust with Citigroup because they could not identify with it. Many left the organisation, which was seen by HR staff as a serious drain of human capital (*ibid.*: 393).

Low levels of organisational trust are linked to perceptions that organisational justice has been broken. Organisational justice is about the way people evaluate the fairness of a decision (Folger and Cropanzano 1998). There are three elements of justice in an organisational context: distributive, procedural and interactional. Distributive justice concerns the fairness of the outcome, procedural justice is about fairness in the way in which the decision is taken, and interactional justice focuses on how decisions are communicated and the extent to which individuals feel treated with respect.

Senior managers can often take the view that the only HR issue of immediate concern in an acquisition announcement is to deal with job security and job loss. This is the question that is always asked by the press. In Hubbard's (1999) acquisition research, there was quite commonly an early announcement that it was to be 'business as usual' and that both companies would be stronger by coming together. This was rarely the case and, at times, announcements to employees of 'business as usual' were at odds with statements to the business press on the need to reduce costs and increase margins. Of course, employees read these and note the incompatibility of the internal with the external statement.

The employee response to an acquisition announcement, especially those in the 'target' firm to be acquired, is much more multi-faceted than a single concern with job security. Hubbard (1999) calls this 'dual expectations theory'. This covers both the individual's perception of their immediate future (what will happen to *me*, do I have a job?) and their concern with their team and the wider social network (what will happen to *us*?). Beyond that, this bifurcation between the individual and the group continues into concerns about assimilation into the new organisation and what sort of firm it is. Thus, for the individual, the issue is 'what sort of job will I have, what type of future, how do I know what is expected of me in terms of performance and will I fit into the new organisational culture?' These concerns of individuals coalesce into wider group or collective worries about the style of the new management. This 'cultural behaviour' means learning about, and internalising as a group, 'the shared patterns of beliefs, assumptions and expectations held by organisational members, and the group characteristic way of perceiving the organisation's environment and its norms, roles and values as they exist outside the individual' (Schwartz and Davis 1981: 33). This is especially difficult in MNCs where differences in language and behavioural expectations are uniquely embedded at the societal level.

The strategic purpose of an acquisition will deeply influence the process and the type of HR issues to be faced. In particular, the crucial issue is the degree of organisational integration required for the combined firms and the underlying reasons for it. The greater the degree of organisational integration, the greater the HR issues that come to the fore since sites are likely to close, rationalisation occurs in department amalgamations (a single sales team, a single finance office, and so on), and there will be 'winners' and 'losers' in the organisational musical chairs that follow (Hubbard and Purcell 2001: 21).

The most frequent way acquisitions are intended to create value, for the shareholder at least, but not for the employee, is by 'resource sharing' (Haspeslagh and Jemison 1991). Primarily, although often dressed up in terms of synergistic value creation, this means a focus on cost reduction, while at times increasing the scope of business activities. 'Resource sharing' is seen, for example, in branch closures where there is overlap in a town, operational rationalisation in the home country or overseas, and contact-centre amalgamations, often linked to offshoring of certain activities. The 'forced' mergers of banks in 2008–9 as part of governments' rescue activities has provided plenty of examples of this. Significant savings, too, can occur within management from specialist departments coming together and from property

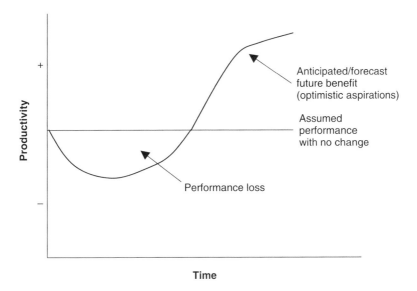

Figure 10.2 The J-curve of productivity loss in the management of change
Source: Adapted from Pil and MacDuffie (1995).

sales and other direct savings such as through shared service centres and offshoring.

The problem is how this can be done quickly, leaving behind a committed, integrated, innovative workforce able to maximise customer service. Performance often dips in a major change programme and in M&As this can be exacerbated because of the loss of institutional trust. The J-curve (Figure 10.2) draws attention to the requirements for 'competency destruction' or 'unlearning' before new learning can occur (Pil and MacDuffie 1996). Where the 'competency destruction' is linked to large redundancies for those that remain, the requirement to learn new operating procedures and deal with new bosses, the slope of the J-curve coming out of the transitional period is tantalising but unachievable. It is often observed that employees who stay in the firm after a major redundancy programme suffer from the 'survivor syndrome' where guilt, a sense of loss and the intensification of work, lead to a collapse of commitment (Baruch and Hind 2000). The loss of productivity or profitability, while anticipated, is both deeper and lasts longer than hoped for, and greatly exceeds that told to the shareholders in the prospectus. It is easy to see how shareholder value is lost, let alone employee value. Cultural integration is especially hard but even IT integration is difficult and requires planning, project teams and high levels of involvement at operational level between employees from the two companies, learning to work together.

Conclusions

Multidivisional organisations are those in which a corporate office of senior executives presides over an array of strategic business units. The fundamental problem for these large multi-business firms is to find an effective way to manage the relationship between the parts of the business and create value in doing so. This is no simple matter. Value is not added simply by owning the assets in a holding company and can, in fact, be squandered. There is the problem of managing vertically, in the relationship between the centre and the subsidiaries, and the problem of managing horizontally, in the way in which the parts of the business collaborate or compete with each other. When M-form companies operate across national boundaries in multinational structures, the complexity is compounded.

We have seen how the logic, in economic terms, of the multidivisional firm has tended to favour decentralisation and the separation of the firm into discrete accounting units, allowing the centre to 'manage by the numbers' in pursuit of financial outcomes. This is a very prevalent philosophy among large Anglo-American firms. It is frequently combined with an emphasis on outsourcing and offshoring, in order to create a more efficient corporation, which can invest in diverse locations and pull out of underperforming sites without too much difficulty. It is a corporate philosophy dominated by strong financial controls over the performance of subsidiary units but limited loyalties to them. This does bring a certain kind of organisational flexibility but it also runs risks. It may over-emphasise short-term profits at the expense of longer-term investment in management development and skill formation across business units. Too little may be invested in professional HR support to the organisation's line managers. At the very least, senior leaders at corporate headquarters need to ensure that a global company of this type can develop and renew its elite human resources, its core group of managerial leaders and technical experts.

An alternative model focuses more on synergistic economies. This includes multidivisional firms that aim to develop core competencies stretching across business units, which can be used to foster innovation in products or processes. When synergies and networks are fostered, the way people, especially managers and expert workers, are managed plays a crucial, if not the crucial, role. Since knowledge sharing is critical, a more liberal, more trusting exchange of it is encouraged through HR practices that facilitate horizontal networking and organisational integration between markets and technologies. The corporation then needs to invest more extensively in the development of its management cadres and in the HR specialists who, in turn, support them.

Quite how far large organisations are moving from the M-form model towards a more networked organisational form is hard to say. Growing by acquisition – rather than organically – makes knowledge-based synergies harder to achieve since different company cultures, labour markets and different operating procedures need to be understood.

As with multidivisional firms, people issues are very central to the strategies of multinational firms, which have the added layer of cross-country complexities. Everyone now realises that globalisation is opening up huge opportunities for multinationals to hire capable workforces at much lower costs. It is possible for powerful firms (and large firms have resources and access to capital denied to smaller organisations) to push for productivity improvements in nearly all countries. This is seen in the emphasis on benchmarking. If they fail, those MNCs which focus on efficiency gains often have the capacity to relocate at relatively low cost, but at a cost to the erstwhile host country. Thus, multinational HR strategies, especially those linked to major cost reductions, can spark widely different responses among employees and citizens in different locations. At the same time as some welcome the choice of their country for a new production site, others will lament the departure of a multinational and the loss of jobs (Edwards and Rees 2006: 39–41).

There has been an enormous amount of interest in the question of whether multinational firms can, and should, export their home-country HR practices. Overall, the research suggests that while multinationals often transfer the key technologies or know-how that gives them a production or service advantage, they come to realise that it is neither possible, not desirable, to impose one way of managing HRM around the world. A substantial degree of adaptation to local labour markets, employment laws and cultural norms is usually essential to run a successful business. The problem for many governments, and for trade unions and community groups, is that multinational firms are only too keen to take advantage of lower labour costs and less demanding employment regulations. Such strategies are often a source of ethical concerns, which are fuelling the growth of regional and global employment standards by which multinational behaviour can be judged.

Many multidivisional and multinational firms pursue growth through mergers and acquisitions. All too often, these are badly handled and end up destroying shareholder value. As tumultuous events, they generate high levels of uncertainty, both for corporations and for workers. Questions of distributive, procedural and interactional justice come strongly into play: for example, in the redundancy programmes associated with corporate restructurings and divestments. Legitimacy issues are inescapable. Local and regional requirements for, and expectations of, employee voice and personal redress are highly salient. Multidivisional and multinational firms are well advised to give careful attention to the management of these changes and the way they affect employees. A disgruntled reaction from employees can damage both the firm's financial performance and its wider reputation as a corporate citizen. Furthermore, the way that decisions are made and communicated will influence the level of trust in the organisation, inevitably affecting its chances of successful change management in the future.

11
Conclusions and implications

The purpose of this final chapter is twofold. First, we summarise the book's most important themes. The book has covered a complex and expanding terrain. We have traversed numerous studies, examined a range of frameworks and theories, and reached a number of important conclusions by the end of each of the chapters. We cannot summarise all of our chapter conclusions but what we do here is underline the most important themes that we would like readers to take away from the book as a whole. In so doing, we take the chance to offer our personal views on some key trends and implications associated with these themes. We then turn to an important 'so what?' question: how can managers in firms improve strategic management processes in their organisations to deal more effectively with the critical HR problems they face and, if possible, to take advantage of the competitive opportunities that HRM presents? This includes a review of the debate over the value of strategic planning and an examination of the question of how to design HR planning systems. It then leads into a discussion of the more integrative approaches to strategic management that have become associated with the notion of the 'balanced scorecard' (Kaplan and Norton 1996).

The main themes of this book

If we were to boil down the book's messages to a few key themes, what would they be? We think seven major themes underpin the book:

Theme one: human resource strategy is an essential element in business strategy, not some kind of dubious appendage to it, and plays a critical role in organisational viability and relative performance.

HRM is about the management of work and people in organisations. It is concerned with how work is organised and it includes all the practices used to manage the people who do it, both individually and collectively. As such, HRM is an essential organisational process, which occurs irrespective of whether the organisation has its own HR specialists, and which has strategic significance in all organisations. Organisations fail if they cannot organise work appropriately and cannot attract, motivate and retain the kind of people they need to meet their goals and develop the organisation over time. A reasonably effective HR strategy is therefore a necessary, though not a sufficient, condition of business survival or viability. In organisations that do survive, the quality of HR strategy has impacts on relative performance. This means that HR strategy may help to lay a basis for sustained competitive advantage.

This theme has implications for the two business disciplines we bring together in this book: strategic management and HRM. In terms of strategic management, we take issue with anyone who thinks HRM lacks strategic significance. We live in an era of knowledge-intensive competition in which HR strategy is assuming more, not less, strategic significance in developed economies. We also live in an era of globalisation and offshoring in which uncompetitive work systems in high-wage countries – in both manufacturing and in services – are under enormous pressure from firms operating in developing countries who are offering more cost-effective and increasingly sophisticated sources of production. Because it is so critical to organisational success, greater attention should be given to HR strategy within the theory, teaching and practice of strategic management.

In terms of HRM, we challenge approaches to teaching and practice that lay too much emphasis on individual techniques and not enough on understanding HRM's role in helping firms manage the strategic problems they face across diverse contexts. This book is not a compendium of 'micro-HR' techniques, organised across the major sub-functions of HRM, such as job analysis, recruitment, selection, training, remuneration and so on. It is often useful for students to take their first course in HRM by looking at a text which covers the main elements of micro-HRM but no one who wishes to contribute meaningfully to the strategic debate and direction in an organisation should limit their reading to this kind of text.

Theme two: the goals of HRM are plural and subject to strategic tensions.

If the first theme underlines the strategic significance of HRM, the second key lesson is that HRM's role should not be thought of only in terms of a single, profit-oriented 'bottom line'. Because the firm is an economic entity located in a social context, a good performance in HRM will always be multidimensional. Certainly, HRM's contribution to short-term economic performance is vital but a good performance in HRM will incorporate more than this. Managers face the need to develop a cost-effective system of labour management to support the firm's economic viability in the industries in which it competes while *at the same time* needing to secure legitimacy in the societies in which the firm operates. Cost-effectiveness and social legitimacy need to be pursued simultaneously.

That social legitimacy is an important goal in its own right, and not simply a means to an end, has been emphasised in this book. At a minimum, firms should employ labour according to legal requirements and should seek to work positively with important social norms for employee management. Reaching the situation where the vast majority of firms operate legitimately in this way would be a major step forward in any society.

On top of cost-effectiveness and social legitimacy, there are other strategic goals that we observe in HRM. Over time, successful firms also embed significant elements of flexibility into their HRM to enable them to cope better with change and develop forms of human resource advantage, although they vary in whether such forms of competitive advantage are based on nurturing an elite group of employees or treating whole workforces as critical assets. The challenge of managing change should never be underestimated. The natural tendency in organisations is to focus on stabilising performance in the immediate context (the 'short-term'). The more this is done, the more difficult it is to generate a capacity to flex the organisation or perform well over the longer term. In the dynamic picture, we also observe management seeking to enhance its power to act. Much of this is rational because firms do depend on having management teams that can react sensibly to change. However, too much emphasis on management power typically compromises the firm's ability to empower other employees and has consequences for trust levels within the organisation.

This theme, therefore, underlines the fact that pursuing multiple goals in HRM inevitably involves grappling with a range of strategic tensions. Among the most important of these are the tensions between employer control and employee motivation, between short-term productivity and long-term adaptability, between corporate survival and employee security, and between the drive for managerial power and the need for social legitimacy. The management of these dilemmas is so important that it is useful to understand the goals of HRM as fundamentally about the management of strategic tensions.

Theme three: managers typically adapt HR strategy to the firm's specific context and they are wise to do so.

A key part of the book's review of the theory of strategic HRM examines the debate between two perspectives: 'best fit' and 'best practice'. Advocates of best fit have emphasised the contingent nature of HRM while advocates of best practice have gone in search of a universally superior set of HR practices. The idea of best practice does not stand up well under close scrutiny, including questions about whose interests are being served by a particular HR practice and how practices evolved in Anglo-American contexts can work in labour markets and cultural contexts where people have different underpinning values or simply have different employment laws. Best-fit is an easy winner in this debate.

When we look at the research and at organisational experience in the widest possible terms, it is readily apparent that firms either adapt their HR strategies to their specific contexts or they risk under-performance and failure. In a nutshell, there is a 'law of context' in HRM, which firms ignore at their peril. Firms are embedded in industries and societies and managers in particular firms never have full control over the shape of their HRM. In this book, we have highlighted a range of important contextual differences in the way HR strategy is shaped. There are typically major differences in HRM between labour-intensive and capital-intensive or high-tech manufacturing: firms are much more likely to recruit selectively, pay high wages and invest heavily in employee development in the latter. Within private-sector services, we see major differentiation in HRM across different types of service markets, ranging from low-skill service markets to highly differentiated service markets in which employees are educated, control-conscious professionals or have fast-changing forms of technical knowledge. There are also important differences in the way HRM is organised in the more highly unionised and organisationally complex public sector.

Two major models of how context affects HRM have been examined in some depth in the book. One deals with the way HR strategy needs to adapt as firms move through the industry life cycle. In the establishment phase, firms typically start as fragile, small and informal organisations. If they build the workforce capabilities they need to survive, they will inevitably need to adapt their HRM to the challenges brought about by the much more bureaucratic mature phrase and then adapt it again to cope with the need for radical change in the renewal phase. Few organisations successfully negotiate all these phases and there are major questions around how HR strategy can help to build organisational agility. We have also looked at models of HRM in multidivisional and multinational firms. There is no HRM context more complex than that faced by these firms. Multidivisional firms have major issues of internal control and coordination and take different approaches to the question of whether synergies, including synergies in management development and social capital, are valuable. On top of this, multinational firms face a much more complex external environment: every different society in which a multinational firm operates will challenge it to adapt its HR strategies in some significant way.

Theme four: while it is not possible to define a universally 'best' set of HR practices, there is still a role for thinking about underpinning principles in HRM.

While we need to dispense with the idea that there can be sets of HR practices that are universally best, it is still possible to take some value out of best-practice thinking. Within an Anglo-American frame of reference, there are some practices which nearly everyone agrees are dumb or dysfunctional. For example, hardly anyone would recommend unstructured employment interviewing over a set of job-relevant questions or, if at all possible, a work-sample test.

   In addition, within particular industry or occupational contexts, it is possible to identify HR systems that have a kind of 'functional equivalence' and which can benefit firms which apply them in a way that involves careful adaptation at the level of particular practices. Thus, it is possible for us to identify critical design features underpinning high-involvement work systems (an emphasis on empowering workers whose jobs have been overly 'Taylorised' and enhancing their skills and performance incentives) while leaving open the question of which HR practices will best serve a particular company and group of workers. For example, there will be some contexts in which managers will see self-managing teamwork as critical to building an HIWS while in others they may well prefer job rotation or off-line problem-solving activities. Similarly, there will be some contexts in which contingent pay systems will be evolved to enhance performance incentives and others in which higher salaries, without contingent components, will be preferred. The role of HR strategy consultants should not be one of selling a static and de-contextualised set of 'best practices' but one of helping firms perceive the underpinning principles of these systems and make sensible adaptations in their unique context.

At the most fundamental level, it is possible to identify some underpinning general principles that can help all firms to improve their HRM. The first and third sections of the book work hard at stressing the general themes that a good performance in HRM depends on meeting multiple goals, that managers typically adapt their HRM to their specific context and that they are wise to do so, and that viable firms can evolve ways of creating superior value through somewhat unique clusters of human and social capital. The middle section of the book is designed to look at more specific principles and theoretical frameworks within the key components of HR systems and within the chain of links that connects HR policies to organisational outcomes. This section underlines the fact that choices about a firm's work systems are inevitably connected to its economic performance and matter enormously to workers, being a principal driver of job satisfaction levels and a major factor in employee turnover. It stresses the importance of voice practices for social legitimacy and underlines research showing that well-embedded voice systems are strongly associated with better levels of discretionary behaviour, job satisfaction and organisational commitment. In terms of understanding the management of individual employment relationships, we stressed the value of the AMO framework, which argues that individual performance improves when individuals have the ability, the motivation and the opportunity to perform. Assuming that firms can effectively recruit the individual capabilities they need (and many cannot), the AMO framework helps to highlight the importance of the ongoing management of motivation in employment relationships. Managing employee motivation requires some thinking about mutuality or reciprocity in the relationship. Employment relationships are more stable when the employee finds the work attractive and there is a fair balance between their efforts and their rewards. The principle of reciprocity also resonates at the collective level. The social climate in workplaces is sensitive to the extent to which employees find that management is open to their voice and the extent to which they find management to be trustworthy over time.

Theme five: HR strategy is usefully understood as a cluster of HR systems, an approach that helps us to analyse strategic HR trends affecting companies and countries.

The HR strategies of firms are usefully thought of as clusters of HR systems. Each HR system is a set of HR practices that has evolved to manage a major hierarchical or occupational group in the firm. The two fundamental building blocks of any HR system are a set of practices for organising work and a set of practices for managing the people to do the work. It is quite common for there to be one HR system for management, another for core operating staff, and one or more models for support workers of various kinds. Questions of social legitimacy and internal political pressures mean there will usually be some overlaps in HR practices across HR systems within an organisation: for example, there may be common ways of handling leave entitlements and common ways of dealing with personal grievances. However, there are also substantial differences that are needed to build and manage a particular type of worker. How managers are identified, developed and incentivised necessarily needs to be somewhat different from how operating workers are selected, motivated and managed. While flexibility is an issue in all models of HRM, models for managing managers should pay particular attention to ways of encouraging creative thinking and collaborative working.

The identification of HR systems or HR models helps us to track changes in patterns of HRM in a way that can be useful for strategic analysis in firms and for public policy making in societies. In small firms, we typically observe a blend of familial and informal HR systems while craft-professional models are critical to professional service firms, to large parts of the public sector and to various niches in manufacturing. Industrial and salaried models emerged first in large-scale manufacturing and then spread to the large 'office factories' of the private sector and the public sector bureaucracy. Key changes in current patterns of HRM include the development of high-involvement models by various manufacturers and service firms in order to support quality-based or knowledge-intensive competition. Such models also help to support higher service levels in parts of the public sector. More controversial is the trend towards outsourcing models of HRM, which are common in globalised and electronically connected production environments where firms seek major reductions in labour costs. Clearly, we are living in an era when managers need to be able to regularly evaluate the fit of their HR systems with their unfolding context if companies are to make astute shifts in HR strategy that help to support their survival.

A key implication we want to stress here is that the interests of governments are not exactly the same as those of companies. Companies ultimately have loyalties to shareholders and this means that they are not necessarily able to commit indefinitely to work sites which have become uneconomic in a particular country. In a globalised environment, company survival comes ahead of the survival of particular production/service sites. Governments, on the other hand, have interests in retaining high-quality work sites in their particular country and keeping local communities viable. For this reason, governments in the high-wage countries increasingly favour the development of high-involvement HR models. To be successful in promoting them, public policy needs to foster the labour-market and societal institutions, including high-quality educational and vocational training systems, that encourage and support firms trying to adopt HIWSs.

Theme six: some degree of idiosyncrasy is inevitable in a firm's HRM and positive, high-quality idiosyncrasies in HRM can be sources of superior performance.

Although requirements for legitimacy in society and for 'table stakes' in particular industries make firms similar, managers inevitably put their own twists on HR systems, and firms build a somewhat idiosyncratic pattern of human and social capital, as the resource-based view (RBV) of the firm indicates. There is always some degree of strategic choice available to managers and particular leadership personalities will inevitably put their mark on HRM, sometimes in ways that generate competitive *dis*advantage rather than competitive advantage. A key interest in this book has been on the question of what it is that can be competitively most valuable in HRM and how such sources of value can be built and defended. The RBV lays emphasis on the ways in which valuable, hard-to-imitate resources are built up over time as a result of critical choices ('path dependency') and thus become socially complex and causally ambiguous. The book's argument is that companies can acquire exceptional strengths in HRM when they attract and retain highly talented individuals (high-quality human capital) and combine their talents through highly positive organisational processes (powerful forms of social capital). The extent to which companies seek to do so in an elite or an egalitarian way is variable, however.

A key implication must be that carefully enacted HR systems, which build human and social capital, can be sources of superior and hard-to-imitate value. Knowledge of individual HR techniques or policies is hardly rare or particularly valuable. However, knowledge of how to build and customise appropriate HR systems (which are clusters of key work and employment practices) and create a positively reinforcing blend of HR systems *within* a particular production or service context is likely to be very rare. The value is greater when these astute HR decisions and processes are complemented by other intangible and tangible assets: senior management commitment, consistent line manager support for critical HR practices over significant time periods, adequate financial resourcing, up-to-date technology, sympathetic management accounting systems, and so on.

Theme seven: in any organisation where management wants to achieve higher value through HRM, careful attention will need to be paid to the chain of critical links between HR policy and performance outcomes.

The previous theme leads directly to this one. Suppose management wants to enhance the quality of products to better serve a niche market or improve the quality of the interactions between employees and customers in order to improve customer satisfaction and retention. How can management enhance the performance of its HR systems in order to create these sources of value? This is often called the 'black box' problem. It centres on the chain of links or set of mediators that leads from HR policies through to whatever type of performance is desired. This chain of links stretches from: (1) management intentions, to (2) management actions, to (3) workforce perceptions and attributions, to (4) workforce responses and outcomes, and, finally, to (5) organisational outcomes. Major gaps between management's espoused intentions and managerial actions will usually engender mistrust and cynicism. Individuals may feel their psychological contracts have been violated and become less committed while trust levels and the quality of cooperation may deteriorate across entire workforces.

Large organisations may have resource and legitimacy advantages but they often have much greater problems than small firms in terms of slippage between HR intentions and performance outcomes. The possibility for gaps between rhetoric and reality underlines the need not only for senior managers in large organisations to figure carefully what they want to achieve and then follow through on their pledges – achieving greater consistency in their own behaviour – but also underlines how dependent they are on lower-level managers to bring HR policies to life and achieve the results they seek. While this includes the roles of both HR specialists and line managers, the latter are particularly important if consistency is going to be high in HRM. How line managers are themselves managed by senior managers is thus critical to the overall effectiveness of the firm's HR systems.

Employees, therefore, are influenced not simply by top management values and formal policies but by the reality of what they experience in their jobs on a daily basis. The individual's perception of the HRM process and how it affects their well-being ('psychological climate') inevitably affects their responses to management. When employees share a collective view of the intentions and trustworthiness of management, we can also talk of the 'social climate' in the workplace, which then becomes an important intervening variable in the links between HRM and organisational performance. Management teams that want to improve the mediating links between their intentions and their outcomes in HRM are well advised to open up more comprehensive channels of employee voice in order to improve their understanding of the strengths and weaknesses in this chain.

Can strategic planning be a valuable resource in the firm?

The final theme we have discussed leads naturally into issues surrounding strategic planning in firms and how data on critical HRM variables, such as employee attitudes to management, can be more effectively incorporated into this process. Before examining this area, we begin with a fundamental question that has attracted controversy in the management literature. The resource-based view (RBV) of the firm has occupied an important role in this book but is it actually supportive of the discipline of strategic planning? Does it suggest that better planning, with all the effort it entails, is a valuable use of executive time and the firm's money? Doesn't the RBV say that 'causal ambiguity' helps to protect a firm's key resources? In which case, does this imply, paradoxically, that we cannot plan for improved performance in HRM? Furthermore, surely Henry Mintzberg's (1990, 1994) stinging criticisms of strategic planning should caution us against bureaucratic planning routines? Could it be that long-range planning suits static rather than dynamic environments and undermines the very flexibility that firms need today?

Like Ansoff (1991) and Wilson (1994), we reject this anti-planning perspective. Chapter 4 considered three barriers to imitation: unique timing and learning, social complexity, and causal ambiguity. It argued that the notion of causal ambiguity is the least significant of the three. Ambiguity around key causes of a firm's success (and especially the way these interact) must be present to some extent in any firm. As Chapter 2 explained, strategic management is cognitively or intellectually challenging. If there were no ambiguities, senior management teams would never make blunders. However, we all know they do, and often with disastrous consequences.

Having said this, we argued that unique timing and learning ('path dependency') and social complexity (patterns of collaboration and teamwork in the firm) are more important barriers to imitation than causal ambiguity. First mover or fast follower strategies, when well executed, build positions of competitive strength, which other firms find very difficult to emulate. There are therefore advantages to be gained from planning to build the firm's human and social capital and create faster learning in the firm.

Research does support this interpretation, as we noted in Chapter 9 in our discussion of the value of planning skills in the mature and renewal contexts of the firm's life cycle. Koch and McGrath's (1996) study of human resource planning practices and business outcomes is instructive. The sample studied consists of 319 business units drawn from the Standard and Poors' database of companies in the USA. Measures of business performance include labour productivity (defined as sales per employee). Their main finding (Koch and McGrath 1996: 350) is that:

> Labor productivity . . . tend[s] to be better in firms that both formally plan how many and what kinds of people they will need, as well as where employers systematically evaluate their recruitment and selection policies . . . *proactive* firms that *plan* for their future labor needs, as opposed to reacting to changes, as well as those firms making investments in getting the right people for the job *at the outset*, tend to be the ones with better labor productivity.

Koch and McGrath (1996) go on to argue that superior HR planning skills, which enhance the quality of the firm's investment in human capital, can provide a form of resource-based advantage.

This is only one study and we should be cautious about concluding anything from a single study. What other evidence is there? A large study of 656 firms located mainly in the USA and in South Africa was set up to examine the debate between Ansoff's 'planning school' and Mintzberg's 'learning school' (Brews and Hunt 1999). While based on executive assessments of planning practice and business performance, the study argues that unstable environments require *more* rather than less planning, thus challenging the idea that planning systems make firms inflexible. It also argues that firms gain greater advantages from planning when they persist with it: benefits are greater after four or more years of working at a planning system (Brews and Hunt 1999: 905). This finding is consistent with the analysis of the US railway companies – the Chicago and North Western (C&NW) and the Chicago, Rock Island and Pacific (Rock Island) – discussed in Chapter 2 (Barr *et al.* 1992). Both firms faced an unstable environment in the 1950s (as railroads faced serious threats from alternative forms of transport) but the directors of C&NW began to change their mental model and take responsibility much more quickly than those at Rock Island (which subsequently went bankrupt).

These studies suggest that 'learning to plan' counts for something. They imply that successful firms find ways of incorporating lessons from learning-by-doing into their planning routines and of making their planning systems more flexible. Formal planning processes, when they involve the key line managers who manage the majority of staff, offer a way of surfacing informal learning about what does and does not work in the management of people. When designed competently, planning sessions provide a means for periodic review: they can be used both to make emergent learning explicit and to consider new external threats and opportunities. Rather than upholding the Mintzbergian criticisms of formal planning, these studies imply that planning systems can be reformed in ways that make them more valuable in changing times. As Brews and Hunt (1999: 906) put it: 'When the going gets tough, the tough go planning: formally, specifically, yet with flexibility and persistence. And once they have learned to plan, they plan to learn.'

The value to be gained does not lie solely in the capacity to improve the analytical abilities of the firm but also has a political dimension, something which is always present in strategic management. As Lam and Schaubroeck (1998) explain, formal planning processes can be used to bring together key constituencies in the firm, thus hammering out new compromises and building commitment for desirable change. We conclude that strategic planning systems should not be abandoned but their design should be reviewed on a regular basis and enhanced. Part of this enhancement should involve improving the way they tackle the HR challenges facing the firm.

This is obviously of great relevance to large firms, including the multi-divisional and multinational firms discussed in Chapter 10, but the principles we will discuss here are also relevant to smaller ones. Small firms do not use the level of formality seen in management processes in large firms. More importantly, small firms are typically at a resource and legitimacy disadvantage (they have fewer resources and are much less well-known). However, as we showed in our discussion of recruitment strategy in Chapter 7 and in the discussion of the establishment and renewal contexts in Chapter 9, their leaders can use proactive thinking and nimble responses in a way that is very hard to do in large organisations. What matters is that managers in small firms regularly take time to examine their context and to think ahead in terms of the threats they face and the opportunities they could grasp.

The design of HR planning processes

The argument that HR planning should be linked to strategic planning did not suddenly emerge with the advent of practitioner and business school interest in HRM in the 1980s. Planning the human aspects of business strategy has a long tradition. For example, the role of planning in personnel management, including planning for recruitment and succession, was emphasised in the publication of the Institute of Personnel Management's booklet on *Functions and Organisation of a Personnel Department* in 1964 (Crichton 1968: 42–3). And it should surely be obvious that military and industrial planning techniques were absolutely central to labour force planning, training and production management in both world wars and, indeed, much earlier than this (Smith and Bartholomew 1988). The idea that we are finally discovering the value of good integration between the planning of organisational goals and labour requirements is an insult to former generations of managers. We are, however, in a position to identify some key lessons about how HR planning can be conducted more effectively.

Improving the quality of HR planning: process principles

Drawing on research and historical learning about HR planning, what principles can be used by executive teams to improve the quality of HR planning in their firm?

The stakeholder principle

As explained in Chapter 1, it is vital to recognise that HRM does not belong to HR specialists. HR planning should aim to meet the needs of the key stakeholder groups involved in people management in the firm. In the broadest sense, stakeholder groups include shareholders, creditors, managers, employees, customers, suppliers, competitors, the local community and environmental interests. In HR planning, however, we need to focus on those stakeholder groups who are most affected by the quality of labour management in the firm. This means the process ought to be designed to consider the interests of:

Senior and lower-level managers

The key issue here is to ensure that HR planning engages the entire management team. Senior managers need to use it to form and express their vision for managing work and people and to learn from the experiences of lower-level managers. As emphasised in Chapter 8, first-line managers manage the vast majority of people in any firm. Their responses and strategies are critical to shaping psychological contracts and the social climate of the firm and, thus, to the success of any major HR initiative. Their views can be canvassed in various ways. For example, all line managers might be surveyed on HR issues in the firm. Alternatively, or in addition, a representative group of line managers might be involved in the planning team. As part of their perspective, line managers should bring into the process an assessment of how other stakeholder groups, such as customers and competitors, are affected by the firm's HR systems.

Employees themselves

It should be obvious that employees and potential recruits are 'clients' of HRM in the firm. Any HR planning process will be better if it allows for employee involvement. A common practice now in large firms is to conduct regular staff surveying, as we shall illustrate further below. Some also use focus groups – smaller samples of staff in a facilitated discussion – to look more qualitatively at key issues. Data on how employees are reacting to HR policies and practices typically helps to improve the quality of HR planning in firms.

The state

Over time, governments play a key role in providing national forms of social capital. In the sense used here, this means the quantity and quality of the country's labour pool and its educational and social infrastructure. In exchange for access to these resources, governments require certain levels of compliance with labour statutes and regulations. The requirements of labour law ought always to influence the design of HR policy in firms.

The involvement principle

The stakeholder principle implies that only through dialogue among those centrally involved in managing people in the firm can the quality of HR planning be improved. As a general rule, the senior management team should drive HR planning (with the chief executive and top team leading but involving key line managers throughout the firm). HR specialists should *facilitate* the process. Managers in other domains will want HR specialists to contribute their specialist expertise (for example, in research reports on the state of internal and external labour markets, on the HR strategies of rival firms and on longer-run plans for management development (Craft 1988), but there is a fine line to be walked here. Senior HR specialists need to provide specialist expertise without creating the situation where strategic HR planning is seen purely as their hobbyhorse or their sectarian interest.

To be valuable, planning processes, in organisations of all sizes, should enhance strategic *understanding* and build strategic *consensus*. They should open up a fertile exchange within the organisation on its context, its past, its problems and its potential. Healthy involvement processes are critical to this. In badly run organisations, strategic planning is driven by the need to have certain planning rituals and to deliver a bureaucratic output (a set of reports containing objectives and milestones). The process can sometimes be forced through quite cynically by the inner elite without any intention to listen to diverse views or face unpalatable truths about a changing environment. It is much better if haste and reporting pressure is de-emphasised and the senior management team leads a process that will allow people to share contrasting views in a supportive environment and expand their openness to a changing world and to creative ideas. As we shall note below, there are ways of reducing the likelihood that this will turn into a 'slug-fest' between rival political groups.

The rivalry principle

HR planning is of little use if it is just navel-gazing. Labour markets are competitive and intelligent rivals will attempt to recruit the best workers and build the best management processes. As a result, the firm's executive team should aim to understand the HR strengths and weaknesses of key competitors (Craft 1988). Does the company have good data on the employment strengths and weaknesses of rivals? While this is a competitive question, it should not simply be seen in a competitive light (Nalebuff and Brandenburger 1996). Rival firms may be competing in the labour market but also have common interests in improving labour supply to the network or cluster of firms, a key reason for co-location of facilities in many industries (see Chapter 9). This is one of the secrets of 'Silicon Valley' in California and of many other examples of co-located firms.

The dynamic principle

As argued in Chapter 1, it is vital to accept that change is inevitable and that some preparation for the future is therefore crucial. We have not so far discussed the issue of the planning horizon but, as in all planning, this is important. Most HRM textbooks cover the techniques of short-term HR planning well and companies typically find they need at least some of them. Some short-term planning is necessary just to stay afloat. Any type of recruitment, for example, involves some kind of thinking in advance about the firm's skill deficits and desirable types of candidate (even if this thinking becomes much sharper as the selection process unfolds). Where firms tend to be much weaker, however, is in the quality of their long-term HR planning (Gratton, Hope-Hailey, Stiles and Truss 1999a, 1999b). As argued in this chapter, planning for the next three to five years is a good thing providing it does not make the organisation unduly inflexible (which it can, if done badly).

The most obvious approach in this context is scenario planning, which can be used to create readiness for a range of competitive futures. One thing that must be accepted about the future is that it is uncertain. As Anthony Giddens repeatedly emphasised in the 1998 BBC Reith lectures on globalisation, we should 'expect the unexpected' and learn to manage risk. The example shown in Box 11.1 involves defining three competitive scenarios and exploring their HR implications. One scenario is based on the most desirable business case. Such scenarios tend to assume that intelligent rivals do not exist and that the environment is generally benign, so it pays to define a second, more likely scenario in which there are competitive rivals and the environment has some surprises. Finally, one can define a least desirable case, a scenario in which there are major downturns or reversals in business fortunes. The bombing of the World Trade Center and the Pentagon in September 2001, and the Icelandic volcanic eruptions of 2010, should remind us that there are factors well beyond business control that can disrupt business performance. Certainly, in the case of airlines, and those in their supply chains, contingency planning for downsizing helps firms to adjust to such undesirable, but all-too-common, circumstances.

Box 11.1   An example of scenario-based HR planning

Step one: identifying long-run business scenarios

- Identify the key rivals in your industry-based 'strategic group'.
- Identify three scenarios that might be played out in the group over the next five years; ((1) benign or most desirable case, (2) competitive or most likely case, and (3) unstable or least desirable case).

Step two: assessing the firm's HR readiness

For each scenario ask:

- What are the HR challenges posed by this scenario (e.g. challenges posed by inadequate social capital, by labour market rivals, or by the attitudes to the firm of current or potential employees)?
- What are our HR strengths to meet these challenges (e.g. existing depth of know-how in a key business area; strength of reputation as an employer)?
- What are our HR weaknesses in relation to these challenges (e.g. recruitment not yet focused on capabilities needed in the future; lack of training for future competitive needs; excessive turnover of core staff)?

Step three: identifying key stakeholder trends relating to HRM

Over the next five years, what are the likely trends in the following and what should the company do to prepare?

- Supply of labour. How might the quantity and quality of the labour pool change across the key occupational groups employed by the firm? How might the needs and aspirations of key workers differ from current needs and aspirations? What should the company do to prepare for these possible changes?
- HR strategies of key rivals. What are the threats they will most likely pose (e.g. 'poaching' of star employees)? What opportunities do they present (e.g. joint training initiatives)?
- Labour law changes. What new forms of employment regulation, locally or internationally, could affect the company?

Step four: planning HR strategies to meet long-term business needs and cope with stakeholder trends

- Focusing on the most desirable business scenario, list the key long-term HR research, review, policy or programme initiatives that must be taken for this scenario to become a reality and develop milestones for them over the next 5 years (e.g. a staged leadership development programme with an increasing annual budget; development of an annual employee attitude survey linked to customer surveying and jointly linked to annual business planning).
- Focusing on the most likely business scenario, identify how key HR systems should be improved to enhance readiness to cope with it.
- Focusing on the least desirable business scenario, identify how key HR systems should be improved to enhance readiness to cope with it.
- Identify HR initiatives that are (a) common across all scenarios, and (b) those that are unique and will require some development of flexible skills and processes in HRM.

In this context, Shell's multiple planning system is a celebrated case (de Geus 1988, Grant 1998). In the aftermath of the 1970s oil shocks, most oil companies in the 1980s planned for a scenario of permanently rising oil prices. Shell did this but also planned for significant price decreases, a scenario that was played out in early 1986 as oil prices fell from US$27 a barrel to $17 in February and $10 in April. As a result of the lateral thinking encouraged by its scenario planning, Shell was better prepared than other companies in the industry. Readers will recognise that the situation in the oil industry has now changed very significantly with concerns about global warming, on the one hand, and problems of oil supply, on the other, both likely to keep prices high. However, this does not rule out the possibility that such factors as alternative technologies and legislation will change the industry dramatically in the future. It is best to be open to such possibilities and this is the point of scenario planning.

The model shown in Box 11.1 deliberately uses three scenarios. As argued by Eisenhardt, Kahwajy and Bourgeois (1997), whose work on strategic decision making is noted in Chapter 2, it helps if more than two options are generated in thinking about the future. Two decision options can degenerate into a political 'slugfest' between two executives or two sides of the team. Three or four options helps to reduce this kind of political in-fighting and to keep us open to the possibility that we might combine ideas from different options in the eventual decisions we take.

The integration principle

The last principle is one that has been continually emphasised in the literature for many years, as noted above. Processes for HR planning ought to be integrated with processes used for:

- long-run strategic planning and business development and
- short-run planning and budgeting.

It is not a question of choosing between short-term and long-term planning systems. Both forms of planning are important and HR planning needs to play an appropriate role in both.

In reality, no one seriously challenges this principle. The key question is always: 'yes, of course, we should integrate – but how?' In the next section, we turn to a closer examination of this issue by considering a key set of ideas about integrating financial and non-financial planning which have become very influential in contemporary strategic management.

Seeking integration: HR planning and the new management accounting

Michael Porter's works – most notably, *Competitive Strategy* (1980) and *Competitive Advantage* (1985) – were landmark contributions to the literature on strategy in the 1980s. These books offered useful analytical frameworks, particularly the notion of 'industry analysis' which helped firms to analyse the economic and political dimensions of industries. Porter's ideas were very much concerned with forging a competitive vision: with strategy as something 'out there'.

From the mid 1990s, another perspective grew up alongside the positioning model, as Chapter 4 explained. In popular reading lists, Hamel and Prahalad's (1994) *Competing for the Future* became a counterpoint alongside Porter's frameworks, encouraging firms to apply some of the internally oriented notions associated with the resource-based view of the firm. Hamel and Prahalad's work, however, has been more difficult to apply in concrete ways. If we want to locate the most practically influential ideas since the 1990s on how to re-shape strategic management they are to be found in the 'new management accounting' associated with a stream of books by Robert Kaplan and David Norton: *The Balanced Scorecard* (1996), *The Strategy-Focused Organization* (2001), *Strategy Maps: Converting Intangible Assets into Tangible Outcomes* (2004), *Alignment: Using the Balanced Scorecard to Create Corporate Synergies* (2006), and *The Execution Premium: Linking Strategy to Operations for Competitive Advantage* (2008). Traditional approaches to management accounting have been roundly criticised for focusing managers on short-term performance and for failing to encourage intelligent management of the links between financial and non-financial variables in the firm (Johnson and Kaplan 1991). As a discipline that heavily influences the strategic management process, traditional management accounting has to be treated with great care if it is not to produce dysfunctional outcomes.

Not unreasonably, Kaplan and Norton start from the premise that it is *executed* strategy that counts in a firm's performance. This, of course, was Mintzberg's (1978) fundamental point in his classic work on emergent strategy. Formulation of strategy may seem incredibly important but what customers and business rivals take most seriously is the strategy that is actually implemented. Business failure is seen to stem mostly from failing to implement and not from failing to have wonderful visions (Kaplan and Norton 2001:1). In their view, good implementation of well-formulated strategy is rare, an argument consistent with the resource-based view of the firm. This stems from lack of consensus about what the firm's strategy actually is. All too often, they argue, senior managers over-estimate what people understand about the firm's espoused strategy.

Balancing performance measures in the firm

There are two fundamental sets of ideas that underpin Kaplan and Norton's (1994, 2001) framework. The first is concerned with balancing the measures

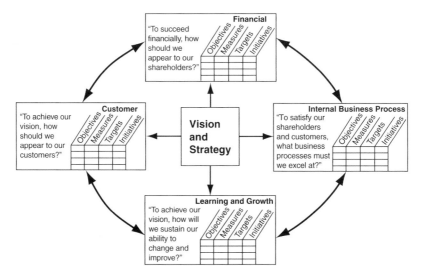

Figure 11.1 The four perspectives in the balanced scorecard

that focus management attention. The balanced scorecard involves a process of developing goals, measures, targets and initiatives in four perspectives on business performance (Figure 11.1).

An edited example of a balanced scorecard, based on a US retail chain store ('Store 24'), is shown in Figure 11.2 (Kaplan and Norton 2001: 82). This edited version is depicted in vertical format rather than as a wheel. It does not show all the links involved and only includes some measures that the company uses (in the top and bottom perspectives). Kaplan and Norton recognise that financial outcomes are important to shareholders (the perspective at the top of the scorecard) but that they are 'lagging' and short-term indicators. To improve a business, management needs to look at desirable long-term outcomes and improve the 'leading indicators' or 'performance drivers' that generate them.

Performance drivers are located in the three perspectives that underpin the financial one. Customers must perceive a 'value proposition' if they are to reward the firm financially. As we noted in our discussion of capabilities or competencies in Chapter 4, this typically involves some 'table stakes' (in common with other firms in the sector) and some differentiators. In the case of Store 24 shown in Figure 11.2, the company's executives tried to differentiate based on providing greater shopping excitement. The motto, posted in every store, became 'Store 24 bans boredom' and special promotions were organised in an attempt to amuse customers.

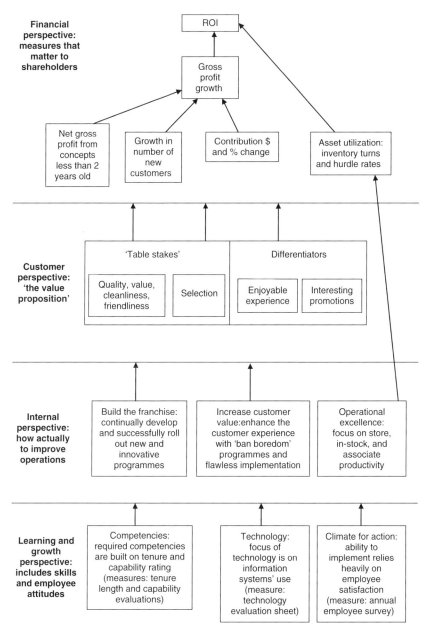

Figure 11.2 Example of a strategy map and some balanced scorecard measures

The customer value proposition depends on carrying out certain key operations. This means that Kaplan and Norton's framework does not demean the role of good operational systems, something we argued is very important in Chapters 2 and 5. In Store 24's case, this was split into three internal operational themes. Two of these were targeted at generating sales growth while the third was focused on productivity or margin improvement. This is fairly typical. Balanced scorecards very often contain dual strategic thrusts: one aimed at raising the top line (revenue) and the other aimed at more effective cost management.

Finally, the balanced scorecard attempts to identify key human resource and technological variables that drive performance. In the 'learning and growth' base of the scorecard, employee skills and satisfaction are nearly always identified as critical to improving internal processes and, thus, enhancing customer satisfaction and financial outcomes. As Kaplan and Norton (2001: 93) describe it:

> The learning and growth strategy defines the intangible assets needed to enable organizational activities and customer relationships to be performed at ever-higher levels of performance. There are three principal categories in this perspective:
>
> 1. Strategic competencies: the strategic skills and knowledge required by the workforce to support the strategy
> 2. Strategic technologies: the information systems, databases, tools, and network required to support the strategy
> 3. Climate for action: the cultural shifts needed to motivate, empower, and align the workforce behind the strategy.
>
> The learning and growth strategies are the true starting point for any long-term, sustainable change.

Although Kaplan and Norton do not use the rubric, their conception of 'learning and growth', including their notions of 'strategic competencies' and 'climate for action', resonates with key ideas in this book: with the 'AMO' model of individual performance and with the issue of building workforce capabilities and social climate (see Figure 8.1 in Chapter 8 which summarises these ideas). In the notion of 'strategic technologies', they also identify part of what it means to provide workers with the opportunity to perform because such tools are needed if people are to work effectively. However, their thinking here does not go as far as we would like. It helps to see the structure of work – the forms of work organisation used in the firm – as facilitating or constraining employee opportunity to make a difference, as we argued in Chapter 5.

Through this kind of framework, therefore, Kaplan and Norton encourage business unit managers to define desirable long-term strategic goals and make short-term plans based on 'milestones' toward long-term goals. This provides a simple, practical way of integrating strategic planning and annual budgeting. Budgeting is a very strong corporate ritual which tends to over-emphasise short-term profitability and undermine long-term efforts to build the business. The balanced scorecard can be used to re-work budgets around steps towards the desired long-term strategy. Some short-term targets are always needed (because survival into the long-term depends on surviving today) but such targets should not create perverse long-term consequences. Given business unit goals, the scorecard can then be used to create departmental and personal scorecards for individual managers.

It can also be used in multidivisional firms to open up a better dialogue between corporate and business unit management about the role of both (Kaplan and Norton 2001, 2006). Rather than simply considering figures on return on investment, balanced scorecards can open up debate around the performance drivers of financial outcomes, including HR variables. Such an approach challenges some of the modes of corporate control discussed in Chapter 10. Corporate or 'enterprise scorecards' in multidivisional firms, argue Kaplan and Norton, should identify synergies across the group (why else have a group?). This includes ways in which central service units (such as corporate finance, IT and HR departments) can add value to particular business units. In those M-form and multinational companies moving to emphasise knowledge sharing through networks, the balanced scorecard could be a valuable tool for identifying synergies across business units and between business units and corporate service centres.

The Kaplan and Norton scorecard is thus better balanced than typical financial reports that only report history and which do not identify underpinning sources of success. Our discussion indicates that it is also better balanced in the sense that it recognises outcomes that matter to other *stake*holders (particularly customers and employees) besides *stock*holders. This emphasis is consistent with a range of contemporary efforts to encourage broader reporting, such as the notion of the 'triple bottom line' (financial, environmental and social) (Elkington 1997).

Building a theory of the business or 'strategy map'

The second key idea in the balanced scorecard is that senior managers should build a 'theory of the business' or what Kaplan and Norton (2001, 2004) call a 'strategy map'. This is a map of causes-and-effects, of performance drivers and their key outcomes. In the edited version of a scorecard depicted in Figure 11.2, key elements of a strategy map become apparent, including the role of skill building and employee motivation in producing good encounters with customers and, thus, better financial returns.

Another example of a strategy map is shown in Figure 11.3. This map depicts the 'service-profit' or 'employee-customer-profit chain' at Sears (Heskett, Jones, Loveman and Schlesinger 1994, Rucci, Kirn and Quinn 1998). Sears uses the idea that the company will become a 'compelling place to invest' if it is a 'compelling place to shop' and a 'compelling place to work'. The map argues that differences in employee satisfaction and capabilities have direct impacts on customer satisfaction in service firms and important indirect impacts on profitability. As Becker, Huselid and Ulrich (2001) note, the links between HR strategy, employee behaviour and what happens to customers are very clear in this kind of service business. The vast majority of employees are working directly with customers and their attitudes to the work and the company become very apparent to them, something to which we can all attest.

The key point about strategy maps is that they open up debate about what really makes the business successful or could make it more successful, particularly when staff at all levels of the business are included in the process (Kaplan and Norton 2001). 'Making strategy everyone's everyday job' is one of the key principles (as opposed to making it the exclusive knowledge of a top-management 'secret society'). Over time, management should postulate and measure various hypotheses about what causes what in the organisation and thus improve their 'theory of the business', something that is emphasised by HR scholars such as David Guest (1997), Becker *et al.* (2001) and Fulmer *et al.* (2003). For example, it helps to collect data at regular intervals on customer satisfaction and employee 'engagement' and develop propositions about cause-and-effect. Do better employee attitudes feed through into customer satisfaction and into financial measures? All this helps to build consensus about how well the organisation is doing and what it should be doing. According to Kaplan and Norton, consensus about where the business should be heading is often lower than people think. 'We cannot expect to implement strategy if we cannot describe it' (Kaplan and Norton 2001: 100).

Strategic HRM and the balanced scorecard: an evaluation

In terms of the practice of strategic HRM, the balanced scorecard is clearly an interesting development. While Kaplan and Norton (1996: 144) are critical of the weak measures often used historically in companies on HR issues, they do

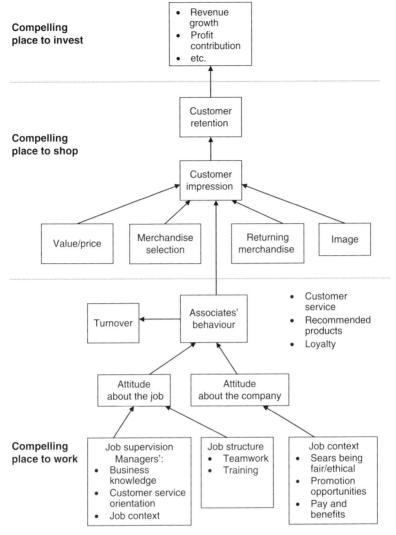

Compelling place to invest
- Revenue growth
- Profit contribution
- etc.

Compelling place to shop

Customer retention

Customer impression

Value/price

Merchandise selection

Returning merchandise

Image

Turnover

Associates' behaviour
- Customer service
- Recommended products
- Loyalty

Attitude about the job

Attitude about the company

Compelling place to work

Job supervision Managers':
- Business knowledge
- Customer service orientation
- Job context

Job structure
- Teamwork
- Training

Job context
- Sears being fair/ethical
- Promotion opportunities
- Pay and benefits

Figure 11.3   The employee-customer-profit chain at Sears

Adapted with permission of Harvard Business School Press. From *The Strategy-Focused Organization* by Kaplan, R. and Norton, D.: Boston, MA, 2001, p. 309 © 2001 by Harvard Business School Publishing Corporation, all rights reserved.

not doubt the fundamental role of HRM in building a business over time. Nor do they doubt the way in which employee skills and commitment can contribute to operational performance, something which is increasingly affirmed in research (for example, Koys 2001, Harrison, Newman and Roth 2006).

The 'learning and growth' perspective is essentially about people management activities. It typically encourages surveying of employee attitudes, recognising the role of these in linking HR activities to performance. The scorecard thus provides a practical methodology for integrating key HR performance drivers into the strategic management framework. There is no doubt this is helpful. Despite the growing attention to HRM over the last 20 years, senior management debates have been hamstrung by lack of agreement on how reports on strategic HR matters should be structured (Purcell and Ahlstrand 1994). This need not remain the case. Tools and techniques inspired by balanced scorecard ideas are increasingly being applied to improve workforce planning. Huselid, Becker and Beatty's (2005) book, *The Workforce Scorecard: Managing Human Capital to Execute Strategy*, provides a number of these, helping senior managers to form and measure a relevant 'workforce strategy' for their firm.

The need for strategic flexibility and 'meta-planning' skills

While seeing the major potential for better HRM–strategy integration through the balanced scorecard, caution should be exercised with some of Kaplan and Norton's ideas, or certainly with a simplistic application of them. The emphasis of the balanced scorecard is very much on improving the quality of the implementation of a *given* strategy. This is important enough, as Kaplan and Norton argue. However, arguments made above about change and dynamic planning suggest it should not be pursued to an inflexible degree. Arguably, those parts of the process which encourage openness to the environment ought to be highlighted more fully. Alongside skills in building particular strategy maps, firms ought to develop what might be called 'meta-planning' skills. These include the ability to sense new environmental directions and to switch to different competitive scenarios, something that was shown to be valuable in our earlier discussion of the US railway cases.

This criticism is increasingly recognised by Kaplan and Norton. In the *Strategy Focused Organisation* (2001: chapter 12), they accept the role and importance of environmental and competitor analysis prior to formulating strategy. They also discuss examples of 'dynamic simulation' and note the value of calibrating scorecard measures against industry rivals (thus benchmarking the firm in terms of industry change). They further argue that the firm's leaders should aim to identify and support the Mintzbergian 'emergent learning' that occurs in their organisation. They note, for example, that Store 24 (Figure 11.2) has now modified its strategy because the 'ban boredom' approach did not impress customers (Kaplan and Norton 2001: 318–19). It turns out that the customers valued fast service and good selection rather than in-store entertainment. The slogan has changed to 'Cause you just can't wait' and the scorecard has been revised accordingly. All these points help to underline the value of strategic flexibility and meta-planning skills.

However, more is needed. Building the capacity for strategic management depends heavily on the quality of the *management* of managers, something we emphasised in Chapters 2, 8 and 10 and which does not figure in typical scorecards. Recruitment, development and team-building activities at the top levels of management (and at the middle and front-line levels which supply them) need to be planned for in astute ways. This point, too, has increasingly been recognised in Kaplan and Norton's later works (for example, 2004: 289–99; 2006: 91–3). The balanced scorecard does contain an emphasis on the management of the non-management workforce and is obviously a way of structuring executive performance measurement. This is absolutely critical but it needs to be complemented with a more comprehensive conception of HR strategy for managing managers, including processes for leadership development and processes for stimulating creative, flexible thinking.

The need to recognise multiple 'bottom lines' in HRM

A second caution is closely related to the first. The importance of productive pursuit of the current strategy is the key theme in Kaplan and Norton's framework. This is, of course, vital in any business. However, this should not make us blind to the fact that some HR policies are not connected directly to cost-effectiveness or indeed to organisational flexibility. Social legitimacy has a role to play in HRM irrespective of competitive goals, one of the key themes of this book. At the very least, all reputable firms should comply with labour laws in their countries of domicile. This means that the firm's scorecard for HRM should never be totally dominated by a single 'bottom line'. Again, Kaplan and Norton have responded somewhat to this point, recognising the importance of regulatory and social processes (2004: chapter 6). They place more emphasis, however, on social legitimacy as a means to an end (building business reputation and shareholder value) and do not go as far as we do in seeing it as an end in itself.

How can firms practically deal with the need for multiple bottom lines in HRM without getting bogged down in too much complexity? We can work with an idea mentioned in Chapter 9. This is Derek Abell's (1993) suggestion that firms should manage with 'dual strategies': 'mastering the present and pre-empting the future'. We depict our thinking in Figure 11.4, which shows HR strategy simultaneously serving two major strategic priorities. Together, these sets of activities contribute to a multi-level understanding of organisational effectiveness.

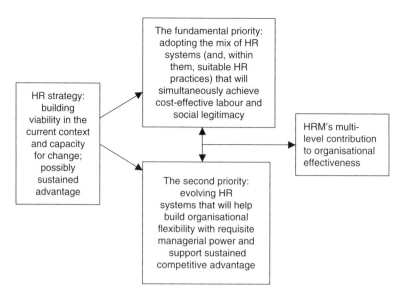

Figure 11.4 Multiple goals in HR strategy and organisational effectiveness

Figure 11.4 argues that the first duty or fundamental priority of HRM is to help the firm adopt a cost-effective and socially legitimate set of HR systems. This is needed to underpin viable operations in the current organisational context. The task here is not simply about picking HR systems out of a framework but requires sensitivity to the particular HR practices that are needed in the specific context. HR systems are broad types which inevitably need to be tailored to the actual environment. A key part of this is ensuring that cost-effectiveness is pursued in socially legitimate ways. At a minimum, this means complying with labour law and important social customs in the countries in which the firm operates. Supporting the firm's viability through cost-effective and socially legitimate HR activities must come first or the firm simply will not survive in the industries and societies in which it is located.

The second priority in HR strategy shown in Figure 11.4 is concerned with preparing for the future and with supporting efforts to build sustained competitive advantage. Building an organisation's flexibility implies there must be an appropriate degree of managerial power but firms need to be careful not to foster the sort of power and reward differences that can alienate employees whose commitment is important. In some cases, steps to support competitive advantage could mean adopting HR systems that foster greater employee involvement in decision making and higher skill levels throughout the organisation. In other cases, it could mean focusing more on the

HR system for managers. For example, a firm may have the kinds of HR systems that are cost effective for its operating workforces but its leaders may find that they are not doing enough to build management succession and development. The response might include fostering forms of management team-building that enhance creative thinking, sponsoring more lateral shifts across the company (including across functions and countries), and reworking its managerial recruitment strategies and career structures.

All of this implies, as argued in Chapter 8, that there will be tensions in any firm's HR strategy: 'internal fit' in the sense of a single, uncomplicated theme is not possible. Multiple themes are needed in an effective HR strategy. At the very least, there needs to be a balancing of economic drivers with the ethical responsibility of the firm to behave in ways that comply with laws and important social customs. And, at the very least, there needs to be some thinking about organisational flexibility given the pervasiveness of change in today's world. As discussed in Chapters 4 and 9, more ambitious and proactive management teams will go beyond the management of these fundamental tensions to try and build the kinds of human and social capital that support sustained competitive advantage.

The need for caution with specific HR practices

A final criticism of the balanced scorecard concerns Kaplan and Norton's assumptions about desirable kinds of HR practice. Like many US best-practice writers, they tend to place too much faith in incentive remuneration (the 'balanced paycheque') (see also Becker *et al.* 2001). The principle of aligning employer and employee interests is, of course, absolutely fundamental but this does not mean that bonus systems are always desirable, a point we covered in our discussion of pay theory in Chapter 7. There are many situations in which the better focus a scorecard can bring will work well alongside high wage levels but without mechanistic bonuses. If, however, the scorecard process encourages firms to find out more about employee motivations (through, for example, encouraging greater use of employee surveying), it should improve the design of work and reward systems over time. The stakeholder and involvement principles we noted earlier in relation to HR planning systems do imply this kind of consultative process. What is needed is a way of identifying that mix or bundle of HR practices that will be relevant in a particular context. While some practices have almost universal relevance in the Anglo-American world (certain kinds of selection practice, for example), others are heavily shaped by organisational, industry and societal contexts.

Conclusions

This chapter has summarised the major themes that underpin this book and then turned to the practical question of how managers can use these ideas to enhance strategic management processes in their firms. While recognising that strategic management is broader than strategic planning, many of the ideas about how to improve strategic management come back to ideas about how to improve planning and decision-making processes in the firm. In most situations, there is competitive value in finding ways to improve the quality of strategic planning, including finding ways in which human resource problems and opportunities can be better understood and tackled. Far from being outdated or inappropriate in changing times, the discipline of strategic planning is something that can yield greater value, particularly when firms show persistence and develop 'meta-planning' skills in environmental analysis and flexible thinking. Scenario planning is important in this regard, particularly those models that involve planning for the HR challenges presented by different scenarios.

At the base of all strategies, there are things that firms need to do with people, as Kaplan and Norton's stream of work on 'balanced scorecards' and 'strategy maps' indicates. Human resources may not be sufficient for competitive success but they are a necessary part of the system of resources that is. There is no doubt that in many firms, the creation and testing of a strategy map would constitute a major breakthrough by helping to identify the key linkages between HRM and a desired competitive position. As the new management accountancy recognises, there is then less likelihood that critical resources, including human ones, will be subject to counter-productive forms of cost-cutting in the firm. Such frameworks represent an important, integrating step forward, one in which management can move beyond mere assertion about the value of human and social capital to a planning regime in which measurement and modelling of causes-and-effects confirm these important assertions by making them specific, data-based and transparent.

As Kaplan and Norton argue, human resource variables, such as employee skills and satisfaction levels, are 'performance drivers' in all firms. However, this perspective cannot encompass all that is important about HR strategy. The strategic goals of HRM should be understood in a broader sense. At the very least, they include cost-effectiveness and social legitimacy in the current context, twin goals that support viability in the firm's industries and the societies in which it is embedded. If the firm wishes to survive, they also involve some measure of flexibility, a functional level of managerial power, and an approach to HRM that supports the firm's particular efforts to build competitive advantage. These goals involve strategic tensions that are never easy to handle even where measurement is improved. The 'bottom line' for HRM in organizations, including both private and public sector ones, is more complex than it first appears. A good performance in HRM is multidimensional. New frameworks in strategic management have lessons for HRM and are more embracing of HRM. The traffic, however, is not all one way. Human resource management also has some enduring lessons for the new strategic management.

References

Abell, D. F. (1993) *Managing with Dual Strategies: Mastering the Present, Preempting the Future.* New York: Free Press.

Adams, J. S. (1965) 'Inequality in social exchange'. In Berkovitz, L. (ed.) *Advances in Experimental Social Psychology, Vol. 2.* New York: Academic Press.

Adler, P. S., Goldolftas, B. and Levine, D. I. (1999) 'Flexibility versus efficiency? A case study of model changeovers with Toyota production system'. *Organization Science* 10(1): 43–68.

Allen, J. and Velden, R. van der (2001) 'Educational mismatches versus skill mismatches: effects on wages, job satisfaction, and on-the-job search', *Oxford Economic Papers*, 3: 434–52.

Alpander, G., Carter, K. and Forsgren, R. (1990) 'Managerial issues and problem-solving in the formative years'. *Journal of Small Business Management* 28(2): 9–19.

Amit, R. and Shoemaker, P. (1993) 'Strategic assets and organizational rent'. *Strategic Management Journal* 14: 33–46.

Ansoff, I. (1991) 'Critique of Henry Mintzberg's "The design school: reconsidering the basic premises of strategic management"'. *Strategic Management Journal* 12(6): 449–61.

Appelbaum, E. and Batt, R. (1994) *The New American Workplace.* Ithaca, NY: ILR Press.

Appelbaum, E., Bailey, T., Berg, P. and Kalleberg, A. (2000) *Manufacturing Advantage: Why High-Performance Systems Pay Off.* Ithaca, NY: ILR Press.

Appelbaum, E. Bernhardt, A. and Murnane, R. (eds) (2003) *Low-Wage America: How Employers are Reshaping Opportunity in the Workplace.* New York: Russell Sage Foundation.

Appleyard, M. and Brown, C. (2001) 'Employment practices and semiconductor manufacturing performance'. *Industrial Relations* 40(3): 436–71.

Armstrong, M. and Baron, A. (1995) *The Job Evaluation Handbook.* London: CIPD.

Arthur, J. (1994) 'Effects of human resource systems on manufacturing performance and turnover'. *Academy of Management Journal* 37(3): 670–87.

Arthur, J. (1999) 'Explaining the variation in human resource practices in the US steel minimills'. In Cappelli, P. (ed.) *Employment Practices and Business Strategy*, New York: Oxford University Press.

Atkinson, J. (1984) 'Manpower strategies for flexible organisations'. *Personnel Management* 28–31 August.

Audit Commission (2002). *Recruitment and Retention.* London: Audit Commission.

Aycan, Z. (2005) 'The interplay between cultural and institutional/structural contingencies in human resource management practices'. *International Journal of Human Resource Management* 16(7): 1083–119.

Bach, S. and Kessler, I. (2007) 'Human resource management and the new public management'. In Boxall, P., Purcell, J. and Wright, P. (eds) *The Oxford Handbook of Human Resource Management.* Oxford: Oxford University Press.

Bacon, N. and Blyton, P. (2001) 'High involvement work systems and job insecurity in the international iron and steel industry'. *Canadian Journal of Administrative Sciences* 18(1): 5–16.

Baden-Fuller, C. (1995) 'Strategic innovation, corporate entrepreneurship and matching outside-in to inside-out approaches to strategy research'. *British Journal of Management* 6(S): 3–16.

Baden-Fuller, C. and Stopford, J. (1994). *Rejuvenating the Mature Business*. London: Routledge.

Baird, L. and Meshoulam, I. (1988). 'Managing two fits of strategic human resource management'. *Academy of Management Review* 13(1): 116–28.

Barker, J. (1993) 'Tightening the iron cage'. *Administrative Science Quarterly* 38(3): 408–37.

Barnard, C. (1938) *The Functions of the Executive*. Boston, MA: Harvard University Press.

Barney, J. (1991) 'Firm resources and sustained competitive advantage'. *Journal of Management* 17(1): 99–120.

Barney, J. (2000) 'Firm resources and sustained competitive advantage'. *Advances in Strategic Management* 17: 203–27.

Barney, J. and Wright, P. (1998) 'On becoming a strategic partner: the role of human resources in gaining competitive advantage'. *Human Resource Management* 37(1): 31–46.

Baron, R. and Kreps, D. (1999) *Strategic Human Resources: Frameworks for General Managers*. New York: Wiley.

Barr, P., Stimpert, J. and Huff. A. (1992) 'Cognitive change, strategic action, and organizational renewal'. *Strategic Management Journal* 13: 15–36.

Barringer, B., Jones, F. and Neubaum, D. (2005) 'A quantitative content analysis of the characteristics of rapid-growth firms and their founders'. *Journal of Business Venturing* 20: 663–87.

Bartlett, C. and Ghoshal, S. (1989) *Managing Across Borders: the Transnational Solution*. Cambridge, MA: Harvard Business School Press.

Bartlett, C. and Ghoshal, S. (1998) *Managing Across Boundaries: The Transnational Corporation*. New York: Random House.

Bartol, K. and Durham, C. (2000) 'Incentives: theory and practice'. In Cooper, C. and Locke, E. (eds) *Industrial and Organizational Psychology*. Oxford: Blackwell.

Baruch, Y. and Hind, P. (2000) 'Survivor syndrome – a management myth?' *Journal of Managerial Psychology* 15(1): 29–45.

Bates, T. (1990) 'Entrepreneur human capital inputs and small business longevity'. *Review of Economics and Statistics* 72(4): 551–9.

Batt, R. (2000) 'Strategic segmentation in front-line services: matching customers, employees and human resource systems'. *International Journal of Human Resource Management* 11(3): 540–61.

Batt, R. (2002) 'Managing customer services: human resource practices, quit rates, and sales growth'. *Academy of Management Journal* 45: 587–97.

Batt, R. (2004) 'Who benefits from teams? Comparing workers, supervisors, and managers'. *Industrial Relations* 43(1): 183–212.

Batt, R. (2005) 'Organizational performance in services'. In Holman, D., Wall, T., Clegg, C., Sparrow, P. and Howard, A. (eds) *The Essentials of the New Workplace*. New York: Wiley.

Batt, R. (2007) 'Service strategies: marketing, operations and human resource practices'. In Boxall, P., Purcell, J. and Wright, P. (eds) *The Oxford Handbook of Human Resource Management*. Oxford: Oxford University Press.

Bauer, T. (2004). 'High performance workplace practices and job satisfaction: evidence from Europe'. Discussion Paper No. 1265, Institute for the Study of Labor (IZA).

Baumeister, A. and Bacharach, V. (2000) 'Early generic educational intervention has no enduring effect on intelligence and does not prevent mental retardation: the infant health and development program'. *Intelligence* 28(3): 161–92.

Becker, B. and Gerhart, B. (1996) 'The impact of human resource management on organizational performance: progress and practice'. *Academy of Management Journal* 39(4): 779–801.

Becker, B. and Huselid, M. (2006) Strategic human resources management: where do we go from here? *Journal of Management* 32(6): 898–925.

Becker, B., Huselid, M., Pickus, P. S. and Spratt, M. F. (1997) 'HR as a source of shareholder value: research and recommendations'. *Human Resource Management* 36(1): 39–47.

Becker, B., Huselid, M. and Ulrich, D. (2001) *The HR Scorecard: Linking People, Strategy, and Performance*. Boston, MA: Harvard Business School Press.

Becker, T., Billings, R., Eveleth, D. and Gilbert, N. (1996) 'Foci and bases of employee commitment: implications for job performance'. *Academy of Management Journal* 39: 464–82.

Beer, M., Spector, B., Lawrence, P., Quinn Mills, D. and Walton, R. (1984) *Managing Human Assets*. New York: Free Press.

Belanger, J., Giles, A. and Murray, G. (2002) 'Towards a new production model: potentialities, tensions and contradictions'. In Murray, G., Belanger, J., Giles, A. and Lapointe, P. (eds) *Work and Employment Relations in the High-Performance Workplace*. London and New York: Continuum.

Belbin, M. (1981) *Management Teams: Why They Succeed or Fail*. Oxford: Butterworth-Heinemann.

Belbin, R.M. (1993) *Team Roles at Work*. Oxford: Butterworth-Heinemann.

Bendix, R. (1956) *Work and Authority in Industry*. Berkeley, CA: UCLA Press.

Benkhoff, B. (1997). 'A test of the HRM model: good for employers *and* employees'. *Human Resource Management Journal* 7(4): 44–60.

Benson, G. and Lawler, E. (2005) 'Employee involvement: utilization, impacts and future prospects'. In Holman, D., Wall, T., Clegg, C., Sparrow, P. and Howard, A. (eds) *The Essentials of the New Workplace: A Guide to the Human Impact of Modern Working Practices*. London: John Wiley.

Benson, J. and Brown, M. (2010) 'Employee voice: does union membership matter?' *Human Resource Management Journal* 20(1): 80–99.

Berg, P. (1999) 'The effects of high performance work practices on job satisfaction in the United States steel industry'. *Relations Industrielles* 54(1): 111–34.

Berggren, C. (1992) *The Volvo Experience: Alternatives to Lean Production in the Swedish Auto Industry*. London: Macmillan (now Palgrave Macmillan).

Bergman, T. and Scarpello, V. (2001) *Compensation Decision Making*. Fort Worth: Harcourt.

Besley, S. and Brigham. E. (2009) *Principles of Finance*. 4th edn. Mason, OH: South Western Cengage Learning.

Bhargava, S. (1994) 'Profit sharing and the financial performance of companies: evidence from UK Panel Data'. *Economic Journal* 104: 1044–56.

Black, S. and Lynch, L. (2001) 'How to compete: the impact of workplace practices and information technology on productivity'. *Review of Economics and Statistics* 83(3): 434–45.

Blasi, J. and Kruse, D. (2006) 'US high-performance work practices at century's end'. *Industrial Relations* 45(4): 547–78.

Blau, P. (1964) *Exchange and Power in Social Life*. New York: Wiley.

Blauner, R. (1964). *Alienation and Freedom: The Factory Worker and His Industry*. Chicago: University of Chicago Press.

Blumberg, M. and Pringle, C. (1982) 'The missing opportunity in organizational research: some implications for a theory of work performance'. *Academy of Management Review* 7(4): 560–9.

Blyton, P. and Turnbull, P. (2004) *The Dynamics of Employee Relations*. London: Palgrave Macmillan.

Boeker, W. (1989) 'Strategic change: the effects of founding and history'. *Academy of Management Journal* 32(3): 489–515.

Bosma, H. *et al.* (1997) 'Low job control and risk of coronary heart disease in Whitehall 11 (prospective cohort) study'. *British Medical Journal* 314:558 (22 February).

Bosma, H. *et al.* (1998) 'Two alternative job stress models and the risk of coronary heart disease'. *American Journal of Public Health* 88(1): 68–74.

Bowen, D. and Ostroff, C. (2004) 'Understanding HRM-firm performance linkages: the role of the "strength" of the HRM system'. *Academy of Management Review* 29: 203–21.

Bowey, A. (1989) *Managing Salary and Wage Systems*. Aldershot: Gower.

Bowey, A. and Thorpe, R. (1986) *Payment Systems and Productivity*. Basingstoke: Macmillan (now Palgrave Macmillan).

Boxall, P. (1992) 'Strategic human resource management: beginnings of a new theoretical sophistication?' *Human Resource Management Journal* 2(3): 60–79.

Boxall, P. (1994) 'Placing HR strategy at the heart of business success'. *Personnel Management* 26(7): 32–5.

Boxall, P. (1995) 'Building the theory of comparative HRM'. *Human Resource Management Journal* 5(5): 5–17.

Boxall, P. (1996) 'The strategic HRM debate and the resource-based view of the firm'. *Human Resource Management Journal* 6(3): 59–75.

Boxall, P. (1998) 'Achieving competitive advantage through human resource strategy: towards a theory of industry dynamics'. *Human Resource Management Review* 8(3): 265–88.

Boxall, P. (1999) 'Human resource strategy and industry-based competition: a conceptual framework and agenda for theoretical development'. In Wright, P., Dyer, L., Boudreau, J. and Milkovich, G. (eds) *Research in Personnel and Human Resource Management (Supplement 4: Strategic Human Resources Management in the Twenty-First Century)*. Stanford, CT and London: JAI Press.

Boxall, P. (2003) 'HR Strategy and competitive advantage in the service sector'. *Human Resource Management Journal* 13(3): 5–20.

Boxall, P. (2007) 'The goals of HRM'. In Boxall, P., Purcell, J. and Wright, P. (eds) *The Oxford Handbook of Human Resource Management*. Oxford: Oxford University Press.

Boxall, P. (2008) 'Trade union strategy'. In Blyton, P., Bacon, N., Fiorito, J. and Heery, E. (eds) *The Sage Handbook of Industrial Relations*. London: Sage.

Boxall, P. and Gilbert, J. (2007) 'The management of managers: a literature review and integrative framework'. *International Journal of Management Reviews* 9(2): 1–21.

Boxall, P. and Haynes, P. (1997) 'Strategy and trade union effectiveness in a neo-liberal environment'. *British Journal of Industrial Relations* 35(4): 567–91.

Boxall, P. and Macky, K. (2009) 'Research and theory on high-performance work systems: progressing the high-involvement stream'. *Human Resource Management Journal* 19(1): 3–23.

Boxall, P. and Purcell, J. (2000) 'Strategic human resource management: where have we come from and where should we be going?'. *International Journal of Management Reviews* 2(2): 183–203.

Boxall, P. and Purcell, J (2009) 'Employee participation: an HRM perspective'. In Wilkinson, A., Gollan, P., Marchington, M and Lewin, D. (eds) *The Oxford Handbook of Participation in Organizations*. Oxford: Oxford University Press.

Boxall, P. and Steeneveld, M. (1999) 'Human resource strategy and competitive advantage: a longitudinal study of engineering consultancies'. *Journal of Management Studies* 36(4): 443–63.

Boxall, P., Freeman, R. and Haynes, P. (2007) 'Conclusions: what workers say in the Anglo-American world'. In Freeman, R., Boxall, P. and Haynes, P. (eds) *What Workers Say: Employee Voice in the Anglo-American World*. Ithaca, NY: Cornell University Press.

Boxall, P., Purcell, J. and Wright, P. (2007) 'Human resource management: scope, analysis, and significance'. In Boxall, P., Purcell, J. and Wright, P. (eds) *The Oxford Handbook of Human Resource Management*. Oxford: Oxford University Press.

Boyer, K., Keong Leong, G., Ward, P. and Krajewski, L. (1997) 'Unlocking the potential of advanced manufacturing technologies'. *Journal of Operations Management* 15: 331–47.

Bracker, J. (1980) 'The historical development of the strategic management concept'. *Academy of Management Review* 5(2): 219–24.

Bradley, K. and Gelb, A. (1983) *Worker Capitalism: The New Industrial Relations*. London: Heinemann Educational.

Bradley, L. and Ashkanasy, N. (2001) 'Formal performance appraisal interviews: can they really be objective and are they useful anyway?'. *Asia Pacific Journal of Human Resources* 39(2): 83–97.

Braverman, H. (1974) *Labor and Monopoly Capital*. New York and London: Monthly Review Press.

Brews, P. and Hunt, M. (1999) 'Learning to plan and planning to learn: resolving the planning school/learning school debate'. *Strategic Management Journal* 20: 889–913.

Brewster, C., Wood, G. and Brookes, M. (2008) 'Similarity or Duality? Recent survey evidence on human resource management policies of multinational corporations'. *British Journal of Management* 19:320–42.

Brown, C. and Reich, M. (1997) 'Micro-macro linkages in high-performance work systems'. *Organization Studies* 18(5): 765–81.

Brown, W. (2009) 'The influence of product markets on industrial relations'. In Blyton, P., Bacon, N., Fiorito, J. and Heery, E. (eds) *The Sage Handbook of Industrial Relations*. London: Sage.

Brown, W., Deakin, S., Hudson, M., Pratten, C. and Ryan, P. (1998) 'The individualisation of the employment contract in Britain'. *Employment Relations Research Series* No. 4. London: Department of Trade and Industry.

Bruce, A. and Buck, T. (1997) 'Executive reward and corporate governance'. In Keasey, K., Thompson, S. and Wright, M. (eds) *Corporate Governance: Economic and Financial Issues*. Oxford: Oxford University Press.

Brynjolfsson, E. and Hitt, L. (2000) 'Beyond computation: information technology, organizational transformation and business performance'. *Journal of Economic Perspectives* 14(4): 23–48.

Bryson, A. (2004a) 'Managerial responsiveness to union and nonunion worker voice in Britain'. *Industrial Relations* 43(1): 213–41.

Bryson, A. (2004b) *A Perfect Union? What Workers Want From Unions*, London: TUC.

Bryson, A. and Freeman, R (2007) 'What voice do British workers want?'. In Freeman, R., Boxall, P. and Haynes, P. (eds) *What Workers Say: Employee Voice in the Anglo-American World*. Ithaca, NY: Cornell University Press.

Bryson, A., Charlwood, A. and Forth, J. (2006) 'Worker voice, managerial response and labour productivity: an empirical investigation'. *Industrial Relations Journal* 37(5): 438–55.

Budd, J. (2004) *Employment with a Human Face*. Ithaca, NY: Cornell University Press.

Buono, A. and Bowditch, J. (1989) *The Human Side of Mergers and Acquisitions*. San Francisco: Jossey-Bass.

Buono, A., Bowditch, J. and Lewis III, J. (1985) 'When cultures collide: the anatomy of a merger'. *Human Relations* 53(5): 477–500.

Burawoy, M. (1979). *Manufacturing Consent*. Chicago: University of Chicago Press.

Burch, G. and Anderson, N. (2004) 'Measuring person-team fit: development and validation of the team selection inventor'. *Journal of Managerial Psychology* 19(4): 406–26.

Burch, G. and Anderson, N. (2008) 'Personality as a predictor of work-related behaviour and performance: recent advances and directions for future research'. *International Review of Industrial and Organizational Psychology* 23: 261–305.

Burgess, S. and Rees, H. (1998) 'A disaggregate analysis of the evolution of job tenure in Britain, 1975–1993'. *British Journal of Industrial Relations* 36(4): 629–55.

Buxton, J. (1998) *Ending the Mother War*. London: Macmillan (now Palgrave Macmillan).

Campbell, D., Campbell, K and Chia, H. (1998) 'Merit pay, performance appraisal, and individual motivation'. *Human Resource Management* 37(2): 131–46.

Campbell, J. P., McCloy, R., Oppler, S. and Sager, C. (1993) 'A theory of performance'. In Schmitt, N. and Borman, W. (eds) *Personnel Selection in Organizations*. San Francisco: Jossey-Bass.

Cappelli, P. and Neumark, D. (2001) 'Do "high performance" work practices improve establishment level outcomes?' *Industrial and Labor Relations Review* 54(4): 737–76.

Cardon, M. and Stevens, C. (2004) 'Managing human resources in small organizations: what do we know?' *Human Resource Management Review* 14: 295–323.

Carless, S. (2005) 'Person-job fit versus person-organization fit as predictors of organizational attraction and job acceptance intentions: a longitudinal study'. *Journal of Occupational and Organizational Psychology* 78(3): 411–29.

Carley, M and Hall, M. (2008) 'European Directive on information and consultation: industrial relations developments in Europe 2007'. European Foundation for the Improvement of Living and Working Conditions. Luxembourg: Office for Official Publications of the European Communities.

Carroll, G. R. and Hannan, M. T. (eds) (1995) *Organizations in Industry: Strategy, Structure and Selection*, New York and Oxford: Oxford University Press.

Cartier, K. (1994) 'The transaction costs and benefits of the incomplete contract of employment'. *Cambridge Journal of Economics* 18: 181–96.

Cartwright, S. and Cooper, C. (1992) *Mergers and Acquisitions: The Human Factor*. Oxford: Butterworth-Heinemann.

Challis, D., Samson, D. and Lawson, B. (2005) 'Impact of technological, organizational and human resource investments on employee and manufacturing performance: Australian and New Zealand evidence'. *International Journal of Production Research* 43(1): 81–107.

Chandler, A. (1962) *Strategy and Structure: Chapters in the History of Industrial Enterprise*. Cambridge, MA: MIT Press.

Chatman, J. and Jehn, K. (1994) 'Assessing the relationship between industry characteristics and organizational culture: how different can you be?' *Academy of Management Journal* 37(3): 522–53.

Chicha, M.-T. (2009) *Promoting Equity: Gender Neutral Job Evaluation for Equal Pay*. Geneva: ILO.

Child, J. (1972) 'Organizational structure, environment and performance: the role of strategic choice'. *Sociology* 6(3): 1–22.

Child, J. (1997) 'Strategic choice in the analysis of action, structure, organizations and environment: retrospect and prospect'. *Organization Studies* 18(1): 43–76.

Child, J. and Smith, C. (1987) 'The context and process of organizational transformation: Cadbury Limited in its sector'. *Journal of Management Studies* 24(6): 564–93.

Clark, A. (2005) 'Your money or your life: changing job quality in OECD countries'. *British Journal of Industrial Relations* 43(3): 377–400.

Clegg, H. (1975) 'Pluralism in industrial relations'. *British Journal of Industrial Relations* 13(3): 309–16.

Clegg, H. (1994) *The History of British Trade Unions since 1889, Vol. III*. Oxford: Oxford University Press.

Clegg, S. and Haugaard, M. (2009). 'Introduction: why power is the central concept of the social sciences. In Clegg, S. and Haugaard, M. (eds) *The Sage Handbook of Power*. Los Angeles: Sage.

Coff, R. (1997) 'Human assets and management dilemmas: coping with hazards on the road to resource-based theory'. *Academy of Management Review* 22(2): 374–402.

Coff, R. (1999) 'When competitive advantage doesn't lead to performance: the resource-based view and stakeholder bargaining power'. *Organization Science* 10(2): 119–33.

Collard, R. and Dale, B. (1989) 'Quality circles'. In Sisson, K. (ed.) *Personnel Management in Britain*. Oxford: Blackwell.

Colli, A., Fernández Pérez, P. and Rose, M. (2003) 'National determinants of family firm development? Family firms in Britain, Spain, and Italy in the nineteenth and twentieth centuries'. *Enterprise and Society* 4: 28–64.

Colling, T. (1995) 'Experiencing turbulence: competition, strategic choice and the management of human resources in British Airways'. *Human Resource Management Journal* 5(5): 18–32.

Collins, C. and Smith, K. (2006) 'Knowledge exchange and combination: the role of human resource practices in the performance of high-technology firms'. *Academy of Management Journal* 49(3): 544–60.

Combs, J., Yongmei, L., Hall, A. and Ketchen, D. (2006) 'Ho much do high-performance work practices matter? A meta-analysis of their effects on organizational performance'. *Personnel Psychology* 59: 501–28.

Commission on the Skills of the American Workforce. (1990) *America's Choice: High Skills or Low Wages!* Rochester, NY: National Center on Education and the Economy.

Conner, K. (1991) 'A historical comparison of resource-based theory and five schools of thought within industrial organization economics: do we have a new theory of the firm?'. *Journal of Management* 17(1): 121–54.

Conyon, M. (1997) 'Institutional arrangements for setting director's compensation in UK companies'. In Keasey, K., Thompson, S. and Wright, M. (eds) *Corporate Governance: Economic and Financial Issues*. Oxford: Oxford University Press.

Cooke, W. (2001) 'The effects of labor costs and workplace constraints on foreign direct investment among highly industrialised countries'. *International Journal of Human Resource Management* 12(5): 697–716.

Cooke, W. (2007a) 'Integrating human resource and technological capabilities: the influence of global business strategies on workplace strategy choices'. *Industrial Relations* 46(2): 241–70.

Cooke, W. (2007b) 'Multinational companies and global human resource strategy'. In Boxall, P., Purcell, J. and Wright, P. (eds) *The Oxford Handbook of Human Resource Management*. Oxford: Oxford University Press.

Cordery, J. and Parker, S. (2007) 'Work organization'. In Boxall, P., Purcell, J. and Wright, P. (eds) *The Oxford Handbook of Human Resource Management*. Oxford: Oxford University Press.

Cox, A., Zagelmeyer, S. and Marchington, M. (2006) 'Embedding employee involvement and participation at work'. *Human Resource Management Journal* 16(3): 250–67.

Coyle-Shapiro, J. (1999) 'Employee participation and assessment of an organizational change intervention'. *Journal of Applied Behavioural Science* 35(4): 439–56.

Coyle-Shapiro, J. and Kessler, I. (2000) 'Consequences of the psychological contract for the employment relationship: a large scale survey'. *Journal of Management Studies* 37(7): 903–30.

Craft, J. (1988) 'Human resource planning and strategy'. in Dyer, L. (ed.) *Human Resource Management: Evolving Roles and Responsibilities*. Washington, DC: Bureau of National Affairs.

Crichton, A. (1968) *Personnel Management in Context*. London: Batsford.

Cronshaw, M., Davis, E. and Kay, J. (1994) 'On being stuck in the middle or good food costs less at Sainsbury's'. *British Journal of Management* 5(1): 19–32.

Croucher, R. and Cotton, E. (2009) *Global Union Global Business: Global Union Federations and International Business*. London: Middlesex University Press.

Cyert, R. and March, J. (1956) 'Organizational factors in the theory of oligopoly'. *Quarterly Journal of Economics* 70(1): 44–64.

Cyert, R. and March, J. (1963) *A Behavioral Theory of the Firm*. Englewood Cliffs, NJ: Prentice Hall.

Danford, A., Durbin, S., Richardson, M., Tailby, S. and Stewart, P. (2009) ' "Everybody's talking about me": the dynamics of information disclosure and consultation in high-skilled workplaces in the UK'. *Human Resource Management Journal* 19(4): 337–54.

Das, A. and Narasimhan, R. (2001) 'Process-technology fit and its implications for manufacturing performance'. *Journal of Operations Management* 19: 521–40.

Datta, D. and Grant, J. (1990) 'Relationships between types of acquisition, the autonomy given to the acquired firm, and acquisition success: an empirical study'. *Journal of Management* 16: 29–44.

Davies, P. and Freedland, M. (2007) *Towards a Flexible Labour Market: Labour Legislation and Regulation since the 1990s*. Oxford, Oxford University Press.

De Cieri, H. (2007) Transnational firms and cultural diversity. In Boxall, P., Purcell, J. and Wright, P. (eds) *The Oxford Handbook of Human Resource Management*. Oxford: Oxford University Press.

De Geus, A. (1988) 'Planning as learning'. *Harvard Business Review* March–April: 70–4.

De Menezes, L., Wood, S. and Gelade, G. (2010) 'The integration of human resource and operation management practices and its link with performance: a longitudinal latent class study'. *Journal of Operations Management*, forthcoming.

Deane, P. (1969) *The First Industrial Revolution*. Cambridge: Cambridge University Press.

Deephouse, D. (1999) 'To be different, or to be the same? It's a question (and theory) of strategic balance'. *Strategic Management Journal* 20: 147–66.

Deery, S. J., Iverson, R. D. and Walsh, J. P. (2002) 'Work relationships in telephone call centers: understanding emotional exhaustion and employee withdrawal'. *Journal of Management Studies* 39(4): 471–97.

Delbridge, R. (2005) 'Workers under lean manufacturing'. In Holman, D., Wall, T., Clegg, C., Sparrow, P. and Howard, A. (eds) *Essentials of The New Workplace*, Chichester: Wiley.

Delbridge, R. (2007) 'HRM and contemporary manufacturing'. In Boxall, P., Purcell, J. and Wright, P. (eds) *The Oxford Handbook of Human Resource Management*. Oxford: Oxford University Press.

Delbridge, R. and Whitfield, K. (2001) 'Employee perceptions of job influence and organizational participation'. *Industrial Relations* 40(3): 472–88.

Delbridge, R., Kenney, M., and Lowe, J. (1998) 'UK manufacturing in the 21st century'. In Delbridge, R. and Lowe, J. (eds) *Manufacturing in Transition*. London: Routledge.

Delery, J. (1998) 'Issues of fit in strategic human resource management: implications for research'. *Human Resource Management Review* 8(3): 289–309.

Delery, J. and Doty, D. (1996) 'Modes of theorizing in strategic human resource management: tests of universalistic, contingency, and configurational performance predictions'. *Academy of Management Journal* 39(4): 802–35.

Delery, J. and Shaw, J. (2001) 'The strategic management of people in work organizations: review, synthesis, and extension'. *Research in Personnel and Human Resources Management* 20: 165–97.

Deming, W. E. (1982) *Out of the Crisis*. Boston, MA: MIT Press.

Dierickx, I. and Cool, K. (1989). 'Asset stock accumulation and sustainability of competitive advantage'. *Management Science* 35(12): 1504–14.

DiMaggio, P. and Powell, W. (1983) 'The iron cage revisited: institutional isomorphism and collective rationality in organizational fields'. *American Sociological Review* 48(2): 147–60.

DiMaggio, P. and Powell, W. (1991) *The New Institutionalism in Organizational Analysis*. Chicago: University of Chicago Press.

Doeringer, P. and Piore, M. (1971) *Internal Labor Markets and Manpower Analysis*. Lexington, MA: Heath.

Doeringer, P., Lorenz, E. and Terkla, D. (2003) 'The adoption of high-performance management: lessons from Japanese multinationals in the West'. *Cambridge Journal of Economics* 27: 265–86.

Donaldson. T. and Preston, L. (1995) 'The stakeholder theory of the corporation: concepts, evidence, and implications'. *Academy of Management Review* 20(1): 65–91.

Doorewaard, H. and Meihuizen, H. (2000) 'Strategic performance options in professional service organisations'. *Human Resource Management Journal* 10(2): 39–57.

Dowling, P. J., Festing, M, and Eagle, A. (2008) *International Human Resource Management.* Fifth Edition. London: Thomson.

Dunning, J. (1993) 'The globalisation of service activities'. In Dunning, J. (ed.), *The Globalisation of Business.* London: Routledge.

Dyer, L. (1984) 'Studying human resource strategy'. *Industrial Relations* 23(2): 156–69.

Dyer, L. and Holder, G. (1988) 'A strategic perspective of human resource management'. In Dyer, L. (ed.) *Human Resource Management: Evolving Roles and Responsibilities.* Washington, DC: Bureau of National Affairs.

Dyer, L. and Reeves, T. (1995) 'Human resource strategies and firm performance: what do we know and where do we need to go?'. *International Journal of Human Resource Management* 6(3): 656–70.

Dyer, L. and Shafer, R. (1999). 'Creating organizational agility: implications for strategic human resource management', in Wright, P., Dyer, L., Boudreau, J. and Milkovich, G. (eds) *Research in Personnel and Human Resource Management (Supplement 4: Strategic Human Resources Management in the Twenty-First Century).* Stanford, CT. and London: JAI Press.

Eaton, S. (2000) 'Beyond "unloving care": linking human resource management and patient care quality in nursing homes'. *International Journal of Human Resource Management* 11(3): 591–616.

Edvinsson, L. and Malone, M. (1997). *Intellectual Capital.* London: Piatkus.

Edwards, P. and Ram, M. (2006) 'Surviving on the margins of the economy: working relationships in small, low-wage firms'. *Journal of Management Studies* 43(4): 895–916.

Edwards, P. and Wright, M. (2001) 'High-involvement work systems and performance outcomes: the strength of variable, contingent and context-bound relationships'. *International Journal of Human Resource Management* 12(4): 568–85.

Edwards, P., Edwards, T., Ferner, A., Marginson, P. and Tregaskis, O. (2006) *Employment Practices of MNCs in Organisational Context: Report of a telephone screening survey.* Available at: http://www2.warwick.ac.uk/fac/soc/wbs/projects/ mncemployment/ conference_papers/telephone_screening_screening_report_20_06_07.pdf.

Edwards, T. (2007) 'The nature of international integration and HR policies in multinational companies'. Paper presented at the 2007 British Academy of Management HRM conference, London, May.

Edwards, T. and Kuruvilla, S. (2005) 'International HRM: national business systems, organizational politics and the international division of labour in MNCs.' *International Journal of Human Resource Management* 16(1): 1–21.

Edwards, T. and Rees, C. (2006) *International Human Resource Management: Globalization, National Systems and Multinational Companies.* Harlow: Pearson Education.

Edwards, T. and Walsh, J. (2009) 'Foreign ownership and industrial relations' in W. Brown, A. Bryson, J. Forth and K. Whitfield (eds) *The Evolution of the Modern Workplace.* Cambridge, Cambridge University Press pp 285–306.

Edwards, T., Coller, X., Ortiz, L., Rees, C. and Wortmann, M. (2006) 'National industrial relations systems and cross-border restructuring: evidence from a merger in the pharmaceuticals sector'. *European Journal of Industrial Relations* 12(1): 69–87.

Eilbert, H. (1959) 'The development of personnel management in the United States'. *Business History Review* 33: 345–64.

Eisenberger, R., Huntingdon, R., Hutchison, S. and Sowa, D. (1986) 'Perceived organizational support'. *Journal of Applied Psychology* 79: 617–26.

Eisenberger, R., Stinglhamber, F., Vandenberghe, C., Sucharski, I. and Rhoades, L. (2002) 'Perceived supervisor support: contributions to perceived organizational support and employee retention'. *Journal of Applied Psychology* 87: 565–73.

Eisenhardt, K. and Bird Schoonhovern, C. (1990) 'Organizational growth: linking founding team, strategy, environment, and growth among US semiconductor ventures, 1978–1988'. *Administrative Science Quarterly* 35(3): 504–29.

Eisenhardt, K. and Zbaracki, M. (1992) 'Strategic decision making'. *Strategic Management Journal* 13: 17–37.

Eisenhardt, K., Kahwajy, J. and Bourgeois, L. (1997) 'How management teams can have a good fight'. *Harvard Business Review* July–August: 77–85.

Elkington, J. (1997) *Cannibals with Forks: The Triple Bottom Line of 21st Century Business*. Oxford: Capstone.

Evans, P. and Genadry, N. (1999) 'A duality-based perspective for strategic human resource management'. In Wright, P., Dyer, L., Boudreau, J. and Milkovich, G. (eds) *Research in Personnel and Human Resources Management (Supplement 4: Strategic Human Resources Management in the Twenty-First Century)*, Stanford, CT and London: JAI Press.

Evans, P., Pucik, V. and Barsoux, J.-L. (2002) *The Global Challenge: Frameworks for International Human Resource Management*. New York: McGraw-Hill.

Eysenck, H. (1953) *Uses and Abuses of Psychology*. London: Penguin.

Farndale, E. and Pauuwe, J. (2007) 'Uncovering competitive and institutional drivers of HRM practice in multinational corporations' *Human Resource Management Journal* 17(4): 355–75.

Farrell, D. (2005) 'Offshoring: value creation through economic change'. *Journal of Management Studies* 42(3): 675–83.

Ferguson, N. (1998) *The Pity of War*. London: Penguin.

Ferlie, E., Ashburner, C., Fitzgerald, L. and Pettigrew, A. (1996) *The New Public Management in Action*. Oxford: Oxford University Press.

Flanders, A. (1970) *Management and Unions*. London: Faber.

Florida, R., Jenkins, D. and Smith, D. (1998) 'The Japanese transplants in North America: production organization, location, and research and development'. In Boyer, R., Chanaron, J.-J., Jurgens, U. and Tolliday, S. (eds) *Between Imitation and Innovation: The Transfer and Hybridization of Production Models in the International Automotive Industry*. Oxford: Oxford University Press.

Folger, R. (2005) 'Justice and employment: moral retribution as a contra-subjugation tendency'. In Coyle-Shapiro, J., Shore, L., Taylor, M., Tetrick, L. (eds) *The Employment Relationship: Examining Psychological and Contextual Perspectives*. Oxford: Oxford University Press.

Folger, R. and Cropanzano, R. (1998) *Organizational Justice and Human Resource Management*. Thousand Oaks, CA: Sage.

Folkman, P., Froud, J., Sukhdev, J. and Williams, K. (2009) 'Private equity: Leveraged on capital or labour?' *Journal of Industrial Relations* 51(4): 517–29.

Forth, J., Bewley, H. and Bryson, A. (2006) *Small and Medium-sized Enterprises: Findings from the 2004 Workplace Employment Relations Survey*. London: Department of Trade and Industry.

Foster, R. (1986) *Innovation: the Attacker's Advantage*. New York: Summit.

Fox, A. (1974). *Beyond Contract: Work, Power and Trust Relations*. London: Faber and Faber.

Freeman, J. (1995) 'Business strategy from the population level'. In Montgomery, C. (ed.) *Resource-Based and Evolutionary Theories of the Firm: Towards a Synthesis*, Boston, MA: Kluwer.

Freeman, J. and Boeker, W. (1984) 'The ecological analysis of business strategy'. *California Management Review* 26(3): 73–86.

Freeman, R. (2007) 'Can the US clear the market for representation and participation?'. In Freeman, R., Boxall, P. and Haynes, P. (eds) *What Workers Say: Employee Voice in the Anglo-American World*. Ithaca, NY: Cornell University Press.

Freeman, R. and Medoff, J. (1984) *What Do Unions Do?* New York: Basic Books.

Freeman, R., Boxall, P. and Haynes, P. (eds) (2007) *What Workers Say: Employee Voice in the Anglo-American World*. Ithaca, NY: Cornell University Press.

Frege, C. and Kelly, J. (2004) 'Union strategies in comparative context'. In Frege, C. and Kelly, I. (eds) *Varieties of Unionism: Strategies for Revitalization in a Globalizing Economy*, Oxford: Oxford University Press.

Frenkel, S., Korczynski, M., Shire, K. and Tam, M. (1999) *On the Front Line: Organization of Work in the Information Economy*. Ithaca, NY: ILR Press.

Fulmer, I., Gerhart, B. and Scott, K. (2003) 'Are the 100 best better? An empirical investigation of the relationship between being a "great place to work" and firm performance'. *Personnel Psychology* 56: 965–93.

Gallie, D. (2005) 'Work pressure in Europe 1996–2001: trends and determinants'. *British Journal of Industrial Relations* 43(3): 351–75.

Gallie, D. and White, M. (1993) *Employee Commitment and the Skills Revolution*. London: Policy Studies Institute.

Gallie, D., White, M., Cheng, Y. and Tomlinson, M. (1998) *Restructuring the Employment Relationship*. Oxford: Clarendon Press.

Gamble, J. (2010) 'Transferring Organisational Practices and the Dynamics of Hybridisation: Japanese Retail Multinationals in China' *Journal of Management Studies* 47(4): 705–33.

Geare, A. (1977) 'The field of study of industrial relations'. *Journal of Industrial Relations* 19(3): 274–85.

Gelade, G. and Ivery, M. (2003) 'The impact of human resource management and work climate on organizational performance'. *Personnel Psychology* 56: 383–404.

Gerhart, B. (2007a) 'Modelling HRM and performance linkages'. In Boxall, P., Purcell, J. and Wright, P. (eds) *The Oxford Handbook of Human Resource Management*. Oxford: Oxford University Press.

Gerhart, B. (2007b) 'Horizontal and vertical fit in human resource systems'. In Ostroff, B. and Judge, T. (eds) *Perspectives on Organizational Fit*. New York: Lawrence Erlbaum Associates.

Gersick, C. (1991) 'Revolutionary change theories: a multilevel exploration of the punctuated equilibrium paradigm'. *Academy of Management Review* 16(1): 10–36.

Ghemawat, P. and Costa, J. E. (1993) 'The organizational tension between static and dynamic efficiency'. *Strategic Management Journal* 14: 59–73.

Ghoshal, A. and Nahapiet, J. (1998) 'Social capital, intellectual capital and the organizational advantage'. *Academy of Management Review* 23(2): 242–66.

Giangreco, A. and Peccei, R. (2005) 'The nature and antecedents of middle manager resistance to change: evidence from an Italian context'. *International Journal of Human Resource Management* 16(10): 1812–29.

Gilbert, J. and Boxall, P. (2009) 'The management of managers: challenges in a small economy'. *Journal of European Industrial Training* 33(4): 323–40.

Gilligan, C. (1982) *In a Different Voice: Psychological Theory and Women's Development*. Cambridge, MA: Harvard University Press.

Gittell, J. and Bamber, G. (2010) 'High- and low-road strategies for competing on costs and their implications for employment relations: international studies in the airline industry'. *International Journal of Human Resource Management* 21(2): 165–79.

Godard, J. (1991) 'The progressive HRM paradigm: a theoretical and empirical re-examination'. *Relations Industrielles* 46(2): 378–400.

Godard, J. (2001) 'Beyond the high-performance paradigm? An analysis of variation in Canadian managerial perceptions of reform programme effectiveness'. *British Journal of Industrial Relations* 39(1): 25–52.

Godard, J. (2004) 'A critical assessment of the high-performance paradigm'. *British Journal of Industrial Relations* 42(2): 349–78.

Godard, J. and Delaney, J. (2000) 'Reflections on the "high performance" paradigm's implications for industrial relations as a field'. *Industrial and Labor Relations Review* 53(3): 482–502.

Gohler, G. (2009) ' "Power to" and "power over" '. In Clegg, S. and Haugaard, M. (eds) *The Sage Handbook of Power*. Los Angeles: Sage.

Gollan, P., Poutsma, E. and Veersma, U. (2006) 'Editors' introduction: new roads in organizational participation?'. *Industrial Relations* 45(4): 499–511.

Gooderham, P., Nordhaug, O. and Ringdal, K. (1999) 'Institutional and rational determinants of organizational practices: human resource management in European firms'. *Administrative Science Quarterly* 44: 507–31.

Gooderham, P., Morley, M., Brewster, C. and Mayrhofer, W. (2004) 'Human resource management: a universal concept?' In Brewster, C., Mayrhofer, W. and Morley, M. *Human Resource Management in Europe: Evidence of Convergence?* Oxford: Elsevier.

Goold, M. (1991) 'Strategic control in the decentralised firm'. *Sloan Management Review* 32(2): 69–81.

Goold, M. and Campbell, A. (1987) *Strategies and Styles: The Role of the Centre in Managing Diversified Corporations*. Oxford: Blackwell.

Goold, M., Campbell, A. and Alexander, M. (1994) *Corporate-level Strategy: Creating Value in the Multibusiness Company*. New York: Wiley.

Gordon, G. and DiTomaso, N. (1992) 'Predicting corporate performance from organizational climate'. *Journal of Management Studies* 26(6): 783–98.

Gospel, H. (1973) 'An approach to a theory of the firm in industrial relations'. *British Journal of Industrial Relations* 11(2): 211–28.

Gospel, H. and Pendleton, A. (2003). 'Finance, corporate governance and the management of labour: a conceptual and comparative analysis'. *British Journal of Industrial Relations* 42(3): 557–82.

Gottschalg, O. and Zollo, M. (2007) 'Interest alignment and competitive advantage'. *Academy of Management Review* 32(2): 418–37.

Gouldner, A. (1960) 'The norm of reciprocity: a preliminary statement'. *American Sociological Review* 25: 161–78.

Granovetter, M. (1985) 'Economic action and social structure: the problem of embeddedness'. *American Journal of Sociology* 91(3): 481–510.

Grant, D. (1999) 'HRM, rhetoric and the psychological contract: a case of "easier said than done" '. *International Journal of Human Resource Management* 10(2): 327–50.

Grant, R. (1991) 'The resource-based theory of competitive advantage: implications for strategy formulation'. *California Management Review* 33(2): 114–35.

Grant, R. (1996) 'Toward a knowledge-based theory of the firm'. *Strategic Management Journal* 17: 109–22.

Grant, R. (1999*) Contemporary Strategy Analysis*. Oxford and Malden, MA: Blackwell.

Grant, R. (2005) *Contemporary Strategy Analysis*. Oxford and Malden, MA: Blackwell.

Gratton, L., Hope-Hailey, V., Stiles, P. and Truss, C. (1999a) 'Linking individual performance to business strategy: the people process model'. *Human Resource Management* 38(1): 17–31.

Gratton, L., Hope-Hailey, V., Stiles, P. and Truss, C. (1999b) *Strategic Human Resource Management: Corporate Rhetoric and Human Reality*. Oxford: Oxford University Press.

Green, F. (2001) 'It's been a hard day's night: the concentration and intensification of work in late twentieth-century Britain'. *British Journal of Industrial Relations* 39(1): 53–80.

Green, F. (2008) 'Leeway for the loyal: a model of employee discretion'. *British Journal of Industrial Relations* 46(1): 1–32.

Green, F. and McIntosh, S. (2001) 'The intensification of work in Europe'. *Labour Economics* 8: 291–308.

Greenwood, R., Hinings, C. and Brown, J. (1990) 'P2-form strategic management: corporate practices in professional partnerships'. *Academy of Management Journal* 33(4): 725–55.

Griffeth, R., Hom, P. and Gaertner, S. (2000) 'A meta-analysis of the antecedents and correlates of employee turnover: update, moderator tests, and research implications for the next millennium'. *Journal of Management* 26(3): 563–88.

Grimshaw, D. and Rubery, J. (2007) 'Economics and HRM'. In Boxall, P., Purcell, J. and Wright, P. (eds) *The Oxford Handbook of Human Resource Management*. Oxford: Oxford University Press.

Grimshaw, D., Marchington, M., Willmott, H. and Rubery, J. (2005) 'Introduction: fragmenting work across organizational boundaries'. In Marchington, M., Grimshaw, D., Rubery, J. and Willmott, H. (eds) *Fragmenting Work: Blurring Organizational Boundaries and Disordering Hierarchies*. Oxford: Oxford University Press.

Guest, D. (1987) 'Human resource management and industrial relations'. *Journal of Management Studies* 24(5): 503–21.

Guest, D. (1995) 'Human resource management, trade unions and industrial relations'. In Storey, J. (ed) *Human Resource Management: A Critical Text*. London: Routledge.

Guest, D. (1997) 'Human resource management and performance: a review and research agenda'. *International Journal of Human Resource Management* 8(3): 263–76.

Guest, D. (1998) 'Is the psychological contract worth taking seriously?'. *Journal of Organizational Behavior* 19: 649–64.

Guest, D. (2007) 'Human resource management and the worker: towards a new psychological contract?'. In Boxall, P., Purcell, J. and Wright, P. (eds) *The Oxford Handbook of Human Resource Management*. Oxford: Oxford University Press.

Guest, D. and Bryson, A. (2009) 'From industrial relations to human resource management: the changing role of the personnel function'. In Brown, W., Bryson, A., Forth, J. and Whitfield, K. (eds) *The Evolution of the Modern Workplace*. Cambridge: Cambridge University Press.

Guest, D. and Conway, N. (1997) 'Employee motivation and the psychological contract'. *Issues in People Management No. 21*. London: CIPD.

Guest, D. and Conway, N. (2002) *The State of the Psychological Contract*. London: CIPD.

Gumbrell-McCormick, R. and Hyman, R. (2006) 'Embedded collectivism? Workplace representation in France and Germany'. *Industrial Relations Journal* 37(5): 473–91.

Guthrie, J. (2001) 'High-involvement work practices, turnover, and productivity: evidence from New Zealand'. *Academy of Management Journal* 44(1): 180–90.

Guthrie, J. (2007) 'Remuneration: pay effects at work'. In Boxall, P., Purcell, J. and Wright, P. (eds) *The Oxford Handbook of Human Resource Management*. Oxford: Oxford University Press.

Guy, F. (2003) 'High-involvement work practices and employee bargaining power'. *Employee Relations* 25(5): 453–69.

Hackman, J. R. and Oldham, G. R. (1980) *Work Redesign*. Reading, MA: Addison-Wesley.

Hall, M. (2006) 'A cool response to the ICE regulations? Employer and trade union approaches to the new legal framework for information and consultation'. *Industrial Relations Journal* 37(5): 456–72.

Hall, M. (2010) 'EU Regulation and the UK employee consultation framework' *Economic and Industrial Democracy*, forthcoming.

Hall, M. and Edwards, P. (1999) 'Reforming the statutory redundancy consultation procedure' *Industrial Law Journal* 28(4): 299–318.

Hall, M., Hutchinson, S., Parker, J., Purcell, J. and Terry, M. (2007) *Implementing information and consultation: early experience under the ICE Regulations*. Employment Relations Research Series 88, London: Department for Business, Enterprise and Regulatory Reform.

Hall, M., Hutchinson, S., Purcell, J., Terry, M. and Parker, J. (2009) *Implementing information and consultation: evidence from longitudinal case studies in organisations with 150 or more employees.* Employment Relations Research Series 105, London: Department for Business, Innovation and Skills.

Hall, P. and Soskice, D. (2001) 'An introduction to varieties of capitalism'. In Hall, P. and Soskice, D. (eds) *Varieties of Capitalism: the Institutional Foundations of Comparative Advantage.* Oxford: Oxford University Press.

Hall, R. (1993) 'A framework linking intangible resources and capabilities to sustainable competitive advantage'. *Strategic Management Journal* 14: 607–18.

Hambrick, D. (1987) 'The top management team: key to strategic success'. *California Management Review* 30(1): 88–108.

Hambrick, D. (1995) 'Fragmentation and the other problems CEOs have with their top management teams'. *California Management Review* 37(3): 110–27.

Hamel, G. and Prahalad, C. (1993). 'Strategy as stretch and leverage'. *Harvard Business Review* 71(2): 75–84.

Hamel, G. and Prahalad, C. (1994) *Competing for the Future.* Boston, MA: Harvard Business School Press.

Hannan, M. (1995) 'Labor unions'. In Carroll, G. R. and Hannan, M. T. (eds) *Organizations in Industry: Strategy, Structure and Selection.* Oxford and New York: Oxford University Press.

Hardy, C. and Clegg, S. (1996) 'Some dare call it power'. In Clegg, S., Hardy, C. and Nord, W. (eds) *Handbook of Organization Studies.* London: Sage.

Harley, B. (2001) 'Team membership and the experience of work in Britain: an analysis of the WERS98 data'. *Work, Employment and Society* 15(4): 721–42.

Harrison, D., Newman, D. and Roth, P. (2006) 'How important are job attitudes? Meta-analytic comparisons of integrative behavioural outcomes and time sequences'. *Academy of Management Journal* 49(2): 305–25.

Hart, S. (1992) 'An integrative framework for strategy-making processes'. *Academy of Management Review* 17(2): 327–51.

Hart, S. and Banbury, C. (1994) 'How strategy-making processes can make a difference'. *Strategic Management Journal* 15: 251–69.

Harvey, G. and Turnbull, P. (2010) 'On the go: walking the high-road at a low cost airline'. *International Journal of Human Resource Management* 21(2): 230–41.

Haspeslagh, P. and Jemison, D. (1991) *Managing Acquisitions: Creating Value through Corporate Renewal.* New York: Free Press.

Haworth, N. and Hughes, S. (2003) 'International political economy and industrial relations', *British Journal of Industrial Relations* 41(4): 665–82.

Hayes, R. and Pisano, G. (1996) 'Manufacturing strategy: at the intersection of two paradigm shifts', *Production and Operations Management* 5(1): 25–41.

Haynes, P. and Allen, M. (2000) 'Partnership as union strategy: a preliminary evaluation'. *Employee Relations* 23(2): 164–87.

Haynes, P. and Fryer, G. (2000) 'Human resources, service quality and performance: a case study'. *International Journal of Contemporary Hospitality Management* 12(4): 240–8.

Hedlund, G. (1994) 'A model of knowledge management and the N-Form corporation'. *Strategic Management Journal* 15: 73–90.

Heery, E. and Simms, M. (2010) 'Employer responses to union organising: patterns and effects'. *Human Resource Management Journal* 20(1): 3–22.

Helfat, C. and Peteraf, M. (2003) 'The dynamic resource-based view: capability life cycles'. *Strategic Management Journal* 24: 997–1010.

Heller, F., Pusic, E., Strauss, G. and Wilpert, B. (1998) *Organizational Participation: Myth and Reality.* Oxford: Oxford University Press.

Henderson, R. (1995) 'Of life cycles real and imaginary: the unexpectedly long old age of optical lithography'. *Research Policy* 24: 631–43.

Hendry, C., Arthur, M. and Jones, A. (1995). *Strategy Through People.* London and New York: Routledge.

Herzberg, F. (1968) 'One more time: How do you motivate employees?'. *Harvard Business Review* 46: 53–63.

Herzenberg, S., Alic, J. and Wial, H. (1998) *New Rules for a New Economy: Employment and Opportunity in Postindustrial America*. Ithaca, NY: ILR Press.

Heskett, J., Jones, T., Loveman, G. and Schlesinger, A. (1994) 'Putting the service-profit chain to work'. *Harvard Business Review* 72(2): 164–74.

Hill, C. and Jones, T. (1992) 'Stakeholder-agency theory'. *Journal of Management Studies* 29(2): 131–54.

Hill, C. and Pickering, J. (1986) 'Divisionalisation, decentralisation and performance of large United Kingdom companies' *Journal of Management Studies* 23(1): 26–50.

Hill, S. (1991) 'Why quality circles failed but total quality management might succeed'. *British Journal of Industrial Relations* 29(4): 541–68.

Hird, M., Marsh, C. and Sparrow, P. (2009) 'HR Delivery systems: re-engineered or over engineered?' Centre for Performance-led HR, Lancaster University Management School.

Hochschild, A. (1986) *The Managed Heart: Commercialization of Human Feeling*. Berkeley, CA: University of California Press.

Hofstede, G. (1980) *Culture's Consequences: International Differences in Work-Related Values*. Thousand Oaks: Sage.

Hofstede, G. (1983) 'The cultural relativity of organizational practices and theories.' *Journal of International Business Studies* 14(2): 73–89.

Hofstede, G. and Bond, M, H. (1988) 'The Confucius connection: from cultural roots to economic growth', *Organizational Dynamics* 16: 5–21.

Holbrook, D., Chen, W., Hounshell, D. and Klepper, S. (2000) 'The nature, sources, and consequences of firm differences in the early history of the semiconductor industry'. *Strategic Management Journal* 21: 1017–41.

Hom, P., Tsui, A., Wu, J., Lee, T., Zhang, A., Fu, P., Lan, L. (2009) 'Explaining employment relationships with social exchange and job emdeddedness'. *Journal of Applied Psychology* 94(2): 277–97.

Hood, C. (1991) 'A public management for all seasons'. *Public Administration* 69(1): 3–19.

Hoopes, D., Madsen, T. and Walker, G. (2003) 'Guest editors' introduction to the special issue: why is there a resource-based view? Toward a theory of competitive heterogeneity'. *Strategic Management Journal* 24: 889–902.

Hope-Hailey, V., Gratton, L., McGovern, P., Stiles, P. and Truss, C. (1997) 'A chameleon function? HRM in the '90s'. *Human Resource Management Journal* 7(3): 5–18.

Hornsby, J. and Kuratko, D. (2003). 'Human resource management in US small businesses: a replication and extension'. *Journal of Developmental Entrepreneurship* 8(1): 73–92.

Hoskisson, R., Hitt, M., Wan, W. and Yiu, D. (1999). 'Theory and research in strategic management: swings of a pendulum'. *Journal of Management* 25(3): 417–56.

Hubbard, N. (1999) *Acquisition Strategy and Implementation*. Basingstoke: Macmillan (now Palgrave Macmillan).

Hubbard, N. and Purcell, J. (2001) 'Managing employee expectations during acquisitions'. *Human Resource Management Journal* 11(2): 17–33.

Huber, V. and Fuller, S. (1998) 'Performance appraisal'. In Poole, M. and Warner, M. (eds) *The IEBM Handbook of Human Resource Management*. London: Thomson Business Press.

Hughes, S. (2002) 'Coming in from the cold: labour, the ILO and the international labour standards regime'. In Wilkinson, R. and Hughes, S. *Global Governance: Critical Perspectives*. London: Routledge, 155–71.

Hughes, S. (2005) 'The International Labour Organisation'. *New Political Economy* 10(3): 413–25.

Hunt, J. and Boxall, P. (1998) 'Are top human resource specialists 'strategic partners'? Self-perceptions of a corporate elite'. *International Journal of Human Resource Management* 9(5): 767–81.

Hunt, J. W., Lees, S., Grümber, J. and Vivian, P. (1987) *Acquisitions: The Human Factor*. London: London Business School and Egon Zehnder International.

Hunt, S. (1995) 'The resource-advantage theory of competition'. *Journal of Management Inquiry* 4(4): 317–22.

Hunter, J. and Hunter, R. (1984) 'Validity and utility of alternate predictors of job performance'. *Psychological Bulletin* 96: 72–98.

Hunter, J., Schmidt, F. and Judiesch, M. (1990) 'Individual differences in output variability as a function of job complexity'. *Journal of Applied Psychology* 75(1): 28–42.

Hunter, J., Schmidt, F., Rauschenberger, J. and Jayne, M. (2000) 'Intelligence, motivation, and job performance'. In Cooper, C. and Locke, E. (eds) *Industrial and Organizational Psychology*. Oxford: Blackwell.

Hunter, L. (2000) 'What determines job quality in nursing homes?'. *Industrial and Labor Relations Review* 53(3): 463–81.

Huselid, M., Becker, B. and Beatty, R. (2005) *The Workforce Scorecard: Managing Human Capital to Execute Strategy*. Boston: Harvard Business School Press.

Hutchinson, S., Kinnie, N., Purcell, J., Rees, C., Scarbrough, H. and Terry, M. (1996) *The People Management Implications of Leaner Ways of Working*. Issues in People Management No. 15. London: Institute of Personnel and Development.

Hutchinson, S., Kinnie, N., Purcell, J., Collinson, M., Scarborough, H. and Terry, M. (1998) *Getting Fit, Staying Fit: Developing Lean and Responsive Organisations*. London: Institute of Personnel and Development.

Hyman, J. (2000) 'Financial participation schemes'. In White, G. and Drucker, J. (eds) *Reward Management: A Critical Text*. London: Routledge.

Hyman, R. (1975) *Industrial Relations: a Marxist Introduction*. London: Macmillan (now Palgrave Macmillan).

Hyman, R. (1987) 'Strategy or structure? Capital, labour and control'. *Work, Employment and Society* 1(1): 25–55.

Ichniowski, C. and Shaw, K. (1999) 'The effects of human resource management systems on economic performance: an international comparison of US and Japanese plant'. *Management Science* 45(5): 704–21.

Ichniowski, C., Shaw, K. and Prennushi, G. (1997) 'The effects of human resource management practices on productivity: a study of steel finishing lines'. *American Economic Review* 87(3): 291–313.

Isenberg, D. J. (1984) 'How senior managers think'. *Harvard Business Review* November–December: 81–90.

Jackson, S. and Schuler, R. (1995) 'Understanding human resource management in the context of organizations and their environments.' *Annual Review of Psychology* 46: 237–64.

Jacoby, S. (1984) 'The development of internal labor markets in American manufacturing firms'. In Osterman, P. (ed.) *Internal Labor Markets*. Cambridge, MA: MIT Press.

Jacoby, S. (2004) *Employing Bureaucracy: Managers, Unions, and the Transformation of Work in the 20th Century*. Mahwah, NJ: Lawrence Erlbaum.

Jacoby, S. (2005) *The Embedded Corporation: Corporate Governance and Employment Relations in Japan and the United States*. Princeton, NJ: Princeton University Press.

James, L. A. and James, L. R. (1989) 'Integrating work environment perceptions: explorations into the measurement of meaning'. *Journal of Applied Psychology* 74(5): 739–51.

James, L. R., Choi, C., Ko, C-H., McNeil, P., Minton, M., Wright, M. and Kim, K. (2008) 'Organizational and psychological climate: a review of theory and research'. *European Journal of Work and Organizational Psychology* 17(1): 5–32.

Janis, I. (1972) *Victims of Groupthink*. Boston, MA: Houghton Mifflin.

Jany-Catrice, F., Gadrey, N. and Pernod, M. (2005) 'Employment systems in labour-intensive activities: the case of retailing in France'. In Bazen, S., Lucifora, C. and Salverda, W. (eds) *Job Quality and Employer Behaviour*. Basingstoke and New York: Palgrave Macmillan.

Jarzabkowski, P. and Balogun, J. (2009) 'The practice and process of delivering integration through strategic planning'. *Journal of Management Studies* 46(8): 1255–88.

Jayaram, J., Droge, C. and Vickery, S. (1999) 'The impact of human resource management practices on manufacturing performance'. *Journal of Operations Management* 18: 1–20.

Jelinek, M. (1979) *Institutionalizing Innovation: A Study of Organizational Learning*. New York: Praeger.

Jensen, J. and Kletzer, L. (2005) 'Tradable services: understanding the scope and impact of services offshoring'. www.brookings.edu/es/commentary/journals/tradeforum/agenda 2005.htm.

Jensen, M. and Meckling, W. (1976). 'Theory of the firm: managerial behavior, agency costs and ownership structure'. *Journal of Financial Economics* 3: 305–60.

Johnson, H. and Kaplan, R. (1991) *Relevance Lost: the Rise and Fall of Management Accounting*. Boston, MA: Harvard Business School Press.

Jones, S. (1994) 'The origins of the factory system in Great Britain: technology, transaction costs or exploitation?' In Kirby, M. and. Rose, M. (eds) *Business Enterprise in Modern Britain*. London: Routledge.

Judge, T., Higgins, C., Thoresen, C. and Barrick, M. (1999) 'The big five personality traits, general mental ability, and career success across the life span'. *Personnel Psychology* 52: 621–52.

Juravich, T. and Hilgert, J. (1999) 'UNITE's victory at Richmark: community-based union organizing in communities of color'. *Labor Studies Journal* 24(1): 27–41.

Kalleberg, A., Marsden, P., Reynolds, J. and Knoke, D. (2006). 'Beyond profit? Sectoral differences in high-performance work practices'. *Work and Occupations* 33(3): 271–302.

Kamoche, K. (1996). 'Strategic human resource management within a resource-capability view of the firm'. *Journal of Management Studies* 33(2): 213–33.

Kaplan, R. and Norton, D. (1996) *The Balanced Scorecard: Translating Strategy into Action*. Boston, MA: Harvard Business School Press.

Kaplan, R. and Norton, D. (2001) *The Strategy-Focused Organization*. Boston, MA: Harvard Business School Press.

Kaplan, R. and Norton, D. (2004) *Strategy Maps: Converting Intangible Assets into Tangible Outcomes*. Boston, MA: Harvard Business School Press.

Kaplan, R. and Norton, D. (2006) *Alignment: Using the Balanced Scorecard to Create Corporate Synergies*. Boston, MA: Harvard Business School Press.

Kaplan, R. and Norton, D. (2008) *The Execution Premium: Linking Strategy to Operations for Competitive Advantage*. Boston, MA: Harvard Business School Press.

Karasek, R. (1979) 'Job demands, job decision latitude, and mental strain: implications for job redesign'. *Administrative Science Quarterly* 24: 285–308.

Karasek, R. and Theorell, T. (1990) *Healthy Work: Stress, Productivity, and the Reconstruction of Working Life*. New York: Basic Books.

Katz, H. and Darbishire, O. (2000) *Converging Divergences: Worldwide Changes in Employment Systems*. Ithaca, NY: Cornell University Press.

Kaufman, B. (2001) 'The employee participation/representation gap: an assessment and proposed solution'. *University of Pennsylvania Journal of Labor and Employment Law* 3(3): 491–550.

Kaufman, B. (2004) 'Prospects for union growth in the United States in the early 21st Century'. In Verma, A. and Kochan, T. (eds) *Unions in the 21st Century*. Basingstoke and New York: Palgrave Macmillan.

Kaufman, B. (2010) 'SHRM theory in the post-Huselid era: why it is fundamentally misspecified'. *Industrial Relations* 49(2): 286–313.

Kay, J. (1993) *Foundations of Corporate Success*. Oxford: Oxford University Press.

Kaysen, C. (1960) 'The corporation: how much power? What scope?' In Mason, E. (ed.) *The Corporation in Modern Society*. Cambridge: Harvard University Press.

Kazis, R and Miller, M. (eds) *Low-Wage Workers in the New Economy.* Washington, DC: The Urban Institute Press.

Keenoy, T. (1992) 'Constructing control'. In Hartley, J. and Stephenson, G. (eds) *Employment Relations: The Psychology of Influence and Control at Work.* Oxford: Blackwell.

Keenoy, T. and Anthony, P. (1992) 'HRM: metaphor, meaning and morality'. In Blyton, P. and Turnbull, P. (eds) *Reassessing Human Resource Management.* London: Sage.

Kelley, M. (2000) 'The participatory bureaucracy: a structural explanation for the effects of group-based employee participation programs on productivity in the machined products sector'. In Ichniowski, C., Levine, D., Olson, C. and Strauss, G. (eds) *The American Workplace: Skills, Compensation and Employee Involvement.* Cambridge: Cambridge University Press.

Kelly, J. (1998) *Rethinking Industrial Relations: Mobilization, Collectivism and Long Waves.* London: Routledge.

Kenney, M., Goe, W., Contreras, O., Romero, J. and Bustos, M. (1998) 'Learning factories or reproduction factories? Labor-management relations in the Japanese consumer electronics maquiladoras in Mexico'. *Work and Occupations* 25(3): 269–304.

Kepes, S. and Delery, J. (2007) 'HRM systems and the problem of internal fit'. In Boxall, P., Purcell, J. and Wright, P. (eds) *The Oxford Handbook of Human Resource Management.* Oxford: Oxford University Press.

Kersley, B., Alpin, C., Forth, J., Bryson, A., Bewley, H., Dix, G. and Oxenbridge, S. (2006) *Inside the Workplace: Findings from the 2004 Workplace Employment Relations Survey.* London: Routledge.

Kessler, I. (1998) 'Payment systems'. In Poole, M. and Warner, M. (eds) *The IEBM Handbook of Human Resource Management.* London: Thomson Business Press.

Kessler, I. and Purcell, J. (1992) 'Performance-related pay: objectives and application'. *Human Resource Management Journal* 2(3): 16–33.

Kessler, I. and Purcell, J. (1996) 'The value of joint working parties'. *Work, Employment and Society* 10(4): 663–82.

Kets de Vries, M. and Miller, D. (1984) *The Neurotic Organization.* San Francisco: Jossey-Bass.

Kidruff, M. (2001) 'The European Corporation: Strategy, Structure and Social Science – Review' *Administrative Science Quarterly* 46(20): 338–340.

Kilgour, J. (2008) 'Job evaluation revisited: the point factor method'. *Compensation and Benefits Review* 40(4): 37–48.

Kim, Y. and Gray, S. (2005) 'Strategic factors influencing international human resource management and host-country nationals' *International Journal of Human Resource Management* 16(5): 809–30.

King, A. and Zeithaml, C. (2001) 'Competencies and firm performance: examining the causal ambiguity paradox'. *Strategic Management Journal* 22: 75–99.

Kinnie, N., Hutchinson, S., Purcell, J., Swart, J. and Rayton, B. (2005) 'Satisfaction with HR practices and commitment to the organisation: why one size does not fit all'. *Human Resource Management Journal* 15(4): 9–29.

Kinnie, N., Swart, J., Lund, M., Morris, S., Snell, S. and Kang, S. (2006) *Managing Knowledge and People in Professional Services Firms.* London: CIPD.

Kintana, M. Alonso, A. and Olaverri, C. (2006) 'High-performance work systems and firms' operational performance: the moderating role of technology'. *International Journal of Human Resource Management* 17(1): 70–85.

Kirkpatrick, I.. Ackroyd, S. and Walker, R. (2005) *The New Managerialism and Public Service Professions.* Basingstoke: Palgrave Macmillan.

Knox, A. and Walsh, J. (2005) 'Organisational flexibility and HRM in the hotel industry: evidence from Australia'. *Human Resource Management Journal* 15(1): 57–75.

Koch, M. and McGrath, R. (1996) 'Improving labor productivity: human resource management policies do matter'. *Strategic Management Journal* 17: 335–54.

Kochan, T. (2007) 'Social legitimacy of the human resource management profession: a U.S. perspective'. In Boxall, P., Purcell, J. and Wright, P. (eds) *The Oxford Handbook of Human Resource Management*. Oxford: Oxford University Press.

Kohler, G. (2003) 'Foreign Direct Investment and its employment opportunities in perspective: meeting the great expectations of developing countries?' in Cooke, W. (ed.) *Multi-national Companies and Global Human Resource Strategies*. Westport CT: Greenwood Press, pp 21–42.

Konzelmann, S., Forrant, R., and Wilkinson, F. (2004) 'Work systems, corporate strategy and global markets: creative shop floors or "a barge mentality"?'. *Industrial Relations Journal* 35(3): 216–32.

Korczynski, M. (2001). 'The contradictions of service work: call centre as customer-oriented bureaucracy.' In Sturdy, A., Grugulis, I. and Willmott, H. (eds) *Customer Service: Empowerment and Entrapment*. Basingstoke: Palgrave Macmillan.

Kossek, E. and Pichler, S. (2007) 'EEO and the management of diversity'. In Boxall, P., Purcell, J. and Wright, P. (eds) *The Oxford Handbook of Human Resource Management*. Oxford: Oxford University Press.

Kostova, T. and Zaheer, S. (1999) 'Organizational legitimacy under conditions of complexity: the case of the multinational enterprise'. *Academy of Management Review* 24(1): 64–81.

Kotha, S. and Swamidass, P. (2000) 'Strategy, advanced manufacturing technology and performance: evidence from US manufacturing firms'. *Journal of Operations Management* 18: 257–77.

Kotler, P. and Keller, K. (2006) Marketing Management. *Twelfth Edition*. Upper Saddle River, NJ: Pearson Prentice Hall.

Koys, D. (2001) 'The effects of employee satisfaction, organizational citizenship behavior, and turnover on organisational effectiveness: a unit-level, longitudinal study'. *Personnel Psychology* 54: 101–14.

KPMG (1999) 'Unlocking shareholder value: the key to success', in *Mergers and Acquisitions: A Global Research Report*. London: KPMG.

Kristof, A. (1996) 'Person-organization fit: an integrative review of its conceptualisations, measurement, and implications'. *Personnel Psychology* 49: 1–49.

Krugman, P. (1997) *Pop Internationalism*. Cambridge, MA.: MIT Press.

Lacey, R. (1986). *Ford: The Men and the Machine*. London: Heinemann.

Lam, S. and Schaubroeck, J. (1998) 'Integrating HR planning and organisational strategy'. *Human Resource Management Journal* 8(3): 5–19.

Landes, D. (1998) *The Wealth and Poverty of Nations*. London: Abacus.

Lane, C. (1990) 'Vocational training and new production concepts in Germany: some lessons for Britain'. *Industrial Relations Journal* 21(4): 247–59.

Lashley, C. (1998). 'Matching the management of human resources to service operaions'. *International Journal of Contemporary Hospitality Management* 10(1): 24–33.

Latham, G. and Latham, S. (2000) 'Overlooking theory and research in performance appraisal at one's peril: much done, more to do'. In Cooper, C. and Locke, E. (eds) *Industrial and Organizational Psychology*. Oxford: Blackwell.

Latham, G. and Pinder, C. (2005) 'Work motivation theory and research at the dawn of the twenty-first century'. *Annual Review of Psychology* 56: 485–516.

Latham, G., Sulsky, L. and MacDonald, H. (2007) 'Performance management'. In Boxall, P., Purcell, J. and Wright, P. (eds) *The Oxford Handbook of Human Resource Management*. Oxford: Oxford University Press.

Lawler, E. (1986) *High-Involvement Management*. San Francisco: Jossey-Bass.

Lazear, E. (1999) 'Personnel economics: past lessons and future directions'. *Journal of Labor Economics* 17(2): 199–236.

Leana, C. and Van Buren, H. (1999) 'Organizational social capital and employment practices'. *Academy of Management Review* 24(3): 538–55.

Lees, S. (1997) 'HRM and the legitimacy market'. *International Journal of Human Resource Management* 8(2): 226–43.

Legge, K. (1978) *Power, Innovation, and Problem-solving in Personnel Management.* London: McGraw-Hill.

Legge, K. (1995) *Human Resource Management: Rhetorics and Realities.* Basingstoke: Macmillan (now Palgrave Macmillan).

Legge, K. (2005) *Human Resource Management: Rhetorics and Realities.* Basingstoke and New York: Palgrave Macmillan.

Lengnick-Hall, M. and Lengnick-Hall, C. (2005) 'International human resource management research and social network/social capital theory'. In Bjorkman, I. and Stahl, G. (eds) *Handbook of Research into International HRM.* Cheltenham: Edward Elgar.

Leonard, D. (1992) 'Core capabilities and core rigidities: a paradox in managing new product development'. *Strategic Management Journal* 13: 111–25.

Leonard, D. (1998) *Wellsprings of Knowledge: Building and Sustaining the Sources of Innovation.* Boston, MA: Harvard Business School Press.

Lepak, D. and Snell, S. (1999) 'The strategic management of human capital: determinants and implications of different relationships'. *Academy of Management Review* 24(1): 1–18.

Lepak, D. and Snell, S. (2002) 'Examining the human resource architecture: the relationships among human capital, employment, and human resource configurations'. *Journal of Management* 28: 517–43.

Lepak, D. and Snell, S. (2007) 'Employment sub-systems and the "HR architecture"'. In Boxall, P., Purcell, J. and Wright, P. (eds) *The Oxford Handbook of Human Resource Management.* Oxford: Oxford University Press.

Lepak, D., Liao, H., Chung, Y. and Harden, E. (2006). 'A conceptual review of human resource management systems in strategic human resource management research'. *Research in Personnel and Human Resources Management*, 25: 217–71.

Leung, A., Zhang, J., Wong, P. and Foo, M. (2006) 'The use of networks in human resource acquisition for entrepreneurial firms: multiple 'fit' considerations'. *Journal of Business Venturing* 21: 664–86.

Levinson, D. (1978) *The Seasons of a Man's Life.* New York: Knopf.

Levinson, D. and Levinson, J. (1996) *The Seasons of a Woman's Life.* New York: Knopf.

Levinthal, D. and Myatt, J. (1994) 'Co-evolution of capabilities and industry: the evolution of mutual fund processing'. *Strategic Management Journal* 15: 45–62.

Li, A. and Cropanzano, R. (2009) 'Do East Asians respond more/less strongly to organisational justice than North Americans? A meta-analysis'. *Journal of Management Studies* 46(5): 787–805.

Liden, R., Bauer, T. and Erdogan, B. (2004) 'The role of leader-member exchange in the dynamic relationship between employer and employee: implications for employee socialization, leaders, and organizations'. In Coyle-Shapiro, J. Shore, L. Taylor, S. and Tetrick, L. (eds) *The Employment Relationship: Examining Psychological and Contextual Perspectives.* Oxford, Oxford University Press.

Littler, C. (1982) *The Development of the Labour Process in Capitalist Societies: A Comparative Study of the Transformation of Work Organization in Britain, Japan, and the USA.* London: Heinemann.

Lloyd, C. (2005) 'Competitive strategy and skills: working out the fit in the fitness industry'. *Human Resource Management Journal* 15(2): 15–34.

Locke, E. and Latham, G. (1990) *A Theory of Goal Setting and Task Performance.* Englewood Cliffs, NJ: Prentice Hall.

Lockett, A., Thompson, S. and Morgenstern, U. (2009) 'The development of the resource-based view of the firm: a critical appraisal'. *International Journal of Management Reviews* 11(1): 9–28.

Longenecker, C., Sims, H. and Gioia, D. (1987) 'Behind the mask: the politics of employee appraisal'. *Academy of Management Executive* 1(3): 183–93.

Lorenz, E. and Valeyre, A. (2005) 'Organisational innovation, human resource management and labour market structure: a comparison of the EU-15'. *Journal of Industrial Relations*, 47(4): 424–42.

Lovas, B. and Ghoshal, S. (2000) 'Strategy as guided evolution'. *Strategic Management Journal* 21: 875–96.

Lovelock, C., Patterson, P. and Walker, R. (2007) *Services Marketing.* Fourth Edition. Sydney: Pearson Education Australia.

MacDuffie, J. (1995) 'Human Resource bundles and manufacturing performance: organizational logic and flexible production systems in the world auto industry'. *Industrial and Labor Relations Review* 48(2): 197–221.

MacKenzie, G. (1973) *The Aristocracy of Labor: The Position of Skilled Craftsmen in the American Class Structure.* London: Cambridge University Press.

Mackie, K., Holahan, C. and Gottlieb, N. (2001) 'Employee involvement management practices, work stress, and depression in employees of a human services residential care facility'. *Human Relations* 54(8): 1065–92.

Macky, K. and Boxall, P. (2007) 'The relationship between high-performance work practices and employee attitudes: an investigation of additive and interaction effects'. *International Journal of Human Resource Management* 18(4): 537–67.

Macky, K. and Boxall, P. (2008). 'High-involvement work processes, work intensification and employee well-being: A study of New Zealand worker experiences.' *Asia Pacific Journal of Human Resources* 46(1): 38–55.

MacLeod, D. and Clarke, N. (2009) *Engaging for Success: Enhancing Performance through Employee Engagement.* A report to Government. London: Department for Business, Innovation and Skills.

MacNeil, I. (1985) 'Relational contract: what we do and do not know'. *Wisconsin Law Review* 3: 483–525.

Maguire, S. and Phillips, N. (2008) '"Citibankers" at Citigroup: a study of the loss of institutional trust after a merger' *Journal of Management Studies* 45(2): 372–401.

Mahoney, J. and Pandian, J. (1992). 'The resource-based view within the conversation of strategic management'. *Strategic Management Journal* 13(5): 363–80.

Main, B. (1990) 'The new economics of personnel'. *Journal of General Management* 16(2): 91–103.

Malos, S. and Campion, M. (2000) 'Human resource strategy and career mobility in professional service firms: a test of the option-based model'. *Academy of Management Journal* 43: 749–60.

March, J. (1962) 'The business firm as a political coalition'. *The Journal of Politics* 24(4): 662–78.

Marchington, M. (1989) 'Joint consultation in practice'. In Sisson, K. (ed.) *Personnel Management in Britain.* Oxford: Blackwell.

Marchington, M. (1995) 'Involvement and participation'. In Storey, J. (ed.) *Human Resource Management: A Critical Text.* London: Routledge.

Marchington, M. (2007) 'Employee voice systems'. in Boxall, P., Purcell, J. and Wright, P. (eds) *The Oxford Handbook of Human Resource Management.* Oxford: Oxford University Press.

Marchington, M. and Grugulis, I. (2000). '"Best practice" human resource management: perfect opportunity or dangerous illusion?'. *International Journal of Human Resource Management* 11(6): 1104–24.

Marchington, M. and Wilkinson, A. (2000) 'Direct participation'. In Bach, S. and Sisson, K. (eds) *Personnel Management: A Comprehensive Guide to Theory and Practice.* Oxford: Blackwell.

Marchington, M., Carroll, M. and Boxall, P. (2003) 'Labour scarcity and the survival of small firms: a resource-based view of the road haulage industry'. *Human Resource Management Journal* 13(4): 3–22.

Marchington, M., Wilkinson, A., Ackers, P. and Dundon, T. (2001) *Management Choice and Employee Voice*. Research report, London: CIPD.

Marginson, P. (1993) 'The multi-divisional structure and corporate control: explaining the degree of corporate coordination over decisions in labour relations'. *Papers in Organization* No. 12. Copenhagen:Institute of Organization and Industrial Sociology, Copenhagen Business School.

Marginson, P. and Meardi, G. (2010) 'Multinational Companies: Transforming national industrial relations?' In Colling, T. and Terry, M. (eds) *Industrial Relations: Theory and Practice*. Chichester: John Wiley and Sons.

Marginson, P., Edwards, P., Martin, R., Purcell, J. and Sisson, K. (1988) *Beyond the Workplace. Managing Industrial Relations in the Multi-Establishment Enterprise*. Oxford: Blackwell.

Marginson, P., Armstrong, P., Edwards, P. and Purcell, J. with Hubbard, N. (1993) 'The control of industrial relations in large companies: an initial analysis of the second company level industrial relations survey'. *Warwick Papers in Industrial Relations No. 45* Coventry: University of Warwick.

Marginson, P., Hall, M., Hoffman, A. and Muller, T. (2004) 'The impact of European works councils on management decision-making in UK and US multinationals: a case study comparison'. *British Journal of Industrial Relations.* 42(2): 209–33.

Marginson, P., Edwards, P., Edwards, T., Ferner, A. and Tregaskis, O. (2010) 'Employee representation and consultative voice in multi-national companies operating in Britain.' *British Journal of Industrial Relations* 48(1): 151–80.

Marks, A., Findlay, P., Hine, J., McKinlay, A. and Thompson, P. (1998) 'The politics of partnership? Innovation in employment relations in the Scottish spirits industry'. *British Journal of Industrial Relations* 36(2): 209–26.

Marshall, V. and Wood, R. (2000) 'The dynamics of effective performance appraisal: an integrated model'. *Asia Pacific Journal of Human Resources* 38(3): 62–90.

Marsick, V. and Watkins, K. (1990) *Informal and Incidental Learning in the Workplace*. London and New York: Routledge.

Martell, K. and Carroll, S. (1995) 'Which executive human resource management practices for the top management team are associated with higher firm performance?'. *Human Resource Management* 34(4): 497–512.

Martin, J. (1992) *Cultures and Organizations: Three Perspectives*. New York: Oxford University Press.

Martin, R. (1981) *New Technology and Industrial Relations in Fleet Street*. Oxford: Clarendon Press.

Martínez Lucio, M. and Stuart, M. (2004) 'Swimming against the tide: social partnership, mutual gains and the revival of "tired" HRM'. *International Journal of Human Resource Management* 15(2): 410–24.

McConnell, C. and Brue, S. (1995) *Contemporary Labor Economics*. New York: McGraw-Hill.

McGee, J. (2003) 'Strategic groups: theory and practice'. In Faulkner, D. and Campbell, A. (eds) *The Oxford Handbook of Strategy*. Oxford: Oxford University Press.

McGovern, P., Gratton, L., Hope-Hailey, V., Stiles, P. and Truss, C. (1997). 'Human resource management on the line?'. *Human Resource Management Journal* 7(4): 12–29.

McKay, P., Avery, D. And Morris, M. (2009) 'A tale of two climates: diversity climate from subordinates' and managers' perspectives and their role in store unit performance.' *Personnel Psychology* 62: 767–91.

McKersie, R. and Hunter, L. (1973) *Pay, Productivity and Collective Bargaining*. London: Macmillan (now Palgrave Macmillan).

McLean Parks, J. and Kidder, D. (1994). ' "Till death us do part . . ." ': changing work relationships in the 1990s'. In Cooper, C. and Rousseau, D. (eds) *Trends in Organizational Behaviour, Vol. 1.* New York: Wiley.

McMillan, J. (1992) *Games, Strategies and Managers.* Oxford and New York: Oxford University Press.

McWilliams, A. and Smart, D. (1995) 'The resource-based view of the firm: does it go far enough in shedding the asssumptions of the S-C-P paradigm?'. *Journal of Management Inquiry* 4(4): 309–16.

Meardi, G., Marginson, P., Fitcher, M., Frybes, M., Stonojevic, M. and Toth, A. (2009) 'Varieties of multinationals'. *Industrial Relations* 48(3): 489–511.

Meyer, A., Tsui, A. S. and Hinings, C. R. (1993) 'Configurational approaches to organizational analysis'. *Academy of Management Journal* 36(6): 1175–95.

Meyer, S. (1981). *The Five Dollar Day: Labor Management and Social Control in the Ford Motor Company 1908–1921.* Albany, NY: State University of New York Press.

Michailova, S. (2002) 'When common sense becomes uncommon: participation and empowerment in Russian companies with Western participation'. *Journal of World Business* 37: 180–7.

Miles, G., Snow, C. and Sharfman, M. (1993) 'Industry variety and performance'. *Strategic Management Journal* 14: 163–77.

Miles, R. and Snow, C. (1984) 'Designing strategic human resources systems'. *Organizational Dynamics* Summer: 36–52.

Milkovich, G. and Newman, J. (2004) *Compensation.* Boston: Irwin/McGraw Hill.

Miller, D. (1981) 'Toward a new contingency approach: the search for organizational gestalts'. *Journal of Management Studies* 18(1): 1–26.

Miller, D. (1992) 'Generic strategies; classification, combination and context'. *Advances in Strategic Management* 8: 391–408.

Miller, D. and Friesen, P. (1980) 'Momentum and revolution in organizational adaptation'. *Academy of Management Journal* 23(4): 591–614.

Miller, D. and Shamsie, J. (1996) 'The resource-based view of the firm in two environments: the Hollywood film studios from 1936 to 1965'. *Academy of Management Journal* 39(3): 519–43.

Millward, N. and Stevens, M. (1986) *British Workplace Industrial Relations 1080–1984: The DE/ESRC/PSI/ACAS Surveys.* Aldershot: Gower.

Millward, N., Bryson, A. and Forth, J. (2000) *All Change at Work: British Employment Relations 1980–1998 as portrayed by the Workplace Industrial Relations Survey Series.* London: Routledge.

Mintzberg, H. (1978) 'Patterns in strategy formation'. *Management Science* 24(9): 934–48.

Mintzberg, H. (1990) 'The design school: reconsidering the basic premises of strategic management'. *Strategic Management Journal* 11(3): 171–95.

Mintzberg, H. (1994) 'Rethinking strategic planning part 1: pitfalls and fallacies'. *Long Range Planning* 27(3): 12–21.

Morgan, G. (1997) *Images of Organization.* Thousand Oaks, CA: Sage.

Morris, J., Wilkinson, B. and Gamble, J. (2009) 'Strategic international human resource management or the "bottom line"? The cases of electronics and garments commodity chains in China'. *International Journal of Human Resource Management* 20(2): 348–71.

Mueller, D. (1997) 'First-mover advantages and path dependence'. *International Journal of Industrial Organization* 15(6): 827–50.

Mueller, F. (1996) 'Human resources as strategic assets; an evolutionary resource-based theory'. *Journal of Management Studies* 33(6): 757–85.

Mueller, F. and Purcell, J. (1992) 'The Europeanization of manufacturing and the decentralisation of bargaining: multinational management strategies in the European automobile industry'. *International Journal of Human Resource Management* 3(2): 15–35.

Murphy, K. and Cleveland, J. (1991) *Performance Appraisal: An Organizational Perspective*. Boston, MA: Allyn and Bacon.

Murray, A. (1988), 'A contingency view of Porter's "generic strategies"'. *Academy of Management Review* 13(3): 390–400.

Nalebuff, B. and Brandenburger, A. (1996) *Co-opetition*. London: HarperCollins Business.

Nelson, R. (1991) 'Why do firms differ, and how does it matter?'. *Strategic Management Journal* 12: 61–74.

Nelson, R. and Winter, S. (1982) *An Evolutionary Theory of Economic Change*. Cambridge, MA: Belknap Press.

Newman, K. And Nollen, S. (1996) 'Culture and congruence: the fit between management practices and national culture'. *Journal of International Business Studies* 27(4): 753–79.

Nishii, L. Lepak, D. and Schneider, B. (2008) 'Employee attributions of the "why" of HR practices: their effects on employee attitudes and behaviors, and customer satisfaction'. *Personnel Psychology* 61: 503–45.

Nissen, B. (2000) 'Living wage campaigns from a "social movement" perspective: the Miami case'. *Labor Studies Journal* 25(3): 29–50.

Noe, R., Hollenbeck, J., Gerhart, B. and Wright, P. (2005) *Human Resource Management: Gaining a Competitive Advantage*. Boston, MA: Irwin McGraw-Hill.

Norburn, D. and Birley, S. (1988) 'The top management team and corporate performance'. *Strategic Management Journal* 9: 225–37.

Oakeshott, R. (2000) *Jobs and Fairness: The Logic and Experience of Employee Ownership*. Norwich: Michael Russell.

Odiorne, G. (1985) *Strategic Management of Human Resources*. San Francisco: Jossey-Bass.

Ogbonna, E. and Harris, L. (1998) 'Managing culture: compliance or genuine change?'. *British Journal of Management* 9(4): 273–89.

Ogbonna, E. and Wilkinson, B. (1990) 'Corporate strategy and corporate culture: the view from the checkout'. *Personnel Review* 19(4): 9–15.

Ohmae, K. (1985) *Triad Power: the Coming Shape of Global Competition*. New York: Free Press.

Ohno, T. (1988) *Just-in-Time: For Today and Tomorrow*. Cambridge, MA: Productivity Press.

Oliver, C. (1997) 'Sustainable competitive advantage: combining institutional and resource-based views'. *Strategic Management Journal* 18(9): 697–713.

O'Neill, G. (1995) 'Linking pay to performance: conflicting views and conflicting evidence'. *Asia Pacific Journal of Human Resources* 33(2): 20–35.

Organ, D. (1988) *Organizational Citizenship Behavior: The Good Soldier Syndrome*. Lexington, MA: Lexington Books.

Orlitzky, M. (2007) 'Recruitment strategy'. In Boxall, P., Purcell, J. and Wright, P. (eds) *The Oxford Handbook of Human Resource Management*. Oxford: Oxford University Press.

Orlitzky, M. and Frenkel, S. J. (2005) 'Alternative pathways to high-performance workplaces'. *International Journal of Human Resource Management* 16(8): 1325–48.

Osterman, P. (1987) 'Choice of employment systems in internal labor markets'. *Industrial Relations* 26(1): 46–67.

Osterman, P. (1994) 'How common is workplace transformation and who adopts it?'. *Industrial and Labor Relations Review* 47(2): 173–88.

Osterman, P. (2000) 'Work reorganization in an era of restructuring: trends in diffusion and effects on employee welfare'. *Industrial and Labor Relations Review* 53(2): 179–96.

Osterman, P. (2001) 'Employers in the low-wage/low-skill labor market'. In Kazis, R and Miller, M. (eds.) *Low-Wage Workers in the New Economy*. Washington, DC: The Urban Institute Press.

Osterman, P. (2006) 'The wage effects of high performance work organization in manufacturing'. *Industrial and Labor Relations Review* 59(2): 187–204.

Ouchi, W. (1980) 'Markets, bureaucracies and clans'. *Administrative Science Quarterly* 25: 129–41.

Paauwe, J. (2004) *HRM and Performance: Achieving Long-Term Viability*. Oxford: Oxford University Press.

Paauwe, J. and Boselie, P. (2003) 'Challenging "strategic HRM" and the relevance of the institutional setting'. *Human Resource Management Journal* 13(3): 56–70.

Paauwe, J. and Boselie, P. (2007) 'Human resource management and societal embeddedness'. In Boxall, P., Purcell, J. and Wright, P. (eds) *The Oxford Handbook of Human Resource Management*. Oxford: Oxford University Press.

Parker, S. (2003) 'Longitudinal effects of lean production on employee outcomes and the mediating role of work characteristics'. *Journal of Applied Psychology* 88(4): 620–34.

Parker, S. and Wall, T. (1998) *Job and Work Design: Organizing Work to Promote Well-being and Effectiveness*. Thousand Oaks, CA.: Sage.

Pascale, R. (1985) 'The paradox of "corporate culture": reconciling ourselves to socialization'. *California Management Review* 27(2): 26–41.

Peel, S. and Boxall, P. (2005) 'When is contracting preferable to employment? An exploration of management *and* worker perspectives'. *Journal of Management Studies* 42(8): 1675–97.

Pendleton, A. (2000) 'Profit sharing and employee share ownership', in Thorpe, R. and Homan, G. (eds) *Strategic Reward Systems*. Harlow: Pearson Education.

Pendleton, A. (2006) 'Incentives, monitoring and employee stock ownership plans: new evidence and interpretations'. *Industrial Relations* 45(4): 753–77.

Pendleton, A., Kaarsemaker, E. and Poutsma, E. (2010) 'Employee participation and share ownership' in A. Wilkinson, M. Marchington, P, Gollan and D, Lewin (eds) *Oxford Handbook of Participation in Organisations*. Oxford: Oxford University Press.

Penn, R., Rose, M. and Rubery, J. (eds) (1994) *Skill and Occupational Change*. Oxford: Oxford University Press.

Penrose, E. (1959) *The Theory of the Growth of the Firm*. Oxford: Blackwell.

Peteraf, M. (1993) 'The cornerstones of competitive advantage: a resource-based view'. *Strategic Management Journal* 14: 179–91.

Peteraf, M. and Shanley, M. (1997) 'Getting to know you: a theory of strategic group identity'. *Strategic Management Journal* 18(S): 165–86.

Pfeffer, J. (1994) *Competitive Advantage through People*. Boston, MA: Harvard Business School Press.

Pfeffer, J. (1998) *The Human Equation: Building Profits by Putting People First*. Boston, MA: Harvard Business School Press.

Pil, F. K. and MacDuffie, J. P. (1996) 'The adoption of high involvement work practices'. *Industrial Relations* 35(3): 423–55.

Pinfield, L. and Berner, M. (1994) 'Employment systems: toward a coherent conceptualisation of internal labour markets'. In Ferris, G (ed.) *Research in Personnel and Human Resources Management*. Stanford, CT and London: JAI Press.

Piore, M. and Sabel, C. (1984) *The Second Industrial Divide: Prospects for Prosperity*. New York: Basic Books.

Polanyi, M. (1962) *Personal Knowledge*. New York: Harper.

Poole, M. (1986) *Industrial Relations: Origins and Patterns of National Diversity*. London: Routledge.

Poole, M. (1990) 'Editorial: human resource management in an international perspective'. *International Journal of Human Resource Management* 1(1): 1–15.

Porter, M. (1980) *Competitive Strategy*. New York: Free Press.

Porter, M. (1985) *Competitive Advantage: Creating and Sustaining Superior Performance*. New York: Free Press.

Porter, M. (1990) *The Competitive Advantage of Nations*. London: Macmillan (now Palgrave Macmillan).

Porter, M. (1991) 'Towards a dynamic theory of strategy'. *Strategic Management Journal* 12(S): 95–117.

Porter, M. (1996) 'What is strategy?'. *Harvard Business Review* November–December: 61–78.

Poutsma, E., Ligthart, P. and Veersma, U. (2006) 'The diffusion of calculative and collaborative HRM practices in European firms'. *Industrial Relations* 45(4): 513–46.

Prahalad, C. and Hamel, G. (1990) 'The core competence of the corporation'. *Harvard Business Review* May–June: 79–91.

Priem, R. and Butler, J. (2001) 'Is the resource-based "view" a useful perspective for strategic management research?'. *Academy of Management Review* 26(1): 22–40.

Purcell, J. (1974) *Good Industrial Relations: Theory and Practice.* Basingstoke: Macmillan (now Palgrave Macmillan).

Purcell, J. (1987) 'Mapping management styles in employee relations'. *Journal of Management Studies* 24(5): 533–48.

Purcell, J. (1989) 'The impact of corporate strategy on human resource management'. In Storey, J. (ed) *New Perspectives on Human Resource Management.* London: Routledge.

Purcell, J. (1995) 'Ideology and the end of institutional industrial relations: evidence from the UK.' In Crouch, C. and Traxler, F. (eds) Organized Industrial Relations in Europe: What Future? Aldershot, Avebury Basingstoke: Macmillan.

Purcell, J. (1996) 'Contingent workers and human resource strategy: rediscovering the core/periphery dimension'. *Journal of Professional HRM* 5: 16–23.

Purcell, J. (1999) 'The search for "best practice" and "best fit": chimera or cul-de-sac?'. *Human Resource Management Journal* 9(3): 26–41.

Purcell, J. and Ahlstrand, B. (1994) *Human Resource Management in the Multidivisional Company,* Oxford: Oxford University Press.

Purcell, J. and Georgiades, K. (2007) 'Why should employers bother with worker voice?'. In Freeman, R., Boxall, P. and Haynes, P. (eds) *What Workers Say: Employee Voice in the Anglo-American World.* Ithaca, NY: Cornell University Press.

Purcell, J. and Hutchinson, S. (2007) 'Front-line managers as agents in the HRM-performance causal chain: theory, analysis and evidence'. *Human Resource Management Journal* 17(1): 3–20.

Purcell, J. and Kinnie, N. (2007) 'HRM and business performance'. In Boxall, P., Purcell, J. and Wright, P. (eds) *The Oxford Handbook of Human Resource Management.* Oxford: Oxford University Press.

Purcell, J., Kinnie, N., Hutchinson, S., Swart, J. and Rayton, B. (2003) *Understanding the People and Performance Link: Unlocking the Black Box.* London: CIPD.

Purcell, J., Purcell, K. and Tailby, S. (2004) 'Temporary work agencies: here today, gone tomorrow?'. *British Journal of Industrial Relations* 42(4): 705–25.

Purcell, J., Kinnie, N., Swart, J., Rayton, B. and Hutchinson, S. (2009) *People Management and Performance.* London: Routledge.

Quinn, J. B. (1980) *Strategies for Change: Logical Incrementalism.* Homewood, IL: Irwin.

Ramsay, H. (1977) 'Cycles of control: worker participation in sociological and historical perspective.' *Sociology* 11(3): 481–506.

Redman, T. and Snape, E. (2005) 'Unpacking commitment: multiple loyalties and employee behaviour'. *Journal of Management Studies* 42(2): 301–28.

Reed, R. and DeFillippi, R. (1990) 'Causal ambiguity, barriers to imitation, and sustainable competitive advantage'. *Academy of Management Review* 15(1): 88–102.

Rees, C. and Edwards, T. (2009) 'Management strategy and HR in international mergers: choice, constraint and pragmatism' *Human Resource Management Journal* 19(1): 24–39.

Reynolds, P. (1987) 'New firms: societal contribution versus survival potential'. *Journal of Business Venturing* 2: 231–46.

Riordan, M. and Hoddeson, L. (1997) *Crystal Fire: the Birth of the Information Age.* New York: Norton.

Robertson Cooper Ltd (2003) *Teamable Technical Manual.* © Robertson Cooper Ltd.

Robinson, S. (1996) 'Trust and the breach of the psychological contract'. *Administrative Science Quarterly* 41(4): 574–99.

Robinson, S. and Rousseau, D. (1994) 'Violating the psychological contract: not the exception but the norm'. *Journal of Organizational Behavior* 15: 245–59.

Rock, M. (1984) *Handbook of Wage and Salary Administration.* New York: McGraw-Hill.

Roehling, M. (2005) 'Legal theory: contemporary contract law perspectives and insights for employment relationship theory'. In Coyle-Shapiro, J., Shore, L., Taylor, M., Tetrick, L. (eds) *The Employment Relationship: Examining Psychological and Contextual Perspectives.* Oxford: Oxford University Press.

Rose, M. (1994) 'Job satisfaction, job skills, and personal skills'. In Penn, R., Rose, M. and Rubery, J. (eds) *Skill and Occupational Change.* Oxford: Oxford University Press.

Rose, M. (2000) 'Work attitudes in the expanding occupations'. In Purcell, K. (ed.) *Changing Boundaries in Employment.* Bristol: Bristol Academic Press.

Rose, M. (2003) 'Good deal, bad deal? Job satisfaction in occupations'. *Work, Employment and Society* 17(3): 503–30.

Rosen, C., Case, J. and Staubus, M. (2005) *Equity: why Employee Ownership is Good for Business.* Boston, MA: Harvard Business School Press.

Rosenthal, P. (2004) 'Management control as an employee resource: the case of front-line service workers'. *Journal of Management Studies* 41(4): 601–22.

Rosenthal, P., Hill, S. and Peccei, R. (1997) 'Checking out service: evaluating excellence, HRM and TQM in retailing'. *Work, Employment and Society* 11(3): 481–503.

Rousseau, D. (1995) *Psychological Contracts in Organizations.* Thousand Oaks, CA: Sage.

Rowlinson, M. (1997) *Organisations and Institutions: Perspectives in Economics and Sociology.* London: Macmillan (now Palgrave Macmillan).

Rubery, J. (1994) 'Internal and external labour markets: towards an integrated analysis'. In Rubery, J. and Wilkinson, F. (eds) *Employer Strategy and the Labour Market.* Oxford: Oxford University Press.

Rubery, J. and Grimshaw, D. (2003) *The Organization of Employment.* Basingstoke and New York: Palgrave Macmillan.

Rubery, J., Earnshaw, J. and Marchington, M. (2005) 'Blurring the boundaries of the employment relationship: from single to multi-employer relationships'. In Marchington, M., Grimshaw, D., Rubery, J. and Willmott, H. (eds) *Fragmenting Work: Blurring Organizational Boundaries and Disordering Hierarchies.* Oxford: Oxford University Press.

Rucci, A., Kirn, S. and Quinn, R. (1998) 'The employee-customer-profit chain at Sears'. *Harvard Business Review* 76(1): 82–97.

Rumelt, R. (1982) 'Diversification strategy and profitability'. *Strategic Management Journal* 3: 359–69.

Rumelt, R. (1987) 'Theory, strategy and entrepreneurship'. In Teece, D. (ed.) *The Competitive Challenge.* New York: Harper and Row.

Rutherford, M., Buller, P. and McMullen, P. (2003) 'Human resource management over the life cycle of small to medium-sized firms'. *Human Resource Management* 42(4): 321–35.

Rynes, S., Barber, A. and Varma, G. (2000) 'Research on the employment interview: usefulness for practice and recommendations for future research'. In Cooper, C. and Locke, E. (eds) *Industrial and Organizational Psychology.* Oxford: Blackwell.

Sako, M. (1998) 'The nature and impact of employee "voice" in the European car components industry'. *Human Resource Management Journal* 8(2): 6–13.

Samuel, P. and Bacon, N. (2010) 'The contents of partnership agreements in Britain 1990–2007' *Work, Employment and Society*, forthcoming.

Schein, E. (1977) 'Increasing organizational effectiveness through better human resource planning and development'. *Sloan Management Review* 19(1): 1–20.

Schein, E. (1978) *Career Dynamics: Matching Individual and Organizational Needs.* Reading, MA: Addison-Wesley.

Schmidt, J. (ed.) (2002) *Making Mergers Work: the Strategic Importance of People*. Alexandria: Towers Perrin/SHRM Foundation.

Schmitt, N. and Kim, B. (2007) 'Selection decision making'. In Boxall, P., Purcell, J. and Wright, P. (eds) *The Oxford Handbook of Human Resource Management*. Oxford: Oxford University Press.

Schnaars, S. (1994) *Managing Imitation Strategies*. Basingstole and New York: Macmillan (now Palgrave Macmillan).

Schuler, R. (1989) 'Strategic human resource management and industrial relations'. *Human Relations* 42(2): 157–84.

Schuler, R. (1996) 'Market-focused management: human resource management implications'. *Journal of Market-Focused Management* 1: 13–29.

Schuler, R. and Jackson, S. (1987) 'Linking competitive strategies and human resource management practices'. *Academy of Management Executive* 1(3): 207–19.

Schumpeter, J. (1950) *Capitalism, Socialism and Democracy*. New York: Harper and Row.

Schwartz, H. and Davis, S. (1981) 'Matching corporate culture and business strategy'. *Organizational Dynamics* 60: 30–48.

Scott, W. (2008) *Institutions and Organizations: Ideas and Interests*. Third Edition. Los Angeles: Sage.

Segal-Horn, S. (2003) 'Strategy in service organisations'. In Faulkner, D. and Campbell, A. (eds) *The Oxford Handbook of Strategy*. Oxford: Oxford University Press.

Seifert, A. (2008) 'Global employee information and consultation procedures in worldwide enterprises'. *International Journal of Comparative Labour Law and Industrial Relations*. 24: 327–37.

Shah, R. and Ward, P. (2003) 'Lean manufacturing: context, practice bundles, and performance. *Journal of Operations Management* 21: 129–49.

Sheehy, G. (1977) *Passages: Predictable Crises of Adult Life*. New York: Bantam.

Sherer, P. and Leblebici, H. (2001). 'Bringing variety and change into strategic human resource management'. *Research in Personnel and Human Resources Management*, 20: 199–230.

Shibata, H. (2008) 'The transfer of Japanese work practices to plants in Thailand'. *International Journal of Human Resource Management* 19(20): 330–45.

Shore, L., Tetrick, L., Taylor, S., Coyle-Shapiro, J., Liden, R., McLean Parks, J., Wolfe Morrison, E., Porter, L., Robinson, S., Roehling, M., Rousseau, D., Schalk, R., Tsui, A. and Van Dyne, L. (2004) 'The employee–organization relationship: a timely concept in a period of transition'. *Research in Personnel and Human Resources Management* 23: 291–370.

Short, J., Payne, G. and Ketchen, D. (2008) 'Research on organizational configurations: past accomplishments and future challenges'. *Journal of Management* 34(6): 1053–79.

Siebert, W. and Zubanov, N. (2009) 'Searching for the optimal level of employee turnover: a study of a large UK retail organization.' *Academy of Management Journal* 52(2): 294–313.

Siegrist, J. (1996) 'Adverse heath effects of high-effort/low-reward conditions'. *Journal of Occupational Health Psychology* 1(1): 27–41.

Simon, H. (1947) *Administrative Behavior*. New York: Free Press.

Simon, H. (1985) 'Human nature in politics: the dialogue of psychology with political science'. *American Political Science Review* 79(2): 293–304.

Sisson, K. (2000) *Direct Participation and the Modernisation of Work Organisation*. Dublin: European Foundation for the Improvement of Living and Working Conditions.

Sisson, K. and Purcell, J. (2010) 'Management: caught between competing views'. In Colling, T. and Terry, M. (eds) *Industrial Relations Theory and Practice*. Third Edition, Chichester: Wiley.

Smith, A. (2001) 'Perceptions of stress at work'. *Human Resource Management Journal* 11(4): 74–86.

Smith, A. R. and Bartholomew, D. J. (1988). 'Manpower planning in the United Kingdom: an historical review'. *Journal of the Operational Research Society* 39(3): 235–48.

Smith, P. (2004) 'Nations, cultures and individuals: new perspectives and old dilemmas'. *Journal of Cross-Cultural Psychology* 35(1): 6–12.

Snape, E., Redman, T. and Wilkinson, A. (1993) 'Human resource management in building societies: making the transformation?'. *Human Resource Management Journal* 3(3): 44–61.

Snell, S. (1999) 'Social capital and strategic HRM: it's who you know'. *Human Resource Planning* 22(1): 62–5.

Snell, S. and Dean, J. (1992) 'Integrated manufacturing and human resources management: a human capital perspective'. *Academy of Management Journal* 35(3): 467–504.

Snell, S., Youndt, M. and Wright, P. (1996). 'Establishing a framework for research in strategic human resource management: merging resource theory and organizational learning'. *Research in Personnel and Human Resources Management* 14: 61–90.

Soderberg, A-M. and Vaara, E. (eds) (2003) *Mergers Across Borders: People, Cultures and Politics,* Copenhagen, Copenhagen University Press.

Solar, P. (2006) 'Shipping and economic development in nineteenth century Ireland'. *Economic History Review* 59(4): 717–42.

Sparrow, P. and Braun, W. (2007) 'Human resource strategy in international context'. In Harris, M. (ed.) *Handbook of Research in International Human Resource Management.* Mahwah, NJ: Lawrence Erlbaum.

Sparrow, P., Brewster, C. and Harris, H. (2004) *Globalizing Human Resource Management.* London: Routledge.

Spender, J.-C. (1989) *Industry Recipes.* Oxford: Blackwell.

Sprigg, C., Jackson, P. and Parker, S. (2000) 'Production teamworking: the importance of interdependence and autonomy for employee strain and satisfaction'. *Human Relations* 53(11): 1519–43.

Steedman, H. and Wagner, K. (1989) 'Productivity, machinery and skills: clothing manufacture in Britain and Germany'. *National Institute Economic Review* May: 40–57.

Stewart, T. A. (1998) *Intellectual Capital.* London: Nicholas Brealey.

Stiglitz, J. (2010) *Freefall: Free Markets and the Sinking of the Global Economy.* London: Allen Lane.

Stinchcombe, A. (1965) 'Social structure and organizations'. In March, J. (ed.) *Handbook of Organizations.* Chicago: Rand McNally.

Storey, D. (1985) 'The problems facing new firms'. *Journal of Management Studies* 22(3): 327–45.

Storey, J. (1995) *Human Resource Management: A Critical Text.* London: Routledge.

Strauss, G. (2006) 'Worker participation: some under-considered issues'. *Industrial Relations* 45(4): 778–803.

Streeck, W. (1987) 'The uncertainties of management in the management of uncertainty: employers, labour relations and industrial adjustment in the 1980s'. *Work, Employment and Society* 1(3): 281–308.

Suarez, F. and Utterback, J. (2005) 'Dominant designs and the survival of firms'. *Strategic Management Journal* 16: 415–30.

Suchman, M. (1995) 'Managing legitimacy: strategic and institutional approaches'. *Academy of Management Review* 20(3): 571–610.

Sun, L.-Y., Aryee, S. and Law, K. (2007) 'High-performance human resource practices, citizenship behaviour, and organizational performance: a relational perspective'. *Academy of Management Journal* 50(3): 558–77.

Swart, J. (2007) 'HRM and knowledge workers'. In Boxall, P., Purcell, J. and Wright, P. (eds) *The Oxford Handbook of Human Resource Management.* Oxford: Oxford University Press.

Swart, J. and Kinnie, N. (2003) 'Sharing knowledge in knowledge-intensive firms'. *Human Resource Management Journal* 13(2): 60–75.

Tailby, S. and Winchester, D. (2000) 'Management and trade unions: towards social partnership?'. In Bach, S. and Sisson, K. (eds) *Personnel Management: A Comprehensive Guide to Theory and Practice*. Oxford: Blackwell.

Taira, K. (1993) 'Japan'. In Rothman, M., Briscoe, D. and Nacamulli, R. (eds) *Industrial Relations Around the World*, Berlin: de Gruyter.

Tayeb, M. (1995) 'The competitive advantage of nations: the role of HRM and its socio-cultural context'. *International Journal of Human Resource Management* 6(3): 588–605.

Taylor, M. and Collins, C. (2000) 'Organizational recruitment: enhancing the intersection of research and practice'. In Cooper, C. and Locke, E. (eds) *Industrial and Organizational Psychology*. Oxford: Blackwell.

Taylor, S., Beechler, S. and Napier, N. (1996) 'Toward an integrative model of strategic international human resource management'. *Academy of Management Review* 21: 959–85.

Teece, D., Pisano, G. and Shuen, A. (1997) 'Dynamic capabilities and strategic management'. *Strategic Management Journal* 18(7): 509–33.

Thompson, P. and Harley, B. (2007) 'HRM and the worker: labor process perspectives'. In Boxall, P., Purcell, J. and Wright, P. (eds) *The Oxford Handbook of Human Resource Management*. Oxford: Oxford University Press.

Toh, S., Morgeson, F. and Campion, M. (2008). 'Human resource configurations: investigating fit with the organizational context'. *Journal of Applied Psychology* 93(4): 864–82.

Tomer, J. (2001) 'Understanding high-performance work systems: the joint contribution of economics and human resource management'. *Journal of Socio-Economics* 30: 63–73.

Towers, B. (1997) *The Representation Gap: Change and Reform in the British and American Workplace*. Oxford: Oxford University Press.

Trevor, C., Gerhart, B. and Boudreau, J. (1997) 'Voluntary turnover and job performance: curvilinearity and the moderating influences of salary growth and promotions'. *Journal of Applied Psychology* 82: 44–61.

Trist, E. and Bamforth, K. (1951) 'Some social and psychological consequences of the long-wall method of coal-getting'. *Human Relations* 4: 3–38.

Trompenaars, F. and Hampden-Turner, C. (1997) *Riding the Waves of Culture: Understanding Cultural Diversity in Business*. London: Nicholas Brealey.

Truss, K. (2001) 'Complexities and controversies in linking HRM with organisational outcomes'. *Journal of Management Studies* 38(8): 1121–49.

Tuchman, B. (1996) *The March of Folly: From Troy to Vietnam*. London: Papermac.

Turnbull, P., Woolfson, C. and Kelly, J. (1992) *Dock Strike: Conflict and Restructuring in British Ports*. Aldershot: Avebury.

Tushman, M., Newman, W. and Romanelli, E. (1986). 'Convergence and upheaval: managing the unsteady pace of organizational evolution'. *California Management Review* 29(1): 29–44.

Uhl-Bien, M., Graen, G. and Scandura, L. (2000) 'Indicators of leader–member exchange (LMX) for strategic human resource management systems'. *Research in Personnel and Human Resources Management* 18: 137–85.

UNCTAD (2008) *World Investment Report 2008*. Geneva: UNCTAD.

Utterback, J. (1994) *Mastering the Dynamics of Innovation*. Boston, MA: Harvard Business School Press.

Van de Voorde, K., Paauwe, J. and Van Veldhoven, M. (2010) 'Predicting business unit performance using employee surveys: monitoring HRM-related changes'. *Human Resource Management Journal* 20(1): 64–79.

Vandenberg, R. J., Richardson, H. A. and Eastman, L. J. (1999) 'The impact of high involvement work processes on organizational effectiveness: a second-order latent variable approach'. *Group & Organization Management* 24(3): 300–39.

Veliyath, R. and Srinivasan, T. (1995) 'Gestalt approaches to assessing strategic coalignment: a conceptual integration'. *British Journal of Management* 6(3): 205–19.

Volberda, J. (1998) *Building the Flexible Firm: How to Remain Competitive*. New York: Oxford University Press.

Waddington, J. (2006) 'The performance of European works councils in engineering: perspectives of the employee representatives'. *Industrial Relations* 45(4): 681–708.

Walker, G. (2003) *Modern Competitive Strategy*. Boston, MA: McGraw-Hill.

Wall, T., Corbett, M., Martin, R., Clegg, C. and Jackson, P. (1990). 'Advanced manufacturing technology, work design and performance: a change study'. *Journal of Applied Psychology* 75(6): 691–7.

Wall, T., Jackson, P. and Davids, K. (1992) 'Operator work design and robotics system performance'. *Journal of Applied Psychology* 77(3): 353–62.

Wallace, T. (1998) 'Fordism'. in Poole, M. and Warner, M. (eds) *The IEBM Handbook of Human Resource Management*. London: Thomson Business Press.

Walton, R. (1985) 'From control to commitment in the workplace'. Harvard Business Review 63(2): 77–84.

Walton, R. and McKersie, R. (1965) *A Behavioural Theory of Labor Negotiations*. New York: McGraw-Hill.

Walton, R., Cutcher-Gershenfeld, J. and McKersie, R. (1994) *Strategic Negotiations: A Theory of Change in Labor–Management Relations*. Boston, MA: Harvard Business School Press.

Warner, M. (1998) 'Taylor, Frederick Winslow (1856–1915)'. In Poole, M. and Warner, M. (eds) *The IEBM Handbook of Human Resource Management*. London: Thompson Business Press.

Warr, P. (2007). *Work, Happiness, and Unhappiness*. London: Lawrence Erlbaum.

Watson, T. (1986) *Management, Organization and Employment Strategy: New Directions in Theory and Practice*. London: Routledge.

Watson, T. (2005) 'Organizations, strategies and human resourcing'. In Leopold, J., Harris, L. and Watson, T. (eds) *The Strategic Managing of Human Resources*. Harlow: Pearson Education.

Watson, T. (2007) 'Organization theory and HRM'. In Boxall, P., Purcell, J. and Wright, P. (eds) *The Oxford Handbook of Human Resource Management*. Oxford: Oxford University Press.

Way, S. (2002) 'High performance work systems and intermediate indicators of firm performance within the US small business sector'. *Journal of Management* 28(6): 765–85.

Webb, S. and Webb, B. (1902) *Industrial Democracy*. London: Longman.

Wernerfelt, B. (1984). 'A resource-based view of the firm'. *Strategic Management Journal* 5(2): 171–80.

West, G. and DeCastro, J. (2001) 'The Achilles heel of firm strategy: resource weaknesses and distinctive inadequacies'. *Journal of Management Studies* 38(3): 417–42.

West, M., Patterson, M. and Dawson, J. (1999) 'A path to profit? Teamwork at the top'. *CentrePiece* 4(3): Winter.

Wever, K. (1995) *Negotiating Competitiveness: Employment Relations and Organizational Innovation in Germany and the United States*, Boston, MA: Harvard Business School Press.

Whitener, E. (2001) 'Do "high commitment" human resource practices affect employee commitment? A cross-level analysis using hierarchical liner modelling'. *Journal of Management* 27: 515–35.

Whitener, E., Brodt, S. E., Korsgaard, M. A. and Werner, J. M. (1998) 'Managers as initiators of trust: an exchange relationship framework for understanding managerial trustworthy behaviour'. *Academy of Management Review* 23(3): 513–30.

Whittaker, S. and Marchington, M. (2003) 'Devolving HR responsibility to the line: threat, opportunity or partnership?'. *Employee Relations* 36(3): 245–61.

Whittington, R. (1993) *What is Strategy – And Does it Matter?* London: Routledge.

Whittington, R. and Mayer, M. (2000) *The European Corporation: Strategy, Structure and Social Science.* Oxford: Oxford University Press.

Wilkinson, A. and Willmott, H. (1995) *Making Quality Critical: New Perspectives on Organisational Change.* London: Routledge.

Wilkinson, B., Gamble, J., Humphrey, J., Morris, J. and Anthony, D. (2001) 'The new international division of labour in Asian electronics: work organization and human resources in Japan and Malaysia'. *Journal of Management Studies* 38(50): 675–95.

Williams, J. (1992) 'How sustainable is your competitive advantage?'. *California Management Review* 34(3): 29–51.

Williamson, O. (1964) *The Economics of Discretionary Behavior: Managerial Objectives in a Theory of the Firm.* Englewood Cliffs, NJ: Prentice Hall.

Williamson, O. (1970) *Corporate Control and Business Behavior.* Englewood Cliffs, NJ: Prentice-Hall.

Williamson, O., Wachter, M. L. and Harris, J. E. (1975) 'Understanding the employment relation: the analysis of idiosyncratic exchange'. *Bell Journal of Economics* 6(1): 250–78.

Wilson, I. (1994) 'Strategic planning isn't dead – it changed'. *Long Range Planning* 27(4): 12–24.

Windolf, P. (1986). 'Recruitment, selection, and internal labour markets in Britain and Germany'. *Organization Studies* 7(3): 235–54.

Winterton, J. (2007) 'Training, development and competence'. In Boxall, P., Purcell, J. and Wright, P. (eds) *The Oxford Handbook of Human Resource Management.* Oxford: Oxford University Press.

Wolfe Morrison, E. and Robinson, S. (1997) 'When employees feel betrayed: a model of how psychological contract violation develops'. *Academy of Management Review* 22(1): 226–56.

Womack, J., Jones, D. and Roos, D. (1990) *The Machine that Changed the World: The Triumph of Lean Production.* New York: Rawson Macmillan.

Wood, S. (1996) 'High commitment management and payment systems'. *Journal of Management Studies* 33(1): 53–77.

Wood, S. (2008) 'Job characteristics, employee voice and well-being in Britain.' *Industrial Relations Journal* 39(2): 153–168.

Wood, S. and Bryson, A. (2009) 'High involvement management' in Brown, W., Bryson, A., Forth, J. and Whitfield, K. (eds) *The Evolution of the Modern Workplace.* Cambridge, Cambridge University Press.

Wooldridge, A. (2006) 'The battle for brainpower'. *The Economist* 7 October: 3–20.

Wright, P. and Gardner, T. (2004) 'The human resource – firm performance relationship: methodological and theoretical challenges'. In Holman, D., Wall, T, Clegg, C., Sparrow, P. and Howard, A. (eds) *The New Workplace: A Guide to the Human Impact of Modern Work Practices.* London: John Wiley.

Wright, P. and Nishii, L. (2004) 'Strategic HRM and organizational behaviour: integrating multiple level analysis'. Paper presented at the *What Next for HRM?* conference, Rotterdam, June.

Wright, P. and Snell, S. (1998) 'Toward a unifying framework for exploring fit and flexibility in strategic human resource management'. *Academy of Management Review* 23(4): 756–72.

Wright, P., McMahan, G. and McWilliams, A. (1994). 'Human resources and sustained competitive advantage: a resource-based perspective'. *International Journal of Human Resource Management* 5(2): 301–26.

Wright, P., Gardner, T., Moynihan, L. and Allen, M. (2005) 'The relationship between HR practices and firm performance: examining causal order'. *Personnel Psychology* 58(2): 409–46.

Youndt, M., Snell, S., Dean, J. and Lepak, D. (1996) 'Human resource management, manufacturing strategy, and firm performance'. *Academy of Management Journal* 39(4): 836–66.

Zatzick, C. and Iverson, R. (2006) 'High-involvement management and workforce reduction: competitive advantage or disadvantage?'. *Academy of Management Journal* 49(5): 999–1015.

Author index

Subject index

emotional labour, 150–1
employee ability, 5–6, 193–202, 214, 244
employee autonomy, 27, 131, 136–40, 157, 162, 166, 206, 234–5, 238, 242
employee behaviour, *see* discretionary behaviour/effort
employee commitment, 83, 89, 132, 140, 152, 177, 212, 219–26, 232, 243, 251, 270; *see also* high-commitment management
employee discretion, *see* discretionary behaviour
employee engagement, 93, 165, 167–8, 179, 187, 203, 330; *see also* discretionary behaviour/effort, employee commitment, employee motivation
employee expectations, 19–20, 76, 79, 183, 219–25, 244–6, 293–4, 302
✳ employee health and well-being, 69–70, 130–2, 139–40, 185, 193, 204, 207, 248–9, 315
employee interests, *see* employee motivation, interest alignment, interest trade-offs
employee involvement, *see* employee voice, high-involvement work systems
employee motivation, 5–6, 26–9, 202–27
employee partnerships, 169
employee perceptions, 118, 179, 180, 181, 210, 224–5, 228, 248–52, 301, 315
employee performance, 5–6, 189–227
employee relations styles, 7–9, 250–1, 182–7
employee retention, 43, 79, 116, 155, 184, 191, 192, 207–8, 226, 266–7, 271, 294; *see also* labour turnover
employee rights, 8, 30–2, 159, 170
employee satisfaction, *see* job satisfaction
employee surveying, *see* attitude surveys
employee turnover, *see* employee retention, labour turnover
employee voice
  and trade unions, 173–8
  changes in, 160–78
  defined, 7–8, 160–1
  direct forms of, 161–2, 166–9
  dual systems of, 180, 185, 187
  embedded, 179–80, 182, 185, 187
  history of, 130–1, 161, 166, 169, 173
  impacts of, 178–82
  indirect or representative forms of, 162–73
  management styles in, 182–7
employer of choice, 22, 118
employment ethics, 19–22, 26, 31–2, 90, 161, 187, 231, 249, 297, 305, 335; *see also* social legitimacy
employment regulation, 10–11, 19–22, 30–2, 71–2, 84, 159–61, 169–73, 305, 310

employment relationship, 27–9, 35, 188–227, 312
employment security, 29, 88, 131, 175, 178, 205, 232
employment subsystems, 7
empowerment, *see* high-involvement work systems
engagement, *see* employee engagement
enabling capabilities, 110–1
entrepreneurship, 98, 261, 263–5, 267, 269, 273, 278
Equal Employment Opportunity (EEO), 4, 20, 22
equifinality, 91, 95
equity, 28, 70, 154, 189, 207–10, 215; *see also* organisational justice
equity theory, 222
escaping, 75, 295; *see also* offshoring, outsourcing
establishment context/phase, 259, 262, 263–268
'Ethical Trading Initiative', 32
ethics, *see* employment ethics
European Union, 142, 144, 159, 162, 169–73
European works councils, 170–1, 296–7; *see also* works councils
expectancy theory, 222–5
expressivism, 202, 226
extrinsic motivators, 116, 204–7; *see also* employee motivation

factory system, 127–33
Fairchild Semiconductor, 104, 267–8
fairness, *see* equity, organisational justice
familial model, 232–5, 239–41, 243
family firms, 79, 232, 235, 239–40, 243
fast followers, 259, 264, 316
feminine cultures, 73; *see also* national culture
financial controls/economies, 240, 243, 287–9, 304
finance/funding strategy, 12, 42, 43–45, 49, 61, 250, 257, 264, 265, 269–70
first-mover advantages, 102–3, 264, 316
First World War, 41, 86, 130, 141, 266, 319
first-line managers, *see* line managers
Five Dollar Day, 266
flexible bureaucracies, 240, 242–3, 273, 290
flexible specialisation, 91
flexibility, *see* flexible bureaucracies, flexible specialisation, functional flexibility, organisational agility, organisational flexibility
focus strategy, 80–1
footwear manufacturing industry, 14, 31, 141

forcing and fostering, 177–8
Ford, Henry, *see* Fordism
Fordism, 129–30, 133–4, 157
formalisation, 150, 241, 269
French education system, 75
functional equivalence, *see* equifinality
functional flexibility, 16

General Electric, 40, 289
General Motors, 133, 265, 285
German workforce, 34
gestalt perspective, 49
global financial crisis, 20, 23, 43, 44, 110. 137,
      156, 207, 213, 226, 262, 286
globalisation, 10, 126, 127, 141–6, 238, 253, 281,
      288, 305, 308, 322
goals of HRM, *see* human resource management
governments, *see* employment regulation, public
      sector, social legitimacy, societal fit
Great Depression, 130, 141
Gregg, Samuel, 128
groupthink, 55–6

Harvard framework, 69–71
health, *see* employee health and well-being
health sector, 3, 10, 26, 144, 153, 154–6, 234,
      238, 240, 242, 246
high-commitment management, 9, 14, 89, 140,
      183–4, 212
high-involvement work systems, 89, 134–40,
      146, 157, 166, 195, 198, 311
high-performance work systems, 89–94, 134;
      see also high-involvement work systems
high-tech manufacturing, *see* manufacturing
higher education, 119–20, 193
Hoechst, 266
Hollywood film studios, 99
homo economicus, 51–2
horizontal fit, 71, 228–32; *see also* internal fit
hotel industry, 18, 78, 82, 149, 151–3, 242
human capital, 7, 112–16, 121, 137, 166, 184,
      197, 264, 275, 301, 314, 317
human capital advantage, 18, 113–16, 121
Human Relations School, 131–2
human resource advantage, 17–19, 24–5, 35,
      114–15, 119, 229, 257, 267–8, 270–2, 274–9,
      309, 314, 334–5
human resource architecture, 7, 115–19
human resource cycle, 188–9
human resource management
      analytical approach to, xii
      contextual embeddedness of, 9–11, 63–96,
            310–11

defined, 1–11, 308
goals of, 11–24, 35, 308–9
micro, 188, 308
process of, 2–3, 7, 308
strategic tensions and problems in, 24–36,
      308–9
styles in, 7–9
human resource planning, 271–2, 317–24, 335
human resource policy v. practice, 244–8,
      250–2, 272, 315
human resource specialists, 4, 57, 61, 64, 68, 241,
      246–7, 250–1, 268, 271, 290, 296, 297, 304,
      308, 315, 319–20
human resource strategy
      and 'black box' problem, 243–54
      and competitive advantage, 17–19, 46–8,
            97–121, 333–7
      and industry dynamics, 257–79
      and organisational patterns, 228–43
      and organisational viability, 12–15, 42–6,
            333–7
      and resource-based view, 97–121
      corporate, 68, 287–90
      defined, 64–8, 228–9
      in mergers and acquisitions, 299–303
      in multinational firms, 293–99
human resource systems
      and 'black box' problem, 243–54
      and equifinality/functional equivalence, 91, 95
      and internal fit, 229–32
      and organisational patterns, 239–43
      defined, 7–9, 64–8, 87–8, 228–9
      high-commitment, *see* high-commitment
            management
      high-involvement, *see* high-involvement work
            systems
      high-performance, *see* high-performance
            work systems
      types of, 232–8
human resources portfolio, 191–2
hyper-determinism, 50
hyper-voluntarism, 50

IBM, 72, 259–60, 267
ideology, *see* management ideology
imitation, 100–5, 109, 112, 120, 259, 271–2, 316
implicit contract, 223
individual performance, *see* employee
      performance
individualism, 73, 87, 186, 290
industrial democracy, *see* employee voice
industrial model, 233, 236, 238, 239, 241, 253
industrial psychology, 86, 188

life-cycle theory, *see* adult life-cycle theory, industry evolution

line managers, 4, 64, 113, 138–9, 178–80, 182, 185, 228, 246–8, 252, 272, 288, 304, 315, 318–20

long-run agility, *see* organisational agility

management accounting, 118, 314, 324–37

management consultancy industry, 141, 184

management control, *see* management power

management development, 42, 56–62, 288, 297–9, 304, 311, 320

management hierarchies, 33, 163, 181, 233, 236, 240, 241, 273

management ideology, 9, 12, 22, 34

management of managers, 56–62, 333; *see also* management development

management perception, 98, 270

management power, 22–4, 30–2, 35, 181, 239, 241, 309

management prerogative, *see* management power

management rhetoric *v.* reality, 12, 113, 244–6, 272, 315

management styles, 7–9, 91, 161, 183, 185, 299

manufacturing
capital-intensive/high-technology, 14, 17, 77, 95, 135, 146, 157, 234, 240, 242, 310
labour-intensive, 14, 142, 147, 157, 310
work systems in, 125–146
see also advanced manufacturing technology, lean production, mass production, total quality management

marginal performers, 191–2

market HRM, 70

marketing, 13, 18, 33, 42–5, 49, 61, 80, 84, 98, 163, 241, 250, 257, 258, 261, 265, 283, 284

masculine cultures, 73; *see also* national culture

mass production, 89, 130, 233, 236

mature context/phase, 259–62, 268–72, 275, 278–9

McKinsey, 65

mediation services, 31

medical electronics industry, 92, 138

mergers, 141, 170, 173, 280–2, 299–303, 305–6

meta-planning, 332–3, 336

microcomputer industry, 259

Microsoft, 49, 111

migrant labour, 13, 21, 77, 236, 241

motivated capability, 191, 203

motivation, *see* employee motivation

motorcycle industry, 133

multidivisional firms (M-form), 33, 40, 50, 67–8, 106, 272, 273, 280–90, 304–5, 311, 329

multinational firms, 23, 31, 74–6, 145, 170, 219, 240, 243, 280–1, 290–9, 304–6, 311, 318, 329

multi-skilling, 16

mutuality, 189, 203, 226, 273, 276, 312; *see also* interest alignment, principle of balance, reciprocity

nation states, *see* employment regulation, national culture, social legitimacy, societal fit

national culture, 21, 71, 72–6, 232, 293, 296

neo-liberalism, 186

networked organisation (N-form), 282–3, 289–90, 296, 298, 304–5

'new public management', 144, 155, 240, 242, 243

newspaper industry, 175, 261

non-substitutability, 101

North America Free Trade Agreement (NAFTA), 142

Norwich Union, 127

nuclear power industry, 14

NUMMI (Toyota–GM plant), 137

occupational safety and health (OSH), 22, 30, 32, 163; *see also* employment regulation, employee health and well-being

offshoring, 15, 17, 118,126–7, 141–6, 151, 153, 154, 157–8, 242, 290, 292, 302–4, 308

oil industry, 3

oil shocks, 133, 323

oligopoly, 98, 263

operations management/strategy, 33, 41, 49, 61, 83–4, 126, 143, 145, 156, 250, 257; *see also* production systems, offshoring, outsourcing, work systems

opportunity to perform, 5–6, 190, 217, 244, 251, 312, 328

organisational agility, 275–9, 311; *see also* organisational flexibility

organisational citizenship behaviours, 222

organisational climate, 179, 249, 251–2, 254, 312, 315, 319, 328

organisational commitment, *see* employee commitment

organisational culture, 99, 105, 185, 218, 245–6, 302

organisational ecology, 16, 47, 235

organisational flexibility, 15–7, 24, 181, 251, 276, 304, 333–5; *see also* short-run responsiveness, organisational agility

organisational fit, 79–85

organisational justice, 28, 301, 305; *see also* equity, equity theory

organisational life-cycle, 79; *see also* establishment context, mature context, renewal context, industry evolution

organisational performance, 6, 243–54, 315; *see also* viability, competitive advantage

organisational politics, 54–6; *see also* labour power, management power

organisational process advantage, 18, 114–15; *see also* social capital advantage

organisational survival, 14, 29, 35, 42–6, 61, 64, 68, 76–78, 120, 126, 138, 157, 178, 258, 279, 308–9, 313, 329; *see also* viability

outsourcing, 15, 117, 119, 153, 156, 186, 197, 234, 238, 242, 273, 288–90, 296, 304, 313

outsourcing model, 234, 238

Owen, Robert, 128

parenting advantage, 68, 282, 298

participatory bureaucracies, 240, 242, 245, 274, 289

partnership, *see* social partnership, trade unions

path dependency, 102, 314, 316

'Pax Victoriana', 141

pay equity, 208–9

pay systems, 207–15, 226, 311; *see also* job evaluation, pay equity, performance-related pay

perceived organisational support, 223–4

perfect competition, 46, 98

performance, *see* employee performance, organisational performance

performance appraisal, 73, 87, 94, 152, 154, 202, 210, 214, 215–9, 237, 247

performance drivers, 326–32, 336

performance equation, *see* AMO framework

performance management, 191, 215, 219, 222, 297

performance-related pay, 70, 73, 155, 210–5, 226, 246, 286, 287

performance variation, 194, 211; *see also* employee performance

personal growth, 173, 201–2, 226

person-job fit, 58, 201

personnel management, xi–ii, 11, 42, 70, 85, 318, 319

person-team fit, 58

'Peter Principle', 192

'poaching', 26, 34, 198, 323; *see also* recruitment strategy

politics, *see* organisational politics

power, *see* labour power, management power, organisational politics, power distance

power distance, 73, 167

'powerholic' personality, 218

PricewaterhouseCoopers, 65

principle of balance, 203–4; *see also* interest alignment, mutuality, reciprocity

privatisation, 117, 143, 246

production systems, 13, 74–5, 93, 134–5, 139, 295; *see also* factory system, lean production, mass production, work systems

productivity, 14–15, 26, 29, 33,47, 53, 74, 92–3, 103, 108, 115–16, 130–1, 133, 135, 140, 145, 160, 166, 171, 175–6, 181, 194, 210–11, 226, 251, 296, 303, 305, 309, 317, 327–8

professional service firms, *see* services

profitability, 12

profit-sharing, 179–80, 266

provisioning motive, 207, 226

psychological contracting, 219–26, 244–5, 269

public sector, 3, 7, 10, 15, 40, 76–8, 143, 144, 145, 147, 154–8, 169, 174, 176, 184, 209, 234, 236–40, 242, 243, 246, 253, 254, 262, 280, 286, 310, 313, 337

punctuated equilibrium, 259

'putting-out' system, 128

quality circles, 3,74, 166, 168; *see also* total quality management

rail industry, 53, 317

rater bias, 217

reciprocity, 13, 189, 226, 312; *see also* interest alignment, mutuality, principle of balance

recruitment strategy, 195–7, 318

redundancies, *see* downsizing

regime advantage/competition, 281, 292

regulation, *see* employment regulation

relational contracts, 219–20

remuneration, *see* pay, performance-related pay

renewal context/phase, 261, 272–9, 317, 318

'rent', 101

'reproduction factories', 75

resource-based view (RBV)
  and barriers to imitation, 100–6, 325
  and competitive advantage, 97–121, 314
  and competitive parity, 112–13
  and HR strategy, 112–21, 140, 224
  and industry dynamics, 259, 263–79
  defined, 97–100

strategic HRM – *continued*
  key themes in, 307–16
  see also human resource management, human
    resource strategy
strategic management
  and cognitive problems, 51–4
  and executive appointments, 56–7, 62
  and organisational politics, 54–6
  and team-building, 58–61
  and the resource-based view, 97–121
  defined, 39–50, 61
  in multidivisional/multinational firms,
    280–306
strategic planning, 40, 271, 316–8, 320, 324,
  329, 336
strategic problems, 39–50, 61, 257, 308
strategy
  and the resource-based view, 97–121
  corporate, 50, 282–90
  defined, 39–50, 61
  emergent, 48, 51, 325
  maps, 325, 329–36
  versus operations, 41
  versus strategic plan, 40–1
  versus tactics, 41
  see also strategic management
stress, 26, 85, 139, 145, 150–1, 204, 207, 246,
  251–2; *see also* job strain, work
  intensification
strikes, 14, 27, 29, 30, 292
'success trap', 53
supplemental capabilities, 110
survival, *see* organisational survival, strategic
  problems, viability
survivor syndrome, 303
sustained competitive advantage, *see* competitive
  advantage
'sweetheart unionism', 184–5
SWOT, 99–100
synergistic economies, 288–9, 296, 304
synergy, 65, 88, 286, 288–9, 299
systemic thinking, 52, 84, 88, 97, 107, 121

'table stakes', 43–4, 61, 109–11, 121, 138, 152,
  314, 326–7
tacit knowledge, 113–4, 266
takeovers, *see* acquisitions
Taylorism, 89, 129–30, 135–6, 140, 146, 147–8,
  156–7, 234, 241; *see also* Scientific
  Management
teamwork, 18, 53, 59–60, 74, 88, 103, 106, 132,
  137, 139–40, 222, 230, 267, 271, 311, 316
technical interdependence, 117, 211

technology, *see* advanced manufacturing
  technology, information technology,
  manufacturing
telecommunications industry, 82, 102, 143, 144,
  240, 243
textile industry, 10, 105, 130
Thatcherism, 9, 143, 155
themes of the book, 307–16
theory of the business, 329–30
time-and-motion study, *see* Scientific
  Management, Taylorism
time orientation, 73; *see also* national culture
top-management team building, 58–61, 62; *see
  also* management development
total quality management (TQM), 84, 133, 180,
  296
'town hall' meetings, 8, 168
toy manufacturing industry, 14, 141, 297
Toyota production system, 133–4, 137
trade unions
  and industrial model, 233, 236, 239, 241
  and management style, 182–6
  and multinational firms, 288, 292, 296, 297,
    305
  and 'partnership' agreements, 7, 64, 91, 174–5,
    177, 183–5, 186, 240, 242, 246
  bargaining with, 162–3, 175–8, 296
  decline of, 173–5, 243
  history of, 30–1, 130–1, 161, 241
  in continental Europe, 19–20
  in the public sector, 154–7, 174, 238
  see also collective bargaining, consultative
    committees/forums, employee voice
trade-offs, *see* interest trade-offs
training and development, 22, 197–202, 226,
  288, 297
transactional contracts, 219–20
transnational corporations, *see* multinational
  firms
'triple bottom line', 21, 329
trucking industry, 26, 53, 241
trust-in-management, 6–7, 27–8, 30, 113, 114,
  121, 129, 151, 155, 165, 174, 224–6, 231,
  233, 235, 245, 247, 249–52, 300–3, 312, 315

uncertainty avoidance, 73
Unilever, 298
union-management partnerships, *see* trade
  unions
unions, *see* trade unions
unique timing and learning, 102–3, 316
unit labour costs, *see* labour costs
United Nations (UN), 31

universalism, 13, 63; *see* best-practice school
US firms, 88; *see also* Anglo-American context

value proposition, 326–8
varieties of capitalism, 19, 20, 288
vertical fit, 80; *see also* best-fit school
vertical integration, 283, 289
viability, 1, 12–5, 17, 19, 25, 29, 35, 42–8, 61–2,
    126, 257, 263–7, 269–70, 273–4, 278, 307–9,
    334, 336; *see also* organisational survival,
    strategic problems
vocational education and training (VET), 34, 75,
    76
voice, *see* employee voice
voluntarism, 171
Volvo, 132

wage-work bargain, *see* effort-reward bargain
Wal-Mart Stores, 3
'war for talent', 191
waterfront industry, 175
Welch, Jack, 289
well-being, *see* employee health and well-being
whanau interviewing, 90
women
    and comparable worth, 209
    and diversity climate, 249–50
    and gendered cultural assumptions, 73, 294
    and work-life patterns, 201

work intensification, 27, 145, 154–55, 157, 246
work measurement/study, *see* Scientific
    Management, Taylorism
work-sample tests, 195, 311
work systems
    defined, 6, 125–6
    and globalisation, 141–6, 157
    high-involvement, *see* high-involvement work
        systems
    high-performance, see high-performance
        works systems
    in manufacturing, 77, 89–92, 127–40, 156–7
    in private sector services, 146–54, 157–8
    in public sector services, 154–6, 158
    'motivational model', 132
    types of, 147–9
workaholism, 192, 207
worker cooperatives, 168, 169
worker self-management, 164
workforce capabilities, 6–7, 251, 310, 328
workforce organisation, 6–7, 244
work-life balance, 195, 206, 251
workload, 16, 28, 30, 85
workplace culture, *see* organisational culture
works councils, 8, 19, 20, 85, 91, 92, 167–8,
    170–2, 184–5, 296–7; *see also* European
    works councils
World Bank, 143